P9-DVK-240

lonely planet

Oahu

Ned Friary
Glenda Bendure

LONELY PLANET PUBLICATIONS
Melbourne · Oakland · London · Paris

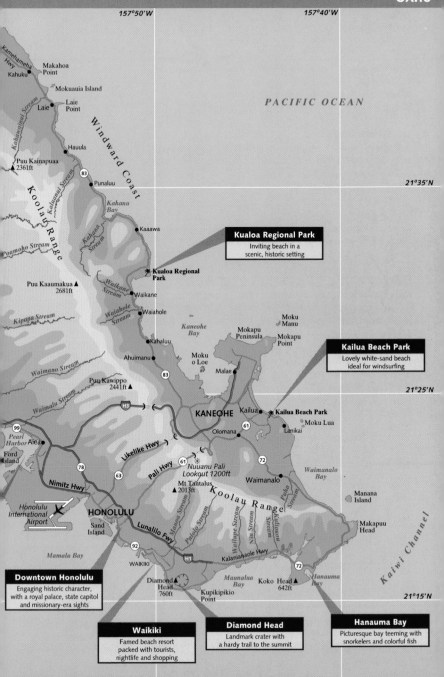

OAHU

157°50'W 157°40'W

PACIFIC OCEAN

21°35'N

21°25'N

21°15'N

Kamehameha Hwy
Makahoa Point
Kahuku
Mokuauia Island
Laie
Laie Point
Windward Coast
Hauula
Koolau Range
Kahawainui Stream
Kailuanui Stream
Puu Kainapuaa 2361ft
Punaluu
Kahana Stream
Kahana Bay
Kaaawa
Poamoho Stream
Waikane Stream
Puu Kaaumakua 2681ft
Kipapa Stream
Waihole Stream
Kualoa Regional Park
Waikane
Waiahole
Kahaluu
Ahuimanu
Kaneohe Bay
Moku o Loe
Waimano Stream
Puu Kawippo 2441ft
Moku Manu
Mokapu Peninsula
Mokapu Point
Malae
Waimalu Stream
H3
KANEOHE
Kailua
Kailua Beach Park
Moku Lua
Lanikai
Olomana
Pearl Harbor
Aiea
Ford Island
99
78
63
Likelike Hwy
Pali Hwy
61
61
Nuuanu Pali Lookout 1200ft
72
Waimanalo
Waimanalo Bay
Manana Island
Nimitz Hwy
Honolulu International Airport
Mt Tantalus 2013ft
Koolau Range
Nuuanu Stream
Waiolu Stream
Niu Stream
Kuliouou Stream
Makapuu Head
HONOLULU
Sand Island
Lunalilo Fwy
92
Palolo Stream
H1
Kalanianaole Hwy
72
Koko Head 642ft
Hanauma Bay
Kaiwi Channel
Mamala Bay
WAIKIKI
Diamond Head 760ft
Kupikipikio Point
Maunalua Bay

Kualoa Regional Park
Inviting beach in a scenic, historic setting

Kailua Beach Park
Lovely white-sand beach ideal for windsurfing

Downtown Honolulu
Engaging historic character, with a royal palace, state capitol and missionary-era sights

Waikiki
Famed beach resort packed with tourists, nightlife and shopping

Diamond Head
Landmark crater with a hardy trail to the summit

Hanauma Bay
Picturesque bay teeming with snorkelers and colorful fish

Oahu
1st edition – March 2000

Published by
Lonely Planet Publications Pty Ltd A.C.N. 005 607 983
192 Burwood Rd, Hawthorn, Victoria 3122, Australia

Lonely Planet Offices
Australia PO Box 617, Hawthorn, Victoria 3122
USA 150 Linden St, Oakland, CA 94607
UK 10a Spring Place, London NW5 3BH
France 1 rue du Dahomey, 75011 Paris

Photographs
Glenda Bendure, Ann Cecil, Ron Dalquist, John Elk III, BJ Formento,
Lee Foster, Ned Friary, Kim Grant, Hawaii State Archives,
Casey & Astrid Witte Mahaney, Douglas Peebles, Andrew Sallmon

Illustrators
Mark Butler, Hugh D'Andrade, Shelley Firth, Hayden Foell,
Rini Keagy, Justin Marler, Hannah Reineck, Wendy Yanagihara

Many of the images in this guide are available for licensing from
Lonely Planet Images.
email: lpi@lonelyplanet.com.au

Front cover photograph
Palms at sunset (Ralph Talmont, Aurora/PNI)

ISBN 1 86450 048 4

text & maps © Lonely Planet 2000
photos © photographers as indicated 2000

Printed by Quebecor Peru S.A., Lima, Peru

Although the authors and Lonely Planet try to make the information as accurate as possible, we accept no responsibility for any loss, injury or inconvenience sustained by anyone using this book.

Contents

2 Contents

MAP INDEX

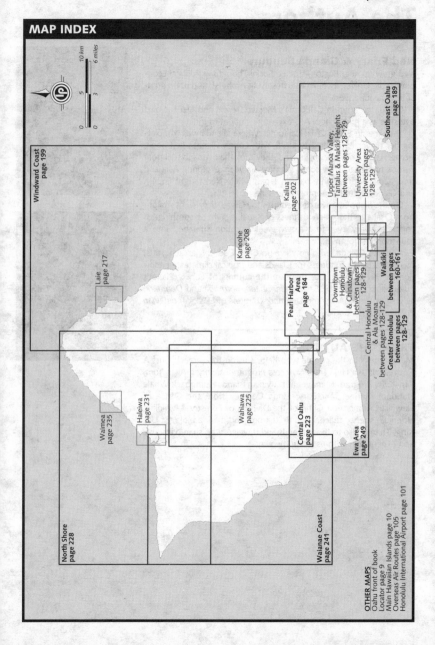

0   5   10 km
0   3   6 miles

Windward Coast
page 199

Laie
page 217

Kaneohe
page 208

Kailua
page 202

Upper Manoa Valley,
Tantalus & Makiki Heights
between pages 128-129

University Area
between pages
128-129

Southeast Oahu
page 189

Downtown
Honolulu
& Chinatown
between pages
128-129

Waikiki
between pages
160-161

Central Honolulu
& Ala Moana
between pages 128-129

Greater Honolulu
between pages
128-129

Pearl Harbor
Area
page 184

Waimea
page 235

Haleiwa
page 231

Wahiawa
page 225

Central Oahu
page 223

Ewa Area
page 249

North Shore
page 228

Waianae Coast
page 241

OTHER MAPS
Oahu front of book
Locator page 9
Main Hawaiian Islands page 10
Overseas Air Routes page 105
Honolulu International Airport page 101

The Authors

Ned Friary & Glenda Bendure

Ned grew up near Boston, studied Social Thought & Political Economy at the University of Massachusetts in Amherst, and upon graduating, headed west.

Glenda grew up in California's Mojave Desert and first traveled overseas as a high school AFS exchange student to India.

They met in Santa Cruz, California, where Glenda was completing her university studies. In 1978, with Lonely Planet's first book, *Across Asia on the Cheap*, in hand, they took the overland trail from Europe to Nepal. They spent the next six years exploring Asia and the Pacific, with a home base in Japan where Ned taught English and Glenda edited a monthly magazine.

On the first of many extended trips to Hawaii, they went straight from Osaka to the green lushness of Kauai, a sight so soothing for concrete-weary eyes that a two-week vacation stretched into a four-month sojourn.

Ned and Glenda, who now live on Cape Cod in Massachusetts, have a particular fondness for islands and tropical climates. In addition to this *Oahu* guide, they are the authors of Lonely Planet's guidebooks to *Hawaii, Eastern Caribbean, Bermuda* and *Denmark*, as well as the Norway and Denmark chapters of LP's *Scandinavian & Baltic Europe* book.

FROM THE AUTHORS

Many thanks to the people who helped us on this project: Curt A Cottrell, Na Ala Hele Trails & Access Program Manager; Allen Tom, Sanctuary Program Manager at Hawaiian Islands Humpback Whale National Marine Sanctuary; Linda Delaney from the Office of Hawaiian Affairs; Jon Giffin of the Division of Forestry & Wildlife; Honolulu science teacher Ted Brattstrom; and marine biologist Lisa King. Thanks also to those friends and travelers who shared insights and experiences with us along the way.

This Book

This 1st edition of *Oahu* was written by Ned Friary and Glenda Bendure. It is based on their earlier books *Hawaii* and *Honolulu*.

FROM THE PUBLISHER

Oahu was produced in Lonely Planet's US office. Maria Donohoe was the editor, with much help and guidance from senior editors Jacqueline Volin and Laura Harger. Kevin Anglin, Wade Fox, Wendy Taylor-Hall, Elaine Merrill and Karen O'Donnell Stein proofread the book, and Ken DellaPenta did the indexing. Chris Gillis was the lead cartographer, with assistance from Colin Bishop, Sean Brandt, Patrick Huerta, Monica Lepe, Patrick Phelan and Eric Thomsen. Amy Dennis and Tracey Croom were the senior cartographers for the project. Shelley Firth and Beca Lafore designed the book, with guidance from Susan Rimerman and Margaret Livingston. Maria, Kevin, Wade, Jacqueline and Laura helped with layout review. The illustrations were drawn by Hugh D'Andrade, Shelley Firth, Hayden Foell, Rini Keagy, Justin Marler, Hannah Reineck and Wendy Yanagihara; some illustrations are from the Hawaii State Archives. The cover was designed by Simon Bracken. Thanks also to Tommie Warren for help with administrative matters.

Foreword

ABOUT LONELY PLANET GUIDEBOOKS

The story begins with a classic travel adventure: Tony and Maureen Wheeler's 1972 journey across Europe and Asia to Australia. Useful information about the overland trail did not exist at that time, so Tony and Maureen published the first Lonely Planet guidebook to meet a growing need.

From a kitchen table, then from a tiny office in Melbourne (Australia), Lonely Planet has become the largest independent travel publisher in the world, an international company with offices in Melbourne, Oakland (USA), London (UK) and Paris (France).

Today Lonely Planet guidebooks cover the globe. There is an ever-growing list of books, and there's information in a variety of forms and media. Some things haven't changed. The main aim is still to help make it possible for adventurous travelers to get out there – to explore and better understand the world.

At Lonely Planet we believe travelers can make a positive contribution to the countries they visit – if they respect their host communities and spend their money wisely. Since 1986 a percentage of the income from each book has been donated to aid projects and human-rights campaigns.

Updates Lonely Planet thoroughly updates each guidebook as often as possible. This usually means there are around two years between editions, although for more unusual or more stable destinations the gap can be longer. Check the imprint page (following the color map at the beginning of the book) for publication dates.

Between editions, up-to-date information is available in two free newsletters – the paper *Planet Talk* and email *Comet* (to subscribe, contact any Lonely Planet office) – and on our website at www.lonelyplanet.com. The *Upgrades* section of the website covers a number of important and volatile destinations and is regularly updated by Lonely Planet authors. *Scoop* covers news and current affairs relevant to travelers. And, lastly, the *Thorn Tree* bulletin board and *Postcards* section of the site carry unverified, but fascinating, reports from travelers.

Correspondence The process of creating new editions begins with the letters, postcards and emails received from travelers. This correspondence often includes suggestions, criticisms and comments about the current editions. Interesting excerpts are immediately passed on via newsletters and the website, and everything goes to our authors to be verified when they're researching on the road. We're keen to get more feedback from organizations or individuals who represent communities visited by travelers.

Lonely Planet gathers information for everyone who's curious about the planet – and especially for those who explore it firsthand. Through guidebooks, phrasebooks, activity guides, maps, literature, newsletters, image library, TV series and website, we act as an information exchange for a worldwide community of travelers.

Research Authors aim to gather sufficient practical information to enable travelers to make informed choices and to make the mechanics of a journey run smoothly. They also research historical and cultural background to help enrich the travel experience and allow travelers to understand and respond appropriately to cultural and environmental issues.

Authors don't stay in every hotel because that would mean spending a couple of months in each medium-size city and, no, they don't eat at every restaurant because that would mean stretching belts beyond capacity. They do visit hotels and restaurants to check standards and prices, but feedback based on readers' direct experiences can be very helpful.

Many of our authors work undercover; others aren't so secretive. None of them accept freebies in exchange for positive write-ups. And none of our guidebooks contain any advertising.

Production Authors submit their raw manuscripts and maps to offices in Australia, the USA, the UK or France. Editors and cartographers – all experienced travelers themselves – then begin the process of assembling the pieces. When the book finally hits the shops, some things are already out of date, we start getting feedback from readers and the process begins again....

WARNING & REQUEST

Things change – prices go up, schedules change, good places go bad and bad places go bankrupt – nothing stays the same. So, if you find things better or worse, recently opened or long since closed, please tell us and help make the next edition even more accurate and useful. We genuinely value all the feedback we receive. Julie Young coordinates a well-traveled team that reads and acknowledges every letter, postcard and email and ensures that every morsel of information finds its way to the appropriate authors, editors and cartographers for verification.

Everyone who writes to us will find their name in the next edition of the appropriate guidebook. They will also receive the latest issue of *Planet Talk*, our quarterly printed newsletter, or *Comet*, our monthly email newsletter. Subscriptions to both newsletters are free. The very best contributions will be rewarded with a free guidebook.

Excerpts from your correspondence may appear in new editions of Lonely Planet guidebooks, the Lonely Planet website, *Planet Talk* or *Comet*, so please let us know if you *don't* want your letter published or your name acknowledged.

Send all correspondence to the Lonely Planet office closest to you:

Australia: PO Box 617, Hawthorn, Victoria 3122
USA: 150 Linden St, Oakland, CA 94607
UK: 10A Spring Place, London NW5 3BH
France: 1 rue du Dahomey, 75011 Paris

Or email us at: talk2us@lonelyplanet.com.au

For news, views and updates, see our website: www.lonelyplanet.com

HOW TO USE A LONELY PLANET GUIDEBOOK

The best way to use a Lonely Planet guidebook is any way you choose. At Lonely Planet, we believe the most memorable travel experiences are often those that are unexpected, and the finest discoveries are those you make yourself. Guidebooks are not intended to be used as if they provided a detailed set of infallible instructions!

Contents All Lonely Planet guidebooks follow the same format. The Facts about the Country chapters or sections give background information ranging from history to weather. Facts for the Visitor gives practical information on issues like visas and health. Getting There & Away gives a brief starting point for researching travel to and from the destination. Getting Around gives an overview of the transport options available when you arrive.

The peculiar demands of each destination determine how subsequent chapters are broken up, but some things remain constant. We always start with background, then proceed to sights, places to stay, places to eat, entertainment, getting there and away, and getting around information – in that order.

Heading Hierarchy Lonely Planet headings are used in a strict hierarchical structure that can be visualized as a set of Russian dolls. Each heading (and its following text) is encompassed by any preceding heading that is higher on the hierarchical ladder.

Entry Points We do not assume guidebooks will be read from beginning to end, but that people will dip into them. The traditional entry points are the list of contents and the index. In addition, however, some books have a complete list of maps and an index map illustrating map coverage.

There may also be a color map that shows highlights. These highlights are dealt with in greater detail later in the book, along with planning questions and suggested itineraries. Each chapter covering a geographical region usually begins with a locator map and another list of highlights. Once you find something of interest in a list of highlights, turn to the index.

Maps Maps play a crucial role in Lonely Planet guidebooks and include a huge amount of information. A legend is printed on the back page. We seek to have complete consistency between maps and text, and to have every important place in the text captured on a map. Map key numbers usually start in the top left corner.

Although inclusion in a guidebook usually implies a recommendation, we cannot list every good place. Exclusion does not necessarily imply criticism. In fact, there are a number of reasons why we might exclude a place – sometimes it is simply inappropriate to encourage an influx of travelers.

Introduction

When people think of Hawaii, many of the places that spring to mind are sights on Oahu – the beaches and high-rise hotels of Waikiki, the WWII memorials at Pearl Harbor and the towering surf at Sunset Beach. The most developed of the Hawaiian Islands, with a population of 880,000 people (nearly 75% of the state's population), Oahu is fittingly nicknamed 'The Gathering Place.'

Although much of Oahu is an urban scene, it's nonetheless a scenic island, with rugged volcanic peaks, tropical forests, fluted mountains, aquamarine bays and valleys carpeted with pineapple fields. It also has some of Hawaii's best beaches – Hanauma Bay is the most-visited snorkeling spot in the Hawaiian Islands; the North Shore has Hawaii's top surfing action; and windward Kailua is Hawaii's most popular windsurfing beach.

The heart of Oahu is vibrant Honolulu. As the capital of Hawaii, it's the political, cultural and economic center of the state. The only US state capital located in the tropics, Honolulu boasts swaying palm trees and balmy weather year-round. It is an attractive city with an intriguing blend of Eastern and Western influences. Cultural offerings range from Chinese lantern parades and traditional hula performances to ballet and good museums. Honolulu has pleasant beaches and parks and the only royal palace in the USA. The city is also a diner's delight, with a wonderful assortment of good ethnic restaurants.

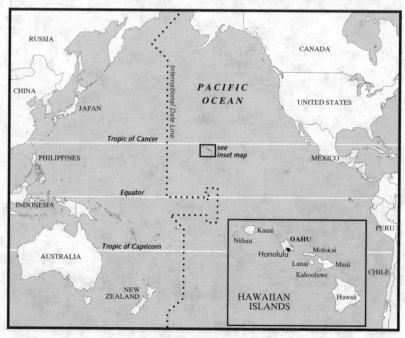

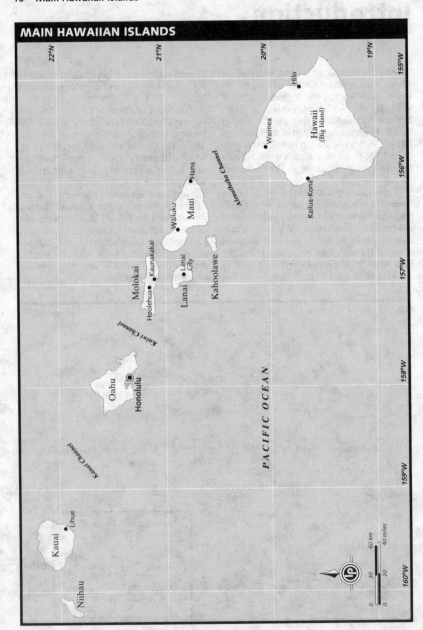

MAIN HAWAIIAN ISLANDS

Hawaii (Big Island)

Hilo

Waimea

Kailua-Kona

Alenuihaha Channel

Hana

Maui

Wailuku

Kahoolawe

Lanai City

Lanai

Molokai

Kaunakakai

Hoolehua

Kalohi Channel

Oahu

Honolulu

Kauai Channel

PACIFIC OCEAN

Lihue

Kauai

Niihau

60 km

40 miles

30

20

0

0

Bustling Waikiki, covering 1½ miles of beachfront at the east side of Honolulu, is one of the biggest resort destinations in the Pacific. Almost all of Oahu's tourist facilities are centered in Waikiki – in fact, Waikiki's hotels play host to nearly half of all visitors to the Hawaiian Islands. A monument to mass tourism, Waikiki packs an amazing array of visitor amenities: seaside restaurants, waterfront hotels, lively entertainment and a variety of beach activities are all close at hand.

Still, there's much more to Oahu than its urban quarters. Lush forest reserves and secluded hiking trails are just 15 minutes from downtown Honolulu. The rest of Oahu's sights are within one or two hours' drive of Honolulu.

Places not to be missed include the Nuuanu Pali Lookout, with its sweeping views; Kailua, with its lovely beach; and the North Shore, with its surfing mania. Oahu also has plenty of enjoyable, off-the-beaten-path attractions too. The community-run Hawaii's Plantation Village, the marketplaces in Chinatown and the county's beautiful botanical gardens are just a few of the spots waiting to be explored.

Facts about Oahu

HISTORY

Hawaii is the northern point of the huge triangle of Pacific Ocean islands known as Polynesia, which means 'many islands.' The other two points of the triangle are Easter Island to the southeast and New Zealand to the southwest.

Because the long path of migration ran from Southeast Asia and east through the islands of the South Pacific before extending north, Hawaii was the last Polynesian island chain to be settled. While parts of southern Polynesia had been colonized as early as 1000 BC, it was another 1500 years before the first settlers arrived in Hawaii.

Archaeological evidence indicates that the first settlers arrived from the Marquesas around 500 AD. They were followed by Tahitians, who arrived in Hawaii in about 1000 AD. Unlike the Marquesans, who had sparse settlements at the northwestern end of the Hawaiian chain, the Tahitians settled all of the main Hawaiian islands.

The Tahitians were thorough colonizers, arriving in double-hulled canoes that were loaded with pigs, chickens, dogs and staple food plants such as taro and bananas.

Adept seafarers who used ocean currents and star patterns to navigate, the Tahitians were not only capable of making the 2700-mile journey north but were also able to memorize the route and retrace it. Vast waves of Tahitian migration occurred throughout the 13th and 14th centuries and archaeologists now believe that Hawaii's population probably reached a plateau of approximately 250,000 by the year 1450. The voyages back and forth continued until around 1500, when all contact between Tahiti and Hawaii appears to have stopped.

Ancient Hawaii

The earliest Hawaiians had simple, animistic beliefs. Good fishing, a safe journey and a healthy child were all considered the result of being in tune with the spirits of nature.

The Menehune

Numerous Hawaiian legends tell of a tribe of happy, elf-like people called *menehunes* who came down out of the mountains to produce great engineering works in stone.

It seems likely that when the first wave of Tahitians arrived in Hawaii in about 1000 AD, they conquered and subjugated the Marquesans who had settled in Hawaii centuries earlier, forcing them to build their temples, irrigation ditches and fishponds.

The Tahitian term for 'outcast' is *manahune*, and the diminutive social status the Marquesans had in the eyes of their conquerors may have given rise to tales of a dwarf-sized race.

The menehunes may have created the temples, but the Tahitian settlers created the legends. While the stonework remains, the true identity of Hawaii's 'little people' has slipped into obscurity.

✽✽✽✽✽✽✽✽✽✽✽✽✽

Their offerings to the gods consisted of prayers and a share of the harvest.

Around the 12th century, a powerful Tahitian *kahuna* (priest), Paao, arrived in Hawaii. Convinced that the Hawaiians were too lax in their worship, Paao introduced the concept of offering human sacrifice to the gods and he built the first *luakini heiau*, a type of temple where these sacrifices took place. He also established the *kapu* system, a practice of taboos that strictly regulated all social interaction.

The kapus forbade commoners from eating the same food or even walking the same ground as the *alii*, or royalty, who were thought to be representatives of the gods. A commoner who crossed the shadow of a king could be put to death. Kapus prohibited all women from eating coconuts, bananas, pork and certain varieties of fish.

This strict system of kapus and social delineation remained intact until after the arrival of the first westerners in the late 18th century.

Religion In the old Hawaiian religion there were four main gods: Ku, Lono, Kane and Kanaloa.

Ku was the ancestor god for all generations of humankind, past, present and future. He presided over all male gods while his wife, Hina, reigned over the female gods. When the sun rose in the morning, it was said to be Ku; when it set in the evening it was Hina. Like Yin and Yang, they were responsible for heaven and earth.

Ku had many manifestations, one as the benevolent god of fishing, Ku-ula (Ku of the abundant seas), and others as the gods of forests and farming. People prayed to Ku when the harvest was scarce. At a time of drought or other such disaster, a temple would be built to appease Ku.

One of the most fearful of Ku's manifestations was Kukailimoku (Ku, the snatcher of land), the war god that Kamehameha the Great worshipped. The temples built for the worship of Kukailimoku were offered sacrifices not only of food, pigs and chickens but also of human beings.

Lono was the god in charge of the elements that brought rain and an abundant harvest. He was also the god of fertility and peace.

Kane created the first man out of the dust of the earth and breathed life into him (the Hawaiian word for man is kane), and it was from Kane that the Hawaiian chiefs were said to have descended.

Ku, Lono and Kane together created the earth, the moon, the stars and the ocean.

Kanaloa, the fourth major god, was often pitted in struggles against the other three gods. When heaven and earth separated, it was Kanaloa who was placed in charge of the spirits on earth. Forbidden from drinking *kava* (a mildly narcotic drink), these spirits revolted and, along with Kanaloa, were driven to the underworld, where Kanaloa became the ruler of the dead.

Below the four main gods, there were 40 lesser gods. The best known of them was Pele, goddess of volcanoes. Her sister Laka was goddess of the hula, and another sister, Poliahu, was the goddess of snow.

The Hawaiians had gods for all occupations and natural phenomena. There was a god for the tapa maker and a god for the canoe builder, as well as shark gods and mountain gods.

Heiaus The temples erected in ancient Hawaii, called heiau, were built in two basic styles, both of which were constructed of lava rock. One was a simple rectangular enclosure of stone walls built directly on the ground. The other was a more substantial structure built of rocks piled high to form raised terraced platforms.

Inside the heiaus were prayer towers, taboo houses and drum houses. These structures were made of ohia wood, thatched with pili grass and tied with cord from the native olona shrub. Tikis, or god images, called *kii*, were carved of wood and placed around the prayer towers.

Heiaus were most commonly dedicated to Lono, the god of harvest, or Ku, the god of war. The heiaus built in honor of Ku were called *luakini heiau* and were the only ones where human sacrifices took place.

Heiaus were built in auspicious sites, often perched on cliffs above the coast or in other places thought to have *mana*, or 'spiritual power.' A heiau's significance focused on the mana of the site rather than the structure itself. When a heiau's mana was gone, it was abandoned.

Westerners Arrive

Hawaii was the last of the Polynesian islands to be 'discovered' by the West. This is due in large part to the fact that early European explorers who entered the Pacific around the tips of either Africa or South America centered their explorations in the Southern Hemisphere. Indeed, the great British explorer Captain James Cook spent the better part of a decade exploring and charting most of the South Pacific before chancing upon Hawaii as he sailed north from Tahiti in search of a northwest passage to the Atlantic.

On January 18, 1778, Captain Cook sighted the islands of Oahu, Kauai and Niihau. The winds favored approaching Kauai, and on January 19, Cook's ships, the *Discovery* and the *Resolution*, sailed into Kauai's Waimea Bay. Cook named the Hawaiian archipelago the Sandwich Islands in honor of the Earl of Sandwich.

The captain was surprised to find that the islanders had a strong Tahitian influence in their appearance, language and culture. The natives were eager to trade fish and sweet potatoes for iron nails and anything else made of metal, which was totally absent from their islands.

Cook, whose arrival in Hawaii happened to coincide with the *makahiki*, an annual harvest festival in honor of the god Lono, was given a warm reception. After two weeks of stocking provisions, Cook's expedition continued its journey north. Failing to find the fabled passages through the Arctic, Cook set sail back to Hawaii, where his arrival date virtually coincided with that of his initial visit to the islands one year earlier.

This time he discovered the remaining Hawaiian islands. On January 17, 1779, Cook sailed into Kealakekua Bay on the Big Island, where a thousand canoes came out to greet him.

When Cook went ashore the next day, he was met by the high priest and guided to a temple lined with skulls. Everywhere the English captain went, people fell face down on the ground in front of him to the chant of 'Lono.'

Not only had Cook once again landed during the makahiki festival, but the tall masts and white sails of Cook's ships, and even the way he had sailed clockwise around the island, all fitted the legendary descriptions of how the god Lono would reappear on the scene.

Whether the priests actually believed Cook was the reincarnated Lono or whether they just used his appearance to enhance their power and add a little flair to the festivities is unknown. What is clear is that Cook never realized that both of his arrivals

to Hawaii had coincided with the makahiki festivals – he assumed this was just the way things were in everyday Hawaii.

There's little wonder that Cook had a favorable impression of the islands. The islanders treated his crew with open hospitality. Hawaiian men invited the sailors to boxing matches and other competitions, and the women performed dances and readily bedded down with Cook's men. For a crew that had just spent months roaming inhospitable frozen tundra, this was paradise indeed.

The expedition's skilled artist, John Webber, was allowed to move freely in the villages. Today, his detailed drawings of native people, costumes and village life constitute the best visual accounts of old Hawaii.

On February 4 the English vessels sailed north out of Kealakekua Bay but soon ran into a storm and the *Resolution* broke a foremast. Cook decided to go back to Kealakekua to repair the mast – a decision that would prove to be a fatal mistake.

The ruling alii seemed upset with the ships' reappearance. Apparently the makahiki was over and not only was Cook's timing inauspicious, but so were the conditions of his return: This time he had arrived in a counter-clockwise direction and with a broken sail.

Thievery became a problem for the British. After a cutter was stolen, Cook set off with a small party to capture the high chief Kalaniopuu with the intention of holding him until the cutter was returned. When Cook took the chief into custody, an angry mob cornered them. Hoping to prevent bloodshed, Cook let the chief go, but fate wasn't with the captain. As Cook was walking towards his boat, he shot at one of the armed Hawaiians who tried to block his way. The pistol misfired and the bullet bounced off the man's chest. The crowd of Hawaiians moved in on Cook with daggers and clubs.

In this freak melee on a shore of the Sandwich Islands, his last discovery, the life of the greatest explorer and navigator of the century came to a bloody end.

It was a bloody ending for Captain Cook.

A week after Cook's death, the expedition's ships set sail, landing briefly on Oahu, Kauai and Niihau before finally leaving Hawaiian waters on March 15, 1779.

Cook and his crew left the Hawaiians a costly legacy in the iron that was turned into weapons, the diseases they introduced that decimated the natives, and the first children of mixed blood. The crews also returned home with charts and maps that allowed others to follow in their wake, and in Britain and Europe, their stories and drawings were published, stirring the public's sense of adventure.

Some of Cook's crew returned to the Pacific, leading their own expeditions. Among them was Captain George Vancouver, who brought the first cattle and horses to Hawaii, and the ill-fated William Bligh, who captained the *Bounty*.

Kamehameha the Great

At the time of the first European contact with Hawaii, the Hawaiian Islands were under the control of a handful of chiefs who were engaged in a struggle for dominance of the island chain. The main rivals were Kamehameha the Great, chief of the island of Hawaii, and Kahekili, the aging king of Maui, who in the 1780s had killed his own stepson in order to take control of Oahu.

After Kahekili died at Waikiki in 1794, a power struggle ensued and his lands were divided between two quarreling relatives. His son Kalanikupule got Oahu, while his half-brother King Kaeokulani of Kauai gained control of Maui, Lanai and Molokai. The two ambitious heirs immediately went to battle with each other, creating a rift that Kamehameha set out to exploit.

In 1795 Kamehameha swept through Maui and Molokai, conquering those islands before crossing the channel to Oahu. He landed his fleet of war canoes on the quiet beaches of Waikiki and marched up towards Nuuanu Valley to meet Kalanikupule, the king of Oahu.

The Oahu warriors were no match for Kamehameha's troops. The first heavy fighting took place around the Punchbowl, where Kamehameha's men quickly circled the fortresslike crater and drove out the Oahuan defenders. Scattered fighting continued throughout the Nuuanu Valley, with the last big battle taking place near the current site of Queen Emma's summer palace, just off the Pali Hwy.

The Oahuans, who were prepared for the usual spear-and-stone warfare, panicked when they realized Kamehameha had brought in a handful of Western sharpshooters with modern firearms. Under Kamehameha's command, the foreigners picked off the Oahuan generals and blasted into their ridge-top defenses.

What should have been the high-ground advantage turned into a death trap for the Oahuans when they found themselves wedged up into the valley, unable to redeploy. Fleeing up the cliffsides in retreat, they were forced to make their last stand at the narrow, precipitous ledge along the current-day Nuuanu Pali Lookout. Hundreds of Oahuans were driven over the top of the *pali* (cliff) to their deaths.

Some Oahuan warriors, including King Kalanikupule, escaped into the upland forests. When Kalanikupule surfaced a few months later, Kamehameha, as an offering to his war god, made a human sacrifice of the fallen king. Kamehameha's taking of Oahu marked the last battle ever fought between Hawaiian troops, as well as Hawaii's emergence as a united kingdom.

Snatcher of Land

In order to amass strength, the warrior chief Kamehameha the Great became the guardian of the war god Kukailimoku, also known as the 'snatcher of land.'

This war god was embodied in a primitively carved wooden image with a bloody red mouth and a helmet of yellow feathers. Kamehameha carried it into battle with him, and it was said that during the fiercest fighting the image would screech out terrifying battle cries.

The effects of Kukailimoku aside, Kamehameha the Great became the most successful warrior in Hawaiian history and the first king to bring all Hawaii's territory under the control of a single ruler.

The Founding of Honolulu

In 1793 the English frigate *Butterworth* became the first foreign ship to sail into what is now called Honolulu Harbor. Its captain, William Brown, named the protected harbor Fair Haven. Ships that followed called it Brown's Harbor. Over time, the name Honolulu, which means 'Sheltered Bay,' came to be used for both the harbor and the seaside district that the Hawaiians had called Kou.

As more and more foreign ships found their way to Honolulu, a harborside village of thatched houses sprang up. The port soon became a focal point for merchant ships plying the seas between the USA and Asia.

In 1809 Kamehameha the Great, who had royal courts throughout the islands, decided to move to the Honolulu Harbor area, which by then had grown into a village of almost 1800 people. Intent on keeping an eye on all the trade that flowed in and out of the harbor, Kamehameha set up a residence near the waterfront on what is today the southern end of Bethel St. With Kamehameha's presence, Honolulu was firmly established as the center of Hawaii's commerce.

Kamehameha traded sandalwood, which was shipped to China, in exchange for weapons and luxury goods. As the trade grew,

Kamehameha built harborside warehouses to store his goods and he introduced wharfage fees to build up his treasury. New England Yankees, who dominated the sandalwood trade, quickly became the main foreign presence in Honolulu.

By the time of Kamehameha's death in 1819, nearly 3500 people lived in Honolulu and it continued to boom as more foreigners arrived on Hawaiian shores.

End of the Old Religion

When Kamehameha the Great died, the crown was passed to his reluctant son Liholiho, who was proclaimed Kamehameha II (1819-24). In reality, however, the power passed to Kaahumanu, who was Kamehameha's favorite of his 21 wives.

Kaahumanu was an ambitious woman, determined to break down the ancient kapu system of taboos that restricted her powers. Less than six months after Kamehameha's death, Kaahumanu threw a feast for the royal women. Although one of the most sacred taboos strictly forbade men from eating with women, Kaahumanu forcefully persuaded Liholiho to sit beside her and join in the meal.

It was an otherwise uneventful meal, and not a single angry god manifested itself. But in that one act, the old religion was cast aside, along with 600 years of taboos and restrictions. Hawaiians no longer feared being put to death for violating the kapus, and a flurry of temple smashing and idol burning quickly followed.

The chiefs and kahunas who resisted her were easily squelched by Liholiho, who used the powerful army that Kamehameha left behind. It was the end of an era.

Liholiho (Kamehameha II)

With Kaahumanu holding the real power, in November 1823 a floundering Liholiho set sail for England with his favorite wife to pay a royal visit to King George – although he failed to inform anyone in England of his plans.

When Liholiho arrived unannounced in London, misfitted in Western clothing and lacking in royal etiquette, the British press roasted him with racist caricatures. While being prepped in the social graces for their audience with the king, Liholiho and his wife came down with measles. They died in England within a few weeks of each other in July 1824, having never met King George.

Missionaries & Sinners

By 1820 whaling ships sailing the Pacific began to pull into Honolulu for supplies, liquor and women. To meet their needs, shops, taverns and brothels sprang up around the harbor.

Much to the ire of the whalers, their arrival was soon followed by that of Christian missionaries. The first missionary ship to land in Hawaii, the *Thaddeus*, sailed into Honolulu on April 14, 1820. The minister in charge of the Honolulu mission was Hiram Bingham, a staunch Calvinist who was set on putting an end to the heathen ways of the Hawaiians.

The missionaries befriended Hawaiian royalty and made their inroads quickly. When Queen Kaahumanu, the widow of Kamehameha the Great, became seriously unwell,

The Sandalwood Trade

In the early 1790s American sea captains discovered that Hawaii had great stocks of sandalwood that were worth a premium in China.

A lucrative three-way trade developed. From Honolulu the ships sailed to Canton and traded loads of the fragrant sandalwood in exchange for Chinese silk and porcelain, which were then carried back to New England ports and sold at high prices. In New England the ships were reloaded with goods to be traded to the Hawaiians.

Hawaii's forests of sandalwood were so vast at this time that the Chinese name for Hawaii was *Tahn Heong Sahn* – the 'Sandalwood Mountains.'

In an effort to maintain the resource, Kamehameha the Great took total control over the sandalwood forests, but even under his shrewd management, the bulk of the profits ended up in the sea captains' pockets. Payment for the sandalwood was in overpriced goods, originally cannons and rifles, and later exotic items such as European furniture.

Although Kamehameha was careful not to deplete all his forests or overburden his subjects, his successor Liholiho allowed local chiefs to get in on the action. These chiefs began purchasing foreign luxuries by signing promissory notes to be paid in future shipments of sandalwood.

To pay off the chiefs' rising 'debts,' commoners were forced into virtual servitude. They were used as packhorses to haul the wood, which was strapped to their backs with bands of ti leaves. The men who carted the wood were called *kua leho*, literally 'callous backs,' after the thick permanent layer of calluses that they developed. It was not uncommon for them to carry heavy loads 20 miles from the interior of the forests to ships waiting on the coast. During the height of the trade, missionaries recorded seeing caravans of as many as 3000 men carting wood.

Within a few short years after Kamehameha's death, Hawaii's sandalwood forests were exhausted. In a futile attempt to continue the trade, Oahu's governor Boki, who had heard of vast sandalwood reserves in New Hebrides, set sail in November 1829 with 500 men on an ill-conceived expedition to harvest the trees. Boki's ship was lost at sea and the expedition's other ship, not too surprisingly, received a hostile welcome in New Hebrides.

In August 1830, 20 emaciated survivors sailed back into Honolulu Harbor. Boki had been a popular, if troubled, leader, in a rapidly changing Hawaii. Hawaiians grieved in the streets of Honolulu when they heard of Boki's tragedy, and his death marked the end of the sandalwood trade.

Whaling in the Pacific

From the 1820s to 1870, Hawaii was the whaling center of the Pacific. It was a convenient way station for whalers hunting in both the Arctic and Japanese whaling grounds. At its peak, between 500 and 600 whaling ships were pulling into Hawaiian ports each year.

Hawaiians themselves made good whalers, and sea captains gladly paid a $200 bond to the Hawaiian government for each *kanaka* (native Hawaiian) allowed to join their crew. Kamehameha IV even set up his own fleet of whaling ships, which flew under the Hawaiian flag.

Whaling in the Pacific peaked in the mid-19th century and quickly began to burn itself out. In a few short years all but the most distant whaling grounds were being depleted and whalers were forced to go farther afield to make their kills. By 1860 whale oil prices were dropping as an emerging petroleum industry began to produce a less expensive fuel for lighting.

The last straw for the Pacific whaling industry came in 1871, when an early storm in the Arctic caught more than 30 ships by surprise, trapping them in ice floes above the Bering Strait. Although more than 1000 seamen were rescued, half of them Hawaiian, the fleet itself was lost.

❋❋❋❋❋❋❋❋❋❋❋❋❋

Hiram's wife, Sybil Bingham, nursed the queen back to health. Shortly after, Kaahumanu showed her gratitude by passing a law forbidding work and travel on the Sabbath.

Although both the missionaries and the whalers hailed from New England, they had little else in common and were soon at odds, with the missionaries intent on saving souls and the whalers intent, after months at sea, on satisfying more earthly desires. In January 1826 the captain of the American warship USS *Dolphin*, having arrived in Honolulu to investigate trade issues, raised a stir with the missionaries by advocating prostitution. In response, Bingham convinced the island chiefs to put a kapu on women, forbidding them to board ships in the harbor. After the sailors stoned Bingham's house, the women were once again allowed free contact with the crews, but the struggles between whalers and missionaries continued.

In time the missionaries gained enough influence with Hawaiian royalty to have more effective laws enacted against drunkenness and prostitution. By the peak whaling years of the mid-1800s, most whaling boats had abandoned Honolulu, preferring to land in Lahaina on Maui, where the whalers had gained an upper hand over the missionaries.

Interestingly, both groups left their marks on Honolulu. To this day the headquarters of the Protestant mission sits placidly in downtown Honolulu, while only minutes away Honolulu's red-light district continues to attracts sea-weary sailors and wayward souls.

Downtown Honolulu also became the headquarters for the emerging corporations that eventually gained control of Hawaii's commerce. It's no coincidence that their lists of corporate board members – Alexander, Baldwin, Cooke and Dole – read like a roster from the first mission ships, for indeed it was the sons of missionaries who became the power brokers in the new Hawaii.

Sugar Plantations

Ko, or sugarcane, arrived in Hawaii with the early Polynesian settlers. Although the Hawaiians enjoyed chewing the cane for its juices, they never refined it into sugar.

The first known attempt at producing sugar in Hawaii was in 1802, when a Chinese immigrant boiled crushed sugarcane in iron pots. Other Chinese soon set up small sugar mills on the scale of neighborhood bakeries.

In 1835 a young Bostonian, William Hooper, saw a bigger opportunity in sugar and set out to establish Hawaii's first sugar plantation. Hooper convinced Honolulu investors Ladd & Company to put up the money for his venture and then worked out a deal with Kamehameha III to lease 980 acres of land on Kauai for $300. His next step was to negotiate with Kauai's alii for the right to use Hawaiian laborers.

In the mid-1830s Hawaii was still largely feudalistic. Commoners fished, farmed and lived on land that was under the domain of the local alii; in exchange the commoners worked when needed for the alii. Therefore, before Hooper could hire any work hands, he had to first pay the alii a stipend to free the Hawaiians from their traditional work obligations.

The new plantation system, which introduced the concept of growing crops for profit rather than subsistence, marked the advent of capitalism and the introduction of wage labor in Hawaii.

The sugar industry emerged simultaneously with the whaling industry. Together they became the foundation for Hawaii's prosperous economy.

By the 1850s sugar plantations were established on Oahu, Maui and the Big Island, as well as on Kauai.

Sugarcane, a giant grass, only flourishes with abundant water. The first plantations were limited to the rainier areas, but irrigation ditches were soon built to carry mountain water into dry plains, converting them into drenched cane fields as well. Today Hawaii is still criss-crossed with hundreds of miles of working ditches and aqueducts built a century ago.

In addition to the irrigation systems, the sugar companies built railroads, such as the Oahu Railway & Land Company, to carry the cane from the fields to the mills. For more than 100 years, sugar formed the backbone of the Hawaiian economy.

Hawaii's Immigrants

As the sugar industry boomed, Hawaii's native population declined, largely as the result of diseases introduced by foreigners.

To expand their operations, the plantation owners began to look overseas for a labor supply. They needed immigrants accustomed to working long days in hot weather and for whom low wages would seem like an opportunity.

In 1852 the plantation owners began recruiting laborers from China. In 1868 they went to Japan and in the 1870s they brought in Portuguese from Madeira and the Azores. After Hawaii's annexation to the USA in 1898 resulted in restrictions on Chinese immigration, plantation owners turned to Puerto Ricans and Koreans. Filipinos were the last group of immigrants brought to Hawaii to work the fields; the first wave came in 1906, the last in 1946.

Although these six ethnic groups made up the bulk of the field hands, a number of South Sea islanders, Scots, Scandinavians, Germans, Galicians, Spaniards and Russians all came in turn as well.

Each group brought its own culture, food and religion. Chinese clothing styles mixed with Japanese kimonos and European bonnets. A dozen languages filled the air and a unique pidgin English developed as a means for the various groups to communicate with one another.

Conditions varied with the ethnic group and the period. At the end of the 19th century, Japanese contract laborers were paid $15 a month. After annexation, the contracts were declared illegal under US law as a form of indentured servitude. Still, wages as low as a dollar a day were common until the 1930s.

In all, approximately 350,000 immigrants came to Hawaii to work on the sugar plantations. A continuous flow of immigrant workers was required to replace those who invariably found better options elsewhere. Although some workers came for a set period to save money and then return home, others fulfilled their contracts and then moved off the plantations to farm their own plots or start their own businesses.

Plantation towns such as Waipahu and Waialua grew up around the mills, with barber shops, beer halls and bathhouses catering to the workers. Even today a drive through these sleepy Oahuan towns, with their now defunct mills (both closed in the 1990s), offers a glimpse of their plantation history.

The major immigrant populations – Japanese, Chinese, Filipino and Western European – came to outnumber the native Hawaiians. Together they created the unique blend of cultures that would continue to characterize Hawaii for generations to come.

Honolulu as Capital

In 1845, Kamehameha III, the last son of Kamehameha the Great, moved the capital of the Kingdom of Hawaii from Maui to Honolulu. Kamehameha III, who ruled from 1825 to 1854, established Hawaii's first national legislature, provided for a supreme court and passed the Great Mahele land act, which established religious freedom and gave all male citizens the right to vote.

Hawaii's only 'invasion' by a foreign power occurred during Kamehameha III's reign. In 1843, George Paulet, an upstart British commander upset about a petty land deal involving a British national, sailed into Honolulu commanding the British ship *Carysfort* and seized Oahu for six months. In that short period, he anglicized street names, seized property and began to collect taxes.

To avoid bloodshed, Kamehameha III stood aside as the British flag was raised and the ship's band played 'God Save the Queen.' Queen Victoria herself wasn't flattered. After catching wind of the incident, she dispatched Admiral Richard Thomas to restore Hawaiian independence. Admiral Thomas re-raised the Hawaiian flag in Honolulu at the site of what is today Thomas Square.

As the flag was raised, Kamehameha III uttered the words *Ua mau ke ea o ka aina i ka pono*, meaning 'The life of the land is perpetuated in righteousness,' which remains Hawaii's official motto.

In an 1853 census, Honolulu registered 11,450 residents, a full 15% of the Hawaiian kingdom's population. Though still a frontier town with dusty streets and simple wooden

The Great Mahele

The Great Mahele of 1848, introduced under the urging of influential missionaries, permanently altered the Hawaiian concept of land rights: For the first time, land became a commodity that could be bought and sold.

Through the provisions of the Great Mahele, the king, who previously owned all land, gave up title to the majority of it. Island chiefs were allowed to buy some of the lands that they had controlled as fiefdoms for the king. Other lands, divided into 3-acre farm plots called *kuleana*, were made available to all Hawaiians. In order to retain title, chiefs and commoners alike had to pay a tax and register the land.

The chiefs had the option of paying the tax in property and many did so. Commoners had no choice but to pay the taxes in cash. Although the act was intended to turn Hawaii into a country of small farms, in the end, only a few thousand Hawaiians carried through with the paperwork and received kuleanas.

In 1850 land purchases were opened to foreigners. Unlike the Hawaiians, the westerners jumped at the opportunity, and before the native islanders could clearly grasp the concept of private land ownership, there was little land left to own. Within a few decades the westerners, who were more adept at wheeling and dealing in real estate, owned 80% of all privately held lands. Sadly, even many of the Hawaiians who went through the process of getting their own kuleana eventually sold it for a fraction of its real value.

Contrary to the bright picture the missionaries painted for Kamehameha III, the Hawaiians became a landless people, drifting into ghettos in the larger towns. In a bitter twist, many of the missionaries ended up with sizable tracts of land and more than a few of them left the church to devote themselves to their new estates.

Although Hawaiian commoners did not have ownership rights to land prior to the Great Mahele, they did have access to it, paying the chief in labor or with a percentage of their crops for their personal use of it. In this way, they lived off the land. After the Great Mahele, they were simply *off* the land.

buildings, Honolulu was both the commercial and political center of the kingdom.

In the decades that followed, Honolulu took on a modern appearance as the monarchy erected a number of stately buildings in the city center, including St Andrew's Cathedral, Iolani Palace and the supreme court building Aliiolani Hale.

By the mid-19th century, Honolulu had a prominent foreign community composed largely of American and British expatriates. These foreigners were not only active in missionary endeavors but were also opening schools and starting newspapers and, more importantly, landing powerful government positions as ministry officials and consuls to the king. As the city continued to grow and westerners wrested increasing control over island affairs from the Hawaiians, the powers of Kamehameha the Great's successors eroded.

Kamehameha IV

Kamehameha IV had a short and rather confusing reign that lasted from 1855 to 1863. He tried to give his rule an element of European regality, à la Queen Victoria, and he and his consort, Queen Emma, established a Hawaiian branch of the Anglican Church of England. He also passed a law mandating that all children be given a Christian name along with their Hawaiian name, a statute that stayed on the books until 1967.

Kamehameha IV's reign was marked by struggles between those wanting to strengthen the monarchy and those wishing to limit it.

Kamehameha V

The most significant accomplishment of Kamehameha V, who reigned from 1863 to 1872, was the establishment of a controversial constitution that gave greater power to the king at the expense of elected officials. It also restricted the right to vote.

Kamehameha V, who suffered a severe bout of unrequited love, was the last king from a royal lineage that dated back to the 12th century. From childhood, he had been enraptured by Princess Bernice Pauahi, who turned down his proposals, opting instead to marry American Charles Reed Bishop. Jolted by the rejection, Kamehameha V never married, yet he also never gave up on the princess. Even on his deathbed he offered Princess Bernice his kingdom, which she declined.

As the bachelor king left no heirs, his death in December 1872 brought an end to the Kamehameha dynasty. Subsequent kings would be elected.

Lunalilo

King Lunalilo's short reign lasted from 1873 to 1874. His cabinet, made up largely of Americans, was instrumental in paving the way for a treaty of reciprocity with the USA.

Although the USA was the biggest market for Hawaiian sugar, US sugar tariffs ate heavily into profit margins. As a means of eliminating the tariffs, most plantation owners favored the annexation of Hawaii to the USA.

The US government was cool to the idea of annexation, but it warmed to the possibility of establishing a naval base on Oahu. In 1872 General John Schofield was sent to assess Pearl Harbor's strategic value. He was impressed with what he saw – the largest anchorage in the Pacific – and enthusiastically reported his findings to Washington.

Although native Hawaiians protested in the streets and the Royal Troops even staged a little mutiny, there would eventually be a reciprocity agreement that would cede Pearl Harbor to the USA in exchange for duty-free access for Hawaiian sugar.

King Kalakaua

King David Kalakaua, who reigned from 1874 to 1891, was Hawaii's last king. Although known as the 'Merrie Monarch,' he ruled in troubled times.

The first challenge to his reign came on election day. His contender was the dowager Queen Emma, and when the results were announced her followers rioted in the streets, requiring Kalakaua to request aid from US and British warships that happened to be in Honolulu Harbor at the time.

Despite the initial turmoil, Kalakaua went on to become a great Hawaiian revivalist.

Hawaii's Alii

Hawaii is the only state in the USA to have been ruled by its own monarchy. Beginning with Kamehameha the Great's 1795 unification of the islands, the reign of Hawaii's *alii* continued until the overthrow of Queen Liliuokalani by American businessmen in 1893. The following are the dates that each of Hawaii's monarchs lived.

NED FRIARY

King Kalakaua

Kamehameha the Great	c1758-1819
Kamehameha II (Liholiho)	1797-1824
Kamehameha III (Kauikeauoli)	1813-1854
Kamehameha IV (Alexander Liholiho)	1834-1863
Kamehameha V (Lot Kamehameha)	1830-1872
Lunalilo (William C Lunalilo)	1832-1874
Kalakaua (David Kalakaua)	1836-1891
Liliuokalani (Lydia Liliuokalani)	1838-1917

He brought back the hula, reversing decades of missionary repression against the 'heathen dance,' and he composed the national anthem *Hawaii Ponoi*, which is now the state song. Kalakaua also tried to ensure some self-rule for native Hawaiians, who had become a minority in their own land.

Although he was unwaveringly loyal to the interest of native Hawaiians, Kalakaua was realistic about the current-day realities he faced. The king proved himself a successful diplomat by traveling to Washington, DC, and persuading President Ulysses Grant to accept a treaty giving Hawaiian sugar growers tariff-free access to US markets, which the US Congress had been resisting. In so doing, Kalakaua gained, at least temporarily, the support of the sugar plantation owners, who controlled most of Hawaii's agricultural land.

During his trip Kalakaua also managed to postpone the ceding of Pearl Harbor for eight years. He returned to Hawaii a hero – to the business community for negotiating the treaty, and to the Hawaiians for simply making it back alive (the last king to leave the islands, Kamehameha II, came back in a coffin).

The king became a world traveler, visiting India, Egypt, Europe and Southeast Asia. Kalakaua was well aware that Hawaii's days as an independent Polynesian kingdom were numbered. To counter the Western powers

that were gaining hold of Hawaii, he made a futile attempt to establish a Polynesian-Pacific empire. On a visit with the emperor of Japan, he even proposed a royal marriage between his niece Princess Kaiulani and a Japanese prince, but the Japanese declined.

Visits with other foreign monarchs gave Kalakaua a taste for royal pageantry. He returned to build Iolani Palace for what the business community thought was an extravagant $360,000. To many influential whites, the king was perceived as a lavish spender fond of partying and throwing public luaus.

As Kalakaua incurred debts, he became increasingly less popular with the sugar barons whose businesses were now the backbone of the economy. In 1887 they formed the Hawaiian League and developed their own armies, which stood ready to overthrow Kalakaua. The league presented Kalakaua with a list of demands and forced him to accept a new constitution strictly limiting his powers. It also limited suffrage to property owners, which at that time excluded the vast majority of Hawaiians.

On July 30, 1889, a group of about 150 Hawaiians attempted to overthrow the new constitution by occupying Iolani Palace. Called the Wilcox Rebellion after its part-Hawaiian leader, it was a confused and futile attempt and the rebels were forced to surrender. Kalakaua died in San Francisco in 1891, bringing an end to the Hawaiian monarchy.

Overthrow of Queen Liliuokalani

Kalakaua was succeeded by his sister, Liliuokalani, wife of Oahu's governor John O Dominis.

Queen Liliuokalani (1891-93) was even more determined than Kalakaua to strengthen the power of the monarchy. She charged that the 1887 constitution was illegally forced upon King Kalakaua. In a controversial decision, the Hawaii Supreme Court upheld her contention.

In January 1893, Queen Liliuokalani was preparing to proclaim a new constitution to restore royal powers when a group of armed US businessmen occupied the supreme court and declared the monarchy overthrown. They announced a provisional government, led by Sanford Dole, son of a pioneer missionary.

A contingent of US sailors came ashore, ostensibly to protect the property of US citizens, but instead of going to neighborhoods where Americans lived, they marched on the palace and positioned their guns at the queen's residence. The queen opted to avoid bloodshed and stepped down.

The provisional government immediately appealed to Washington for annexation, while the queen appealed to the same powers to restore the monarchy. To the dismay of Dole's representatives, the timing seemed to be to the queen's advantage. Democratic president Grover Cleveland had just replaced a Republican administration and his sentiments favored the queen. Cleveland sent an envoy to investigate the situation and received Queen Liliuokalani's niece Princess Kaiulani, who, at the time of the coup, was in London being prepared for the throne. The beautiful 18-year-old princess eloquently pleaded the monarchy's case. She also made a favorable impression on the American press, which largely caricatured those involved in the overthrow as dour, greedy buffoons.

Cleveland ordered that the US flag be taken down and the queen restored to her throne. However, the provisional government, now firmly in power, turned a deaf ear, declaring that Cleveland was meddling in 'Hawaiian' affairs.

On July 4, 1894, Dole stood on the steps of Iolani Palace and announced that Hawaii was now a republic and he was its president. A disapproving Cleveland initially favored reversing the situation, but he realized that the US public's sense of justice was weak and that ousting a government of white Americans and replacing them with native Hawaiians could backlash on his own political future. Consequently, his actions were largely limited to rhetoric.

Weary of waiting for outside intervention, in early 1895 a group of Hawaiian royalists attempted a counter-revolution that was easily squashed. Liliuokalani was accused of being a conspirator and placed under arrest.

To humiliate her, the queen was tried in her own palace and referred to only as Mrs John O Dominis. She was fined $5000 and sentenced to five years of hard labor, later reduced to nine months of house arrest at the palace.

Liliuokalani spent the rest of her life in her husband's residence, Washington Place, one block from the palace. When she died in November 1917, all of Honolulu came out for the funeral procession. To most islanders, Liliuokalani was still their queen.

Annexation

With the Spanish-American War of 1898, Americans acquired a taste for expansionism, and Hawaii was an interesting prospect.

Not only was Hawaii attractive because of Pearl Harbor, it took on a new strategic importance being midway between the USA and its newly acquired possession, the Philippines. The annexation of Hawaii was approved by the US Congress on July 7, 1898, and Hawaii entered the 20th century as a territory of the USA.

In just over a century of Western contact, the native Hawaiian population was decimated by foreign diseases to which it had no immunities. It began with the venereal disease introduced by Captain Cook's crew in 1778. The whalers followed with cholera and smallpox, and Chinese immigrants, who came to replace Hawaiian laborers, brought leprosy. By the end of the 19th century, the native Hawaiian population was reduced from an estimated 300,000 to less than 50,000.

Descendants of the early missionaries first took over the land and then the government. Without ever fighting a single battle against a foreign power, Hawaiians lost their islands to ambitious foreigners. All in all, as far as the native Hawaiians were concerned, the annexation wasn't anything to celebrate.

The Chinese and Japanese were also uneasy. One of the reasons for the initial reluctance of the US Congress to annex Hawaii was the racial mix of the islands' population. There were already restrictions on Chinese immigration to the USA, and restrictions on Japanese immigration were expected to follow.

In a rush to avoid a labor shortage, the sugar plantation owners quickly brought 70,000 Japanese immigrants into Hawaii. By the time the immigration wave was over, the Japanese accounted for more than 40% of Hawaii's population.

In the years after the reciprocity agreement negotiated by King Kalakaua, sugar production increased tenfold. Those who ruled the land ruled the government, and closer bonding with the USA didn't change the formula. In 1900, President McKinley appointed Sanford Dole the first territorial governor.

World War I

Soon after annexation, the US Navy set up a huge Pacific headquarters at Pearl Harbor and built Schofield Barracks, the largest US army base anywhere. The military quickly became the leading sector of Oahu's economy.

The islands were relatively untouched by WWI, even though the first German prisoners of war 'captured' by the USA were in Hawaii. They were escorted off the German gunboat *Grier*, which had the misfortune to be docked at Honolulu Harbor when war broke out.

The war affected people in Hawaii in other ways. Heinrich Hackfeld, a German sea captain long settled in the islands, had established Hawaii's most successful merchandise stores, BF Ehler's & Company. During WWI, anti-German sentiments forced Hackfeld to liquidate his holdings, and American Factors (Amfac) took over his stores, ironically renaming them Liberty House.

Pineapples & Planes

In the early 20th century, pineapple emerged as Hawaii's second major export crop. James Dole, a cousin of Sanford Dole, purchased the island of Lanai in 1922 and turned it into the world's largest pineapple plantation. He also established similar operations on Oahu. Although sugar remained Hawaii's top crop in export value, the more labor-intensive pineapple eventually surpassed it in terms of employment.

In 1936, Pan American flew the first passenger flights from the US mainland to Hawaii, an aviation milestone that ushered in the transpacific air age. Hawaii was now only hours away from the US West Coast.

World War II

On December 7, 1941, a wave of Japanese bombers attacked Pearl Harbor, jolting the USA into WWII. The devastating strike, which lasted two hours, caught the US fleet by surprise. A total of 2335 US soldiers were killed and 21 ships and nearly 350 planes were lost.

After the smoke cleared, Hawaii was placed under martial law and Oahu took on the face of a military camp. Already heavily militarized, vast tracts of Hawaii's land were turned over to the US armed forces for expanded military bases, training and weapons testing. Much of that land would never be returned. Throughout the war, Oahu served as the command post for the USA's Pacific operations.

Following the attack on Pearl Harbor, a wave of suspicion landed on the *nisei* (people of Japanese descent) in Hawaii. While sheer numbers prevented the sort of internment practices that took place on the mainland, the Japanese in Hawaii were subject to interrogation, and their religious and civic leaders were sent to mainland internment camps.

Japanese language schools were closed, and many of the teachers arrested. Posters were hung in restaurants and other public places warning islanders to be careful about speaking carelessly in front of anyone of Japanese ancestry. Nisei were dismissed from posts in the Hawaiian National Guard and prevented from joining the armed services.

Eventually Japanese-Americans were allowed to volunteer for a segregated regiment, although they were kept on the mainland and out of the action for much of the war's duration.

During the final stages of the war, when fighting was at its heaviest, the nisei were given the chance to form a combat unit. Volunteers were called and more than 10,000 nisei signed up, forming two distinguished Japanese-American regiments. One of these, the 442nd Second Regimental Combat Team, which was sent into action on the European front, became the most decorated fighting unit in US history.

The veterans returned to Hawaii with different expectations. Many went on to college using the GI bill, and today they account for some of Hawaii's most influential lawyers, judges and civic leaders. Among the veterans of the 442nd is Hawaii's senior US senator, Daniel Inouye, who lost an arm in the fighting.

Unionizing Hawaii

The mainland-based International Longshoremen's and Warehousemen's Union (ILWU) began organizing Hawaiian labor in the 1930s.

After WWII, the ILWU organized an intensive campaign against the 'Big Five' – C Brewer, Castle & Cooke, Alexander & Baldwin, Theo Davies and Amfac – Hawaii's biggest businesses and landholders, all of which had roots in the sugar industry.

The ILWU's six-month waterfront strike in 1949 virtually halted all shipments to and from Hawaii. The union went on to organize plantation strikes that resulted in Hawaii's sugar and pineapple workers becoming the world's highest paid.

The new union movement helped develop political opposition to the staunchly Republican landowners, who had maintained a stronghold on the political scene since annexation.

In the 1950s, McCarthyism, the fanatical wave of anti-Communism that swept the mainland, spilled over to Hawaii. In the fallout, the leader of the ILWU in Hawaii, Jack Hall, was tried and convicted of being a Communist.

Statehood

WWII brought Hawaii closer to the center stage of American culture and politics.

The prospect of statehood was long the central topic in Hawaiian political circles. Three decades had passed since Prince Jonah Kuhio Kalanianaole, Hawaii's first delegate to the US Congress, introduced the first statehood bill in 1919. It received a cool reception in Washington at that time, and there were mixed feelings in Hawaii as well. However, by the time the war was over, opinion polls showed that two out of three Hawaiian residents favored statehood.

Still, Hawaii was too much of a melting pot for many politicians to support statehood, particularly those from the rigidly segregated southern states. To the overwhelmingly white and largely conservative Congress, Hawaii's multiethnic community was too exotic and foreign to be thought of as 'American.'

Congress was also concerned with the success of Hawaiian labor strikes and the growth of membership in the ILWU. These factors combined to keep statehood at bay until the end of the 1950s.

In March 1959 the US Congress finally passed legislation to make Hawaii a state. On June 27 a plebiscite was held in Hawaii, with more than 90% of the islanders voting for statehood.

On August 21, 1959, after 61 years of territorial status, Hawaii became the 50th state of the USA.

Hawaiian Sovereignty

Over the past decade, a Hawaiian sovereignty movement, intent on righting some of the wrongs of the past century, has become a forefront political issue in Hawaii. Growing

Hawaiian Home Lands

In 1920, under the sponsorship of Prince Jonah Kuhio Kalanianaole, the congressional delegate for the Territory of Hawaii, the US Congress passed the Hawaiian Homes Commission Act. The act set aside almost 200,000 acres of land for homesteading by native Hawaiians, who were by this time the most landless ethnic group in Hawaii. The land was but a small fraction of the crown lands that were taken from the Kingdom of Hawaii when the USA annexed the islands in 1898.

Under the legislation, people of at least 50% Hawaiian ancestry were eligible to apply for 99-year leases at $1 a year. Originally, most of the leases were for 40-acre parcels of agricultural land, although more recently residential lots as small as a quarter of an acre have been allocated.

Hawaii's prime land, already in the hands of the sugar barons, was excluded from the act, and much of what was designated for homesteading was on far more barren turf. Still, many Hawaiians were able to make a go of it. Presently, there are about 6500 native Hawaiian families living on about 30,000 acres of homestead lands.

Like many acts established to help native Hawaiians, administration of the Hawaiian Home Lands has been riddled with abuse. The majority of the land has not been allocated to native Hawaiians but has been leased out at bargain rates to big business, ostensibly as a means of creating an income for the administration of the program.

In addition, the federal, state and county governments have illegally, and with little or no compensation, taken large tracts of Hawaiian Home Lands for their own use. The Lualualei Naval Reservation alone constitutes one-fifth of all homestead lands on Oahu, despite the fact that more than 5000 Oahuans of native Hawaiian descent remain on the waiting list – some for as long as 30 years.

discontent over the mismanagement of Hawaiian Home Lands and the heightened consciousness created by the 1993 centennial anniversary of Queen Liliuokalani's overthrow have served as rallying points. Things are still in a formative stage, and a consensus on what form sovereignty should take has yet to emerge.

Ka Lahui Hawaii, the largest of the many Hawaiian sovereignty groups, has adopted a constitution for a Hawaiian nation within the USA, similar to that of 300 Native American groups on the mainland who have their own tribal governments and lands. Ka Lahui Hawaii wants all Hawaiian Home Lands, as well as the title to much of the crown land taken during annexation, turned over to native Hawaiians. These lands include nearly 1¾ million acres that were held by the Hawaiian Kingdom at the time of the 1893 overthrow.

Other native Hawaiian groups are also calling for self-determination. Some favor

the restoration of the monarchy, others focus on monetary reparations, but the majority are looking at some form of a nation-within-a-nation model.

One sovereignty demand was addressed in November 1993, when US president Bill Clinton signed a resolution apologizing 'to Native Hawaiians for the overthrow of the Kingdom of Hawaii on January 17, 1893, with participation of agents and citizens of the United States, and the deprivation of the rights of Native Hawaiians to self-determination.' The apology went on to 'acknowledge the ramifications of the overthrow' and expressed a commitment to 'provide a proper foundation for reconciliation.'

Ka Lahui introduced state legislation to establish their group as the stewards of a new Hawaiian nation, and two other sovereignty bills were also introduced. In part to sort out the disparity between the three bills, the state legislature established the Hawaiian Sovereignty Advisory Commission to create a mechanism for native Hawaiians to determine what form sovereignty should take.

The commission itself, however, became a source of conflict, as all 20 of the commission members were chosen by the governor, and only 12 of those were selected from nominees submitted by native Hawaiian organizations. Consequently, some groups, such as Ka Lahui and Nation of Hawaii, refused to participate in the commission.

In the summer of 1996, a commission-sponsored mail-in vote, open to all people of Hawaiian ancestry, was held on the ballot question, 'Shall the Hawaiian People elect delegates to propose a native Hawaiian government?' It was a first-step vote to determine if native Hawaiians wanted to establish a sovereignty process that would be based on electing delegates and holding a convention to chart out their future.

Of the 80,000 ballots mailed to native Hawaiians worldwide, some 30,000 were returned. The initiative passed, with 73% voting yes and 27% against, but in many ways it was a far more divided vote. Some native Hawaiians, including members of Ka Lahui, felt the process was co-opted by the state, which had provided funding for the ballot, and they boycotted the vote. The controversial commission itself disbanded after the vote, and the state declared it would not provide funding for the delegate elections and convention. A nonprofit group, Ha Hawaii, which includes former members of the commission, then spent two years raising funds for that purpose.

In 1999, the Ha Hawaii-organized election took place for the selection of 85 delegates to form a Hawaiian Convention aimed at charting the sovereignty course. However, many groups boycotted this election as well, claiming the Ha Hawaii vote was influenced by the state and the process itself was flawed. Consequently, the voter turnout was only 8.7% – fewer than 9000 of the 102,000 eligible voters participated. With so few people embracing the election, the future of the convention remains in doubt, and there's still no clear consensus on a forum for debating sovereignty issues.

Although attitudes may change once the movement takes shape, polls show that a significant majority of all Hawaii residents support the concept of Hawaiian sovereignty if it's within the framework of a nation-within-a-nation. Interestingly, support for the sovereignty movement doesn't vary greatly along ethnic lines.

Incidentally, the Hawaiian flag flown upside down as a sign of distress has come to represent the Hawaiian sovereignty movement.

GEOGRAPHY

The Hawaiian Islands stretch 1523 miles in a line from Kure Atoll in the northwest to the Big Island in the southeast. Hawaii is the southernmost state in the USA.

The equator is 1470 miles south of Honolulu, and all the main Hawaiian islands are in the tropic of Cancer. Hawaii shares the same latitude as Hong Kong, Bombay and Mexico's Yucatán Peninsula. Honolulu is 2557 miles from Los Angeles, 3847 miles from Tokyo and 5070 miles from Sydney.

Hawaii's eight major islands are, from largest to smallest, Hawaii (the Big Island), Maui, Oahu, Kauai, Molokai, Lanai, Niihau and Kahoolawe. Together, they have a land area of 6470 sq miles, which includes 96 small nearshore islands with a combined area of less than 3 square miles. Hawaii's boundaries also include the Northwestern Hawaiian Islands, 33 tiny islands that lie scattered across a thousand miles of ocean west of Kauai; their combined land area is just 5 square miles. In total, Hawaii is a bit smaller than Fiji and a bit larger than the US state of Connecticut.

Oahu, which covers 594 sq miles, is the third-largest Hawaiian island. It basically has four sides, with distinct windward and leeward coasts and north and south shores. The island's extreme length is 44 miles, its width 30 miles.

Two separate volcanoes arose to form Oahu's two mountain ranges, Waianae and Koolau, which slice the island from the northwest to the southeast. Oahu's highest point, Mt Kaala at 4020 feet, is in the Waianae Range.

GEOLOGY

The Hawaiian Islands are the tips of massive mountains created by a crack in the earth's mantle that has been spewing out molten rock for more than 25 million years. The hot spot is stationary, but the ocean floor is part of the Pacific Plate, which is moving northwest at the rate of about three inches a year. (The eastern edge of this plate is California's San Andreas fault.)

As weak spots in the earth's crust pass over the hot spot, molten lava bursts through as volcanoes, building underwater mountains. Some of them finally emerge above the water as islands.

Each new volcano eventually creeps northward past the hot spot that created it. The farther from the source, the lower the volcanic activity, until the volcano is eventually cut off completely and turns cold.

Once the lava stops, it's a downhill battle. The forces of erosion (wind, rain and waves) slowly wash the mountains away. In addition, the settling of the ocean floor causes the land to gradually recede.

While the main Hawaiian islands still have impressive topography, the once mountainous Northwestern Hawaiian Islands, the oldest in the Hawaiian chain, are now flat atolls that in time will be totally submerged.

The Big Island, Hawaii's southernmost island, is still in the birthing process. Its most active volcano, Kilauea, is directly over the hot spot. In its latest eruptive phase, which began in 1983 and still continues, Kilauea has pumped out more than 2 billion cubic yards of lava, making this the largest known volcanic eruption in Hawaii's history.

In addition, a new Hawaiian island appears to be in the making. Less than 30 miles southeast of the Big Island, an emerging seamount named Loihi has already built up 15,000 feet on the ocean floor. It now lies about 3100 feet below the surface of the water. The growing mounds of lava are expected to break the ocean surface within 10,000 years; however, if it were to get hyperactive, it could emerge within a century or two.

Hawaii's volcanoes are shield volcanoes, which form not by explosion but by a slow buildup of layer upon layer of lava. They rise from the sea with gentle slopes and a relatively smooth surface. It's only after eons of facing the elements that their surfaces become sharply eroded. It's for this reason that the most fluted cliffs in Hawaii – those on the Na Pali Coast on Kauai and the Koolau Range on Oahu – are on the two oldest main Hawaiian islands.

CLIMATE

Hawaii's climate is typically warm and sunny. It's unusually pleasant for the tropics, as near-constant trade winds prevail throughout the year. Although there can be spells of stormy weather, particularly in the winter, much of the time the rain falls as short daytime showers accompanied by rainbows.

In Honolulu the average daily maximum temperature is 84°F and the minimum is 70°F. Temperatures are a bit higher in summer and a few degrees lower in winter. The highest temperature on record is 94°F and the lowest is 53°F.

Rainfall varies greatly with elevation, even within short distances. Waikiki has an average annual rainfall of only 25 inches, whereas the Lyon Arboretum in the upper Manoa Valley, at the north side of Honolulu,

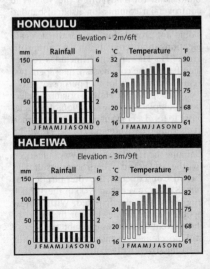

averages 158 inches. Mid-afternoon humidity averages 56%.

Average water temperatures in Waikiki are 77°F in March, 82°F in August.

The National Weather Service provides recorded weather forecasts for Honolulu (☎ 973-4380), for all Oahu (☎ 973-4381) and for marine conditions (☎ 973-4382). You can also see what's happening with the weather in the Hawaiian Islands by going online (www.hawaii.edu/news/hhp.weather.html).

ECOLOGY & ENVIRONMENT

Hawaii has one of the world's most isolated and fragile ecosystems. Hawaiian native species are highly sensitive to habitat degradation and over the past century numerous species became extinct, including more than a third of all native forest birds. Today, fully half of Hawaii's native flora and fauna is either threatened or endangered.

Vast tracts of native forest have long been buried under to give way to the monocrop cultures of sugarcane and pineapple. In the 1960s the advent of mass tourism posed new challenges to the environment, most notably in the rampant development of land-hungry golf courses. In the past two decades the number of golf courses on Oahu has jumped from just a handful to 36, and the total acreage given over to these golf courses now rivals that used for plantation agriculture.

In terms of air quality, Oahu has no polluting heavy industry. However, Honolulu, being on the dry and less windy leeward side of the island, occasionally has moderate levels of vehicle-related pollution. As for general aesthetics, roadside billboards are not allowed and overall, the level of environmental awareness is more advanced than on much of the US mainland.

There are more than 150 environmental groups in Hawaii, running the gamut from chapters of international organizations fighting to save the rain forests to neighborhood groups working to protect local beaches from impending development.

One of the broadest-based is the Hawaii chapter of the Sierra Club, whose activities range from political activism on local environmental issues to weekend outings for eradicating invasive plants from the island's native forests.

Also in the forefront is the nonprofit Earthjustice Legal Defense Fund (formerly the Sierra Club Legal Defense Fund), which presses legal challenges against abuses to Hawaii's fragile environment. For instance, in conjunction with Greenpeace Hawaii, they've forced the state of Hawaii to prohibit jet skis in waters used by endangered humpback whales.

In 1999, the Earthjustice Legal Defense Fund, together with the Center for Marine Conservation and the Sea Turtle Restoration Project, filed a lawsuit to stop the ongoing killing of sea turtles by an emerging longline fishing industry. Most of the longline ships in Hawaii's waters arrived in the 1990s after depleting fishing stocks in the Atlantic. Although their target is swordfish or tuna, these ships lay fishing lines up to 30 miles long that carry thousands of baited hooks that catch anything going for the bait, including seabirds, marine mammals and hundreds of endangered sea turtles.

A different approach is taken by the Nature Conservancy of Hawaii, which protects Hawaii's rarest ecosystems by buying up vast tracts of land and working out long-term stewardships with prominent landholders. On Oahu, the Nature Conservancy manages Ihiihilauakea Preserve, a 30-acre site containing a crater with a unique vernal pool above Hanauma Bay, and the Honouliuli Preserve, a 3692-acre tract on the southeast slope of the Waianae Mountains that's home to 45 rare plant and animal species.

FLORA & FAUNA

The Hawaiian island chain, 2500 miles from the nearest continental land mass, is the most geographically isolated place in the world.

All living things that reached Hawaii's shores were carried across the ocean on the wind or the waves – seeds clinging to a bird's feather, a floating hala plant, or insect eggs in a piece of driftwood. Fern and moss spores, able to drift thousands of miles in the air, were probably the first plant life to arrive on the newly emerged volcanic islands.

It's estimated that before human contact, a new species managed to take hold in Hawaii only once every 100,000 years. New arrivals found specialized habitats ranging from desert to rain forest and elevations climbing from sea level to nearly 14,000 feet. Each species evolved to fit a specific niche in its new environment.

Over 90% of Hawaii's native flora and fauna are found exclusively in Hawaii, but some have evolved so thoroughly that it's not possible to trace them to any continental ancestor. Many of Hawaii's birds may have evolved from a single species, as is thought to have been the case with the more than 30 species of native honeycreeper (*Drepanididae*).

Having evolved with limited competition and few predators, Hawaii's native species generally fare poorly among more aggressive introduced flora and fauna. They are also highly sensitive to habitat destruction. When westerners first came to Hawaii, the islands had 70 native bird species. Of those, 24 are now extinct and an additional 36 are threatened with extinction.

The first Polynesian settlers to arrive weren't traveling light. They brought food and medicinal plants, chickens, dogs and pigs. The pace of introducing exotic species escalated with the arrival of Europeans, starting with Captain Cook, who dropped off goats and left melon and pumpkin seeds. The next western visitors left cattle and horses.

Prior to human contact, Hawaii had no land mammals save for monk seals and hoary bats. The introduction of free-ranging pigs, cattle and goats, who grazed and foraged at will, devastated Hawaii's fragile ecosystems and spelled extinction for many plants.

Released songbirds and game birds spread avian diseases to the native Hawaiian birds who did not have the immunities to fight off foreign pathogens. Erosion, deforestation and the thousands of introduced plants that compete with and choke out native vegetation have all taken their toll.

Today, more than 25% of all the endangered species in the USA are Hawaiian plants and animals. Of the approximately 2400 different native plants, half are either threatened or endangered.

Flora

Oahu is abloom year-round with colorful tropical flowers. Perhaps no flower is more closely identified with Hawaii than the hibiscus, whose lush blooms are worn by women tucked behind their ears. Thousands of varieties of hibiscus bushes grow in Hawaii; on most, the flowers bloom early in the day and drop before sunset. The variety most frequently seen is *Hibiscus rosa-sinensis*, commonly known as the red (or Chinese) hibiscus; it is used as a landscape hedge throughout Oahu.

Other flowers seen in gardens and yards include blood-red anthurium, brilliant orange bird-of-paradise, colorful bougainvillea, red ginger, torch ginger, shell ginger, fragrant jasmine and gardenia and various heliconias with bright orange and red bracts. Monkeypod, plumeria and poinciana are three of the more common flowering trees.

Native coastal plants include *pohuehue* (*Ipomoea brasiliensis*), a beach morning glory with pink flowers that's found on the sand just above the wrack line; beach *naupaka* (*Scaevola sericea*), a shrub with oval leaves and a small white five-petal flower that looks as if it's been torn in half; and Oahu's official flower, the low-growing *ilima* (*Sida fallax*), which has delicate yellow-orange blossoms.

There are a number of native forest trees that are also easy to identify. The *ohia lehua* (*Metrosideros collina*), with its red pompom flowers, grows in barren areas as a shrub and on more fertile land as a tree. The *Koa* (*Acacia koa hawaiiensis*), found at higher elevations, grows up to 100 feet high and is unusual in that the young saplings have fernlike compound leaves, while mature trees have flat crescent-shaped phyllodes. The *kukui* tree (*Aleurites moluccana*), brought to the island by the early Polynesian settlers, has oily nuts the Hawaiians used for candles, hence its common name, candlenut tree; it's recognizable in the forest by its light silver-tinged foliage.

Humpback Whales

Hands-down, the most popular wintering visitor to Hawaii is the humpback whale (*Megaptera novaeangliae*), which is the state's official marine mammal. Humpbacks, the fifth largest of the great whales, reach lengths of 45 feet and weigh 40 to 45 tons.

They're great performers, known for their acrobatic displays, which include arching dives, lobtailing, breaching and fin splashing. In breaching, humpbacks jump almost clear out of the water and then splash down with tremendous force.

They save the best performances for breeding time. Sometimes several bull whales will do a series of crashing breaches to gain the favor of a cow, often bashing into one another, even drawing blood, before the most impressive emerges the winner.

Once one of the most abundant of the great whales, humpbacks were hunted almost to extinction and are now an endangered species. At the end of the 19th century an estimated 15,000 humpbacks remained. They were still being hunted as late as 1966, when the International Whaling Commission enforced a ban on their slaughter.

The entire population of North Pacific humpbacks is now thought to be about 4000. An estimated two-thirds of those winter in Hawaii, while most of the others migrate to Mexico.

Humpbacks feed all summer in the plankton-rich waters off Alaska, developing a layer of blubber that sustains them through the winter. One of the toothless whales, humpbacks gulp huge quantities of water and then strain it back out through the filterlike baleen in their mouths, trapping krill and small fish. They can eat close to a ton of food a day.

During their winter sojourn in the warm tropical waters off Hawaii, humpbacks mate and give birth. The gestation period is 10 to 12 months.

Mothers stay in shallow waters once their calves are born, apparently as protection from shark attacks. At birth calves are about 12 feet long and weigh 3000 pounds. They are nursed for about six months and can put on 100 pounds a day in the first few weeks. Adults go without eating while wintering in Hawaii.

Humpbacks don't arrive in Hawaii en masse, but start filtering in around November. They can be found throughout the islands, including Oahu, but their most frequent wintering spot is in the shallow waters around Maui and Molokai.

For information on whale-watching cruises, see the Cruises section in the Activities chapter.

Two trees found along the coast that were well utilized in old Hawaii are *hala* (*Pandanus odoratissimus*), also called pandanus or screw pine, whose spiny leaves were used for thatching and weaving; and the coconut palm, or *niu* (*Cocos nucifera*), which thrives in coral sands and produces about 75 coconuts a year.

Also expect to see *kiawe* (*Prosopis pallida*), a non-native tree found in dry coastal areas. A member of the mesquite family, kiawe is useful for making charcoal but is a nuisance for beachgoers, as its sharp thorns easily pierce soft sandals.

If you want to learn more about Hawaii's flora, Oahu has some excellent botanical gardens. Foster Garden in the Chinatown area and the Lyon Arboretum on the north side of Honolulu both have unique native and exotic species, some of which can no longer be found in the wild.

Fauna

The most prominent urban birds are pigeons, doves, red-crested cardinals and common mynas. The myna (*Acridotheres tristis*), introduced from India, is a brown, speckled bird that congregates in noisy flocks, walks rather than hops, and is plentiful even around hotels.

For those who get into the woods, Oahu has a few native forest birds worth seeking out. The *elepaio* (*Chasiempis sandwichensis*), a brownish bird with a white rump, and the *amakihi* (*Hemignathus virens*), a small yellow-green bird, are the most common endemic forest birds on Oahu. The *apapane* (*Himatione sanguinea*), a vivid red honey-creeper, and the *iiwi* (*Vestiaria coccinea*), a bright vermilion bird, are less common.

From the Brink of Extinction

One of the Pacific's rarest marine creatures is the Hawaiian monk seal (*Monachus schauinslandi*), so named for the cowl-like fold of skin at its neck and for its solitary habits. The Hawaiian name for the animal is *ilio holo kai*, meaning 'the dog that runs in the sea.'

The species has remained nearly unchanged for 15 million years, though in the past century it has been in danger of dying out completely. The annual birth rate for Hawaiian monk seal pups is between 150 and 175 a year, though due to shark attacks and other predators, the majority of pups don't reach maturity.

Fortunately, conservation efforts, including the relocation of some seals to create a better male-female ratio, appear to be bringing the seals back from the edge of extinction. The Hawaiian monk seal population has risen about 15% in the past decade to a total of approximately 1300 seals.

Although their prime habitat is the uninhabited Northwestern Hawaiian Islands, monk seals do occasionally haul up on Oahu's more remote northwest beaches, near Kaena Point.

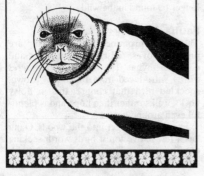

Most of the islets off Oahu's windward coast are sanctuaries for seabirds, including terns, noddies, shearwaters, Laysan albatrosses, tropicbirds, boobies and frigate birds. Moku Manu ('Bird Island'), off Mokapu Peninsula in Kaneohe, has the greatest variety of species, including a large number of sooty terns (*Sterna fuscata oahuensis*) that lay their eggs directly on the ground. Because the nesting birds are sensitive to human disturbance, visitors are not allowed at all on Moku Manu and are restricted on the other islands.

However, if you have a pair of binoculars you can enjoy birding right from the coast. Great frigate birds (*Fregata minor palmerstoni*), aerial pirates that snatch food from other birds in midair, are commonly seen circling above Waimanalo Bay; graceful in flight, they are easily identifiable by their 7-foot wingspan and distinctively forked tail. Another bird that can be spotted soaring along the cliffs of the windward coast is the red-tailed tropicbird (*Phaethon rubricauda rothschildi*), which has a white body with a trailing red tail.

Oahu has an endemic genus of tree snail, the *Achatinella*. In former days the forests were loaded with these colorful snails, which clung like gems to the leaves of trees. They were too attractive for their own good, however, and up until the early 20th century, hikers were collecting them by the handfuls. The deforestation of habitat and the introduction of a cannibal snail and predatory rodents have been even more devastating. Of 41 *Achatinella* species, only 19 remain and all are endangered.

Oahu has wild pigs and goats in its mountain valleys. A more interesting introduced species is the brush-tailed rock wallaby (*Petrogale penicillata*), accidentally released in 1916 and now residing in the Kalihi Valley, north of Honolulu. Although rarely seen, the wallabies are of keen interest to zoologists because they may be the last members of a subspecies that's now extinct in their native Australia.

Hawaii has a rich and varied marine life. Almost 700 fish species live in Hawaiian waters, with nearly one-third of those found

Aaaaaahhhhh!

An estimated 3000 wild peacocks live in the Makaha Valley, on the Waianae Coast.

Hibiscus

NED FRIARY

Plumeria flowers

LEE FOSTER

Vanda orchid

NED FRIARY

Red ginger

NED FRIARY

Red bombax

LEE FOSTER

Bird of paradise

NED FRIARY

Not to be missed – the dramatic view from the Nuuanu Pali Lookout, on the windward coast

nowhere else in the world. Oahu's nearshore waters harbor large rainbow-colored parrotfish, some 20 different kinds of butterfly fish, numerous varieties of wrasses, bright yellow tangs, odd-shaped filefish and ballooning pufferfish, just to list a few. There are also green sea turtles, manta rays and moray eels.

Several types of whales frequent Hawaiian waters, though it is the migrating humpback (*Megaptera novaeangliae*), with its acrobatic breaches and tail flips, that everyone wants to see. Luckily for whale watchers, humpback whales are coast-huggers, preferring waters with depths of less than 600 feet. They can sometimes be seen in winter from the beaches along Oahu's west coast. See boxed text 'Humpback Whales.' Other migratory whales in Hawaiian waters include the fin whale (*Balaenoptera physalus*), minke whale (B *acutorostrata*) and right whale (*Balaena glacialis*); all are baleen whales.

Hawaii's year-round resident whales, which are all toothed whales, include the sperm whale (*Physeter macrocephalus*), false killer whale (*Pseudorca crassidens*), pigmy killer whale (*Feresa attenuata*), beaked whale (*Ziphius cavirostris*), melonhead whale (*Peponocephala electra*) and, most common of all, the pilot whale (*Globicephala macrorhynchus*). The latter is a small whale that often travels in large pods and, like most whales, prefers deep offshore waters.

Numerous dolphins – including spinner (*Stenella longirostris*), bottlenose (*Tursiops truncatus*), slender-beaked, spotted (*S attenuata*), striped (*S caeruleoalba*) and roughtoothed (*Steno bredanensis*) varieties – are found in the waters around Hawaii.

GOVERNMENT & POLITICS

Hawaii has three levels of government: federal, state and county. Honolulu is the seat of both state and county government.

Hawaii has a typical state government with executive power vested in the governor, who is elected to a four-year term. The present governor, Benjamin Cayetano, who has been in office since December 1994, is the first state governor in the USA to be of Filipino ancestry.

The state's lawmaking body is a bicameral legislature. The senate includes 25 members, elected for four-year terms from the state's 25 senatorial districts. The house of representatives has 51 members, each elected for a two-year term.

For local administration, Hawaii is divided into four county governments. Unlike the mainland states, Hawaii has no separate municipal governments, so the counties provide services, such as police and fire protection, that elsewhere in the USA are usually assigned to cities.

The City & County of Honolulu is the unwieldy name attached to the single political entity governing all of Oahu. It is administered by a mayor and a nine-member council, elected for four-year terms.

ECONOMY

Tourism is Hawaii's largest industry and accounts for about one-third of the state's income. Hawaii gets about 6.7 million visitors a year, and approximately half of them visit Oahu. In total they spend about $10 billion in the state, but not all at the same rate. The 3.7 million visiting Americans spend an average of $150 a day, while the 1.8 million Japanese spend nearly double that. Since the onset of the Asian economic downturn, dubbed the 'Asian flu,' visitor arrivals from Japan and other Asian nations have dropped 10%. Although there's been a 4% rise in the number of North American and European tourists coming to Hawaii, that hasn't been enough to offset stagnation in Hawaii's tourism industry.

The second largest sector in the economy is the US military, pumping out about $3 billion annually. Agriculture is a distant third.

Sugar and pineapple, which once formed the backbone of Hawaii's economy, have been scaled back dramatically in recent years. Currently, the two crops account for around $175 million in sales, less than half of their value a decade ago. On Oahu, pineapple production still takes place, but sugar has disappeared from the landscape.

Meanwhile, diversified crops, defined as all crops except sugar and pineapple, have increased twofold in the state over the past decade and have a combined sales value of nearly $300 million. Tropical flowers and macadamia nuts accounted for more than a third of that total. Other sizable crops include vegetables, tropical fruit, coffee and seed corn.

Hawaii's unemployment rate hovers around 6%, which is nearly 2% higher than the US average. Oahu fares a bit better than the other Hawaiian islands, with an unemployment rate of 5%. In terms of employment on Oahu, tourism accounts for about 30% of the jobs, followed by defense and other government employment, which together account for 22% of all jobs.

The cost of living is 20% higher in Honolulu than in the average US mainland city, while wages are 9% lower. For those stuck in service jobs, which represent the most rapidly growing sector of the Hawaiian economy, it is tough to get by.

Although sugar production, no longer considered profitable, was phased out entirely in 1996, nearly one-fifth of Oahu is still used for agricultural purposes, mostly for growing pineapples. On the North Shore, around Haleiwa and Waialua, coffee trees have been introduced into former cane fields.

The Military Presence

Hawaii is the most militarized state in the nation. In total, the military has a grip on about 250,000 acres of Hawaiian land. The greatest holding is on Oahu, where nearly 25% of the island is controlled by the armed forces and where there are more than a hundred installations, from ridge-top radar stations to Waikiki's Fort DeRussy Beach.

Oahu is the hub of the Pacific Command, which directs military activities from western USA to the eastern Africa. The navy, which accounts for 40% of Hawaii's military presence, is centered at Pearl Harbor, home of the Pacific Fleet.

Despite the end of the Cold War, the military still spends about $3 billion annually in the state. There are 45,000 military personnel and an additional 50,000 military dependents living on the islands.

Hawaii's politicians, although otherwise liberal-leaning, generally embrace the military presence. The Chamber of Commerce of Hawaii even has a special military affairs council that lobbies in Washington, DC, to draw still more military activity to Hawaii.

POPULATION & PEOPLE

Oahu's population is 880,000, with Honolulu accounting for nearly half of the total. Other sizable population centers are Pearl City, Kailua, Kaneohe, Kapolei, Aiea, Waipahu and Mililani. There is no ethnic majority – everyone belongs to a minority. Honolulu's ethnic breakdown is 24% Caucasian, 21% Japanese, 17% mixed ancestry other than part-Hawaiian, 16% part-Hawaiian (less than 1% pure Hawaiian), 7% Filipino and 6% Chinese, with numerous other Pacific and Asian minorities.

Hawaii's people are known for their racial harmony. Race is generally not a factor in marriage. On average, islanders have a 50/50 chance of marrying someone of a race different than their own, and the majority of children born in Hawaii are *hapa*, or of mixed blood.

EDUCATION

Hawaii is the only US state to have a public education system run by the state, rather than county or town education boards. Education accounts for approximately one-third of the state budget.

Under Hawaii state law, all children between the ages of six and 18 are expected to attend school. More than 80% of all students are enrolled in the state's public school system, with the remainder in private schools.

Schools operate on a two-semester system; the first semester is from the first week of September to late December, the second from early January to the first week in June.

About a quarter of all adults living in Hawaii have completed at least four years of college. As with secondary education, the state is the main provider of higher education. Approximately 20,000 students attend the state-run University of Hawaii (UH) at Manoa, north of Waikiki. There are also four community college campuses on Oahu: Honolulu Community College, Kapiolani Community College, Leeward Community College and Windward Community College.

In addition, there are three small private colleges operating on Oahu: a Hawaii campus of Brigham Young University, in Laie; Chaminade University, in Honolulu; and Hawaii Pacific University, also in Honolulu.

ARTS
Hula

Perhaps no art form is more uniquely Hawaiian than the hula. There are many different schools of hula, all very disciplined and graceful in their movements.

Most ancient hula dances expressed historical events, legendary tales and the accomplishments of the great alii. Facial expressions, hand gestures, hip sway and dance steps all conveyed the story. They were performed to rhythmic chants and drum beatings, serving to connect with the world of spirits. Eye movement was very important; if the story was about the sun, the dancer's eyes would gaze upward, and if about the netherworld, they would gaze downward. One school, the *hula ohelo*, was very sensual, with movements suggesting the act of procreation.

Traditional hula dancers wore tapa cloth – not the now familiar grass skirts, which were introduced from Micronesia only a hundred years ago.

The Christian missionaries found the hula too licentious and suppressed it. The dance might have been lost forever if not for King David Kalakaua, the 'Merrie Monarch,' who revived it in the latter half of the 19th century.

Hula *halaus* (schools) have experienced an influx of new students in recent years. Some practice in public places, such as school grounds and parks, where visitors are welcome to watch. Although many of the halaus rely on tuition fees, others receive sponsorship from hotels and shopping centers and give weekly public performances in return.

There are also numerous island-wide hula competitions, one of the biggest being the Prince Lot Hula Festival held each July at the Moanalua Gardens.

Music

Contemporary Hawaiian music gives center stage to the guitar, which was first introduced to the islands by Spanish cowboys in the 1830s. The Hawaiians made it uniquely their own, however. In 1889, Joseph Kekuku, a native Hawaiian, designed the steel guitar, one of only two major musical instruments invented in what is now the USA. (The other is the banjo.) The steel guitar is usually played with slack-key tunings and carries the melody throughout the song.

Slack-key guitar, a type of tuning in which some strings are slackened from the conventional tuning to produce a harmonious, soulful sound, is also a 19th-century Hawaiian creation and one that has come back into the spotlight in recent times. Some of Hawaii's more renowned slack-key guitar players include Cyril Pahinui, Keola Beamer,

---

Traditional Musical Instruments

The *pahu hula*, a knee drum carved from a breadfruit or coconut log, with a sharkskin drum head, was traditionally used solely at hula performances. Other hula musical instruments include *ke laau* sticks, used to keep the beat for the dancers; *iliili*, stone castanets; *puili*, rattles made from split bamboo; and *uliuli*, gourd rattles decorated with colorful feathers.

The early Hawaiians were a romantic lot. Instruments used for courting included the *ohe*, a nose flute made of bamboo, and the *ukeke*, a musical bow with a couple of strings.

Raymond Kane, Peter Moon and Atta Isaacs Jr, and the late Gabby Pahinui and Sonny Chillingworth.

The ukulele, which is so strongly identified with Hawaiian music, was actually derived from the braginha, a Portuguese instrument introduced to Hawaii in the 19th century. In Hawaiian, the word 'ukulele' means 'jumping flea.'

Both the ukulele and the steel guitar were essential to the lighthearted, romantic music popularized in Hawaii from the 1930s to the 1950s. *My Little Grass Shack, Lovely Hula Hands* and *Sweet Leilani* are classic examples. Due in part to the 'Hawaii Calls' radio show, which for more than 30 years was broadcast worldwide from the Moana Hotel in Waikiki, this music became instantly recognizable as Hawaiian, conjuring up images of hula dancers swaying under palm trees in a tropical paradise. Troy Fernandez and Ledward Kaapana are among the present-day masters of the ukulele.

A current sound in Hawaii is Jawaiian, a blending of Hawaiian music and Jamaican reggae. One hot new group with an emphasis on Jawaiian is the Oahu-based Kulana, but many other well-known musicians incorporate elements of Jawaiian, including Bruddah Waltah, the Kaau Crater Boys and Hoaikane. Other popular contemporary Hawaiian musicians include vocalist-composer Henry Kapono; Hapa, the duo of Kelii Kanealii and Barry Flanagan, who fuse folk, rock and traditional Hawaiian elements; the Hawaiian Style Band, who merge Hawaiian influences with rock; and Kealii Reichel, a charismatic vocalist and hula dancer who sings Hawaiian ballads and love songs as well as poetic chants.

Painting & Sculpture

Many artists draw inspiration from Hawaii's rich cultural heritage and natural beauty.

Well-known Hawaiian painter Herb Kawainui Kane creates detailed oil paintings that focus on the early Polynesian settlers and Kamehameha the Great's life. His works are mainly on display in museums and at gallery collections in resorts.

Another notable native Hawaiian artist is Rocky Kaiouliokahihikoloehu Jensen, who does wood sculptures and drawings of Hawaiian gods, ancient chiefs and early Hawaiians with the aim of creating sacred art in the tradition of *makaku*, or 'creative artistic mana.'

Honolulu artist Pegge Hopper paints traditional Hawaiian women in relaxed poses using a distinctive graphic design style and bright washes of color. Her work has been widely reproduced on posters and postcards.

Crafts

Some of Hawaii's most impressive crafts are ceramics, particularly raku work, a style of Japanese earthenware; bowls made of native woods, such as koa and milo; and baskets woven of native fibers.

Hawaiian quilting is another unique art form. The concept of patchwork quilting was introduced by the early missionaries, but the Hawaiians, who had only recently taken to Western cotton clothing, didn't have a surplus of cloth scraps – and the idea of cutting up new lengths of fabric simply to sew them back together again in small squares seemed absurd. Instead, the Hawaiian women created their own designs using larger cloth pieces, typically with stylized tropical flora on a white background.

Leis, or garlands, are a more transitory art form. Although the leis most visitors wear are made of fragrant flowers such as plumeria and tuberose, traditional leis of mokihana berries and maile leaves were more commonly worn in old Hawaii. Both types are still made today.

See the Shopping section in the Facts for the Visitor chapter for information on buying crafts.

Literature

A Hawaiian Reader, edited by A Grove Day and Carl Stroven, is an excellent anthology with 37 selections, both fiction and nonfiction, about the authors' experiences in Hawaii. It starts with a log entry by Captain James Cook and includes writings from early missionaries as well as Mark Twain,

Ancient Crafts

Tapa Weaving In ancient Hawaii, women spent much of their time beating *kapa* (tapa cloth) or preparing *lauhala* for weaving.

Tapa made from the *wauke* (paper mulberry tree) was the favorite material. The bark was carefully stripped, then pounded with wooden beaters. The beaters were carved with different patterns that then became the pattern of the tapa. Dyes were made from charcoal, flowers and sea urchins.

Tapa had many uses in addition to clothing, from food containers to burial shrouds. After the missionaries introduced cotton cloth and western clothing, the art of tapa making slowly faded away. Today, most of the tapa for sale in Hawaii is from Samoa and has bold designs, unlike traditional Hawaiian tapa, which had more delicate patterns.

Lauhala Weaving Lauhala weaving uses the *lau* (leaves) of the *hala* (pandanus) tree. Preparing the leaves for weaving is hard, messy work due to the razor-sharp spines along the leaf edges and down the center.

In old Hawaii, lauhala was woven into mats and floor coverings, but today smaller items like hats, placemats and baskets are most common.

Wooden Bowls The Hawaiians had no pottery and made their containers using either gourds or wood. Wooden food bowls were most often made of kou or milo, two native woods which didn't leave unpleasant tastes.

Hawaiian bowls were free of designs and carvings. Their beauty lay in the natural qualities of the wood and in the shape of the bowl alone. Cracked bowls were often expertly patched with dovetailed pieces of wood. Rather than decrease the value of the bowl, patching suggested heirloom status and such bowls were amongst the mostly highly prized.

Featherwork & Leis The Hawaiians were known for their elaborate featherwork. The most impressive items were the capes worn by chiefs and kings. The longer the cape, the higher the rank of its wearer. Capes made from the yellow feathers of the now extinct *mamo* bird were the most highly prized.

The mamo was a predominantly black bird with a yellow upper tail. An estimated 80,000 mamo birds were caught to create the cape that Kamehameha the Great wore. It's said that bird catchers would capture the birds, pluck the desired feathers and release them otherwise unharmed. Feathers were also used to make helmets and leis.

The *lei palaoa*, a necklace traditionally worn by Hawaiian royalty, was made of finely braided human hair. It had a smoothly carved whale tooth pendant shaped like a curved tongue hanging from it.

Jack London, Somerset Maugham, David Malo, Isabella Bird, Martha Beckwith and others. If you only have time to read one book about Hawaii, this inexpensive paperback is a great choice.

OA Bushnell is one of Hawaii's best-known contemporary authors. The University of Hawaii Press has published his titles *The Return of Lono*, a historical novel of Captain Cook's final voyage; *Kaaawa*, about Hawaii in the 1850s; *The Stone of Kannon*, about the first group of Japanese contract laborers to arrive in Hawaii; and its sequel *The Water of Kane*.

Stories of Hawaii is a collection of 13 of Jack London's yarns about the islands.

Talking to the Dead, by Sylvia Watanabe, is an enjoyable read about growing up as a second-generation Japanese-American in post-war Honolulu.

SOCIETY & CULTURE

In many ways, contemporary Hawaiian culture resembles contemporary culture in the rest of the USA.

Hawaiians listen to the same pop music and watch the same TV shows as Americans on the mainland. Honolulu has dance clubs and ballroom dancing, rock bands and classical orchestras, junk food and nouvelle cuisine. The wonderful thing about Hawaii, however, is that the mainland influences largely stand beside, rather than engulf, the culture of the islands.

Not only is traditional Hawaiian culture an integral part of the social fabric, but so are the customs of the ethnically diverse immigrants who have made the islands their home. Honolulu is more than just a meeting place of East and West; it's a place where the cultures merge, typically in a manner that brings out the best of both worlds.

The 1970s saw the start of a Hawaiian cultural renaissance that continues today. Hawaiian language classes are thriving and there is a concerted effort to reintroduce Hawaiian words into modern speech. Hula classes are concentrating more on the nuances behind hand movements and facial expressions than on the dramatic hip-shaking that sells tickets to dance shows. Many Hawaiian artists and craftspeople are returning to traditional mediums and themes.

Certainly the tourist centers have long been overrun with packaged Hawaiiana that seems almost a parody of island culture, from plastic leis to theme-park luaus. But fortunately for the visitor, the growing interest in traditional Hawaiiana is having an impact on the tourist industry, and authentic performances by hula students and Hawaiian musicians are increasingly easier to find.

RELIGION

Oahu's population is diverse in terms of religion. In addition to the standard Christian denominations, the island has numerous Buddhist temples and Shinto shrines. There are also Hindu, Taoist, Tenrikyo, Jewish and Muslim houses of worship.

Christianity has the largest following, with Catholicism being the predominant religious denomination. Interestingly, the United Church of Christ, which includes the Congregationalists who initially converted the islands, now claims only about half as many members as the Mormons and one-tenth as many as the Catholics.

LANGUAGE

The main language of Hawaii is English, although it's liberally peppered with Hawaiian phrases, words borrowed from the various immigrant languages and pidgin slang. However, it's not uncommon to hear islanders speaking other languages, as the first language in one out of every four Hawaiian homes is a tongue other than English.

The Hawaiian language itself is still spoken, among family members, by about 9000 people.

Closely related to other Polynesian languages, Hawaiian is melodic, phonetically simple and full of repeated syllables and vowels.

Some 85% of all place names in Hawaii are in Hawaiian and often have interesting translations and stories behind them.

The Hawaiians had no written language until the 1820s, when Christian missionaries arrived and wrote down the spoken language in roman letters.

Pronunciation

The written Hawaiian language has just 12 letters. Pronunciation is easy and there are few consonant clusters.

Vowel sounds are about the same as in Spanish or Japanese, more or less as follows:

a ah, as in 'father' or uh, as in 'above'
e ay, as in 'gay' or eh, as in 'pet'
i ee, as in 'see'
o oh, as in 'go'
u oo, as in 'noon'

Hawaiian has diphthongs, created when two vowels join together to form a single sound. The stress is on the first vowel, although in general, if you pronounce each vowel separately, you'll be easily understood.

The consonant *w* is usually pronounced like a soft English *v* when it follows the letters *i* and *e* (the town Haleiwa is pronounced Haleiva) and like the English *w* when it follows *u* or *o*. When *w* follows *a* it can be pronounced either *v* or *w* – thus you will hear both Hawaii and Havaii.

The other consonants – *h, k, l, m, n, p* – are pronounced about the same way as they are pronounced in English.

Glottal Stops & Macrons Written Hawaiian uses both glottal stops and macrons, although in modern print they are often omitted.

The glottal stop (') indicates a break between two vowels, producing an effect similar to saying 'oh-oh' in English. A macron, a short straight line over a vowel, stresses the vowel.

Glottal stops and macrons not only affect pronunciation, but can give a word a completely different meaning. For example *ai* can mean 'sexual intercourse' or 'to eat,' depending on the pronunciation.

All this takes on greater significance when you learn to speak Hawaiian in depth. If you're using Hawaiian words in an English-language context ('this *poi* is *ono*'), there shouldn't be a problem.

Compounds Hawaiian may seem more difficult than it is because many proper names are long and look similar. Many begin with *ka*, meaning 'the,' which over time simply became attached to the beginning of the word.

When you break each word down into its composite parts, some of which are repeated, it all becomes much easier. For example: *Kamehameha* consists of the three components Ka-meha-meha. *Humuhumunukunukuapuaa*, which is Hawaii's state fish, is broken down into humu-humu-nuku-nuku-a-pu-a-a.

Some words are doubled to emphasize their meaning. For example: *wiki* means 'quick,' and *wikiwiki* means 'very quick.'

There are some easily recognizable compounds repeatedly found in place names and it can be fun to learn a few. For instance, *wai* means 'freshwater' – Waikiki means 'spouting water,' so named for the freshwater springs that were once there. *Kai* means 'seawater' – Kailua means 'two seas.' *Lani* means 'heavenly' – Lanikai means 'heavenly sea.' *Hana* means 'bay' – Hanalei means 'crescent bay.'

Common Hawaiian Learn these words first: *aloha* and *mahalo*, which are everyday pleasantries; *makai* and *mauka*, commonly used in giving directions; and *kane* and *wahine*, often on toilet doors. Check the glossary in the back of the book for other useful words.

Pidgin

Hawaii's early immigrants communicated with each other in pidgin, a simplified, broken form of English. It was a language born of necessity, stripped of all but the most needed words.

Modern pidgin is better defined as local slang. It is extensive, lively and ever-changing. Whole conversations can take place in pidgin, or often just a word or two is dropped into a more conventional English sentence.

Even Shakespeare's *Twelfth Night* has been translated (by local comedian James Grant Benton) to *Twelf Nite O Wateva*.

Shaka Sign

Islanders greet each other with the shaka sign, which is made by folding down the three middle fingers to the palm and extending the thumb and little finger. The hand is then usually held out and shaken in greeting. It's as common as waving.

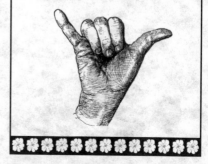

Malvolio's line 'My masters, are you mad?' becomes 'You buggahs crazy, o wat?'

Short-term visitors will rarely win friends by trying to speak pidgin. It's more like an insider's code that you're allowed to use only after you've lived in Hawaii long enough to understand the nuances.

Some characteristics of pidgin include: a fast staccato rhythm, two-word sentences; dropping the soft 'h' sound from words that start with 'th'; use of words borrowed from many languages (often Hawaiian); and double meanings that frequently confuse the uninitiated.

Some of the more common words and expressions include the following:

blalah – big Hawaiian fellow
brah – brother, friend; also used for 'hey you'
broke da mouth – delicious
buggah – guy
chicken skin – goose bumps

coconut wireless – word of mouth
cockaroach – steal
da kine – that kind of thing, whatchama-callit, etc; used whenever you can't think of the word you want but you know the listener knows what you mean
geev em – go for it, beat them
grinds – food, eat; *ono grinds* is good food.
haolefied – become like a *haole*
how you stay? – how are you?
howzit? – hi, how's it going?
humbug – a real hassle
like beef? – wanna fight?
mo' bettah – much better, the best
slippahs – flip-flops, thongs
stick – surfboard
stink eye – dirty look, evil eye
talk story – any kind of conversation, gossip, tales
tanks – thanks; most commonly used in the phrase *tanks brah*.
tree – three

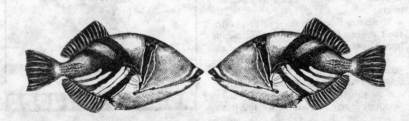

Facts for the Visitor

HIGHLIGHTS

Vibrant Waikiki is the venue for scores of tourist activities, with sunbathing, water sports and people-watching among its highlights. At the less-touristed end of Waikiki is Kapiolani Park, a grand public park with an aquarium, zoo and facilities for everything from concerts to tennis.

Don't miss a stroll through downtown Honolulu's historic district, which sports the state capitol, early mission church sites and the only royal palace in the USA. Another delightful place is the adjacent Chinatown area, with its lively markets and ethnic restaurants. While you're there, stroll through Foster Botanical Garden, which has some of the island's loftiest trees and rarest plants.

For a city of its size, Honolulu has some surprisingly good museums. Spending a few hours at the renowned Bishop Museum will give you a great introduction to Hawaiian culture. The Honolulu Academy of Arts has a high-quality fine arts collection, while the more recently established Contemporary Museum displays modern art in a lovely estate setting.

The most visited attraction in all of Hawaii is the USS *Arizona* Memorial at Pearl Harbor, the site of the surprise Japanese attack that brought Americans into WWII.

A trip around southeast Oahu offers fine scenery and a glimpse of one of the less-developed sides of the island, including Hanauma Bay with its striking scenery and easy-access snorkeling.

For phenomenal surf, you can't beat the North Shore, which draws the world's top surfers with its monstrous winter waves. If you'd rather try your hand at windsurfing, then Kailua's superb beach, with its steady breezes, is the place to go.

PLANNING
When to Go

Oahu is a great place to visit any time of the year. Although the busiest tourist season is in winter, that has more to do with weather elsewhere, as many visitors are snowbirds escaping cold winters back home. Essentially, the weather in Hawaii is agreeable year-round. It's a bit rainier in the winter and a bit hotter in the summer, but there are no extremes as cooling trade winds modify the heat throughout the year.

In terms of cost, spring through fall can be a bargain, because many hotels drop prices around the first of April, and most of the prices don't climb back up again until mid-December.

Naturally, for certain activities there are peak seasons. For instance, if you're a board surfer, you'll find the biggest waves in winter, whereas if you're a windsurfer, you'll find the best wind conditions in summer.

Maps

There are simple island maps in the ubiquitous free tourist magazines, but if you're going to be renting a car and doing any exploring at all it's worth picking up a good road map, especially for navigating around Honolulu.

Detailed Gousha road maps (which are recommended because they show numbered highway exits) and Rand McNally road maps are sold in stores throughout Oahu for a couple of dollars. Members of the American Automobile Association (AAA) or an affiliated automobile club can get a free Gousha road map from the AAA office (Map 3; ☎ 593-2221), 1270 Ala Moana Blvd, Honolulu.

The 200-page *Bryan's Sectional Maps Oahu* atlas, which maps out and indexes virtually every street on the island, is the most comprehensive source, but it's more detailed than most visitors will need. *Bryan's* can be purchased at bookstores around Oahu.

The University of Hawaii (UH) Press publishes a visitor-oriented relief map of Oahu that not only covers roads, but also beaches, historical sites and major hiking trails. It has insets for Waikiki, Honolulu, Kaneohe-Kailua and southeast Oahu. This

Official Oahu

Oahu's nickname is 'The Gathering Place.' The island's official color is yellow-orange, which is the same color as the delicate blossoms of the native ilima, Oahu's official flower. Ilima, a ground cover, grows wild on the island.

handy map costs $4 and is readily available in bookstores and shops frequented by tourists.

The United States Geological Survey (USGS) publishes topographical maps of Oahu, both as full-island and detailed sectional maps. Despite the precise geographic detail, the practical use of these maps is limited for casual visitors by their unruly size and infrequent updates. Maps can be ordered from the USGS (☎ 888-275-8747, fax 303-202-4693, infoservices@usgs.gov), Box 25286, Denver Federal Center, Denver, CO 80225. The USGS also has a website (www.usgs.gov). Maps cost $4 per sheet, plus a $3.50 mailing fee per order. In Honolulu, USGS maps, nautical charts and other specialty maps can be purchased at the Pacific Map Center (☎ 545-3600), 560 N Nimitz Hwy, suite 206A.

What to Bring

Oahu has balmy weather and a casual attitude towards dress so, for the most part, packing is a breeze. It's essentially summer all year long. For tourist activities, shorts, sandals and a cotton shirt are the standard day dress. A light jacket or sweater will be the warmest clothing you'll need.

Pack light. You can always pick up something with a floral Hawaiian print when you get there and dress island-style. An aloha shirt and lightweight slacks for men, and a cotton dress for women, is pretty much regarded as 'dressing up' in Hawaii. Only a few of the most exclusive restaurants require anything fancier.

If you have plans for excursions to the Neighbor Islands, note that the 'upcountry' areas of both Maui and the Big Island can get quite nippy and warrant an extra layer of clothing.

If you plan on camping on Oahu, public campgrounds require tents (they're a good idea anyway because of mosquitoes), but you won't need anything more than the lightest sleeping bag.

Consider bringing binoculars for watching dolphins, whales and birds. You may want to bring along a snorkel, mask and fins, although you can also buy or rent them at reasonable prices once you get there. Actually, you don't need to worry too much about what to bring, because just about anything you forget to pack you can easily buy in Oahu.

TOURIST OFFICES

The Hawaii Visitors and Convention Bureau (HVCB) provides free tourist information. On request, they'll mail you a magazine containing general Hawaii-wide tourist information and a booklet listing member hotels and restaurants. HVCB information is also available on their website at www.gohawaii.com.

Local Tourist Offices

The administrative office of the Hawaii Visitors and Convention Bureau (☎ 923-1811, fax 924-0290), in Waikiki at 2270 Kalakaua Ave, suite 801, Honolulu, HI 96815, will mail you general tourist information on Oahu and the rest of Hawaii.

To pick up tourist brochures in person, go to the HVCB's visitor information office (☎ 924-0266), which is in Waikiki in the Royal Hawaiian Shopping Center, 2201 Kalakaua Ave, suite A401A. It's open 8 am to 5 pm Monday through Friday.

On the US mainland, HVCB maintains an office (☎ 415-248-3800, 800-353-5846, fax 415-248-3808) at 180 Montgomery St, suite 2360, San Francisco, CA 94104. In addition, you can order a free, glossy tourist magazine containing visitor-related information on Oahu by calling 800-624-8678.

Tourist Offices Abroad

The Hawaii Visitors and Convention Bureau frequently changes its overseas agents. The following are the current addresses for HVCB representatives abroad.

Australia
(☎ 02-9955-2619, fax 02-9955-2171)
c/o The Sales Team, suite 2, level 2,
34 Burton St, Milsons Point,
NSW 2061

Canada
(☎ 604-669-6691, fax 604-669-6075)
c/o Comprehensive Travel Industry Services,
1260 Hornby St, suite 104,
Vancouver, BC V6Z 1W2

China
(☎ 21-6466-1077, fax 21-6466-7501)
East-West Marketing, 38 Da Pu Rd,
Hai Hua Garden, No 4 Bldg 27C,
Shanghai 200023

Germany
(☎ 61-02-722-411, fax 61-02-722-409)
c/o American Venture Marketing,
Siemenstrausse 9,
63263 Neu Isenburg

Japan
(☎ 3-3201-0430, fax 3-3201-0433)
Kokusai Building, 2nd floor,
1-1 Marunouchi 3-chome, Chiyoda-ku,
Tokyo 100

Korea
(☎ 2-773-6719, fax 2-757-6783)
c/o Travel Press, Seoul Center Building,
12th floor, 91-1 Sokong-dong, Chung-ku,
Seoul 100-070

New Zealand
(☎ 9-379-3708, fax 9-309-0725)
c/o Walshes World, Dingwall Building,
87 Queen St, 2nd floor,
Auckland

Taiwan
(☎ 22-506-7043, fax 22-507-5816)
c/o Federal Transportation Company, 8th floor,
61 Nanking East Rd, Section 3,
Taipei

UK
(☎ 0181-941-4009, fax 0181-941-4011)
Box 208, Sunbury on Thames,
Middlesex TW16 5RJ

VISAS & DOCUMENTS

The conditions for entering Hawaii are the same as for entering any other state in the USA.

Passport & Visas

Canadians must have proper proof of Canadian citizenship, such as a citizenship card with photo ID or a passport. Visitors from other countries must have a valid passport, and most visitors also need a US visa.

However, there is a reciprocal visa-waiver program in which citizens of certain countries may enter the USA for stays of 90 days or less without first obtaining a US visa. Currently these countries are: Andorra, Argentina, Australia, Austria, Belgium, Brunei, Denmark, Finland, France, Germany, Iceland, Ireland, Italy, Japan, Liechtenstein, Luxembourg, Monaco, Netherlands, New Zealand, Norway, Portugal, San Marino, Singapore, Slovenia, Spain, Sweden, Switzerland, the UK and Uruguay.

As we go to press, Greece is being considered for inclusion as well. Under the visa-waiver program you must have a roundtrip ticket that is nonrefundable in the USA and you will not be allowed to extend your stay beyond the 90-day period.

Other travelers will need to obtain a visa from a US consulate or embassy. In most countries the process can be done by mail.

Your passport should be valid for at least six months longer than your intended stay in the USA and you'll need to submit a recent photo (37mm x 37mm) with the application. Documents of financial stability and/or guarantees from a US resident are sometimes required, particularly for those from third world countries.

Visa applicants may be required to 'demonstrate binding obligations' that will ensure their return back home. Because of this requirement, those planning to travel through other countries before arriving in the USA are generally better off applying for their US visa while they are still in their home country rather than while on the road.

The validity period for US visitor visas depends on what country you're from. The length of time you'll be allowed to stay in the USA is ultimately determined by US immigration authorities at the port of entry.

Visa Extensions If you want to stay in the USA longer than the date stamped on your passport, apply for an extension by contacting the Honolulu office of the Immigration & Naturalization Service (INS; ☎ 532-3721), 595 Ala Moana Blvd, *before* the expiration date stamped in your passport.

Travel Insurance

Foreign visitors should be aware that health care in the USA is expensive. It's a good idea to take out a travel insurance policy, which usually covers medical expenses, luggage theft or loss and cancellation or delays in your travel arrangements. There are a wide variety of policies available and the exact coverage depends on the policy you buy, so get your insurer or travel agent to explain the details.

Check the small print because some policies exclude 'dangerous activities,' which can include scuba diving, motorcycling and anything to do with parachutes.

Although you may find a policy that pays doctors or hospitals directly, be aware that many doctors and medical clinics in Hawaii will demand payment at the time of service. If you have to make a claim later, be certain to keep all documentation.

It's best to purchase travel insurance as early as possible. If you buy it the week before you fly, you might find, for instance, that you're not covered for delays to your flight caused by a strike that may have been in force before you took out the insurance.

Purchasing your ticket with a credit card often provides travel accident insurance and may also give you the right to reclaim your payment if the operator doesn't deliver. Ask your credit card company, or the issuing bank, for details.

Photocopies

All important documents (passport data page and visa page, credit cards, travel insur-

ance policy, air tickets, driver's license, etc) should be photocopied before you leave home. Leave one copy with someone at home and keep another with you, separate from the originals.

Other Documents

All visitors, including Americans, should keep in mind that all US airlines, including Hawaii's inter-island carriers, now require passengers to present a photo ID as part of the airline check-in procedure.

All foreign visitors (other than Canadians) must bring their passport. US and Canadian citizens may want to bring along a passport as well, in the event they are tempted to extend their travels beyond Hawaii.

All visitors should bring their driver's license and any health insurance or travel insurance cards.

Members of Hostelling International (HI) will be able to take advantage of lower hostel rates at Oahu's two HI hostels by bringing their membership cards.

Although Hawaii doesn't offer a lot of student discounts, if you have a student card, bring it along anyway, as flashing it may occasionally win you a discount at museums and other sights.

Members of senior citizen organizations such as the American Association of Retired Persons (AARP) and the Canadian Association of Retired Persons (CARP) can get an occasional hotel or car rental discount by showing their cards.

Members of the American Automobile Association (AAA) or other affiliated automobile clubs can get car rental, airfare and some sightseeing admission discounts with their membership cards.

Divers should bring their certification cards with them.

CUSTOMS

US Customs allows each person over the age of 21 to bring one quart of liquor and 200 cigarettes duty-free into the USA. Most fresh fruits and plants are restricted from entry into Hawaii and there's a strict quarantine on animals.

MONEY

There are 10 banks with around 150 branches throughout Oahu, so it's never a problem finding a bank in the major towns. The Bank of Hawaii (☎ 643-3888), Hawaii's largest bank, has a branch at the airport and at 2220 Kalakaua Ave in central Waikiki. Elsewhere around Oahu, banks can easily be found in central areas and in shopping centers.

For information on banking hours, see Business Hours, later in this chapter.

Currency

As is true throughout the USA, the US dollar is the only currency used in Hawaii.

The US dollar ($) is divided into 100 cents (¢). Coins come in denominations of 1¢ (the penny), 5¢ (nickel), 10¢ (dime), 25¢ (quarter) and 50¢ (half dollar). Notes ('bills') come in denominations of $1, $5, $10, $20, $50 and $100. There is also a one-dollar coin that the government has tried unsuccessfully to bring into mass circulation and a two-dollar note that is out of favor but still occasionally seen.

Exchange Rates

At press time, exchange rates were as follows:

country	unit		US dollars
Australia	A$1	=	US$0.63
Canada	C$1	=	US$0.66
France	1FF	=	US$0.16
Germany	DM1	=	US$0.55
Hong Kong	HK$1	=	US$0.13
Japan	¥100	=	US$0.83
New Zealand	NZ$1	=	US$0.54
UK	UK£1	=	US$1.61
euro	€1	=	US$1.05

Exchanging Money

Cash If you're carrying foreign currency, it can be exchanged for US dollars at larger banks, such as the ubiquitous Bank of Hawaii, or at the Honolulu International Airport.

Traveler's Checks The main benefit of traveler's checks is that they provide protection from theft and loss. Large companies such as

American Express and Thomas Cook generally offer efficient replacement policies.

Foreign visitors who carry traveler's checks will find it much easier to use them if the checks are in US dollars. Restaurants, hotels and most stores accept US dollar traveler's checks as if they're cash, so if that's what you're carrying, odds are you'll never have to use a bank or pay an exchange fee.

Keeping a record of the check numbers and those you have used is vital when it comes to replacing lost checks, so keep this information separate from the checks themselves. For refunds on lost or stolen American Express traveler's checks, call ☎ 800-221-7282; for lost MasterCard traveler's checks, call ☎ 800-223-9920.

ATMs Automatic teller machines (ATMs) are a handy alternative to traveler's checks. The small service charge for withdrawing money from an ATM is less than the 1% fee charged for exchanging traveler's checks, and using an ATM card eliminates the necessity of carrying around a bundle of checks.

Major banks such as Bank of Hawaii and First Hawaiian Bank have extensive ATM networks throughout Oahu that will give cash advances on major credit cards (MasterCard, Visa, American Express, Discover and JCB) and allow cash withdrawals with affiliated ATM cards. Most ATM machines in Hawaii accept bank cards from both the Plus and Cirrus systems, the two largest ATM networks in the USA.

In addition to traditional bank locations, you can also find ATMs at most large grocery stores, in mall-style shopping centers and in a growing number of convenience stores.

Credit Cards Major credit cards are widely accepted throughout Hawaii, including at car rental agencies and most hotels, restaurants, gas stations, shops and larger grocery stores. Most recreational and tourist activities can also be paid for by credit card.

The most commonly accepted cards in Hawaii are Visa, MasterCard and American Express, although JCB, Discover and Diners Club cards are also accepted by a fair number of businesses.

Note, however, that many Bed & Breakfast establishments and some condominiums, particularly those handled through rental agencies, do not accept credit cards, so call in advance to inquire.

Although some tourism businesses, such as car rental agencies, require customers to have a credit card, many other places that accept Visa and MasterCard are also likely to accept debit cards. Unlike a credit card, a

Embassies & Consulates

US Embassies Abroad

Australia
(☎ 02-6214-5600, www
.usisaustralia.gov/embassy.html)
21 Moonah Place. Yarralumla,
Canberra, ACT 2600

Belgium
(☎ 2-513-3830)
27 Boulevard du Regent,
B-1000 Brussels

Canada
(☎ 613-238-5335,
www.usembassycanada.gov)
100 Wellington St,
Ottawa, Ontario K1P 5T1

Denmark
(☎ 35 55 31 44,
www.usembassy.dk)
Dag Hammarskjolds Allé 24,
2100 Copenhagen

Federated States of Micronesia
(☎ 320-2187) PO Box 1286,
Pohnpei, FSM 96941

Finland
(☎ 0-171-931,
www.usembassy.fi)
Itainen Puistotie 14A,
Helsinki 00140

France
(☎ 01 43 12 22 22,
www.amb-usa.fr)
2 avenue Gabriel,
75382 Paris Cedex 08

Germany
(☎ 228-3391,
www.usembassy.de)
Deichmanns Aue 29,
53170 Bonn

Hong Kong
(☎ 2523-9011)
26 Garden Rd,
Hong Kong

Indonesia
(☎ 21-360-360)
Medan Merdeka Selatan 5,
Jakarta

Ireland
(☎ 1-668-8777)
42 Elgin Rd,
Ballsbridge, Dublin

Israel
(☎ 3-517-4338,
www.usis-israel.org.il)
71 Hayarkon St,
Tel Aviv

Italy
(☎ 64 67 41, www.usis.it)
Via Veneto 119/A,
00187 Rome

Japan
(☎ 3-224-5000)
10-5, Akasaka 1-chome,
Minato-ku, Tokyo

Korea
(☎ 2-397-4114)
82 Sejong-Ro,
Chongro-ku,
Seoul

Malaysia
(☎ 248-9011)
376 Jalan Tun Razak,
50400 Kuala Lumpur

Mexico
(☎ 5-211-0042,
www.usembassy.org.mx)
Paseo de la Reforma 305,
Colonia Cuauhtémoc
06500 Mexico City

Netherlands
(☎ 70-310-9209,
www.usemb.nl)
Lange Voorhout 102,
2514 EJ The Hague

New Zealand
(☎ 4-472-2068)
29 Fitzherbert Terrace
PO Box 1190, Thorndon,
Wellington

Norway
(☎ 22 44 85 50)
Drammensveien 18,
0244 Oslo 2

Philippines
(☎ 2-521-7116)
1201 Roxas Blvd,
Ermita Manila 1000

Singapore
(☎ 65-476-9100)
27 Napier Rd,
Singapore 258508

Spain
(☎ 1-577-400)
Calle Serrano 75,
28006 Madrid

Sweden
(☎ 08-783-53-00,
www.usis.usemb.se)
Strandvagen 101,
115 89 Stockholm

Switzerland
(☎ 31-357-70-11)
Jubilaeumstrasse 93,
3005 Bern

Thailand
(☎ 2-205-4000)
120 Wireless Rd, Bangkok

UK
(☎ 020-499-9000,
www.usembassy.org.uk)
24/31 Grosvenor Square,
London W1A 1AE

Western Samoa
(☎ 21-631) 5th floor,
Beach Rd, Box 3430, Apia

debit card deducts payment directly from the user's checking account. Instead of an interest rate, users are charged a minimal fee for the transaction. Be sure to check with your bank to confirm that your debit card will be accepted in other states – debit cards from large commercial banks can often be used worldwide.

If you lose your credit cards or they are stolen, contact the company immediately.

Embassies & Consulates

Consulates on Oahu

American Samoa
American Samoa Office-Hawaii
(☎ 847-1998)
1427 Dillingham Blvd, suite 210

Australia
Consulate-General of Australia
(☎ 524-5050)
1000 Bishop St

Austria
Consulate of Austria
(% 923-8585)
1314 S King St, suite 1260

Belgium
Consulate of Belgium
(☎ 533-6900)
745 Fort St Mall, 18th floor

Brazil
Consulate of Brazil
(☎ 235-0571)
44-166 Nanamoana

Chile
Consulate of Chile
(☎ 949-2850)
1860 Ala Moana Blvd, suite 1900

Denmark
Consulate of Denmark
(☎ 545-2028)
1001 Bishop St, suite 2626

Federated States of Micronesia
Federated States of Micronesia Office
(☎ 836-4775)
3049 Ualena, suite 408

Germany
Consulate of Germany
(☎ 946-3819)
2003 Kalia Rd, suite 1I

India
Consulate-General of India
(☎ 262-0292)
306 Hahani St

Italy
Consulate of Italy
(☎ 531-2277)
735 Bishop St, suite 201

Japan
Consulate-General of Japan
(☎ 523-7495)
1742 Nuuanu Ave

Kiribati
Consulate of the Republic of Kiribati
(☎ 521-7703)
850 Richards St, suite 503

Korea
Consulate-General of Korea
(☎ 595-6109)
2756 Pali Hwy

Mariana Islands
Mariana Hawaii Liaison Office
(☎ 592-0300)
1221 Kapiolani Blvd, suite 730

Marshall Islands
Republic of the Marshall Islands Office
(☎ 545-7767)
1888 Lusitana, suite 301

Mexico
Consulate of Mexico
(☎ 524-4390)
677 Ala Moana Blvd, suite 501

Netherlands
Consulate of the Netherlands
(☎ 535-8450)
700 Bishop St, 21st floor

Norway
Consulate of Norway
(☎ 593-1240)
1314 S King St, suite G4

Papua New Guinea
Consulate-General of Papua New Guinea
(☎ 524-5414)
1154 Fort St Mall, suite 300

Philippines
Consulate-General of the Philippines
(☎ 595-6316)
2433 Pali Hwy

Sweden
Consulate of Sweden
(☎ 528-4777)
737 Bishop St, suite 2600

Switzerland
Consulate of Switzerland
(☎ 737-5297)
4231 Papu Circle

Thailand
Royal Thai Consulate-General
(☎ 845-7332), 287A Kalihi

Tonga
Tonga Consular Agency
(☎ 521-5149)
220 S King St, suite 1230

See the toll-free directory at the back of this book for the phone numbers for the main credit card companies.

International Transfers Transferring money from your home bank will be easier if you've authorized someone back home to access your account. Specify the town, the bank and the branch to which you want your money directed, or ask your home bank to tell you where there's a suitable one, and make sure you get the details right. You can find some of the necessary information on the websites of Hawaii's two largest banks: Bank of Hawaii (www.boh.com) and First Hawaiian Bank (www.fhb.com).

Costs

How much money you need for your trip to Oahu depends on your traveling style. Some people get by quite cheaply while others rack up huge balances on their credit cards.

Airfare to Hawaii is usually one of the heftier parts of the budget. Fares vary greatly, particularly from the US mainland, so shop around. (Note that Honolulu stopovers are often thrown in free, or for a nominal charge, on trips between North America and Asian or Pacific countries.)

If you want to rent a car, budget about $50 a day for the rental fee, gas and parking. However, a car is not essential for exploring most of the island, as Oahu has a good, inexpensive bus system that charges just $1 no matter how far you travel.

The Waikiki/Honolulu area has a wide range of accommodations. The least expensive places to stay are the two HI-affiliated youth hostels and the handful of private hostel-type places – all of them have dorm beds for about $16. After that, there are rooms at Ys for $30 and a few budget Waikiki hotels that start around $50. Waikiki has lots of middle-range hotels in the $75 to $125 range, as well as luxury beachfront hotels that fetch triple that rate.

Because much of Hawaii's food is shipped in, grocery prices average 25% higher than on the US mainland. Due to the shipping costs, bulky items such as cereal have the highest markups, while compact items such as canned tuna have the lowest. Waikiki restaurants generally reflect these higher food prices, but Oahu's plethora of less-touristed neighborhood restaurants are an excellent value, with prices generally comparable to those you'll find on the mainland.

The good news for visitors is that lots of things in Oahu are free. There are no parking or entrance fees at beaches or state parks (except for Hanauma Bay); free hula shows abound in Waikiki; and a few of Oahu's main sightseeing attractions – such as the *Arizona* Memorial and the Aloha Tower – don't charge admission.

Tipping & Bargaining

Tipping practices are the same as in the rest of the USA. In restaurants, waiters expect a tip of about 15%, while 10% is generally sufficient for taxi drivers, hair stylists and the like. Hotel bellhops are typically tipped about $1 per bag.

In Hawaii, prices are generally fixed. However, some bargaining takes place in markets where you buy from individual vendors, such as the Aloha Flea Market at Aloha Stadium and at the International Market Place in Waikiki.

For Business Travelers

Those traveling on business will find that some of the larger Waikiki hotels, such as Hilton Hawaiian Village, offer personal computer rentals and other specialized services geared for business travelers. Some of the hotels in the Outrigger chain have small business centers where guests can rent work desks equipped with computers, printers and modem hookups and arrange other business services.

One city hotel, the Executive Centre Hotel in downtown Honolulu, is geared specifically for business travelers. The rooms at the Executive have private-line phones with voice mail, and the hotel's business center has work stations, laptop rentals and secretarial services.

In addition, the chain business center Kinko's, which is open 24 hours a day, offers reasonably priced on-site computer rentals, with major word processing programs, scanning and color output. It also has inexpensive photocopying services. Kinko's has a branch downtown (Map 2; ☎ 528-7171), 1050 Bishop St, one near the university (Map 4; ☎ 943-0005), 2575 S King St, and another just north of the Ala Moana Center (Map 3; ☎ 944-8500), 1500 Kapiolani Blvd.

If you have any last-minute business needs as you're leaving Hawaii, the business center (☎ 831-3600) in the central departure lobby of Honolulu International Airport offers photocopy, fax and mail services and work station rentals.

Most major rental car agencies in Honolulu offer short-term cellular phone rentals, as do some local cellular phone specialists such as Digital Connection (☎ 922-3000) and Business Services Center (☎ 955-9555).

If you're hoping to set up a business in Hawaii, there are a couple of organizations that can provide assistance. The state's Department of Business, Economic Development & Tourism (☎ 586-2545, fax 586-2544), 1130 N Nimitz Hwy, suite A-254, Honolulu, HI 96817, will send you a packet that includes information on business regulations, starting a business in Hawaii and assistance provided by state agencies. The Chamber of Commerce of Hawaii (☎ 545-4300), 1132 Bishop St, suite 200, Honolulu, HI 96813, provides more general background information and support.

Taxes

Hawaii has a 4.17% state sales tax that is tacked onto virtually everything, including all meals, groceries, car rentals and accommodations. An additional 7.24% room tax brings the total tax added to accommodation bills to 11.41%. Another tax targeted at visitors is a $2-a-day 'road use' tax imposed upon all car rentals.

POST & COMMUNICATIONS

By world standards, the US Postal Service is both reliable and inexpensive.

There are 35 post offices on Oahu. The main Honolulu post office is not in central Honolulu, but is at the side of the airport at 3600 Aolele St, opposite the inter-island terminal. It's open 7:30 am to 8:30 pm weekdays and 8 am to 2:30 pm on Saturday.

You can get detailed 24-hour postal information, including the business hours for every post office in Hawaii, by dialing toll-free ☎ 800-275-8777.

Private shippers such as United Parcel Service (UPS; ☎ 800-742-5877) and Federal Express (FedEx; ☎ 800-463-3339) also ship to both domestic and foreign locations.

Postal Rates

Postage rates for first-class mail within the USA are 33¢ for letters up to 1oz (22¢ for each additional ounce) and 20¢ for postcards. First-class mail between Hawaii and the mainland goes by air and usually takes three to four days.

International airmail rates are $1 for a 1oz letter, 60¢ for a half-ounce letter and 50¢ for a postcard to any foreign country with the exception of Canada and Mexico. Letters to Canada cost 55¢ for a 1oz letter, 48¢ for a half-ounce letter and 45¢ for a postcard. Letters to Mexico cost 46¢ for a 1oz letter and 40¢ for either a half-ounce letter or a postcard.

The cost for parcels airmailed anywhere within the USA is $3.20 for 2 pounds or less. For heavier items, rates differ according to the distance mailed.

Receiving Mail

All general delivery mail sent to you in Honolulu must be picked up at the main Honolulu post office, next to the airport. Note that any mail sent general delivery to the Waikiki post office or other Honolulu branches will either go to the main post office or be returned to the sender. If you're receiving mail in Honolulu, have it addressed to you as follows:

Your name

c/o General Delivery, Main Post Office
3600 Aolele St, Honolulu, HI 96820-3600

It's also possible to have general delivery mail sent to you in Kailua. To do so, have it addressed to you as follows:

Your name

c/o General Delivery, Kailua Post Office
335 Hahani St, Kailua, HI 96734-9998

For general delivery service, domestic mail will usually be held for 10 days, international mail for 30 days. You'll need to present photo identification to collect your mail.

Most hotels will also hold mail for incoming guests. In addition, the American Express office (☎ 926-5441) at the Hyatt Regency hotel in Waikiki will hold mail for 30 days for American Express card and traveler's check holders. They will not accept parcels or anything that must be signed for. Their office is open 8 am to 8 pm daily.

Have mail addressed to you as follows:

Your name

c/o American Express, Client Mail Service
2424 Kalakaua Ave, Honolulu, HI 96815

Telephone

All phone numbers within the USA consist of a three-digit area code followed by a seven-digit number. However, all of the Hawaiian islands share the same area code (808), making it unnecessary to use it when making calls on the same island.

All phone numbers listed in this book beginning with 800, 877 or 888 are toll-free numbers from the US mainland, unless otherwise noted. The same numbers are sometimes toll free from Canada as well.

Pay phones can readily be found in public places such as shopping centers and beach parks. Local calls cost 35¢ at pay phones. Any call made from one point on Oahu to any other point on Oahu is a local call. Calls from Oahu to the other Hawaiian islands are long distance.

There are several companies that provide pay phone service, the most common being GTE. To dial direct from one Hawaiian island to another from a GTE pay phone, the rate is $1.45 for the first minute and 15¢ for each additional minute. The cost drops to $1.35 for the first minute and 10¢ for each extra minute from 5 pm to 8 am weekdays and all day on Saturday and Sunday.

Most hotels add a service charge of 50¢ to $1 for each local call made from a room phone and most also have hefty surcharges for long-distance calls. Public phones, which can be found in most hotel lobbies, are always cheaper. You can pump in coins, use a phonecard or make collect calls from pay phones.

In Hawaii you can make toll-free calls (those that begin with 800, 877 or 888) from pay phones without inserting any money.

For directory assistance for Oahu phone numbers dial ☎ 1-411 and for elsewhere in Hawaii dial ☎ 1-808-555-1212. To find out if there's an inter-island toll-free number for a business, dial ☎ 1-800-555-1212.

International Calls To make an international call direct from Hawaii, dial ☎ 011 + country code + area code + number. (An exception is to Canada, where you instead dial ☎ 1 + area code + number.) For international operator assistance dial ☎ 0 (zero).

Area Code for Hawaii

The telephone area code for all of Hawaii is 808. The area code is not used when making calls on the same island, but it must be added to all Hawaiian phone numbers when calling from outside the state and when calling from one Hawaiian island to another.

Because the area code cannot be dialed when making a local call, the phone numbers in this book do not include the area code, but it should be understood that it is 808.

The operator can provide specific rate information and tell you which time periods are the cheapest for calling – these vary with the country being called.

If you're calling Hawaii from abroad, the international country code for the USA is '1,' and all calls to Hawaii are then followed by the area code 808 and the seven-digit local number.

Phonecards There's a wide range of local and international phonecards. Lonely Planet's eKno Communication Card (see the insert at the back of this book) is aimed specifically at travelers and provides cheap international calls, a range of messaging services and free email (for local calls, you're usually better off with a local card). You can join online at www.ekno.lonelyplanet.com, or by phone from Oahu by dialing ☎ 1-800-294-3676. Once you have joined, to use eKno from Oahu, dial ☎ 1-800-527-6786.

Fax

Faxes can be sent and received through the front desks of most hotels. There are also business centers that offer reasonably priced fax services, such as Kinko's, which is open 24 hours a day and has branches in downtown Honolulu, just north of the Ala Moana Center and near the University of Hawaii. See the boxed text 'For Business Travelers' for additional information.

Email & Internet Access

Traveling with a portable computer is a great way to stay in touch with home, but unless you know what you're doing, it's fraught with potential problems. If the power supply voltage in your home country is different than in Hawaii (see Electricity later in this chapter), bring a universal AC adapter, which will enable you to plug in the computer without frying its innards. You may also need a plug adapter, which is often easiest to buy before you leave home.

Also, your PC-card modem may not work once you leave your home country, but you won't know for sure until you try. The safest option is to buy a reputable 'global' modem before you leave home. Keep in mind that the telephone socket may be different from that at home as well, so ensure that you have at least a US RJ-11 telephone adapter that works with your modem. You can almost always find an adapter that will convert from RJ-11 to the local variety. For more information on traveling with a portable computer, see www.teleadapt.com or www.warrior.com.

Major Internet service providers such as America Online (www.aol.com) and CompuServe (www.compuserve.com) have dial-in nodes throughout the USA; it's best to download a list of the dial-in numbers before you leave home. If you access your Internet email at home through a smaller ISP, your best option is either to open an account with a global ISP, like those mentioned above, or to rely on public access points to collect your mail.

To use public access points to get your email, you'll need to know your incoming (POP or IMAP) mail server name, your account name and your password. A final option to collect mail through public access points is to open a free Web-based email account such as HotMail (www.hotmail.com) or Yahoo! Mail (mail.yahoo.com). You can then access your mail from anywhere in the world from any Internet-connected machine running a standard Web browser.

If you're carrying a laptop, you may want to check with your hotel in advance to see if the room comes with a phone jack that can accommodate modem hookups; these are becoming more common as hotels upgrade and renovate.

Cybercafes Cybercafes in Honolulu have about the life expectancy of a fly, falling by the wayside quickly.

One exception is Coffee Haven (☎ 732-2090, sip@coffee-haven.com), at 1026 Kapahulu Ave near the H-1 Fwy overpass, which owes its success to providing good coffee and homemade pies along with Internet access. There are four Macs available for $4 an hour and one IBM for $6 an hour. The minimum charge is 50¢, which covers five to seven minutes. It's open 8 am to 10 pm Monday through Thursday, 8 am to midnight on Friday and Saturday and 9 am to 5 pm on Sunday.

Coffee Cove On Line (Map 4; ☎ 955-2683, online@coffeecove.com), 2600 S King St, is an invitingly casual setting near the University of Hawaii campus where you can get coffee and muffins while you check your email. The cost is $1.50 per 15 minutes. It's open 7 am to midnight on weekdays, 10 am to midnight on weekends.

For other Internet access options, see the boxed text 'For Business Travelers,' earlier in this chapter and Libraries, later in this chapter.

Kinko's (www.kinkos.com) business centers provide email access, as well as computer work stations, for $12 an hour, but there's no minimum charge so you pay only for the minutes you use. It's open 24 hours a day and has branches a block north of the Ala Moana Center (☎ 944-8500), 1500 Kapiolani Blvd, and near the university (☎ 943-0005), 2575 S King St, and in downtown Honolulu (☎ 528-7171).

INTERNET RESOURCES

The World Wide Web is a rich resource for travelers. You can research your trip, hunt down bargain airfares, book hotels, check on weather conditions or chat with locals and other travelers about the best places to visit (or avoid!).

There's no better place to start your Web explorations than the Lonely Planet website (www.lonelyplanet.com). Here you'll find succinct summaries on traveling to most places on earth, postcards from other travelers and the Thorn Tree bulletin board, where you can ask questions before you go or dispense advice when you get back. You can also find travel news and updates to many of our most popular guidebooks, and the subWWWay section links you to the most useful travel resources elsewhere on the Web.

In addition, www.hawaii.net and www.planet-hawaii.com are useful websites that have links to a wealth of Hawaii information. Other websites are given throughout this book under specific topics.

BOOKS

There is a wealth of books available on everything from culture and history to Oahu's best beaches and surfing spots. The books that follow are just a few of the recommended titles.

Lonely Planet

If you're planning to visit any of the Hawaiian islands other than Oahu, you'll want to pick up Lonely Planet's *Hawaii*, which is packed with comprehensive information on traveling throughout Hawaii.

History, People & Culture

Hawaii's Story by Hawaii's Queen, by Queen Liliuokalani (Mutual Publishing), written in 1897, is an autobiographical account of Liliuokalani's life and the circumstances surrounding her 1893 overthrow.

The Betrayal of Liliuokalani: Last Queen of Hawaii, 1838-1917, by Helena G Allen (Mutual Publishing), is an insightful account not only of the queen's life, but also of missionary activity and foreign encroachment in Hawaii.

Hawaiian Antiquities, by David Malo (Bishop Museum Press), written in 1838, was the first account of Hawaiian culture written by a Hawaiian. It gives an in-depth history of Hawaii before the arrival of the missionaries.

Shoal of Time, by Gavan Daws (University of Hawaii Press), is a comprehensive and colorful history covering the period from Captain Cook's 'discovery' of the islands to statehood.

Fragments of Hawaiian History, by John Papa Ii and translated by Mary Kawena Pukui (Bishop Museum Press), is a firsthand account of old Hawaii under the *kapu* system. Ii lived in Hawaii at the time of Kamehameha the Great and the arrival of the first westerners.

The Hawaiian Kingdom, by Ralph S Kuykendall (University of Hawaii Press), is a three-volume set written from 1938 to 1967. It covers Hawaiian history from 1778 to 1893 and is considered the definitive work on that period.

Keneti, by Bob Krauss (University of Hawaii Press), is a biography of Kenneth 'Keneti' Emory, the esteemed Bishop Museum archaeologist who, over the years, sailed with writer Jack London, worked with anthropologist Margaret Mead and surfed with Olympian Duke Kahanamoku. He spent much of his life uncovering the ruins of villages and temples throughout the Pacific, recording them before they disappeared forever. Emory died in 1992.

Na Wahi Pana O Koolau Poko, by Anne Kapulani Landgraf (University of Hawaii Press), focuses on the historical sites of windward Oahu. The book has 82 high-quality duotone photographs accompanying a Hawaiian/English text.

Nana I Ke Kumu (Look to the Source), by Mary K Pukui, EW Haertig and Catherine A Lee (Hui Hanai), is a fascinating two-volume collection of information on Hawaiian cultural practices, social customs and beliefs.

Merchant Prince of the Sandalwood Mountains, by Bob Dye (University of Hawaii Press), tells the story of Chun Afong, Hawaii's first Chinese millionaire, in the context of the turbulent social and economic changes of the 18th century.

Mythology

The Kumulipo, by Martha Beckwith (University of Hawaii Press), is a translation of the Hawaiian chant of creation. The chant of 2077 lines begins in the darkness of the spirit world and traces the genealogy of an *alii*

(royal) family said to be the ancestors of humankind.

Hawaiian Mythology, also by Martha Beckwith (University of Hawaii Press), has comprehensive translations of Hawaii's old myths and legends.

The Legends and Myths of Hawaii (Mutual Publishing) is a collection of legends as told by King David Kalakaua, with a short introduction to Hawaiian culture and history as well.

Natural History

The Many-Splendored Fishes of Hawaii, by Gar Goodson (Stanford University Press), is one of the better of several small, inexpensive fish-identification books on the market and has good descriptions and 170 color drawings.

Hawaii's Fishes: A Guide for Snorkelers, Divers and Aquarists, by John P Hoover (Mutual Publishing), a more expensive and comprehensive field guide, covers more than 230 reef and shore fishes of Hawaii. It's fully illustrated with color photographs and gives insights on island dive sites.

The Hawaii Audubon Society's *Hawaii's Birds* is the best pocket-sized guide to the birds of Hawaii. It includes color photos and descriptions of all the native birds and many of the species that have been introduced to the Hawaiian Islands.

For a more comprehensive book, there's *A Field Guide to the Birds of Hawaii & the Tropical Pacific* by H Douglas Pratt, Phillip L Bruner and Delwyn G Berrett (Princeton University Press). The book contains nearly 50 pages of color plates.

Mammals in Hawaii, by P Quentin Tomich (Bishop Museum Press), is an authoritative book on the mammals in Hawaii, with interesting stories on how they arrived in the islands. Coverage includes whales, dolphins and such oddities as the Australian rock-wallabies that were accidentally released in 1916 and now reside in Oahu's Kalihi Valley.

Plants and Flowers of Hawaii, by S Sohmer and R Gustafson (University of Hawaii Press), has good-quality color photos and descriptions of more than 130 native plants of Hawaii, including information on their habitats and evolution.

The new *Manual of the Flowering Plants of Hawaii*, by Warren L Wagner, Derral R Herbst and SH Sohmer (Bishop Museum Press), has in-depth information on Hawaiian flora, including some of the rare and endangered species that have recently been categorized.

Practical Folk Medicine of Hawaii, by LR McBride (Petroglyph Press), has descriptions of many native medicinal plants and their uses.

A good general book on flora and fauna is *Plants and Animals of Hawaii* by local biologist Susan Scott (Bess Press). It discusses various environments, including reefs, shorelines, forests and wetlands, and details plants and animals of the islands, both native and introduced. There are interesting tidbits on medicinal uses, origins and the like.

See the Flora and Fauna sections, in the Facts about Oahu chapter for additional information.

Outdoor Activities

Diving and Snorkeling Hawaii, written by Casey Mahaney and Astrid Witte Mahaney, (Lonely Planet Pisces Books), is an informative guide to both diving and snorkeling in Hawaii. It includes color photos illustrating sites and fish.

The Beaches of Oahu, by John RK Clark (University of Hawaii Press), is a comprehensive book detailing the island's coastline and every one of its beaches, including water conditions, shoreline geology and local history.

Surfer's Guide to Hawaii: Hawaii Gets All the Breaks, by Greg Ambrose (Bess Press), describes the top surfing spots throughout the islands, including Oahu's world-famous Sunset Beach and Banzai Pipeline. Written in an entertaining style, it's packed with everything you need to know about surfing in Hawaii.

The Hiker's Guide to Oahu, by Stuart Ball (University of Hawaii Press), covers 53 hikes in Oahu. The author, a former president of the Hawaiian Trail & Mountain Club, gives information on length, difficulty and direction to the trailhead for each hike. Walks are described in detail and accompanied by topographical maps.

Also worth considering is *Oahu Trails*, by Kathy Morey (Wilderness Press), which covers 43 hikes and provides maps and detailed directions for each, including curious tidbits of information.

Mountain Biking the Hawaiian Islands, by Oahu resident John Alford (Ohana Publishing), is an excellent resource for mountain bikers, covering the public trails open to bikers, with maps and descriptions.

General

From the Skies of Paradise, Oahu is an aerial photography book with color plates by renowned photographer Douglas Peebles and text by Glen Grant (Mutual Publishing). All parts of Oahu – cities, beaches, mountains and fields – are beautifully photographed, with accompanying narratives that incorporate Hawaiian myths and legends.

Architecture in Hawaii, by Rob Sandler (Mutual Publishing), is a coffee-table book with striking color photographs of Hawaii's most notable buildings, the majority of which are in Honolulu. More than 150 buildings are detailed, from thatched cottages to the royal palace, covering some two centuries of island architecture. There are also biographies of Hawaii's top architects.

Another good large-format book is *Hawaii: The Islands of Life* (Signature Publishing), which has beautiful photos of the flora, fauna and landscapes being protected by the Nature Conservancy of Hawaii. The text is by respected author Gavan Daws.

Reference

The recently revised 350-page *Atlas of Hawaii* (University of Hawaii Press), by the University of Hawaii's Department of Geography, is loaded with data, maps and tabulations covering everything from land ownership to seasonal ocean wave patterns.

Place Names of Hawaii, by Mary Kawena Pukui, Samuel H Elbert and Esther T Mookini (University of Hawaii Press), is a glossary of 4000 Hawaiian place names. The meaning and background of each name is explained.

Hawaiian Dictionary, by Mary Kawena Pukui and Samuel H Elbert (University of Hawaii Press), is the authoritative work on the Hawaiian language. It's written in both Hawaiian-English and English-Hawaiian, with 30,000 entries. There's also an inexpensive pocket-sized version, with 10,000 Hawaiian words.

There are many other Hawaiian-language books on the market, including grammar texts, conversational self-study guides and books on pidgin.

Mail-Order Sources

Island Bookshelf (☎ 503-297-4324, 800-967-5944, fax 503-297-1702), Box 91003, Portland, OR 97291, specializes in books on Hawaii and will mail out a comprehensive catalog on request. They also have a website (www.islandbookshelf.com) from which you can order books.

The following Hawaiian publishers will send catalogs of titles that can be ordered by mail:

Bess Press
(☎ 734-7159, 800-910-2377, fax 732-3627, www.besspress.com) 3565 Harding Ave, Honolulu, HI 96816

Bishop Museum Press
(☎ 848-4134, fax 841-8968) 1525 Bernice St, Honolulu, HI 96817

University of Hawaii Press
(☎ 956-8255, 888-847-7377, fax 988-6052, www2.hawaii.edu/uhpress) 2840 Kolowalu St, Honolulu, HI 96822

FILMS

Dozens of feature movies have been filmed on Hawaii, and scores of others have used footage of Hawaii as the backdrop. Although the island of Kauai, with its lush landscapes and striking Na Pali Cliffs, is the darling of the movie industry, Oahu has played a role in a handful of notable films as well.

Picture Bride (1993), which stars Yuki Kudoh, with a cameo by Toshiro Mifune, is one of the few films to insightfully delve into island life. Filmed on Oahu, it depicts the blunt realities of 19th-century Hawaiian plantation life for a Japanese mail-order bride.

The following movies were filmed at least partially on Oahu: *From Here to Eternity* (1953), starring Burt Lancaster and Deborah Kerr, with its classic love scene on the beach at Halona Cove; *Hawaii* (1966), filmed in part on the Waianae Coast of Oahu and starring Julie Andrews and Max von Sydow; *Tora! Tora! Tora!* (1970), starring Jason Robards, about the surprise Japanese attack on Pearl Harbor; and *Godzilla* (1998), starring Matthew Broderick, and Steven Spielberg's *Jurassic Park* (1993), both of which shot scenes at Kualoa Ranch on Oahu's windward coast.

NEWSPAPERS & MAGAZINES

Hawaii's two main papers are the *Honolulu Advertiser* (www.thehonoluluadvertiser.com), which is published each morning, and the *Honolulu Star-Bulletin* (www.starbulletin.com), which comes out in the afternoon Monday to Saturday. An excellent website is www.starbulletin.com, which allows you to browse the *Star-Bulletin* online.

In addition, Oahu has numerous weekly or monthly newspapers, many of which can be picked up for free around the island. These include the *Honolulu Weekly* (www.honoluluweekly.com), a progressive paper with an extensive entertainment section; *The Waikiki News*, with Waikiki-related news and upcoming events; and other regional rags such as the *Windward Oahu News* and the *Kailua Sun Press*.

Several mainland newspapers are also widely available, including *USA Today*, the *Wall Street Journal* and the *Los Angeles Times*. Look for them in the lobbies of larger hotels and in convenience stores. The best place to get international newspapers is at Borders bookstore, which carries an impressive selection from around the world.

As for magazines, *Honolulu*, *Aloha* and *Hawaii Magazine* are the main general interest publications about Hawaii. *Honolulu* is geared more towards residents and is published monthly. *Aloha* and *Hawaii Magazine* have more visitor-oriented feature articles and are both published six times a year.

All of these magazines can be purchased at news racks and bookstores around the island.

There are also numerous free tourist magazines, such as *This Week Oahu* and *Spotlight's Oahu Gold*, which can readily be found at the airport and in street-corner racks all around Waikiki. Although the tourist magazines are mostly composed of paid advertising, they can still be a good source of visitor information. For example, they contain simple maps, a bit of current event information and discount coupons for everything from hamburgers to sunset cruises.

RADIO & TV

Oahu has 17 commercial AM radio stations, 12 commercial FM radio stations and three public radio stations. Radio station Da KINE (105.1 FM) plays classic Hawaiian music. Hawaii Public Radio is on KHPR (88.1 FM), KKUA (90.7 FM) and KIPO (89.3 FM).

Hawaii has commercial TV stations representing all the major US networks and cable network stations, including tourist information and Japanese language channels. Almost anything you can watch on the mainland you can watch in Hawaii. Cable channels 8 and 10 feature continuous visitor information and ads geared to tourists.

Baywatch Hawaii

After 10 years of lolling on Southern California beaches, the popular TV series *Baywatch* packed up its bags and moved to Hawaii. The show is now filmed against the backdrop of Haleiwa Alii Beach Park on Oahu's North Shore.

It's not the first television series to be filmed in Hawaii, of course – two of TV's top-drawing police/detective series, *Hawaii Five-0* and *Magnum PI*, were Hawaii home-growns. But TV's heyday in Hawaii is a fading memory – since the closing episode of *Magnum PI*, more than a decade ago, no TV series has made a successful go of it from the islands.

That's likely to change with the arrival of *Baywatch*, which boasts the

They've rescued just about everyone in LA, so it's on to Oahu.

broadest viewership of any syndicated TV action program in the world. The show is translated into 41 languages – three in China alone – and is broadcast in nearly 150 countries.

So how did Hawaii attract this top-rated TV series? It took more than the North Shore's phenomenal surf and picturesque beaches. The state coughed up about $2 million in capital improvement incentives, offering to refurbish the old *Hawaii Five-0* stage into a *Baywatch* studio and to build a new 'Lifeguard Beach' set at Haleiwa. And the Hawaii Visitors and Convention Bureau, eager for the 'free' advertising, donated another million dollars.

In return, *Baywatch* plans to film 22 episodes on Oahu each year – pumping about $20 million into the local economy and giving Hawaii a volume of television exposure that tourism officials claim will be worth even more. The show also agreed to add 'Hawaii' to its name and to add a couple of Hawaiian characters to the cast.

For some local flavor, the evening news on Channel 2 ends with some fine slack-key guitar music by Keola and Kapono Beamer and clips of people waving the shaka sign (see the boxed text 'Shaka Sign,' in the Facts about Oahu chapter).

PHOTOGRAPHY & VIDEO
Film & Equipment
Both print and slide film are readily available on Oahu. If you're going to be in Hawaii for any length of time, consider having your film developed there, because the high temperature and humidity of the tropics greatly accelerate the deterioration of exposed film. The sooner it's developed, the better the results.

Kodak and Fuji have labs in Honolulu, and drugstores and camera shops usually send film to those labs. Longs Drugs is one of the cheapest places for both purchasing film and having it developed. Slides generally take two to three days, prints a day or two, and the cost is cheaper than at camera shops. Although there are no branches in Waikiki, there's a Longs Drugs on the upper level of the Ala Moana Center and another at 2220 S King St, across from the Chiang Mai restaurant, between downtown Honolulu and the university. There are also numerous places in Waikiki that do one-hour photo processing.

Videotapes can be readily purchased throughout Hawaii. However, foreign visitors should be aware that North America uses the NTSC system, which is incompatible with the PAL system used in Europe, Asia and Australia.

Technical Tips
Oahu is a great place for photography. There is an abundance of interesting subjects, from the architecture in downtown Honolulu to landscapes, hula dancers and beach scenes.

Because of the sunny climate, a few precautions are needed. Most important, don't leave your camera in direct sun any longer than necessary. A locked car can heat up like an oven in just a few minutes, seriously damaging the film.

Sand and water are intense reflectors and in bright light they'll often leave foreground subjects shadowy. You can try compensating by adjusting your f-stop (aperture) or attaching a polarizing filter, or both, but the most effective technique is to take photos in the gentler light of early morning and late afternoon.

TIME
When it's noon in Honolulu, the time in other parts of the world is as follows: 1 pm in Anchorage, Alaska; 2 pm in Los Angeles, California; 5 pm in New York, New York; 10 pm in London, England; 11 pm in Bonn, Germany; 7 am the next day in Tokyo, Japan; 8 am the next day in Sydney and Melbourne, Australia; and 10 am the next day in Auckland, New Zealand.

Hawaii does not observe daylight saving time. Therefore, the time difference is one hour greater during those months when other countries observe daylight saving. For example, from April to October, when it's noon in Honolulu, it's 3 pm in Los Angeles and 6 pm in New York; and from November to March, when it's noon in Honolulu, it's 9 am in Melbourne and 11 am in Auckland.

Hawaii has about 11 hours of daylight in midwinter and almost 13½ hours in midsummer. In midwinter, the sun rises at about 7 am and sets at about 6 pm. In midsummer, it rises before 6 am and sets after 7 pm.

And then there's 'Hawaiian Time,' which is either a slow-down-the-clock pace or a euphemism for being late.

ELECTRICITY
Electricity is 110/120V, 60 cycles, and a flat two-pronged plug is used, the same as everywhere else in the USA.

WEIGHTS & MEASURES
Hawaii, like the rest of the USA, uses the imperial system of measurement. Distances are in feet, yards and miles. Three feet equals 1 yard (.914m); 1760 yards or 5280 feet are 1 mile. Dry weights are in ounces (oz), pounds (lb) and tons (16oz are 1 pound; 2000lb are 1 ton), but liquid measures differ from dry measures. One pint

equals 16 fluid oz; 2 pints equal 1 quart, a common measure for liquids such as milk, which is also sold in half gallons (2 quarts) and gallons (4 quarts). Gasoline is measured in US gallons (1 gallon = 3.79L).

For those unaccustomed to the imperial system, there is a metric conversion table on the inside back cover of this book.

LAUNDRY
Many hotels and hostels have coin-operated washers and dryers. In addition, there are numerous public coin laundries. The average cost is about $1 to wash a load of clothes and another dollar to dry.

TOILETS
The sanitation standard is very high in Hawaii. Public toilets are free to use and easy to find – at least in comparison to the US mainland. Virtually every beach park has toilet facilities (also referred to as rest rooms), as do larger shopping centers and most hotel lobbies. Fast-food restaurants are another possibility, though they're generally intended for customers only.

HEALTH
Hawaii is a very healthy place to live and to visit. Because Oahu is 2500 miles from the nearest industrial center, there's little air pollution. The main exception – and it's quite rare – occurs when unfavorable winds carry ash and haze from eruptions at Kilauea volcano on the Big Island over to Oahu.

Hawaii ranks first out of all the 50 US states in life expectancy, which is currently about 76 years old for men and 81 years old for women.

There are few serious health concerns. The islands have none of the tropical nasties like malaria, cholera or yellow fever, and you can drink water directly out of the tap, although all stream water needs to be boiled or treated.

No immunizations are required to enter Hawaii or any other port in the USA.

Be aware that there are many poisonous plants in Hawaii, so you should never taste a plant that you cannot positively identify as edible.

If you're new to the heat and humidity, you may find yourself easily fatigued and more susceptible to minor ailments. Acclimatize yourself by slowing down your pace and setting your body clock to the more kicked-back 'Hawaiian Time.' Drink plenty of liquids.

If you're planning on a long outing or anything strenuous, take enough water and don't push yourself.

Emergency Medical Care
Oahu has several hospitals with 24-hour emergency services, including Queen's Medical Center (☎ 538-9011), 1301 Punchbowl St, and Straub Clinic & Hospital (☎ 522-4000), 888 S King St at Ward Ave, both in Honolulu. For 24-hour service in Kailua, there's the Castle Medical Center (☎ 263-5500) at 640 Ulukahiki St.

Divers with the bends are brought to the UH Hyperbaric Treatment Center (☎ 587-3425), 347 N Kuakini St, Honolulu.

Everyday Health

Normal body temperature is up to 98.6°F (37°C); more than 4°F (2°C) higher indicates a high fever. The normal adult pulse rate is 60 to 100 beats per minute (children 80 to 100, babies 100 to 140). As a general rule, the pulse increases about 20 beats per minute for each 2°F (1°C) rise in fever.

Respiration (breathing) rate is also an indicator of illness. Count the number of breaths per minute: between 12 and 20 is normal for adults and older children (up to 30 for younger children, 40 for babies). People with a high fever or serious respiratory illness breathe more quickly than normal. More than 40 shallow breaths a minute may indicate pneumonia.

A suicide and crisis line (☎ 521-4555) operates 24 hours a day. Dial ☎ 911 for all ambulance emergencies.

Medical Problems & Treatment

Sunburn Sunburn is always a concern in the tropics, because the closer you get to the equator the fewer of the sun's rays are blocked out by the atmosphere. Don't be fooled by what appears to be a hazy overcast day – you can get sunburned surprisingly quickly, even through clouds.

Sunscreen with an SPF (sun protection factor) of 10 to 15 is recommended if you're not already tanned. If you're going into the water, put on one that's water-resistant. Snorkelers may want to wear a T-shirt if they plan to be out in the water a for long time. You'll not only be protecting yourself against sunburn, but also potential skin cancer and premature aging of the skin.

Fair-skinned people can get both first- and second-degree burns in the hot Hawaiian sun, and wearing a sun hat for added protection is a good idea. The most severe sun is between 10 am and 2 pm.

Prickly Heat Prickly heat is an itchy rash caused by excessive perspiration trapped under the skin. It usually strikes people who have just arrived in a hot climate and whose pores have not yet opened sufficiently to cope with increased sweating. Keeping cool by bathing often or resorting to air-con may help until you acclimatize.

Heat Exhaustion Dehydration or salt deficiency can cause heat exhaustion. Take time to acclimatize to high temperatures and make sure you get sufficient liquids. Salt deficiency is characterized by fatigue, lethargy, headaches, giddiness and muscle cramps, and in this case salt tablets (available at drugstores) may help. Vomiting or diarrhea can deplete your liquid and salt levels.

Heat Stroke This serious, sometimes fatal condition occurs when the body's heat regulating mechanism breaks down and the body temperature rises to dangerous levels. Long, continuous periods of exposure to high temperatures can leave you vulnerable to heat stroke. Avoid strenuous activity in open sun when you first arrive. The symptoms of heat stroke include feeling unwell, sweating very little or not at all and a high body temperature (102°F to 106°F). When sweating has ceased, the skin becomes flushed and red. Severe, throbbing headaches and lack of coordination will also occur, and the sufferer may be confused or aggressive. Eventually the victim may become delirious or convulsive. Hospitalization is essential, but meanwhile get patients out of the sun, remove their clothing, cover them with a wet sheet or towel and then fan them continually.

Fungal Infections The same climate that produces lush tropical forests also promotes a prolific growth of skin fungi and bacteria. Hot-weather fungal infections are most likely to occur between the toes or fingers or in the groin.

To prevent fungal infections, it's essential to keep your skin dry and cool and allow air to circulate. Choose loose cotton clothing rather than artificial fibers, and sandals rather than shoes. If you do get an infection, wash the infected area daily with a disinfectant or medicated soap. Rinse and dry well and then apply an antifungal powder.

Motion Sickness Eating lightly before and during a trip will reduce the chances of motion sickness. If you are prone to motion sickness, try to find a place that minimizes disturbance – near the wing on aircraft or close to the midpoint on boats. Fresh air usually helps; breathing cigarette smoke or reading doesn't. Commercial antimotion sickness preparations, which can cause drowsiness, have to be taken before the trip commences; when you're feeling sick it's too late. Ginger is a natural preventative and is available in capsule form.

Jet Lag When we travel long distances rapidly, our bodies take time to adjust to the 'new time' of our destination and we may experience fatigue, disorientation, insomnia, anxiety, impaired concentration and loss of appetite. These effects will usually be gone

Medical Kit

A small first-aid kit is a sensible thing to carry. A basic kit should contain the following: aspirin or Panadol for pain or fever; an antihistamine (such as Benadryl) for use as a decongestant, to relieve the itch from insect bites or to help prevent motion sickness; an antiseptic ointment for cuts and scratches; calamine lotion or aluminum sulfate spray to ease the irritation from bites and stings; bandages and Band-Aids; scissors; tweezers; insect repellent; and sunblock.

Be sure to also bring adequate supplies of any prescription medicine or contraceptive pills you may already be taking.

within three days of arrival, but there are ways of minimizing the impact of jet lag:

- Rest for a couple of days prior to departure; try to avoid staying up late and last-minute dashes for traveler's checks and the like.
- Try to select flight schedules that minimize sleep deprivation; arriving late in the day means you can go to sleep soon after you arrive. For very long flights, try to organize a stopover.
- Avoid excessive eating (which bloats the stomach) and alcohol (which causes dehydration) during the flight. Instead, drink plenty of noncarbonated, nonalcoholic drinks such as fruit juice or water.
- Make yourself comfortable by wearing loose-fitting clothes and perhaps bringing an eye mask and ear plugs to help you sleep.

HIV & AIDS Infection with the human immunodeficiency virus (HIV) may lead to acquired immune deficiency syndrome (AIDS), which is a fatal disease. Any exposure to blood, blood products or body fluids may put the individual at risk. The disease is often transmitted through sexual contact or dirty needles – vaccinations, acupuncture, tattooing and body-piercing can be as dangerous as intravenous drug use.

If you have any questions regarding AIDS while on Oahu, contact the AIDS/STD Hotline at ☎ 922-1313.

Cuts & Scratches Cuts and skin punctures are easily infected in Hawaii's hot and humid climate, and infections can be persistent. Keep any cut or open wound clean and treat it with an antiseptic solution. Keep the area protected, but where possible avoid bandages, which can keep wounds wet.

Coral cuts are even more susceptible to infection because tiny pieces of coral can get embedded in the skin. These cuts are notoriously slow to heal, as the coral releases a weak venom into the wound.

Pesky Creatures Hawaii has no land snakes, but it does have its fair share of annoying mosquitoes, as well as centipedes, which can give an unpleasant bite. There are also bees and ground-nesting wasps, which, like the centipede, generally pose danger only to those who are allergic to their stings. (For information on stinging sea creatures, see Ocean Safety, under Dangers & Annoyances, later in this chapter.)

This being the tropics, cockroaches are plentiful, and although they don't pose much of a health problem, they do little for the appetite. Lodgings with kitchens tend to have the most problems. If you find that the place where you're staying is infested, you can always call the manager or the front desk and have them spray poisons – which are no doubt more dangerous than the roaches!

While sightings are not terribly common, Hawaii has two dangerous arachnids: the black widow spider and the scorpion. Found in much of the USA, the black widow is glossy black and has a body that's a half-inch in diameter with a characteristic red hourglass mark on its abdomen. It weaves a strong, tangled web close to the ground and inhabits brush piles, sheds and outdoor privies.

Its bite, which resembles the prick of a pin, is barely noticeable, but is followed in about 30 minutes by severe cramping, which causes the abdominal muscles become boardlike, and labored breathing. Other reactions include vomiting, headaches, sweating, shaking and a tingling sensation in the fingers. In severe cases, the bite can be fatal. If you think that you have been bitten by a black widow, seek immediate medical attention.

The scorpion, confined principally to dry regions, is capable of inflicting a painful sting by means of its caudal fang. Like the black widow, the venom contains neurotoxins. Severity of the symptoms generally depends on the age of the victim, and stings can even be fatal for very young children. Symptoms are shortness of breath, hives, swelling and vomiting. Apply diluted household ammonia and cold compresses to the area of the sting and seek immediate medical help.

While the odds of encountering a scorpion are quite low, campers should always check inside their hiking boots before putting them on!

Leptospirosis Visitors to Hawaii should be aware of leptospirosis, a bacterial disease found in freshwater streams and ponds. The disease is transmitted from animals such as rats, mongooses and wild pigs.

Humans most often pick up the disease by swimming or wading in water contaminated by animal urine. Leptospirosis can exist in any fresh water, including idyllic-looking waterfalls, because the water may have washed down the slopes through animal habitats.

Leptospirosis enters the body through the nose, eyes, mouth or cuts in the skin. Wetland taro farmers, swimmers and hikers account for the majority of cases. One precaution is to avoid unnecessary freshwater crossings, especially if you have open cuts.

Symptoms can occur within two to 20 days after exposure and may include fever, chills, sweating, headaches, muscle pains, vomiting and diarrhea. More severe symptoms include blood in the urine and jaundice. Symptoms may last from a few days to several weeks.

There are a few dozen confirmed cases statewide each year. Because symptoms of leptospirosis resemble the flu and hepatitis, other cases probably go unconfirmed. Although deaths have been attributed to the disease, they are relatively rare. Leptospirosis is not specific to Hawaii and can be found on the mainland and in other countries as well.

Leptospirosis can be serious, yet thousands of people swim in Hawaiian streams without contracting it. The state has posted warnings at many trailheads and freshwater swimming areas. Islanders have differing opinions on leptospirosis – some never swim in fresh water because of it, while others consider it such a long shot that they take no precautions at all.

Ciguatera Poisoning Ciguatera is a serious illness caused by eating fish affected by ciguatoxin, which herbivorous fish can pick up from marine algae. There is no ready way of detecting ciguatoxin, and it's not diminished by cooking. Symptoms of food poisoning usually occur three to five hours after eating.

Ciguatoxin is most common among reef fish (which are not commonly served in restaurants) and it hasn't affected Hawaii's deep-sea fish, such as tuna, marlin and mahimahi. The symptoms, if you do eat the wrong fish, include nausea, stomach cramps, diarrhea, paralysis, tingling and numbness of the face, fingers and toes and a reversal of temperature feelings, so that hot things feel cold and vice versa. Extreme cases can result in unconsciousness and even death. Vomit until your stomach is empty and get immediate medical help.

WOMEN TRAVELERS

Women travelers are no more likely to encounter problems in Hawaii than elsewhere in the USA. The usual precautions apply. We advise against hitchhiking, especially women traveling alone, but if you do, size up the situation carefully and don't hesitate to decline a ride from anyone who makes you feel uncomfortable. If you're camping, select your campground carefully; you may want to opt for camping areas with caretakers.

If you are assaulted, call the police (☎ 911). Women who have been abused or sexually assaulted can also call the Sex Abuse Treatment Center's 24-hour hotline at ☎ 524-7273.

GAY & LESBIAN TRAVELERS

Gay marriages in Hawaii? In recent years, it looked as if travelers of all persuasions might be able to tie the knot in Hawaii, as the state took center stage in the movement to legalize same-gender marriages.

In December 1996 a circuit court judge ruled that state prohibitions against same-sex marriages violated the equal protection clause of Hawaii's constitution, which explicitly bans gender discrimination. The implementation of the ruling, however, was postponed pending an appeal to the Hawaii Supreme Court and they have yet to hand down their decision.

Not long after, two related events took place. In July 1997, Hawaii became the first US state to extend broad rights to domestic partners. To make the law more acceptable to the vocal conservatives who oppose gay marriages, it covers any two adults who cannot legally marry, including not just same-sex couples, but also others such as a mother and adult child or two siblings living together. Those who register are covered on an umbrella of items ranging from medical insurance to survivorship rights.

In the eyes of Hawaii legislators, the new domestic partnership law was a compromise, meant to quiet both the pro and con voices in the controversy over gay marriages.

However, in response to the domestic partnership law, conservative members of the state legislature put forth an amendment to Hawaii's state constitution allowing the legislature 'to reserve marriage to opposite-sex couples' only. This amendment was over-whelmingly passed by Hawaii voters in the November 1998 elections.

The issue, however, is far from buried. The Hawaii Supreme Court could still rule favorably on the 1996 circuit court decision striking down the prohibition against same-sex marriages, or the court may even be asked to void the 1998 state constitutional amendment on the grounds that it violates the US Constitution's equal protection clause, so the final battle in this protracted struggle may be years away.

Gay marriages aside, Hawaii is as popular a vacation spot for gays and lesbians as it is for straights. The state has strong minority protections and a constitutional guarantee of privacy that extends to sexual behavior between consenting adults.

Still, most of the gay scene is low key; public hand-holding and other outward signs of affection between gays are not commonplace. In terms of nightlife, the main gay club scene is centered in Waikiki.

The following information sources can help gay and lesbian visitors get oriented to the islands.

Pacific Ocean Holidays (☎ 923-2400, 800-735-6600, fax 923-2499), Box 88245, Honolulu, HI 96830, arranges vacation packages for gay men and women. They also produce a booklet called *Pocket Guide to Hawaii*, which is geared to the gay community and costs $5 when ordered by mail.

The volunteer-run Gay & Lesbian Community Center (☎ 951-7000), 1566 Wilder Ave, Honolulu, HI 96822, is a good source of information on local issues for both women and men. It also has recorded information on the latest gay entertainment venues and will mail a visitor information packet to travelers for $5.

For general information on gay issues, browse www.tnight.com or www.gayhawaii.com on the Web; both have links to a variety of gay and lesbian sites that cover items from travel and entertainment to politics.

DISABLED TRAVELERS

Overall, Hawaii is an accommodating destination for travelers with disabilities, and Waikiki in particular is considered one of the more accessible destinations in the USA. Many of the larger hotels throughout Hawaii have wheelchair-accessible rooms and as more of them renovate their facilities, accessibility improves.

The Commission on Persons with Disabilities (☎ 586-8121), 919 Ala Moana Blvd, room 101, Honolulu, HI 96814, distributes the three-part *Aloha Guide to Accessibility*, which contains detailed travel tips for physically disabled people. Part I contains general information and covers airport access on the major islands. This section is free and can be ordered by mail, and with it you'll receive an order form for purchasing Parts II and III, which list hotels with wheelchair access or specially adapted facilities and detail accessibility to beaches, parks, shopping centers and visitor attractions. Parts II and III cost $15, postage included, or $5 if you just want the section on hotels.

In terms of getting around, about half of Oahu's modern fleet of public buses have wheelchair lifts. To find out which buses have lifts, call ☎ 848-5555 or consult a bus schedule, which uses a wheelchair symbol to indicate routes with lifts. In addition, disabled travelers can contact the Honolulu Public Transit Authority (☎ 454-5050) for information on Handi-Van curb-to-curb service and other provisions for the disabled.

For travel plans in general, Wheelers of Hawaii (☎ 879-5521, 800-303-3750), 186 Mehani Circle, Kihei, HI 96753, is a well-regarded organization that books accessible accommodations, rents accessible vans and arranges various activities for disabled travelers.

Those with a physical disability may want to get in touch with their national support organization (preferably the 'travel officer' if there is one) before leaving home. They often have libraries devoted to travel and can put you in touch with travel agents who specialize in tours for the disabled.

In the USA, the Society for the Advancement of Travel for the Handicapped (SATH; ☎ 212-447-7284), 347 Fifth Ave, suite 610, New York, NY 10016, publishes a quarterly magazine for $13 a year and has various information sheets on travel for the disabled. You can also browse SATH at www.sath.org on the Web.

SENIOR TRAVELERS

Hawaii is a popular destination for retirees and lots of discount schemes are available. The applicable age for discounts has been creeping lower as well.

For instance, Oahu's biggest hotel chain, Outrigger, offers across-the-board discounts of 20% to anyone 50 years of age or older, and if you're a member of the American Association of Retired Persons (AARP), they'll discount it another 5%. Such discounts are available from other hotels as well, so be sure to inquire.

The nonprofit AARP is a good source for travel bargains. For information on joining this advocacy group for Americans 50 years of age and older, contact AARP (☎ 800-424-3410), Membership Center, 3200 E Carson St, Lakewood, CA 90712.

For information on senior bus passes, which can make getting around Oahu a bargain, see the Bus section in the Getting Around chapter.

TRAVEL WITH CHILDREN

Families with children will find lots to do on Oahu. In addition to beaches, swimming pools and a range of water sports, there are lots of other outdoor activities and cool sightseeing attractions for kids of all ages.

Successful travel with young children requires planning and effort. Try not to overdo things; even for adults, attempting to do too much can cause problems. Include children in the trip planning, because if they've helped to work out where you will be going, they will be much more interested when they get there.

For those vacationing with children, Lonely Planet's *Travel with Children*, by Maureen Wheeler, is packed full of valuable tips and interesting anecdotal stories. Also, see the boxed text 'Fun forKids' on the next page.

If you're traveling with infants and come up short once you arrive on Oahu, you can contact Baby's Away (☎ 395-2929), which rents cribs, strollers, play pens, infant seats, high chairs, gates and more. They have a website (www.csd.net/~babyaway).

USEFUL ORGANIZATIONS
State Parks

The Division of State Parks (☎ 587-0300), Box 621, Honolulu, HI 96809, provides a free brochure to Hawaii's state parks, including camping information and a brief description of each park. Information is also available online (www.state.hi.us/dlnr/dsp/dsp.html).

Environmental Groups

The Sierra Club (☎ 538-6616), Box 2577, Honolulu, HI 96803, offers guided hikes,

Fun for Kids

Although tourism officials tend to slant their promotions toward adults, Oahu has plenty of attractions of interest to children. These range from heavily touristed sites like the family-oriented Polynesian Cultural Center and the Hawaiian Waters Adventure Park to low-key local activities that visitors seldom stumble across.

The nonprofit Hawaii Nature Center (☎ 955-0100), 2131 Makiki Heights Drive in Honolulu, at the Makiki Forest baseyard, has a Sunday program of 'Keiki Nature Adventures' that provides a great way for visiting children to join Hawaiian children in nature projects and narrated hikes; activities typically last a few hours and are open to children as young as age five.

If you feel like staying closer to your hotel, Waikiki offers a wide range of activities right at the beach. Older children can take surfing lessons from the pros and children of all ages can hop aboard an outrigger canoe for an easier ride across the surf.

Young children may enjoy visiting the petting section of the Honolulu Zoo, where they can encounter some of the tamer creatures up close. Older children may want to sign up for the zoo's elephant encounter (☎ 971-7174), held at least once daily, which includes a lecture by the keepers on elephant care and behavior as well as the opportunity – when the beasts are in a good mood – for children to feed the elephants.

The nearby Waikiki Aquarium can be a fascinating place – not only does it have the usual colorful array of tropical fish, as well as monk seals and sharks, but there's also a touch tank geared specifically for children.

The free Kodak Hula Show, which like the zoo and aquarium is in Kapiolani Park, offers a fun little music and dance performance and is followed by a photo opportunity where parents can snap photos of their kids posing with the hula dancers.

---

maintains trails and is involved in conservation projects throughout Hawaii. Contact them for recorded information on upcoming hikes. For other information on Sierra Club activities, write or visit the website (www.hi.sierraclub.org).

The Earthjustice Legal Defense Fund (☎ 599-2436), 223 S King St, 4th floor, Honolulu, HI 96813, plays a leading role in protecting Hawaii's fragile environment through court action. To learn more about their present struggles, contact them or visit the website (www.earthjustice.org).

The Nature Conservancy of Hawaii (Map 2; ☎ 537-4508), 1116 Smith St, Honolulu, HI 96817, protects some of Hawaii's endangered ecosystems by acquiring land and arranging long-term stewardships with landowners. On Oahu, they manage a small crater above Hanauma Bay that has a unique vernal pool and is home to a rare species of fern, and, in the Waianae Mountains, they are the stewards of a large tract of land that is the habitat of 45 rare plant and animal species. Contact the Nature Conservancy of Hawaii or visit the website (www.tnc.org) for more information.

American Automobile Association

The American Automobile Association (Map 3; AAA; ☎ 593-2221), 1270 Ala Moana Blvd, Honolulu, can provide AAA members with information on motoring in Hawaii, including detailed Honolulu and Hawaii road maps. Members are also entitled to discounts on car rentals, Aloha Airlines tickets and some hotels and sightseeing attractions. Note: the Honolulu office is the only AAA office in Hawaii; they have a website (www.aaa-hawaii.com).

It also provides members with emergency road service and towing (☎ 800-222-4357).

For information on joining AAA on the mainland before arrival in Hawaii, call ☎ 800-564-6222. Membership dues vary by state but average $55 the first year, $40 for subsequent years.

LIBRARIES

Hawaii has a statewide system of public libraries, with 22 branches in Oahu. The main library is in downtown Honolulu, next to Iolani Palace, and there are also branches in Waikiki and Kailua.

Visitors can check out books only after applying for a Hawaii library card; a visitor's card valid for three months costs $10 and can be issued on the spot. Because the system is unified, not only is the card good at all branches, but you can borrow a book at one branch and return it at another branch.

Most of the libraries have good Hawaiiana sections, with lots of books on culture, history, flora and fauna. Most also subscribe to Hawaii's daily newspapers as well as to a few mainland newspapers such as the *Wall Street Journal* and *USA Today*.

Some libraries have computers that are online. Although a few librarians will sometimes bend the rules, officially you need a library card to use the computers. At many libraries you need to sign up for a particular time slot – sometimes this must be done in advance, and at other times you may be able to walk in and find a computer vacant. For more about Internet access, see the Email & Internet Access section, earlier in this chapter.

DANGERS & ANNOYANCES
Theft & Violence

For the most part, Oahu is a safe place. Honolulu has a lower violent crime rate than most other US cities, but like any city, crime does occur and reasonable precautions are advisable.

Petty theft is one crime that ranks high on Oahu. Watch your belongings and never leave anything unattended on a beach. Most accommodations have a place where you can store your valuables.

It is important to be aware that Hawaii is notorious for rip-offs from parked rental cars. The people who break into these cars are good at what they do and they can pop a trunk or pull out a lock assembly in seconds to get to the loot inside. What's more, they do it not only when you've left your car in a secluded area to go for a long hike, but also in crowded parking lots where you'd expect safety in numbers.

It's certainly best not to leave anything of value in your car any time you walk away from it. If for some reason you feel you must, at least pack things well out of sight *before* you've pulled up to the place where you're going to leave the car.

Other than rip-offs, most hassles encountered by visitors are from drunks. While Waikiki Beach is well patrolled by the police, you should be aware of the environment on other beaches at night and in places where young guys hang out to drink.

Touts

There's been a clampdown on the hustlers who used to push time-shares and other con deals from every other street corner in Waikiki. They're not totally gone – there are just fewer of them (and some have metamorphosed into 'activity centers'). If you see a sign touting car rentals for $5 a day, you've probably found one.

Time-share salespeople will offer you all sorts of deals, from free luaus to sunset cruises, if you'll just come to hear their 'no obligation' pitch. *Caveat emptor*.

Tsunamis

Tsunamis, or tidal waves, are not common in Hawaii but when they do hit they can be severe.

Tsunamis are generated by earthquakes or other natural disasters. The largest tsunami known to have hit Hawaii was in 1946, the result of an earthquake in the Aleutian Islands. Waves reached a height of 55.8 feet, entire villages were washed away and 159 people died. Since that time, Hawaii has installed a modern tsunami warning system, which is aired through yellow speakers mounted on telephone poles. They're tested on the first working day of each month at 11:45 am for about one minute.

Although tsunamis traveling across the Pacific can take hours to arrive, others can be caused by earthquakes or volcanic eruptions within Hawaii. For these there may be little warning. Any earthquake strong enough to cause you to grab onto something to keep

STRONG CURRENT   MAN-OF-WAR   SHARP CORAL

HIGH SURF   DANGEROUS SHOREBREAK   WAVES ON LEDGE

Look for signs warning of dangerous conditions.

from falling is a natural tsunami warning. If you're in a low-lying coastal area when one occurs, immediately head for higher ground.

Tsunami inundation maps in the front of the Oahu white pages phone book show susceptible areas and safety zones.

Ocean Safety

Drowning is the leading cause of accidental death for visitors.

If you're not familiar with the water conditions, ask someone. Most major Oahu beaches have daytime lifeguards, but if there's no lifeguard on duty, local surfers are generally helpful – they'd rather give you the lowdown on water conditions than pull you out later. Of course, it's best not to swim alone in any unfamiliar place.

Shorebreaks Shorebreaks occur where waves break close to or directly on shore. They are formed when ocean swells pass abruptly from deep to shallow waters. If they are only a couple of feet high, they generally don't pose a threat for novice bodysurfers. Otherwise, they're for experienced bodysurfers only.

Large shorebreaks can hit with a hard, slamming downward force. Broken bones, neck injuries, dislocated shoulders and loss of wind are the most common injuries, although anyone wiped out in the water is a potential drowning victim as well.

Rip Currents Rip currents, often referred to as rips, are fast-flowing currents of water within the ocean, moving from shallow nearshore areas out to sea. They are most common in high surf conditions, forming when water from incoming waves builds up near the shore. Essentially, the waves are coming in faster than they can flow back out.

The water then runs along the shoreline until it finds an escape route out to sea, usually through a channel or out along a point. Swimmers caught in the current can be ripped out to deeper water.

Although rips can be powerful, they usually dissipate 50 to 100 yards offshore. Anyone caught in one should either go with the flow until it loses power or swim parallel to shore to slip out of it. Trying to swim against a rip current can exhaust even the strongest of swimmers.

Undertows Undertows are common along steeply sloped beaches when large waves backwash directly into incoming surf. The outflowing water picks up speed as it flows down the slopes. When it hits an incoming wave, the outflow curls under the wave, creating an undertow. Swimmers caught in an undertow can be pulled beneath the surface. The most important thing is not to panic. Go with the current until you get beyond the wave.

Rogue Waves Never turn your back on the ocean. Waves don't all come in with equal height or strength. An abnormally high 'rogue wave' can sweep over shoreline ledges such as those circling Hanauma Bay. You need to be particularly cautious during high tide and in conditions of stormy weather or high surf.

Some people think rogue waves don't exist because they've never seen one. But that's the point – you don't always see them.

Coral Most coral cuts occur when swimmers are pushed onto the coral by rough waves and surges. It's a good idea to wear diving gloves when snorkeling over shallow reefs. Avoid walking on coral, which can not only cut your feet, but also seriously damages the coral.

Sea Urchins *Wana*, or spiny sea urchins, have long brittle spines that can puncture the skin and break off, causing burning and possible numbness. The spines sometimes inflict a toxin and can cause an infection. You can try to remove the spines with tweezers or by soaking the area in hot water, although more serious cases may require surgical removal.

Sharks More than 35 varieties of sharks are found in Hawaiian waters, including nonaggressive whale sharks and basking sharks, which can reach lengths of 50 feet. Because Hawaiian waters are abundant with fish, sharks in Hawaii are well fed and most pose little danger to humans.

Sharks are curious and will sometimes investigate divers, although they generally just check things out and continue on their way. If they start to hang around, however, it's probably time for you to go.

Outside of the rarely encountered great white shark, the most dangerous shark in Hawaiian waters is the tiger shark, which averages about 20 feet in length and is identified by vertical bars along its side. The tiger shark is not terribly particular about what it eats and has been known to chomp down on pieces of wood (including surfboards) floating on the ocean surface.

Should you come face to face with a shark the best thing to do is move casually and quietly away. Don't panic, as sharks are attracted by things that thrash around in water.

Some aquatic officials suggest thumping an attacking shark on the nose or sticking your fingers into its eyes, which may confuse it long enough to give you time to escape. Indeed, some divers who dive in shark waters carry a billy club or bang stick. Swimmers should avoid murky waters. After heavy rains, sharks sometimes come in and linger around river mouths.

Sharks are attracted by blood. Some attacks on humans are related to spearfishing, when a shark is going after a diver's bloody catch and the diver gets in the way. Sharks are also attracted by shiny things and by anything bright red or yellow, which might influence your choice of swimsuit color.

However, unpleasant encounters with sharks are extremely unlikely. According to the University of Hawaii Sea Grant College, only about 30 known unprovoked shark attacks occurred in Hawaii between 1900 and 1990, and about a third of them were fatal. Nevertheless, in recent years, the number of reported sharks and shark attacks has increased, with attacks throughout Hawaii now occurring on average at a rate of about two or three a year.

Jellyfish Take a peek into the water before you plunge in to make sure it's not jellyfish territory. These gelatinous creatures, with saclike bodies and stinging tentacles, are fairly common around Hawaii. They're most apt to be seen eight to 10 days after the full moon, when they come into shallow nearshore waters in places such as Waikiki. They're not keen on the sun, and as the day heats up, they retreat from shallow waters, so beachgoers mostly encounter them in the morning.

The sting of a jellyfish varies from mild to severe, depending on the variety. Unless you have an allergic reaction to their venom, the stings are not generally dangerous.

Portuguese Man-of-War The Portuguese man-of-war is a colonial hydrozoan, or a colony of coelenterates (radially symmetrical invertebrate animals), rather than a solitary coelenterate like the jellyfish. Its body consists of a translucent, bluish, bladder-like float, which in Hawaii generally grows to 4 or 5 inches long. Known locally as 'bluebottles,' they're most often found on the windward coast, particularly after storms.

The sting of a Portuguese man-of-war is very painful, similar to a bad bee sting except that you're likely to get stung more than once from clusters of long tentacles containing hundreds of stinging cells. These tentacles can reach up to 50 feet in length. Even touching a bluebottle a few hours after it's washed up on shore can result in burning stings.

If you do get stung, quickly remove the tentacles and apply vinegar or a meat tenderizer containing papain (derived from papaya) to neutralize the toxins – in a pinch, you could use urine as well. For serious reactions, including chest pains or difficulty in breathing, seek medical attention immediately.

Fish Stings Encounters with venomous sea creatures in Hawaiian waters are rather rare. You should, however, learn to recognize scorpionfish and lionfish, two related fish that can inject venom through their dorsal spines if touched. Both are sometimes found in quite shallow water.

The Hawaiian lionfish, which grows up to 10 inches, is strikingly attractive with vertical orange and white stripes and feathery appendages that contain poisonous spines; it likes to drift along the reef, particularly at night. The scorpionfish is more drab in appearance, has shorter and less obvious spines, is about 6 inches in length, and tends to sit immobile on the bottom or on ledges.

The sting from either fish can cause a sharp burning pain, followed by numbness around the area of the sting, nausea and headaches. Immediately stick the affected area in water that is as hot as you can bear (take care not to unintentionally scald the area due to numbness) and go for medical treatment.

Cone Shells Cone shells – which take their name from their conical shape and most commonly have brown or black patterns – should be left alone unless you're sure they're empty. There's no safe way of picking up a live cone shell, as the animal inside has a long, harpoonlike tail that can dart out and reach anywhere on its shell to deliver a painful sting. The wound should be soaked in hot water and medical attention sought.

A few species, such as the textile cone, whose shell is decorated with brown diamond or triangular shapes, have a venom so toxic that in extreme cases the sting could even be fatal.

Eels *Puhi*, or moray eels, are often spotted by snorkelers around reefs and coral heads. They're constantly opening and closing their mouths to pump water across their gills, which makes them look far more menacing than they actually are.

Eels don't attack, but will protect themselves if they feel cornered by fingers jabbing into the reef holes or crevices where they live. Eels have sharp teeth and strong jaws and may clamp down if someone sticks a hand in their door.

EMERGENCY

For police, fire and ambulance emergencies anywhere in Oahu, dial ☎ 911. The inside front cover of the Oahu phone book lists other vital service agencies, such as poison control and coast guard rescue.

If you're unfortunate enough to have something stolen, report it immediately to the police. If your credit cards or traveler's checks have been taken, notify your bank or the relevant company as soon as possible. For the phone numbers of the major credit card and traveler's check companies, see the Money section, earlier in this chapter.

Foreign visitors who lose their passport should contact their consulate in Honolulu; a list of consulate phone numbers can be found earlier in this chapter.

LEGAL MATTERS

Anyone arrested in Hawaii has the right to have the representation of a lawyer, from the time of their arrest to their trial, and if a person cannot afford a lawyer, the state will provide one for free. If you want to hire a lawyer, the Hawaii State Bar Association (☎ 537-9140) can make referrals; foreign visitors may want to call their consulate for advice.

Drunk driving is against the law. In Hawaii, anyone driving with an alcohol blood level of .08% or greater is guilty of driving 'under the influence.'

As in most places, the possession of marijuana and nonprescription narcotics is illegal in Hawaii. Be aware that US Customs has a zero-tolerance policy for drugs; federal authorities have been known to seize boats after finding even minute quantities of marijuana on board.

For consumer issues, Hawaii's Department of Commerce & Consumer Affairs (☎ 587-1234) has a handy recorded information line that provides information on your rights regarding refunds and exchanges, time-share contracts, car rentals and similar topics.

BUSINESS HOURS

Office hours are usually 8:30 am to 4:30 pm Monday to Friday, although there can be a variance of half an hour in either direction. Shops in central areas and malls, as well as large chain stores, are usually open into the evenings and on weekends, and some grocery stores are open 24 hours.

Banks are generally open 8:30 am to 4 pm Monday to Thursday and from 8:30 am to 6 pm on Friday. However, bank branches

inside grocery stores keep longer hours, typically 10 am to 7 pm on weekdays and 10 am to 3 pm on Saturday and Sunday.

PUBLIC HOLIDAYS & SPECIAL EVENTS

With its diverse cultural heritage and good year-round weather, Oahu has a seemingly endless number and variety of holidays, festivals and sporting events. The highlights are listed here.

As events and venues change a bit from year to year, it's best to check activity schedules in local papers or inquire at the Hawaii Visitors and Convention Bureau. Water sports in particular are reliant on the weather and on the surf, so any schedule is tentative.

Note: when public holidays fall on a weekend, they are often celebrated on the nearest Friday or Monday instead.

January

New Year's Day – firecrackers and fireworks are shot off through the night to welcome the first day of the year (January 1 is a public holiday).

Chinese New Year – begins at the second new moon after winter solstice (mid-January to mid-February) with lion dances and strings of firecrackers. The Narcissus Festival, part of the Chinese New Year celebrations, runs for about five weeks and includes arts, crafts, food booths, a beauty pageant and coronation ball. Events are held all around Honolulu; Chinatown is the center stage.

Martin Luther King Jr Day – this is a public holiday to honor the civil rights leader; it is observed on the third Monday in January.

Morey Bodyboards World Championship – at this competition on the North Shore, some of the world's top bodyboarders hit the Banzai Pipeline's towering waves.

Sony Open in Hawaii – this PGA tour golf tournament takes place in mid-January at the Waialae Country Club in Kahala.

February

Cherry Blossom Festival – this festival runs the entire month and spills over into March. It features a variety of Japanese cultural events at various locations around Oahu, including tea ceremonies, mochi pounding and taiko drummers.

NFL Pro Bowl – the annual all-star game of the National Football League is held at Aloha Stadium near the beginning of the month.

Hawaiian Ladies Open – this PGA Tour golf tournament takes place in mid-February at Kapolei Golf Course.

Presidents' Day – this public holiday is observed on the third Monday in February.

Great Aloha Run – this is a popular 8.2-mile fun run from Aloha Tower to Aloha Stadium held on Presidents' Day, the third Monday in February.

March

St Patrick's Day – March 17 is celebrated with a parade of bagpipers and marching bands from Fort DeRussy, down Kalakaua Ave in Waikiki to Kapiolani Park.

Prince Kuhio Day – this state holiday on March 26 honors Prince Jonah Kuhio Kalanianaole, Hawaii's first delegate to the US Congress.

Good Friday – this day, the Friday before Easter, is a public holiday.

April

International Bed Race – this offbeat wheeled-bed race from Fort DeRussy to Kapiolani Park is held in late April.

May

May Day – this is Lei Day in Hawaii. On the first day of the month, everybody dons a lei. There are lei-making competitions and Oahu crowns a lei queen at Kapiolani Park.

Molokai Challenge – held in late May, this 32-mile kayak race across the treacherous Kaiwi Channel starts at Kaluakoi Resort on Molokai and finishes at Koko Marina on Oahu.

Memorial Day – held on the last Monday in May, this public holiday honors soldiers killed in battle. At the National Memorial Cemetery of the Pacific at Punchbowl, there's a service with taps, a 21-gun salute and a flyover by fighter planes; music is usually by the Royal Hawaiian Band.

50th State Fair – this event features games, rides and exhibits and runs for four weekends from late May into June at the Aloha Stadium.

June

King Kamehameha Day – this is a state holiday celebrated on or near June 11. The statue of Kamehameha opposite the Iolani Palace is ceremoniously draped with leis and there's a parade from downtown Honolulu to Kapiolani Park, where there are hula shows, music and crafts.

King Kamehameha Hula & Chant Competition – this is one of Hawaii's biggest hula contests and is held in Honolulu near the end of June.

July

Independence Day – the Fourth of July is celebrated with fireworks at Ala Moana Beach Park and a parade to Kapiolani Park; it is a public holiday.

Prince Lot Hula Festival – this event is held at Moanalua Gardens on the third Saturday of the month and features hula competitions amongst Hawaii's major hula schools and traditional Hawaiian games.

Transpacific Yacht Race – on the July 4 weekend of odd-numbered years, sailboats leave southern California and arrive in Honolulu 10 to 14 days later. The race, which has been held for nearly a century, is the country's oldest long-distance sailboat race.

August

Obon – observed in July and August, this event is marked by Japanese 'bon odori' dances to honor deceased ancestors. The final event is a floating lantern ceremony at Waikiki's Ala Wai Canal on the evening of August 15.

Hawaiian Slack-Key Guitar Festival – this features Hawaii's top slack-key guitarists in a concert at Ala Moana Beach Park.

Admission Day (the anniversary of Hawaiian statehood) – this day is observed on the third Friday in August and is a public holiday.

September

Labor Day – this holiday is observed the first Monday in September and is a public holiday.

Aloha Week – a celebration of all things Hawaiian, with cultural events, contests, canoe races and Hawaiian music. Festivities, held in mid-September, include a street fair in downtown Honolulu and a parade in Waikiki.

Na Wahine O Ke Kai – Hawaii's major annual women's outrigger canoe race starts at sunrise at Kaluakoi, Molokai, and ends 40 miles later at Waikiki's Fort DeRussy Beach. It's held near the end of the month.

October

Na Molokai Hoe – Hawaii's major men's outrigger canoe race is held near midmonth. It starts after sunrise on Molokai and finishes at Waikiki's

Fort DeRussy Beach about five hours later. Teams from Australia, Germany and the US mainland join Hawaiian teams in this annual competition, which was first held in 1952.

Discoverers Day (Columbus Day on the mainland) – this public holiday is observed on the second Monday in October.

November

General Election Day – this falls on the second Tuesday in November (during election years) and is a public holiday.

Veterans Day – honoring the nation's veterans, this public holiday is observed on November 11.

Hawaii International Film Festival – features about 150 films from Pacific Rim and Asian nations. Films are shown throughout Oahu for a week around mid-November, with the schedule listed in the Honolulu papers.

Triple Crown of Surfing – consists of three professional competitions that draw the world's top surfers to Oahu's North Shore. The events begin in November and run through December, with the exact dates and locations depending on when and where the surf's up.

Thanksgiving – this national holiday is celebrated on the fourth Thursday in November.

December

Bodhi Day – the Buddhist Day of Enlightenment is celebrated on the 8th with ceremonies at Buddhist temples.

Honolulu Marathon – in terms of the number of runners, this is the second-largest marathon in the USA. It's run midmonth along a 26-mile course from the Aloha Tower to Kapiolani Park.

Christmas – festivals and craft fairs are held around Oahu throughout the whole month; December 25 is a public holiday.

Aloha Bowl – this is a big collegiate football game held at Aloha Stadium on Christmas Day and televised nationally.

COURSES

In Oahu, the main venue for courses is the University of Hawaii, which offers both full-time university attendance and summer school. The university's Campus Leisure Programs are perhaps of most interest to visitors. The program provides summer courses, typically a month in duration, and one-day workshops in such things as Hawaiian music, crafts and sailing. For details, see

Hawaiian Weddings

Many visitors come to Hawaii not only for their honeymoon, but to make their wedding vows as well.

Getting married in Hawaii is a straight-forward process. The state requires that the prospective bride and groom appear in person together before a marriage license agent and pay $50 for a license, which is given out on the spot. There's no waiting period and no residence, citizenship or blood-test requirements. The legal age for marriage is 18, or 16 with parental consent.

Full information and forms are available from the Department of Health (☎ 586-4544), Marriage License Office, Box 3378, 1250 Punchbowl St, Honolulu, HI 96813. The office is open 8 am to 4 pm weekdays.

Numerous companies provide wedding services. One of these, Affordable Weddings of Hawaii (☎ 923-4876, 800-942-4554, fax 396-0959), PO Box 26475, Honolulu, HI 96825, will mail out a brochure with helpful tips on planning your wedding, choosing a location, photography and other services. The Reverend KC Russ of Affordable Weddings can provide a nondenominational service, starting at $95 for a simple weekday ceremony and going up to $800 for more elaborate packages.

For something more romantic, you can sail off the coast of Honolulu at sunset on Capt Ken's Love Boat, a private 40-foot yacht. One reader recommending the service reported that the captain made the day a lot of fun and was appropriately serious when it came to the ceremony. The whole thing, with flowers, champagne, dinner, limousine service and a three-hour cruise, costs around $1000. It's arranged through Tradewind Charters-Wedding at Sea (☎ 973-0311, 800-829-4899, fax 396-5094, captken@pixi.com), 1098 Kumukumu St, suite E, Honolulu, HI 96825.

the 'University Information' boxed text in the Honolulu chapter.

While short-term visitors can't join a traditional hula *halau* (school), where students commit themselves for years to the tutelage of their instructor, even the casual visitor can learn the basics of hula by taking the free lessons offered at the Royal Hawaiian Shopping Center in Waikiki. The instructors are patient and cater to both visitors there for a short period and Waikiki residents who attend classes on a more regular basis.

For those staying in Waikiki who want to casually try their hand at other Hawaiian crafts, the Royal Hawaiian Shopping Center also offers free mini-classes in ukulele playing, lei making and Hawaiian quilting. See the Free Entertainment section in the Waikiki chapter for details.

For courses in a more natural setting, the Hawaii Nature Center (☎ 955-0100), 2131 Makiki Heights Drive in Honolulu, at the Makiki Forest baseyard, holds weekend workshops. Topics include such things as ancient Hawaiian games, taro patch farming, ikebana (Japanese flower arranging) and jewelry making with natural fibers and shells. Though most of their participants are islanders, visitors are also welcome. Classes typically last two hours, and the cost is $7 for nonmembers.

WORK

US citizens can pursue employment in Hawaii as they would in any other state. Foreign visitors who are in the USA for tourist purposes are not legally allowed to take up employment.

As Hawaii has had a relatively slow economy for the past few years, the job situation is not particularly rosy. Much of the economy is tied to the service industry, with wages hovering close to the minimum wage. For visitors, the most common work is waiting on tables, and if you're young and energetic there are job possibilities in restaurants and clubs.

If you're hoping to find more serious 'professional' employment, note that Hawaii is considered a tight labor market, with a lack of diversified industries and a relatively immobile labor force. Professional jobs that do open up are generally filled by established Hawaii residents.

A good online resource is www.surfhawaii .com, which contains the 'help wanted' ads from Oahu's two dailies, the *Honolulu Advertiser* and the *Honolulu Star-Bulletin*.

For more information on employment in Hawaii, contact the State Department of Labor & Industrial Relations (☎ 586-8700) at 830 Punchbowl St, Honolulu, HI 96813.

ACCOMMODATIONS

Oahu has a wide range of accommodations, from inexpensive hostels to high-priced luxury resorts.

Unless otherwise noted, the accommodation rates given throughout this book are the same for singles and doubles and don't include the 11.41% room tax.

Reservations

A reservation will guarantee the specific dates for which you need accommodations. Be aware, however, that most reservations require deposits. Once you have either sent a deposit or guaranteed it with a credit card, there may be restrictions on getting a refund if you change your mind.

Many B&Bs, hotels and condominiums will only refund your money if they receive your cancellation a set number of days in advance; three days for a hotel and 30 days for other accommodations is typical, but this varies widely among places. Some places may issue only a partial refund, and in some cases, you may forfeit your entire deposit altogether. Be sure to clearly establish the cancellation policies and other restrictions before making a deposit.

Camping

Camping is allowed at numerous county beach parks, one botanical garden and four state parks. There are, however, no full-service private campgrounds of the KOA type that are popular on the US mainland. Although Oahu's campgrounds are fairly well spread around the island, none of them are in Waikiki or the central Honolulu area.

Travel Clubs

Travel clubs provide handsome discounts on accommodations. Essentially, hotels try to fill vacant rooms at the last minute by offering cut rates to members of these clubs. In many cases, you aren't allowed to book more than 30 days in advance and room availability is limited during the busiest periods. A few places even black out winter dates altogether.

Many of Hawaii's largest hotel chains, including Outrigger, participate in the two travel clubs listed below. Both clubs allow members to book hotels directly, so they're easier to use than travel clubs that act more like reservation services.

By far the most prominent club is the Entertainment program, which produces an annual book to Hawaii that lists scores of hotels that offer members 50% off standard published rates. It also includes about 50 Oahu restaurants with two-for-one meals (or 50% off meals for single diners) and numerous coupons for other discounts. The book, which includes a membership card, can be ordered by phone (☎ 800-374-4464) for $40 or purchased in Hawaii at bookstores and a few other places (☎ 737-3252 for Hawaii locations).

Another popular club, Encore (☎ 800-638-0930), offers the same 50% room discounts and a similar list of hotels as Entertainment, but the dining benefits are more marginal. Annual membership costs $60.

One important difference between the two clubs is that Entertainment membership is valid for a one-year period beginning and ending December 1 – a problem for travelers who arrive in November and stay into December. Encore, on the other hand, is valid for 12 months from the time you enroll.

Keep in mind that the number of businesses participating in these programs varies significantly with the economy. When hotel occupancy is low, participation booms, and when the economy is brisk, more businesses pull out of the clubs or add restrictions.

Certainly these clubs work best for those who visit Hawaii for longer periods of time, are traveling outside the peak winter season and have flexibility with hotel preferences and dates.

❀❀❀❀❀❀❀❀❀❀❀❀❀❀❀ ❀❀❀❀❀❀❀❀❀❀❀❀❀❀❀

All county and state campgrounds on Oahu are closed on Wednesday and Thursday nights, ostensibly for maintenance, but also to prevent permanent encampments.

Campgrounds are busiest on weekends, particularly three-day holiday weekends, and throughout the summer, as those are the times Hawaii residents are most apt to camp.

Although thousands of visitors use these campsites each year without incident, rip-offs are not unknown, especially at roadside campgrounds, so keep an eye on your belongings. Because of turf issues and an undercurrent of resentment by some residents against outsiders, camping along the Waianae Coast is not recommended for nonresidents.

State Parks Oahu has four state parks, and camping in them is free by permit. Sand Island State Recreation Area and Keaiwa Heiau State Recreation Area are on the out-skirts of Honolulu, and Malaekahana State Recreation Area and Kahana Valley State Park are both on the windward coast. Keaiwa Heiau, north of Pearl Harbor, is a good choice for an inland park.

Camping is limited to five nights per month in each park. Another camping permit for the same park will not be issued until 30 days have elapsed.

Permit applicants must be at least 18 years old and provide their address and phone number as well as an identification number (driver's license, passport or social security number) for each camper in the group.

Permit applications can be made no more than 30 days before the first camping date. As permits are issued on a first-come, first-served basis, it's best to apply as soon as possible; if you have a change of plans, be sure to cancel so that other campers get a chance to use the space.

Applications may be made by phone or mail to the Division of State Parks (☎ 587-0300), Box 621, Honolulu, HI 96809, or in person at 1151 Punchbowl St, room 131 between 8 am and 3:30 pm weekdays.

County Beach Parks Camping is free with a permit at the following county beach parks: Mokuleia and Kaiaka beach parks on the North Shore; Hauula, Swanzy and Kualoa beach parks on the windward side; Bellows Field, Waimanalo and Waimanalo Bay beach parks in southeast Oahu; and Nanakuli, Lualualei (summer only) and Keaau beach parks on the Waianae Coast.

Camping is allowed 8 am Friday to 8 am Wednesday, except at Swanzy and Bellows Field beach parks, which are open only on weekends.

County camping permits are not available by mail but can be picked up between 7:45 am and 4 pm weekdays at the Department of Parks & Recreation (☎ 523-4525), 650 S King St, in downtown Honolulu in the Honolulu Municipal Building (the tall gray building on the corner of King and Alapai Sts). The office for permits is on the ground floor.

Camping permits are also available from satellite city halls, including the one at the Ala Moana Center (☎ 973-2600), 1450 Ala Moana Blvd, Honolulu, which is open 9 am to 4:30 pm Monday to Thursday, 9 am to 5:45 pm Friday, and 8 am to 4 pm Saturday. Other satellite city halls are in Kailua (☎ 261-8575), Keolu Shopping Center, 1090 Keolu Drive; Kaneohe (☎ 235-4571), 46-024 Kamehameha Hwy; and Wahiawa (☎ 621-0791), 330 N Cane St. All three offices are open 7:45 am to 4:30 pm weekdays.

County Botanical Garden Hoomaluhia Park (☎ 233-7323), an inland park in Kaneohe at the base of the Koolau Range, is unique among the county campgrounds in that it's operated by the botanical gardens division. With a resident caretaker and gates that close to noncampers at 4 pm, the park is one of the safest places to camp on Oahu. Like other county campgrounds, there's no fee.

Camping is allowed on Friday, Saturday and Sunday nights only. You can get a permit in advance at any satellite city hall, or simply go to the park between 9 am and 4 pm Monday to Saturday to get a permit; if you decide to go straight to the park, call first to be sure space is available.

For more details on the botanical garden, see the Hoomaluhia Park section in the Windward Oahu chapter.

Backcountry Camping The state forestry division allows backcountry camping along some valley and ridge trails, including in Hauula on the windward coast (see the Hauula section in the Windward Coast chapter for more details).

All backcountry camping requires a permit from the Division of Forestry & Wildlife (☎ 587-0166), 1151 Punchbowl St, room 325, Honolulu, HI 96813. Permits are issued between 7:45 am and 4 pm weekdays. There are no fees.

Fellow hikers on backcountry trails are likely to be pig hunters.

Camping Supplies The Bike Shop (Map 3; ☎ 596-0588), 1149 S King St, rents internal-frame backpacks and lightweight, two-person tents. The rate for each is $15/35/70 per day/weekend/week.

Omar The Tent Man (☎ 677-8785), 94-158 Leoole St, Waipahu, HI 96797, has weekly rates of $30 for lightweight, two-person dome tents, $20 to rent sleeping bags or external-frame backpacks and $18 for stoves or lanterns. Three-day rates for these items are $25, $15 and $14, respectively.

Hostels

There are two Hostelling International/American Youth Hostels (HI/AYH) hostels in Oahu: Hostelling International Waikiki in the center of Waikiki and Hostelling International Honolulu near the University of Hawaii.

US citizens/residents can join HI/AYH (☎ 202-783-6161, fax 783-6171, hiayhserv@hiayh.org), PO Box 37613, Washington, DC, 20013, by calling and requesting a membership form or by downloading a form from the website (www.hiayh.org) and mailing or faxing it.

Non-US residents can buy a HI membership in their home countries. If you do not already have a membership when you arrive, you can still stay in US hostels by purchasing 'Welcome Stamps' for each night you stay in the hostel. When you have six stamps, your stamp card becomes a valid one-year membership card valid at HI hostels around the world. The stamps cost $3 each and the price is added to your nightly stay. Thus, if you're a nonmember, you'll pay $15.50 to stay at Hostelling International Honolulu (whereas members pay $12.50). You receive a stamp for each night you stay.

In addition to the two HI hostels, there are a number of private businesses providing hostel-like dormitory accommodations around Waikiki. These make finding a cheap place to crash much easier than it has been in days past. Most of these places occupy older apartment buildings; some have a cluster of units, while others have taken over the whole complex. They all cater to backpackers and draw a fairly international crowd. There are no curfews or other restrictions, except that to avoid taking on local boarders, some places require travelers to show a passport or an onward ticket.

Despite the 'hostel' in their names, these private businesses are not members of the Hostelling International association, and in most cases, visitors should expect lower standards than those found in US mainland or European hostels.

Hosteling is a very fluid scene on Oahu. There are few businesses in Hawaii that change as quickly – a change in management can see a shabby operation become newly respectable, or a good place quickly become uninviting. All factors considered, it may be wise to avoid making a long-term commitment (advance payments typically aren't refunded) until after you arrive and have had a look around.

YMCAs/YWCAs

Although much overlooked, Ys provide another budget accommodation option. In Honolulu, there are three YMCAs and one YWCA that provide lodgings. Unlike the hostels, these Ys are not geared solely for tourists and they offer simple, inexpensive rooms (private or semiprivate) rather than dormitories. Although none are in Waikiki, the Central Branch YMCA is conveniently located just outside Waikiki near the Ala Moana Center. See the Places to Stay section in the Honolulu chapter for details.

One YWCA outside of Honolulu, the YWCA Camp Kokokahi in Kaneohe, also offers visitor accommodations.

B&Bs

Oahu B&Bs are rooms in private homes (or separate units at the side of the home), not full-fledged inns with paid staff or business signs out front. There aren't many B&Bs on Oahu, largely due to strict county restrictions that make it difficult to establish new businesses and limit B&Bs already in operation to renting only two guest rooms.

Many of those that do exist are in the Kailua-Kaneohe area. B&Bs are particularly scarce in Honolulu, although there are a few places available through reservation services, mostly in the city outskirts in areas such as Diamond Head and Manoa Valley.

In consideration of their neighbors and guests, the B&B hosts, who are often not at home during the day, discourage unannounced drop-ins. Because of this, B&Bs are not placed on maps in this book. Even if you're hoping to book for the same day, you'll need to call first, though same-day reservations are usually hard to get, because many places are booked weeks, or even months, in advance.

Prices are typically between $55 and $100 per room. Many require a minimum stay of two or three days.

Because of state codes that place restrictions on serving home-cooked meals, many B&Bs instead offer a continental breakfast (such as coffee, fruit, juice, bread and pastries), or provide food for guests to cook their own.

In this book, we recommend a number of B&Bs that can be booked directly, but there are others that can be booked only through

B&B reservation services. The following are reputable agencies:

Affordable Paradise Bed & Breakfast
(☎ 261-1693, fax 261-7315, afford@aloha.net), Maria Wilson, 226 Pouli Rd, Kailua, HI 96734, books reasonably priced cottages, studios and B&Bs throughout Oahu. Maria speaks German; there is a website (www.aicomm.com/hawaii).

All Islands Bed & Breakfast
(☎ 263-2342, 800-542-0344, fax 263-0308, carlina001@hawaii.rr.com), 823 Kainui Drive, Kailua, HI 96734, books host homes, including many in Kailua. There's a 3% fee if you use a credit card. There is a website (www .hawaiialohaspirit.com/alisbnb).

Bed & Breakfast Hawaii
(☎ 822-7771, 800-733-1632, fax 822-2723, reservations@bandb-hawaii.com), Box 449, Kapaa, HI 96746, is one of the larger statewide services. If you contact them in advance, they'll send a free listing of all the properties they book, or you can simply call and book by phone; they also have a website (www.bandb-hawaii.com).

Hotels

Some 90% of Oahu's 40,000 hotel rooms are in Waikiki. Unlike the other Hawaiian islands where resort hotels are in multiple destinations, all but two of Oahu's resort hotels are found in the Waikiki and Honolulu area.

In many hotels, the rooms and amenities are the same, with only the views varying. Generally, the higher the floor, the higher the price, and an ocean view will commonly bump up the bill by 50% to 100%. If you're paying extra for a view, you might want to ask to see the room first, since Waikiki certainly doesn't have any truth-in-labeling laws governing when a hotel can call a room 'ocean-view.' Although some 'ocean views' are the real thing, others are mere glimpses of the water as seen through a series of high-rise buildings.

Some hotels have different rates for high and low seasons (also called peak season and off-season). The high season is December 15 to April 15, but it can vary by a few weeks in either direction, depending on the hotel. The rest of the year is the low season, although a few hotels switch back to high-season rates in midsummer. During the low season, not only do many places drop their rates, but getting the room of your choice without advance reservations is far easier as well.

In Hawaii, as elsewhere, hotels commonly undercut their standard published rates in order to remain as close to capacity as possible. Some hotels simply offer discounted promotional rates to pick up the slack, but a few of the larger chains, such as Outrigger, often throw in a free rental car. Before booking any room, it's worth asking the hotel if it's running any specials – some places actually have room/car packages for less than the 'standard' room rate!

The Hawaii Visitors and Convention Bureau (see Tourist Offices, earlier in this chapter) will mail you a free annual accommodations guide that lists member hotels, addresses and prices. It includes virtually all of Oahu's top-end hotels and most of those in the moderate price range.

Rental Accommodations

Most tourist accommodations in the Waikiki area are in hotels, not condominiums, so the sort of lease-free monthly condo rentals that are readily found in tourist locales elsewhere in Hawaii are not so easily found here.

Most condos are filled with long-term residents, but you can look in the classified sections of Honolulu's two daily newspapers (see Newspapers, earlier) to see what's available, but just keep in mind that the vacation-rental listings can be meager, particularly in the winter season. If you're willing to sign a lease, the selection will be larger. Expect a modest one-bedroom condo to run about $1000 a month, a studio about $750; Honolulu is one of the most expensive housing markets in the USA.

Another option is to share a house or apartment with others. Start by perusing the 'Rentals to Share' listings in the classified ads. Try also grocery store bulletin boards, which commonly have a notice or two posted by individuals looking for roommates. Another resource is the University of

Hawaii, where there's a board listing rooms for rent in shared student households.

FOOD

Eating in Oahu can be a real treat, since the island's ethnic diversity gives rise to hundreds of different cuisines. You can find every kind of Japanese food, an array of regional Chinese cuisines, spicy Korean specialties, native Hawaiian dishes and excellent Thai and Vietnamese food.

Generally, the best inexpensive food is found outside of Waikiki, Oahu's main tourist area. There are good, cheap neighborhood restaurants to explore throughout greater Honolulu – two particularly rewarding locales are the Chinatown and University of Hawaii areas.

Oahu also has many upscale restaurants run by renowned chefs. Although these feature gourmet foods of all types, including traditional continental fare, the most prevalent influence is the increasingly popular style dubbed 'Pacific Rim' or 'Hawaii Regional' cuisine. This type of cooking incorporates fresh island ingredients, borrows liberally from Hawaii's various ethnic groups and is marked by creative combinations such as *kiawe*-grilled (like mesquite) freshwater shrimp with taro chips, wok-charred ahi with island greens, and Peking duck in ginger-lilikoi sauce.

Hawaiian Food

The traditional Hawaiian feast marking special events is the *luau*. Local luaus are still commonplace in modern Hawaii for events such as baby christenings. In spirit, these local luaus are far more authentic than anything you'll see at a commercial tourist luau, but they're family affairs and the short-stay visitor would be lucky indeed to get an invitation to one.

The main dish at a luau is *kalua pig*, which is roasted in a pitlike earthen oven called an *imu*. The imu is readied for cooking by building a fire and heating rocks in the pit. When the rocks are glowing red, layers of moisture-laden banana trunks and green *ti* leaves are placed over the stones. A pig that has been slit open is filled with some of the hot rocks and laid on top of the bed.

Other foods wrapped in ti and banana leaves are placed around it. It's all covered with more ti leaves and a layer of coconut-frond mats and topped with dirt to seal in the heat, which then bakes and steams the food. The process takes about four to eight hours depending on the amount of food. Anything cooked in this style is called *kalua*.

Wetland taro (a starchy rootstock) is used to make *poi*, a paste pounded from cooked taro corms. Water is added to make it puddinglike and its consistency is measured in one-, two- or three-finger poi – which indicates how many fingers are required to bring it from bowl to mouth, one-finger poi being the thickest. Poi is highly nutritious and easily digestible, but it's a bit of an acquired taste. It is sometimes fermented to give it a zingier flavor.

Laulau is fish, pork and taro wrapped in a ti leaf bundle and steamed. *Lomi* salmon (also sometimes called *lomilomi* salmon) is made by marinating thin slices of raw salmon with diced tomatoes and green onions.

Other Hawaiian foods include baked *ulu* (breadfruit), *limu* (seaweed), *opihi* (the tiny limpet shells that fishers pick off the reef at low tide) and *pipikaula* (beef jerky). *Haupia*, the standard dessert for a Hawaiian meal, is a firm pudding made of coconut cream thickened with cornstarch or arrowroot.

In Hawaiian food preparation, ti leaves are indispensable, functioning as a biodegradable version of both aluminum foil and paper plates: food is wrapped in it, cooked in it and served on it.

Because it's harder to find than other ethnic cuisines, many visitors only taste traditional Hawaiian food at expensive tourist luaus or by sampling a dollop of poi at one of the more adventurous hotel buffets. Still, Oahu does have a few neighborhood restaurants that specialize in Hawaiian food, including Ono Hawaiian Food, on Kapahulu Ave at the edge of Waikiki, and Helena's Hawaiian Foods, across town on the north side of Honolulu. See the Places to Eat sections of the respective chapters for more information.

Tropical Fruit

Avocado Hawaii has three main types of avocado: the West Indian, a smooth-skinned variety, which matures in summer and autumn; the rough-skinned Guatemalan, which matures in winter and spring; and the Mexican variety, which has a small fruit and smooth skin. Many of the avocados available in Hawaii are a hybrid of the three. Local fruit tends to be larger and more watery than the avocados grown in California.

Breadfruit The Hawaiian breadfruit is a large, round, green fruit. It's comparable to the potato as a source of carbohydrates, and it is prepared in much the same way. In old Hawaii, as in much of the Pacific, breadfruit was one of the traditional staples.

Guava The common guava is a yellow, lime-shaped fruit, about 2 to 3 inches in diameter. It has a moist, pink, seedy flesh, all of which is edible. Guavas can be a little tart but tend to sweeten as they ripen. They're a good source of vitamin C and niacin and can be found along roadsides and trails.

Lilikoi Also known as passion fruit, lilikoi is from a vine with beautiful flowers that grow into small, round fruits. The thick skin of the fruit is generally purple or yellow and wrinkles as it ripens. The pulp inside is juicy, seedy and slightly tart. The slimy texture can be a bit of a put-off the first time, but once you taste it you'll be hooked.

Mango Big, old mango trees are abundant on Oahu, found both in home gardens and in remote valleys. The juicy, oblong fruits are about 3 inches in diameter and 4 to 6 inches long. The fruits start out green but take on deeper colors as they ripen, usually reddening to an apricot color. Mangoes are a good source of vitamins A and C. Two popular varieties, Pirie and Haden, are less stringy than those found in the wild. Mangoes are mainly a summer fruit.

Mountain Apple The mountain apple is a small, oval fruit a couple of inches long. It is related to the guava, although the fruit is completely different, with a crispy white flesh and a pink skin. The mountain apple tree bears fruit in the summer and is common along trails.

Papaya Papayas come in several varieties. One of the best available in grocery stores is the Solo, a small variety with pale strawberry-colored flesh. The flavor of a papaya depends largely on where it's grown. The most prized are from Oahu's Kahuku area. Papayas, which are a good source of calcium and vitamins A and C, are harvested year-round.

Pineapple Oahu's number-one fruit crop is the pineapple. Most Hawaiian pineapples are of the smooth cayenne type and weigh a good 5lbs. Pineapples are fairly unique among fruits in that they don't continue to ripen after they're picked. Although they're harvested year-round, the long sunny days of summer produce the sweetest pineapples.

Starfruit The carambola, or starfruit, is a translucent, yellow-green fruit with five ribs like the points of a star. It has a crisp, juicy pulp and can be eaten without being peeled.

Local Food

The distinct style of food called 'local' usually refers to a fixed plate lunch with 'two scoop rice,' a scoop of macaroni salad and a serving of beef stew, mahimahi or teriyaki chicken, generally scoffed down with chopsticks. A breakfast plate might have Spam, eggs, *kimchi* (a vegetable pickle) and, always, two scoops of rice.

These plate meals are the standard fare in diners and lunch wagons. If it's full of starches, fats and gravies, you're probably eating local.

Snacks

Pupus is the local term used for all kinds of munchies or hors d'oeuvres. Boiled peanuts, soy-flavored rice crackers called *kaki mochi* and *sashimi* (thinly sliced raw fish) are common pupus.

Another island favorite is *poke*, which is raw fish marinated in soy sauce, oil, chili peppers, green onions and seaweed. It comes in many varieties – sesame ahi is a particularly delicious one that goes well with beer.

Another popular snack is crack seed, a Chinese food that can be sweet, sour, salty or some combination of the three. It's often made from dried fruits such as plums and apricots, although more exotic ones include sweet and sour baby cherry seeds, pickled mangoes and *li hing mui*, one of the sour favorites. Crack seed shops commonly sell dried cuttlefish, roasted green peas, candied ginger, beef jerky and rock candy as well.

Shave ice is similar to mainland snow cones, only better. The ice is shaved as fine as powdery snow, packed into a paper cone and drenched with sweet fruit-flavored syrups. Many islanders like the ones with ice cream and/or sweet adzuki beans at the bottom, while kids usually opt for rainbow shave ice, which has colorful stripes of different syrups.

DRINKS
Nonalcoholic Drinks

Tap water is safe to drink, although some people prefer the taste of bottled water, which is readily available in grocery stores and at the ubiquitous ABC discount stores.

Fish

Fresh fish is readily available throughout Oahu. It is generally expensive at fancy places that cater to tourists, but it can be quite reasonable at neighborhood restaurants. Some of the most popular locally caught fish include the following:

Hawaiian Name	Common Name
ahi	yellowfin tuna
aku	skipjack tuna
au	swordfish, marlin
kaku	barracuda
mahimahi	a fish called 'dolphin' (not the mammal)
mano	shark
onaga	red snapper
ono	wahoo
opah	moonfish
opakapaka	pink snapper
papio or ulua	jack fish
uhu	parrotfish
uku	gray snapper

Cans of Hawaiian-made fruit juices such as guava-orange or passion fruit can be found at most stores. If you're touring around, you might want to toss a couple of drinks into your daypack; the juices make a good alternative to sodas since they don't explode when shaken and they taste good even when they're not chilled.

Alcoholic Drinks

The minimum drinking age in Hawaii is 21. It's illegal to have open containers of alcohol in motor vehicles, and drinking in public parks or on the beaches is also illegal. All grocery stores sell liquor as do most of the smaller food marts.

Tedeschi Vineyards, a winery on Maui, makes a surprisingly good pineapple wine that can be picked up at wine shops and grocery stores throughout Oahu.

Honolulu has a couple of microbreweries, the most popular being the waterfront Gordon Biersch, at the Aloha Tower

Marketplace, which brews good German-style lagers, including both light and dark varieties.

And, of course, at every beachside bar you can order one of those popular tropical drinks topped with a fruit garnish and paper umbrella. Three favorites are: *piña colada*, with rum, pineapple juice and cream of coconut; *mai tai*, a mix of rum, grenadine and lemon and pineapple juices; and Blue Hawaii, a vodka drink colored with blue curaçao.

ENTERTAINMENT

Oahu has a lively and varied entertainment scene, ranging from beachside hula shows and traditional Hawaiian music to theater performances and rock concerts. The vast majority of entertainment takes place in Waikiki and central Honolulu.

The best place to look for up-to-date entertainment information is in the free *Honolulu Weekly* newspaper and in the 'TGIF' insert in the Friday edition of the *Honolulu Advertiser*. For detailed information, see the Entertainment sections in the chapters for specific destinations. For festivals, fairs and sporting events, see the Special Events section earlier in this chapter.

Luaus

Oahu's two main commercial luaus, Paradise Cove (☎ 973-5828) and Germaine's Luau (☎ 949-6626), are both huge, impersonal affairs held nightly out in the Kapolei area. Both cost around $50, which includes the bus ride from Waikiki hotels (about one hour each way), a buffet dinner, drinks, a Polynesian show and related hoopla. Children pay about half price.

A pricier, but less crowded, luau is held beachside in Waikiki at the Royal Hawaiian Hotel (☎ 923-7194) on Monday; the cost is $78 for adults, $48 for children ages 5 to 12.

SPECTATOR SPORTS

Some of the most popular spectator sports in Oahu are surfing, boogie boarding and windsurfing contests, many of which command high purses and bring out scores of onlookers. Top events include the Morey Body-boards World Championship, which takes place at the North Shore's Banzai Pipeline in January, and the Triple Crown of Surfing, the world's top surfing event, which takes place at various North Shore locales beginning in late November.

Road races also attract crowds of spectators, especially the Honolulu Marathon, which is held in mid-December and is now the second-largest marathon in the USA.

The University of Hawaii's basketball and volleyball teams have a strong local following; call ☎ 956-4481 for ticket information and schedules..

The state has a winter baseball league that plays from October through December and includes players from Japanese, Korean and US minor-league baseball organizations. One of the four teams, the Honolulu Sharks, has its home field at the University of Hawaii's Rainbow Stadium. For ticket information, call ☎ 956-4481; schedules are printed in the sports pages of the Honolulu papers.

Hawaii does not have teams in the national football, baseball or basketball leagues, but near the beginning of February, Honolulu does host the National Football League Pro Bowl, an all-star game held at the Aloha Stadium. The island also hosts the Aloha Bowl, a nationally televised collegiate football game held on Christmas Day. For ticket information on the bowl games, contact the Aloha Stadium ticket office (☎ 486-9300) as far in advance as possible.

Oahu is also host to PGA events that attract top golfing pros, including the Sony Open in Hawaii, at the Waialae Country Club in Kahala in mid-January, and the Hawaiian Ladies Open at Kapolei Golf Course in mid-February.

SHOPPING

For many people shopping is an integral part of a vacation, and Oahu offers plenty of opportunities.

Honolulu is a large, cosmopolitan city with plenty of sophisticated shops selling designer clothing, jewelry and the like. Most of the more fashionable shops are either in Waikiki or have branches there.

Of course, there are also lots of kitsch souvenir shops selling imitation Polynesian souvenirs, from Filipino shell hangings and carved coconuts to cheap seashell jewelry and wooden tiki statues. Not surprisingly, the largest collection of such shops is in Waikiki.

In addition, Waikiki has no shortage of swimsuit and T-shirt shops or quick-stop convenience marts. The prolific ABC discount stores (33 in Waikiki at last count) are often the cheapest places to buy more mundane items such as macadamia nuts, beach mats, sunblock and other vacation necessities.

Where to Shop

Shopping Centers Hawaii's biggest shopping center is the Ala Moana Center (☎ 955-9517), which has some 200 stores. The center has a wide range of places to shop, from chain department stores such as Sears, Liberty House, Neiman Marcus and JC Penney to fashionable boutiques and specialty shops. Among the brand-name clothing and accessory shops are Guess, Gap, Gucci, Banana Republic, Burberry's, Polo/Ralph Lauren, Christian Dior, Gianni Versace and Emporio Armani. Jewelry shops include Cartier and Tiffany. Danish design is represented at shops featuring Georg Jensen silverwork and Royal Copenhagen porcelain dinnerware.

For Hawaiian influence, the Ala Moana Center has Crazy Shirts, which specializes in T-shirts with island logos; Locals Only and Hawaiian Island Creations, for beachside casual wear; High Performance Kites, for Hawaii-made kites with island designs; and Ala Moana Stamp & Coin, which has an interesting collection of antique Hawaiian stamps and coins.

The two other significant, but much smaller, shopping centers in central Honolulu are the Ward Centre (☎ 591-8411) and the adjacent Ward Warehouse (☎ 593-2376), both on Ala Moana Blvd. The larger of the two is the Ward Warehouse, which has about 60 stores, including a number of boutique clothing shops and a few craft and jewelry shops.

In Waikiki, the biggest shopping center is the Royal Hawaiian Shopping Center (☎ 922-0588), which spans three blocks along Kalakaua Ave. It has a few dozen designer-fashion clothing and jewelry shops as well as numerous gift shops.

The International Market Place (☎ 923-9871), in the center of Waikiki, is an expansive collection of ticky-tacky shops and stalls set beneath a sprawling banyan tree. Although few of the stalls carry high-quality goods, if you're looking for inexpensive jewelry or T-shirts, it's the place to stroll.

The Kahala Mall (☎ 732-7736), on Waialae Ave in Kahala, is another large shopping center with Liberty House, Waldenbooks, Banana Republic, Tower Records and many other stores and clothing shops. See also the Designer Fashions section, later in this chapter.

The Aloha Tower Marketplace (☎ 528-5700), at Honolulu Harbor, has about 50 shops, as well as numerous kiosks selling Hawaiian-made foods, jewelry, sun hats and various knickknacks.

One of the more interesting stores to browse through is Martin & MacArthur, which specializes in upmarket Hawaiiana products including calabashes, quilts, furniture, dolls and koa woodwork. Other stores include Aloha Tower Traders, which has moderately priced Hawaiian clothing and souvenirs; Island Muu Muu, which sells men's and women's aloha clothing (tropical prints); and Magnet Five-O, which displays thousands of refrigerator magnets in the shape of hula dancers, pineapples and palm trees. There are also clothing and gift stores carrying products from the mainland.

Factory Outlets Waikele Premium Outlets (☎ 676-5656), in Waipahu, west of Honolulu, is noted for its factory outlet stores offering discounts on name brands. Don't expect better buys than you'd find at US mainland outlet stores, but the center does attract Japanese tourists who pay a premium for some of these products back home. Shops include a clearinghouse branch of Saks Fifth Avenue, Levi's, Oshkosh B'Gosh, Bugle

Boy, Local Motion, Mikasa, Anne Klein, Donna Karan, Izod, Guess, Geoffrey Beene, Bass, Carter's for Kids, Van Heusen and about 35 more.

To get there from Waikiki, take bus No 2 to downtown Honolulu and change to bus No 48. If driving, take H-1 West to Waipahu exit 8B, stay to the right and merge onto Kamehameha Hwy, then turn left onto Lumiaina St.

Thrift Shops The Waikiki Community Center (☎ 523-1802), at 310 Paoakalani Ave in Waikiki (see Waikiki map), has a small thrift shop open 10 am to 2 pm on Monday, Tuesday, Thursday and Friday. There's a fairly big turnover of items, including inexpensive aloha clothing.

Larger, and with a fairly good selection of used clothing, is the Goodwill (Map 3; ☎ 536-4115) thrift store at 780 S Beretania St in downtown Honolulu, near the Honolulu Academy of Arts; it's open 9 am to 6 pm daily (to 5:30 pm on Sunday).

Keep in mind that aloha clothing is typically made of cotton, and hence many of the items donated to the shops are those that have shrunk after taking one too many trips through the dryer! The larger you are, the less likely you are to find something that fits.

Aloha Flea Market For local flavor, the Aloha Flea Market (☎ 486-1529), at Aloha Stadium out near Pearl Harbor, has some 1500 vendors who sell a wide variety of items, from beach towels and bananas to old Hawaiian license plates. It's open 6 am to 3 pm on Wednesday, Saturday and Sunday. A private shuttle bus picks up passengers from Waikiki hotels every half hour from 7 am to noon and returns from the flea market hourly from 9:30 am to 3:30 pm. Reservations (☎ 455-7300) are required.

Chinatown Chinatown can be a fun place to do some offbeat shopping. A good spot to start is the Maunakea Marketplace, which has a hodgepodge of shops and stalls in and around it. One of the more interesting ones is Bo Wah's Trading Co (☎ 537-2017), 1037 Maunakea, where you can find everything from inexpensive rice bowls and stacked bamboo steamers to jasmine soap and Oriental cookie molds. At Hip Shing Fat, in the Maunakea Marketplace, you can get your own personalized seal with your name carved in Chinese characters. Nearby shops sell snuff bottles, cloisonné jewelry, strings of freshwater rice pearls and numerous trinkets.

Chinatown is also a good place to look for art and antiques; see the Art and Antiques sections, later in this chapter.

Bookstores Oahu has many good bookstores. The Borders bookstore chain has a branch in the Ward Centre (☎ 591-8995) on Ala Moana Blvd and another in the Waikele Center (☎ 676-6698), next to the Waikele Premium Outlets shopping center in Waipahu. These are huge, well-stocked bookstores with comprehensive sections on Hawaiian history, flora and fauna, island literature and outdoor activities, as well as good map and travel sections.

Another large-scale store is Barnes & Noble (☎ 737-3323) at 4211 Waialae Ave in Honolulu.

The Waldenbooks chain has shops at the Ala Moana Center (☎ 955-9517), the Kahala Mall (☎ 737-9550) in Kahala, the Windward Mall (☎ 235-8044) in Kaneohe, the Pearlridge Center (☎ 488-9488) in Pearl City and at the Waikiki Shopping Plaza (☎ 922-4154) in Waikiki. All have good Hawaiiana and travel sections.

For a well-stocked bookstore in downtown Honolulu, there's Bestsellers (Map 2; ☎ 528-2378), which is on the corner of Bishop and S Hotel Sts.

The Bishop Museum (Map 1; ☎ 848-4158), 1525 Bernice St, on the west side of Honolulu, has a collection of general Hawaiiana books as well as more esoteric scholarly works on various aspects of Hawaiian culture.

Rainbow Books & Records (Map 4; ☎ 955-7994), 1010 University Ave, at the corner of Beretania St near the University of Hawaii, is a good place to look for used books of all sorts as well as current travel guides.

If you're on the windward coast, visit Bookends (☎ 261-1996), 590 Kailua Rd, Kailua.

What to Buy

Hawaiiana The Hula Supply Center (Map 4; 941-5379), 2346 S King St in Honolulu, sells feather leis, calabash gourds, bamboo sticks, hula skirts, Tongan tapa cloth and the like. Although they're intended for Hawaiian musicians and dancers, some of the items would make interesting souvenirs and prices are reasonable.

Quilts Hawaii (Map 4; ☎ 942-3195), 2338 S King St, next to the Hula Supply Center, has high-quality Hawaiian quilting, including bedcovers, pillows and wall hangings. It also carries other Hawaiian crafts such as hats, koa chests and dolls. Prices are high but reasonable for the quality.

A gift shop in the Bishop Museum (Map 1; ☎ 848-4158), 1525 Bernice St on the west side of Honolulu, has quality Hawaiian gift items, from inexpensive lauhala (pandanus tree leaves) bookmarks to Niihau shell leis selling for more than a thousand dollars. You'll also find koa-wood items, handmade dolls, Hawaiian musical instruments, feather leis, books on the Pacific and more. See the Honolulu chapter for details on the museum.

The gift shop at the rear of Queen Emma Summer Palace (Map 5; ☎ 595-3603), 2913 Pali Hwy, also sells Hawaiiana books and carries some hand-crafted items such as koa bracelets and native-wood bowls. See the Honolulu chapter for details on the palace.

For Hawaiian-made crafts in Waikiki, there's the Little Hawaiian Craft Shop (☎ 926-2662) in the Royal Hawaiian Shopping Center. It has a full range of items from cheap kukui nut key chains to reasonably priced quilt-pattern kits and expensive, high-quality woodwork.

Handicrafts There are many fine craftspeople in Oahu and choice handicrafts are easily found around the island.

One of the most prized items is native-wood bowls, which are often made of beautifully grained Hawaiian hardwoods, such as koa and milo. Hawaiian bowls are not decorated or ornate, but are shaped to bring out the natural beauty of the wood. The thinner and lighter the bowl, the finer the artistry and greater the value. Wood bowls can run anywhere from $100 to a few thousand dollars. If you're curious to see the various grains of different woods, there's a good display (not for sale) of wooden bowls in the hallway lobby of the Outrigger Reef Hotel, 2169 Kalia Rd in Waikiki.

Oahu has some excellent potters, many influenced by Japanese styles and aesthetics. Good raku (Japanese pottery) work in particular can be found in island shops, and prices are generally reasonable.

Lauhala, the leaves of the pandanus tree, are woven into placemats, hats and baskets – all of which make long-lasting souvenirs.

For general crafts, you'll usually find the best deals at one of the craft shows that periodically take place in city parks (check the newspapers for schedules). Otherwise, there are a number of shops specializing in crafts. A notable one is the Nohea Gallery (Map 3; ☎ 596-0074), in the Ward Warehouse at 1050 Ala Moana Blvd, which has good-quality Hawaiian-made arts and crafts, including pottery, blown glass, woodwork and watercolor paintings.

Art You can buy paintings directly from island artists at the south side of the Honolulu Zoo on Monsarrat Ave in Kapiolani Park. Local artists have been hanging their paintings on the zoo fence each weekend for more than 25 years, and the practice has come to be referred to as 'Art in the Park.' The artwork is on display 10 am to 4 pm on Saturday and Sunday and 9 am to noon on Tuesday. It's possible you might find a great deal here, as many of Hawaii's better painters got their start at the fence.

Perhaps the most recognized contemporary painter in Oahu is Pegge Hopper, whose prints of Hawaiian women adorn many a wall in the islands. At her gallery (Map 2; ☎ 524-1160), 1164 Nuuanu Ave in Chinatown, you can buy signed posters for $40 or originals from $10,000. The gallery also sells coffee mugs with Pegge Hopper designs for $10; not only are the mugs attractive, but the proceeds benefit victims of domestic violence.

A block to the northwest is Ramsay Galleries (Map 2; ☎ 537-2787), at 1128 Smith St, which features finely detailed pen-and-ink drawings of Honolulu by the artist Ramsay as well as changing collections of works by other local artists.

Antiques A good place to browse for antiques is Aloha Antiques (Map 2; ☎ 536-6187) and the adjacent Mahalo Antique Mall (Map 2; ☎ 536-6179), at 926 and 930 Maunakea St near the waterfront on the west side of Chinatown. At this site, about 20 vendors set out their diverse collections, which include jewelry, art deco items, Asian statues, Steuben crystal, Asian ceramics and '50s collectibles. Prices range from $5 for kitsch items to thousands of dollars for rare antiques.

If you're interested in antique furniture and carved Chinese chests, you might also want to check out CS Li Furnishings (☎ 521-2725) in the Chinatown Cultural Plaza, 100 N Beretania St.

Lai Fong Department Store (☎ 537-3497), at 1118 Nuuanu Ave in Chinatown, sells an eclectic collection of antiques, including Chinese porcelain, knickknacks and old postcards of Hawaii dating back to the first half of the 20th century. It also sells antique Chinese clothing, including dragon robes and silk dresses.

In Waikiki, the three-story Island Treasures Antiques (☎ 922-8223), at 2145 Kuhio Ave, has lots of odds and ends, including jewelry, art glass, posters and old paintings. For the location, see the Waikiki map.

Bushido (Map 2; ☎ 941-7239), just west of Waikiki at 1684 Kalakaua Ave, specializes in fine Oriental antiques including an extensive collection of Japanese swords and Korean ceramics.

Aloha Clothing Hawaii's island-style clothing is colorful and light, often with prints of tropical flowers. The classiest aloha shirts are of lightweight cotton with subdued colors (like those of reverse fabric prints). For women there's the muumuu, a loose, comfortable, full-length Hawaiian-style dress.

For new aloha clothing, there are endless shops along the streets in Waikiki. Most department stores also have aloha clothing sections. Liberty House, an upmarket Hawaiian department store, has good-quality clothing, including aloha shirts, at moderate prices and it sometimes runs good sales. Liberty House has branches at 2314 Kalakaua Ave in Waikiki, at the Ala Moana Center, at the Kahala Mall in Kahala and at the Windward Mall in Kaneohe.

For antique and used aloha shirts, Bailey's Antique Shop (☎ 734-7628), 517 Kapahulu Ave (see Waikiki map), has the island's widest selection, with prices from $10 to $3000. It's a great place to go and look around – almost like a museum.

Bargain-hunters can sometimes find used aloha shirts and muumuus at thrift shops.

Designer Fashions There are numerous shops along Kalakaua Ave in Waikiki selling designer clothing, handbags and accessories. The simplest approach is just to stroll the streets and peruse the lobbies of the more expensive hotels. One particularly interesting hotel for this is the Sheraton Waikiki, which has a bustling lobby that resembles an exclusive Tokyo shopping center, lined with expensive jewelry stores and boutiques with French names and fashionable labels.

The Royal Hawaiian Shopping Center in Waikiki also has a good selection of designer fashions, including Donna Karan, Calvin Klein, Max Mara, Versace, Hermes and Chanel. A good place to begin is the center's McInerny Galleria, which has one of the broadest selections of both European and American designer labels.

Just outside of Waikiki, you'll find a sizable concentration of designer-fashion shops at the Ala Moana Center. See also the Shopping Centers section, earlier in this chapter.

Jewelry There are many places specializing in designer jewelry and European watches.

Two Ala Moana Center shops – Cartier and Ben Bridge – carry a wide selection of top-end watches and jewelry. In Waikiki, there are several upmarket jewelry stores at the Royal Hawaiian Shopping Center, and cheaper costume jewelry abounds in the vendor stalls at the nearby International Market Place.

For local-made jewelry, the premium product in Hawaii is the delicate Niihau shell lei. These necklaces are made from tiny shells that wash up on the island of Niihau and are one of the most prized Hawaiiana souvenirs. Elaborate pieces cost thousands of dollars and are sold at top-end jewelry stores around Honolulu.

Music & Instruments CDs and cassettes of Hawaiian music make good souvenirs. You'll find excellent collections of both classic and contemporary Hawaiian music at Borders, which has branches at the Ward Centre in Honolulu and at the Waikele Center in Waipahu, and at Tower Records, which has a branch at the International Market Place in Waikiki and another just north of the Ala Moana Center. Both Borders and Tower Records have handy headphone set-ups that

People's Open Market

Oahu's island-wide public market program was formed in the 1970s to provide local farmers, fishers and aquaculturists opportunities to sell directly to customers. At the People's Open Market, you'll find food that's both significantly fresher and cheaper than at grocery stores – on average, you can expect prices to be about 35% lower.

Not only will you find bargain prices on fruits such as papayas, oranges and avocados, you'll also find items such as passion fruit and exotic ethnic vegetables that simply aren't sold in supermarkets.

The markets are on a fixed schedule, but occasionally there are adjustments; call ☎ 522-7088 for the latest information. Also, markets are closed on public holidays.

As for market etiquette, an air horn is sounded to start the market and the organizers prohibit any sales prior to that point. It's considered bad manners to ask a vendor to reserve anything for you before the market starts. Remember that you're buying directly from the owner, so some of the testing that's commonplace in the supermarket – squeezing fruit, for instance – isn't going to make a good impression.

Try to get there early. As a matter of fact, it's best to be there before the starting time, as once the horn blows, there's a big rush, and people begin to scoop things up quickly. Everything wraps up within an hour.

There are 22 market sites in all. The ones most accessible to visitors are as follows:

Honolulu Area
Monday Manoa Valley District Park, 2721 Kaaipu Ave, 6:45 to 7:45 am; Makiki District Park, 1527 Keeaumoku St, 8:30 to 9:30 am; Mother Waldron Park, 525 Coral St, 10 to 11:15 am; City Hall Parking Lot Deck, Alapai and Beretania Sts, 11:45 am to 12:30 pm

Waikiki Area
Wednesday McCully District Park, 831 Pumehana St, 8:15 to 9:15 am; Queen Kapiolani Park, Monsarrat and Paki Sts, 10 to 11 am

East Coast Area
Thursday Waimanalo Beach Park, 41-741 Kalanianaole Hwy, 7:15 to 8:15 am; Kailua District Park, 21 South Kainalu Drive, 9 to 10 am; Kaneohe District Park, 45-660 Keaahala Road, 10:45 to 11:45 am

to listen to various Hawaiian-
before you buy.

Hula musical instruments, such as nose
flutes and gourd rattles, are uniquely Hawaiian
and make interesting gifts. See the Hula
Supply Center under the Hawaiiana section
earlier in this chapter.

Kamaka Hawaii (Map 2; ☎ 531-3165), at
550 South St in Honolulu, specializes in
hand-crafted ukuleles made on Oahu, priced
from $235. You can also find ukuleles –
imported, but cheaper – at the Hawaiian
Ukulele Co (☎ 536-3228) in the Aloha Tower
Marketplace at the Honolulu Harbor; prices
begin at $80.

Food The standard edible souvenir is
macadamia nuts, either plain or covered in
chocolate. Locally made macadamia nut
butters, lilikoi or poha berry preserves and
mango chutney all make convenient,
compact gift items.

Another popular food item is Hawaiian-
grown coffee. Oahu has recently begun har-
vesting its own crop – Waialua coffee – but
more revered in gourmet circles is Kona
coffee, which is grown on the cool hillsides
of the Big Island. Note that 'Kona blend' is
only 10% Kona coffee – if you want the real
thing, make sure it says 100%. Coffee prices
change with the market, but expect to pay
around $10 a pound.

Pineapples are not a great choice in the
souvenir department. Not only are they
heavy and bulky, but they're likely to be
just as cheap at home. See the boxed text

'Agricultural Inspection' in the Getting
There & Away chapter for information
regarding restrictions on taking agricultural
products out of Hawaii.

For those who enjoy cooking Japanese
food, Hawaii is a good place to pick up
ingredients that might be difficult to find
back home. Most grocery stores have a wide
selection of things such as dried seaweed,
mochi and ume plums.

If you just want to buy a carton of macadamia nuts or a few bags of Kona coffee,
Longs Drugs generally has better prices than
places in Waikiki. There's a Longs at the Ala
Moana Center, one at 2220 S King St in
Honolulu, and numerous other branches
around Oahu.

Flowers Beautiful, fragrant flower leis are
short-lived but delightful to wear. There are
numerous lei shops in Oahu, including some
at the airport, several in Chinatown (where
most leis are made, and the prices are generally cheaper) and in some Waikiki hotel
lobbies.

Tropical flowers such as orchids, anthuri-
ums and proteas make good gifts if you're
flying straight home. Proteas stay fresh for
about 10 days and then can be dried. See the
boxed text 'Agricultural Inspection' in the
Getting There & Away chapter for additional details.

Foreign visitors should check with their
airline in advance, however, as there are
usually restrictions against taking agricultural products across international borders.

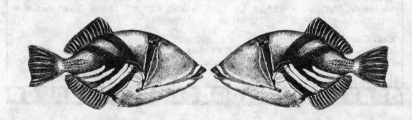

Activities

Oahu has an exhaustive variety of recreational activities available. Of course, it's a great place for most anything that has to do with the water, including swimming, snorkeling, diving, surfing, windsurfing and kayaking. But it also has good opportunities for land-based activities like hiking, jogging, tennis, golf and horseback riding. Or, if you prefer to take to the sky, you could even try your hand at skydiving.

BEACHES & SWIMMING

Oahu has more than 50 beach parks, most of which have rest rooms and showers. About half are patrolled by lifeguards. The island's four distinct coastal areas have their own peculiar seasonal water conditions. When it's rough on one side, it's generally calm on another, so you can find places to swim and surf year-round.

Oahu's south shore extends from Barbers Point to Makapuu Point and encompasses the most popular beaches on the island, including the extensive white sands of Waikiki and Ala Moana.

The windward coast extends from Makapuu Point to Kahuku Point. Lovely Kailua Beach Park, Oahu's busiest windsurfing spot, also has good swimming conditions and is the best all-around beach on the windward side. Other nice windward beaches are at Waimanalo, Kualoa and Malaekahana.

The North Shore extends from Kahuku Point to Kaena Point. Although the North Shore has spectacular waves in winter, it can be as calm as a lake during the summer months. There are attractive sandy strands at Haleiwa, Waimea and Sunset Beach.

The leeward Waianae Coast extends from Kaena Point to Barbers Point. It's the driest, sunniest side of the island, with long stretches of white sands. The most popular beach on this side is Makaha, which sees big surf in the winter but has suitable swimming conditions in summer.

Swimming Pools

The county maintains 18 community swimming pools on Oahu, including ones in Kailua, Kaneohe, Pearl City, Wahiawa and Waipahu. Pools in the greater Honolulu area are at Palolo Valley District Park (☎ 733-7362), 2007 Palolo Ave; Manoa Valley District Park (☎ 988-6868), 2721 Kaaipu Ave; Booth District Park (☎ 522-7037), 2331 Kanealii Ave; and McCully District Park (☎ 973-7268), 831 Pumehana.

SURFING

Hawaii lies smack in the path of all the major swells that race unimpeded across the Pacific, so it comes as no surprise that surfing got its start in these islands hundreds of years ago with the early Hawaiians.

Oahu boasts some 594 defined surfing sites, nearly twice as many as any of the other Hawaiian islands. There's good surfing throughout the year, with the biggest waves hitting from November to February along the North Shore. Summer swells, which break along the south shore, are usually not as frequent and not nearly as large as the northside winter swells.

Oahu's North Shore not only lays claim to Hawaii's top surf action but also plays host to some of the world's top surfing competitions. The winter swells at Waimea, Sunset Beach and the Banzai Pipeline can bring in towering 30-foot waves, creating the conditions that legends are made of. The other hot winter surf spot is at Makaha Beach on the Waianae Coast.

In summer, when the south shore sees its finest surfing waves, Waikiki and Diamond Head have some of the best breaks.

Surf News Network (☎ 596-7873) has a recorded surf line, updated three times a day, reporting winds, wave heights and tides. The National Weather Service (☎ 973-4383) also provides recorded tide and surf conditions. Visit www.seewaves.com for a live, online video surf report.

H30, a monthly magazine that interviews surfers and reports on surfing events and surf conditions, can be picked up at surf shops around Oahu. Annual subscriptions cost $36 in the USA, $72 in other countries. To subscribe, contact *H30* (☎ 488-7873, fax 488-7584), 99-061 Koaha Way, suite 206, Aiea, HI 96701. They also have a website (www.h30.com).

Another good website for surfers to browse is www.holoholo.org/surfnews.

Surfing Lessons & Rentals

The county's Haleiwa Surf Center (☎ 637-5051), at Haleiwa Alii Beach Park on the North Shore, holds free surfing lessons from 9:30 am to noon on most weekends between early September and late May. Surfboards are provided – all you need to bring is a swimsuit and suntan lotion!

Surf-N-Sea (☎ 637-9887) in Haleiwa rents surfboards for $5 for the first hour, $3.50 each additional hour, or $24 a day. In addition, Surf-N-Sea gives surfing lessons for $65, including board rental. Surf-N-Sea and a few other shops in Haleiwa also sell new and used surfboards.

The First Surfers

Surfing is a Hawaiian creation that was as popular in old Hawaii as it is today. When the waves were up, everyone was out. There were royal surfing grounds and spots for commoners as well. There were even coastal temples where Hawaiians paid their respects to the surfing gods before hitting the waves.

Boards used by commoners were made of breadfruit or koa wood and were about 6 feet long. Only the alii were free to use the long *olo* boards, which were up to 16 feet in length and made of *wiliwili*, the lightest of native woods. The boards were highly prized possessions and were carefully wrapped in tapa cloth and suspended from the ceilings of homes.

In Waikiki, surfing lessons can be arranged from beach concession stands such as Star Beach Boys, which is behind the police station, or Aloha Beach Services behind Duke's Canoe Club. The going rate for a private one-hour lesson is $35; the cost drops to $25 per person if there are two or more people. These Waikiki concession stands also rent surfboards for around $8 an hour or $25 a day.

With two locations, Planet Surf (☎ 924-9050), at 159 Kaiulani Ave in Waikiki (see Waikiki map) and opposite Pupukea Beach Park in Waimea (☎ 638-1110), rents surfboards for $20 per 24 hours.

BODYSURFING & BOOGIE BOARDING

Bodysurfing is the technique of surfing a wave without a board, using only your body for riding. With larger, offshore breaks, the arms are typically kept at the sides of the body, while with steep shorebreaks, usually at least one arm is held out in front for control.

The island's two hottest (and most dangerous) spots for expert bodysurfers are Sandy Beach Park and Makapuu Beach Park, both in southeast Oahu. Other top shorebreaks are at Makaha on the Waianae Coast, Waimea Bay on the North Shore, Kalama Beach in Kailua and Pounders in Laie on the windward coast.

Waimanalo Beach Park and nearby Bellows Field Beach Park, on the windward coast, have gentle shorebreaks good for beginning bodysurfers.

In boogie boarding, you ride the waves with your upper body supported by a foam board that's a couple of feet long, with your lower body trailing in the water. A very popular boogie boarding spot is the Kapahulu Groin in Waikiki, near the northern border of Kapiolani Park.

In both bodysurfing and boogie boarding, donning a pair of fins can provide an added measure of propulsion.

Boogie Board Rentals

If you're going to be doing much boogie boarding, you may be better off buying your own board. However, there are plenty of places to rent them.

The concession stands on Waikiki Beach generally charge about $5 an hour, $15 a day for boogie board rentals (see Waikiki map).

A less-expensive option, Planet Surf (☎ 924-9050), at 159 Kaiulani Ave in Waikiki, rents boogie boards for $8 a day, $20 a week. They also sell used boards. There's another branch opposite Pupukea Beach Park on the North Shore.

Surf-N-Sea (☎ 637-9887) in Haleiwa rents boogie boards for $4 for the first hour, $3 for each additional hour.

Kailua Sailboards & Kayaks (☎ 262-2555), 130 Kailua Rd, in the Kailua Beach Center, rents boogie boards for $12 a half day.

DIVING

Hawaiian waters offer good year-round diving. There's excellent visibility, with water temperatures ranging from 72°F to 80°F.

The marine life around the islands is superb. Almost 700 fish species live in Hawaiian waters, and nearly one-third of them are not found anywhere else in the world. In addition to colorful tropical fish, divers often see spinner dolphins, green sea turtles, manta rays and moray eels.

There are all sorts of hard and soft corals, waving anemones, sea urchins, sponges and shellfish. Because of their volcanic origins, the Hawaiian Islands harbor underwater caves, canyons and steep vertical walls.

Oahu's top summer dive spots include the caves and ledges at Three Tables and Shark's Cove in Waimea on the North Shore and the Makaha Caverns off Makaha Beach on the Waianae Coast. On the south shore, Hanauma Bay has calm diving conditions most of the year. There are a number of other popular dive spots between Hanauma and Honolulu that provide good winter diving. Two-tank dives for certified divers average around $85.

If you want to experience diving for the first time, some of the dive operators offer a short beginner's 'try scuba' course for non-divers that includes a brief instruction, followed by a shallow beach or boat dive. The cost generally ranges from $65 to $90,

depending upon the operation and whether a boat is used.

For those who want to jump into the sport wholeheartedly, a number of shops offer full, open-water PADI certification courses, which can sometimes be completed in as little as three days and cost around $400. If you're staying in Waikiki, many dive shops will provide transportation from your hotel.

There are numerous dive shops on Oahu. The following shops are all five-star PADI operations.

Aaron's Dive Shop
  (☎ 262-2333, aarons@aloha.com)
  602 Kailua Rd, Kailua, HI 96734

Aloha Dive Shop
  (☎ 395-5922)
  Koko Marina Shopping Center, 7192 Kalanianaole Hwy, Honolulu, HI 96825

Aquatic Lifestyles
  (☎ 396-9738, aloha@hawaiidive.com)
  377 Keahole St, Hawaii Kai, HI 96825

Bojac Aquatic Center
  (☎ 671-0311)
  94-801 Farrington Hwy, Waipahu, HI 96796

Breeze Hawaii Diving Adventure
  (☎ 735-1857, aloha@breezehawaii.com)
  3014 Kaimuki Ave, Honolulu, HI 96816

Dan's Dive Shop
  (☎ 536-6181)
  660 Ala Moana Blvd, Honolulu, HI 96813

Dive Authority-Honolulu
  (☎ 596-7234)
  333 Ward Ave, Honolulu, HI 96814

Hawaii Dive College
  (☎ 843-2882)
  24 Sand Island Access Rd, Honolulu, HI 96819

Hawaiian Island Aquatics
  (☎ 622-3483)
  1640 Wilikina Drive, Wahiawa, HI 96786

Honolulu Diving Academy
  (☎ 941-4369)
  512-A Atkinson Drive, Honolulu, HI 96814

Island Quest
  (☎ 422-5551, iq@oceanconcepts.com)
  Bldg 1511, Scott Pool, Pearl Harbor, HI 96860

Ocean Concepts
  (☎ 696-7200, ocw@oceanconcepts.com)
  85-371 Farrington Hwy, Waianae, HI 96792

South Sea Aquatics
  (☎ 922-0852)
  2155 Kalakaua Ave, Honolulu, HI 96815

Sunshine Scuba
 (☎ 593-8865, sunshine@lava.net)
 642 Cooke St, Honolulu, HI 96813

Waikiki Diving Center
 (☎ 922-2121)
 424 Nahua St, Honolulu, HI 96815

Windward Dive Center
 (☎ 263-2311, wdc@divehawaii.com)
 789 Kailua Rd, Kailua, HI 96734

Snuba

If you want to get beneath the surface of the water but aren't ready for a dive course, snuba offers an experience in between snorkeling and diving. Snuba utilizes a long air hose attached to an air tank on an inflatable raft that floats on the water's surface. The diver simply wears a mask and weight belt and can dive down as far as the air hose allows.

All snuba programs include elementary dive instruction that essentially explains how to clear your face mask and equalize ear pressure. An instructor is in the water with you during the entire dive. It makes for a quick and easy introduction to the underwater world and can certainly whet one's appetite for more serious diving.

Snuba Tours of Oahu (☎ 396-6163) offers snuba at Hanauma Bay for $85 or at Maunalua Bay in the Hawaii Kai area for $75. Both of these prices include roundtrip transportation from Waikiki; if you get there on your own, the cost for either outing drops to $65. The dive itself lasts about 30 minutes; the whole outing, if you opt for transport from Waikiki, takes about 3½ hours. The company is based at the Koko Marina Shopping Center, 7192 Kalanianaole Hwy, in Hawaii Kai.

SNORKELING

Donning a mask and snorkel allows you to turn the beach into an underwater aquarium, offering a view of coral gardens and abundant reef fish.

Hawaii's nearshore waters harbor hundreds of kinds of tropical fish. Expect to see large rainbow-colored parrotfish munching coral on the sea floor, schools of silver needlefish glimmering near the surface, as well as brilliant yellow tangs, odd-shaped

filefish, ballooning pufferfish and an assortment of butterfly fish.

Because of all the action in the water, Waikiki Beach is not a good place for snorkeling – Sans Souci Beach, on Waikiki's east side, is the best bet as it still has some coral.

However, just a short bus ride from Waikiki is scenic Hanauma Bay in southeast Oahu, which has the island's best year-round snorkeling. Although Hanauma has plenty of fish, keep in mind that it is overcrowded and the marine life ecosystem has been altered by all the tourist activity.

In summer, when the waters are calm, Pupukea Beach Park in Waimea on the North Shore provides excellent snorkeling and far less activity than Hanauma.

Snorkel Gear Rentals

Some travelers cart along their own mask, snorkel and fins, but if you prefer to travel without the extra weight, these can readily be rented once you arrive on Oahu.

Prime Time Sports (☎ 949-8952), a concession stand at Fort DeRussy Beach in Waikiki, rents snorkel sets for $8 for three hours.

A less-expensive option, just a couple of blocks from the beach, is Planet Surf (☎ 924-9050), at 159 Kaiulani Ave in Waikiki, which rents snorkel sets for $5 a day, $13 a week. There's another branch (☎ 638-1110) opposite Pupukea Beach Park on the North Shore.

Snorkel Bob's (☎ 735-7944), 702 Kapahulu Ave, about a mile out of Waikiki, rents basic snorkel sets from $3.50 a day, $9 a week, and better sets with silicone masks for $7 a day, $19 to $29 a week.

Kayak Oahu Adventures (☎ 923-0539), at the New Otani Kaimana Beach Hotel on Waikiki's Sans Souci Beach, rents snorkel sets for $5 a day.

Surf-N-Sea (☎ 637-9887) in Haleiwa rents snorkel sets for $6.50 for a half day, $9.50 for 24 hours.

Kailua Sailboards & Kayaks (☎ 262-2555), 130 Kailua Rd in Kailua, rents snorkel sets for $9 a day. For information on snorkel gear rentals at Hanauma Bay, see the Hanauma Bay Beach Park section in the Southeast Oahu chapter.

Considerations for Responsible Diving

The popularity of diving is placing immense pressure on many sites. Please consider the following tips when diving and help preserve the ecology and beauty of reefs:

- Avoid touching living marine organisms with your body or dragging equipment across the reef. Polyps can be damaged by even the gentlest contact. Never stand on corals, even if they look solid and robust. If you must hold onto the reef, only touch exposed rock or dead coral.

- Be conscious of your fins. Even without contact, the surge from heavy fin strokes near the reef can damage delicate organisms. When treading water in shallow reef areas, take care not to kick up clouds of sand. Settling sand can easily smother the delicate organisms of the reef.

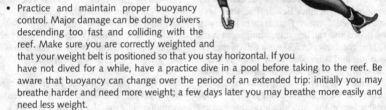

- Practice and maintain proper buoyancy control. Major damage can be done by divers descending too fast and colliding with the reef. Make sure you are correctly weighted and that your weight belt is positioned so that you stay horizontal. If you have not dived for a while, have a practice dive in a pool before taking to the reef. Be aware that buoyancy can change over the period of an extended trip: initially you may breathe harder and need more weight; a few days later you may breathe more easily and need less weight.

- Take great care in underwater caves. Spend as little time within them as possible as your air bubbles may be caught within the roof and thereby leave previously submerged organisms high and dry. Taking turns to inspect the interior of a small cave will lessen the chances of damaging contact.

- Resist the temptation to collect or buy corals or shells. Aside from the ecological damage, taking home marine souvenirs depletes the beauty of a site and spoils the enjoyment of others. The same goes for marine archaeological sites (mainly shipwrecks). Respect their integrity; sites are typically protected from looting by law.

- Ensure that you take home all your rubbish and any litter you may find as well. Plastics in particular are a serious threat to marine life. Turtles can mistake plastic for jellyfish and eat it.

- Resist the temptation to feed fish. You may disturb their normal eating habits, encourage aggressive behavior or feed them food that is detrimental to their health.

- Minimize your disturbance of marine animals. In particular, do not ride on the backs of turtles as this causes them great anxiety. In Hawaii, it also subjects you to stiff penalties.

WINDSURFING

Oahu has lots of windsurfing activity, with some windsurfing spots ideal for beginners and other locales boasting advanced wave-riding conditions.

Kailua Bay is Oahu's number one windsurfing spot. It has good year-round trade winds and both flat-water and wave conditions in different sections of the bay. The very best winds are usually in summer. At that time, Kailua's predominant winds are typically east-to-northeast trades running 8 to 15 knots, though when high-pressure systems come in, they can easily be double that.

Other good windsurfing spots include Diamond Head Beach, for speed and jumps; Laie, for open-water cruising; Mokuleia Beach Park, for consistent North Shore winds; and Backyards, off Sunset Beach, with the island's highest sailable waves. In Waikiki, Fort DeRussy Beach is the main windsurfing spot.

Windsurfing Lessons & Rentals

Naish Hawaii (☎ 262-6068, 800-767-6068), 155A Hamakua Drive, Kailua, HI 96734 – as in windsurfing champion Robbie Naish – has its shop in downtown Kailua, but can deliver equipment to Kailua Beach. The shop sells and rents equipment. Rental rates vary with the board and rig: beginner equipment costs $20 for two hours or $30 for a full day; intermediate and advanced equipment is $35 a half day, $40 to $45 a full day. Naish Hawaii gives introductory group lessons for $35 for three hours. For $55 you can get a 1½-hour private lesson that includes an additional 2½ hours of board use. Naish can also arrange packages that include both windsurfing gear rental and accommodations.

The other major player is Kailua Sailboards & Kayaks (☎ 262-2555, watersports@ aloha.net), 130 Kailua Rd, Kailua, HI 96734, which rents beginner equipment for $29 a half day, $39 for a full day or $160 for a week; high-performance boards cost $39 for a half day, $49 for a day or $199 for a week. Three-hour beginner's lessons cost $49 for a group lesson. Private lessons cost $35 an hour. Kailua Sailboards & Kayaks also offers a package that includes transportation from Waikiki, lessons and gear for $59, leaving Waikiki at 9:30 am and returning at 4:30 pm.

The two main Kailua windsurfing shops set up vans at Kailua Beach Park on weekdays and Saturday mornings, renting boards and giving lessons.

Waikiki Pacific Windsurfing (☎ 949-8952), at the Prime Time Sports concession stand on Fort DeRussy Beach, rents windsurfing equipment for $30 an hour, $80 for a half day; add $10 more for a lesson.

In Haleiwa, Surf-N-Sea (☎ 637-9887), at 62-595 Kamehameha Ave, rents windsurfing equipment at $12 for the first hour and $8 for each additional hour. Two-hour windsurfing lessons are available for $65.

KAYAKING

Ocean kayaking is becoming increasingly popular in Hawaii, spurred in part by the newer types of stable kayaks that are suitable for beginners.

On Oahu, the favorite kayaking spot is Kailua Beach, which has a couple of uninhabited nearshore islands within the reef that you can paddle to. Landings are allowed on Moku Nui, which has a beautiful beach good for sunbathing and snorkeling, and on Popoia Island (Flat Island), which you can walk around. With the Kailua companies listed in the following section, you can arrange to pick up your kayak at the beach.

Busy Waikiki is not the most ideal place for kayaking, but there are kayak rentals available right on the beach there as well. Both Fort DeRussy Beach and Sans Souci Beach have fewer swimmers and catamarans to share the water with, and make a better bet than the central Waikiki Beach strip.

Kayak Rentals

Twogood Kayaks Hawaii (☎ 262-5656), 345 Hahani St in Kailua, rents and sells kayaks. One-person kayaks rent for $25 a half day or $32 a full day; two-person kayaks cost $32/42.

Kailua Sailboard & Kayaks (☎ 262-2555), 130 Kailua Rd in Kailua, has one- and two-person kayaks at the same rate as Twogood. In addition, they offer a $49 package that includes transportation from Waikiki plus the kayak rental and lunch, leaving Waikiki at 9:30 am and returning at 4:30 pm.

Kayak Oahu Adventures (☎ 923-0539) rents kayaks at the New Otani Kaimana Beach Hotel on Waikiki's Sans Souci Beach. Rates for one- and two-person kayaks are $10/20 an hour, $30/40 a half day.

At the other end of Waikiki is Prime Time Sports (☎ 949-8952) on Fort DeRussy Beach, which rents one-person kayaks for $10 an hour, two-person kayaks for $20 an hour.

FISHING

Hawaii has excellent deep-sea fishing. Popular sport fishes include Pacific blue marlin, black marlin, yellowfin tuna, wahoo and mahimahi. Charter fishing boats leave from Kewalo Basin in Honolulu and typically charge about $500 for a day charter that can accommodate up to six people, or $115 per person if you want to join a group. The price includes all gear, but not food or beverages. The Hawaii Charter Skippers Association (☎ 591-9100, hcsa@msn.com) books outings on several boats.

Licenses are not required for saltwater fishing when the catch is for private consumption. There are, however, seasons, size limits and other restrictions on taking *ula* (spiny lobster), crab, octopus (*hee* in Hawaiian, and also called tako or squid), *opihi* (a kind of limpet), *limu* (seaweed) and certain species of fish. Clams and oysters cannot be taken.

Also, seek local advice before eating your catch, as ciguatera poisoning (see Health in the Facts for the Visitor chapter) has become more common in recent years.

In addition to ocean fishing, the state maintains two public freshwater fishing areas on Oahu. The main one is Wahiawa Reservoir in central Oahu and it comprises 300 acres of fishable waters. Stocked fish include largemouth and smallmouth bass, bluegill sunfish, channel catfish, puntat (Chinese catfish), tilapia, carp, tucunare, oscar and pongee. It's open year-round.

Much more restricted is the Nuuanu Reservoir, off the Pali Hwy north of Honolulu, which is open only on selected weekends in May, August and November. Comprising about 25 acres, it's stocked mainly with channel catfish but also has puntat and tilapia.

Licenses are required for freshwater fishing. A 30-day license for nonresidents costs $3.75 (free for those ages 65 and older). To obtain a fishing license, contact the Division of Aquatic Resources (☎ 587-0100), Department of Land & Natural Resources,

1151 Punchbowl St, room 330, Honolulu, HI 96813. The office is open 7:45 am to 3:30 pm weekdays.

The office can also provide full details on public freshwater fishing areas, as well as two free booklets: *Hawaii Fishing Regulations* and *Freshwater Fishing in Hawaii*.

HIKING

Oahu has some good hiking opportunities. Despite all the development on the island, it's surprising how much of the land is still in a natural state. There are numerous trails, including pleasant jaunts just minutes by bus from Waikiki, and backcountry hikes that are farther afield.

Safety & Tips

Some of Oahu's hiking trails take you into steep, narrow valleys with gullies that require stream crossings. The main rule here is that if the water begins to rise, it's not safe to cross, because a flash flood may be imminent.

Flash floods give little warning. Hikers caught in them have reported hearing a sudden loud crack and then seeing a wall of water pour down the stream bed, leaving just

seconds to reach higher ground. If the water starts to rise or you hear a rumbling, get up on a bank immediately and wait it out. Don't try to cross the stream if the water reaches above your knees.

Other than flash floods, landslides and falling rocks are the biggest dangers on trails. Be wary of swimming under high waterfalls, because rocks can dislodge from the top, and be careful on the edge of steep cliffs, since cliffside rock in Hawaii tends to be crumbly.

Darkness sets in soon after sunset in Hawaii, and ridgetop trails are not the place to be caught unprepared for it. It's a good idea to carry a flashlight when you're hiking, just in case. Long pants will protect your legs from the overgrown parts of the trail, and sturdy footwear with good traction is advisable. Hawaiian trails tend to be quite slippery when wet, so a walking stick always makes a good companion.

Oahu has no snakes, no poison ivy, no poison oak and few dangers from wild animals. There's a slim possibility of meeting up with a large boar in the backwoods, but boars are unlikely to be a problem unless cornered.

Trails

The most popular hike on Oahu is the trail that starts inside the Diamond Head crater and climbs three-quarters of a mile up to its summit. It's easy to reach from Waikiki and ends with a panoramic view of the city. See the Diamond Head section of the Southeast Oahu chapter for additional details.

Another nice, short hike is the Manoa Falls Trail, north of Waikiki, where a peaceful walk through an abandoned arboretum of lofty trees leads to a waterfall. See the Upper Manoa Valley section in the Honolulu chapter for more details.

The Tantalus and Makiki Valley area has the most extensive trail network around Honolulu, with fine views of the city and surrounding valleys. Amazingly, although it's just two miles above the city hustle and bustle, this lush forest reserve is unspoiled and offers quiet solitude. See the Tantalus & Makiki Heights section in the Honolulu chapter for more details.

On the western edge of Honolulu, the Moanalua Trail goes deep into the Moanalua Valley. You can hike it on your own or join a guided Sunday walk. See the Other Honolulu Attractions section of the Honolulu chapter for more details.

At Keaiwa Heiau State Park, northwest of Honolulu, the Aiea Loop Trail leads 4½ miles along a ridge that offers views of Pearl Harbor, Diamond Head and the Koolau Range. For additional details on this park, see the Pearl Harbor chapter.

On the westernmost point of Oahu, there's the Kaena Point Trail, a scenic coastal hike through a natural area reserve. It's the most popular hike in that area, but there are also inland forestry trails nearby. See the Kaena Point State Park section in the Waianae Coast chapter for more details.

On Oahu's windward side, a pleasant hour-long hike leads out to Makapuu lighthouse (see the Southeast Oahu chapter for details) and there's another easy coastal trail at Kahana Valley State Park (see the Windward Coast chapter for details). For a hardier walk on the windward coast, there are three forestry trails in the Hauula area, the most popular being the 2½-mile Hauula Loop Trail, which offers nice views of both the coast and forest. See the Hauula section of the Windward Coast chapter for details.

In addition, there are short walks from the Nuuanu Pali Lookout, at Hoomaluhia Park in Kaneohe and along many beaches. See the Pali Hwy and Kaneohe sections of the Windward Coast chapter for details.

Guided Hikes

Notices of hiking club outings are posted in the *Honolulu Star-Bulletin*'s 'Do It Out There' page on Tuesdays, the *Honolulu Advertiser*'s Friday 'TGIF' insert and the *Honolulu Weekly*'s 'Scene' section.

By joining one of these outings, you get to meet and hike with ecology-minded islanders. It may also be a good way to get to the backwoods if you don't have a car, as they often share rides. Wear sturdy shoes and, for the longer hikes, bring lunch and water.

Naturalists from the Hawaii Nature Center (☎ 955-0100), at the Makiki Forest baseyard in Honolulu's Tantalus and Makiki Valley area, lead hikes on either Saturday or Sunday on most weekends. Trails range from short walks of a mile or two, geared for families, to strenuous all-day hikes suitable for fit adults only. The cost is $7 for nonmembers. Reservations are required.

The Sierra Club (☎ 538-6616) leads hikes and other outings on Saturdays and Sundays. These range from easy 2-mile hikes to strenuous 10-mile treks. Most outings meet at 8 am at the Church of the Crossroads (Map 4), 2510 Bingham St, Honolulu. The hike fee is $3.

The Hawaii Audubon Society (☎ 528-1432) leads bird-watching hikes once a month, usually on a weekend. The suggested donation is $2. Binoculars and a copy of *Hawaii's Birds* are recommended.

The Hawaiian Trail & Mountain Club has guided hikes most weekends, although some are for members only. The hike fee is $2. Hikes generally range from 3 to 12 miles and cover the full gamut from novice to advanced in level of difficulty. For a copy of the hiking schedule, send a stamped, self-addressed envelope to the club at Box 2238, Honolulu, HI 96804.

For information on guided walking tours of downtown Honolulu and Chinatown, see those destinations in the Honolulu chapter.

GOLF

A lot of turf on Oahu is given over to golf courses. At last count, the island had a total of 36 courses – six municipal, seven military and 23 others that are either resort, public, private or semi-private courses.

These range from unpretentious municipal courses with affordable fees and relaxed settings to members-only private country clubs with resident pros and ultramanicured surroundings.

One of the private clubs, Waialae Country Club in Kahala, is home to the PGA's Sony Open in Hawaii. Held in January, it's the first full field event of the PGA season and offers a heady $2.6 million purse. The LPGA tour is also represented on Oahu, with the Cup Noodles Ladies Hawaiian Open; it's held in February at the Kapolei Golf Course in Kapolei and has a $650,000 purse.

Municipal Courses

Of Oahu's six municipal golf courses, five have 18 holes. Greens fees at these courses are $40 per person, plus an optional $14 for a gas-powered cart. The fee for the other municipal golf course, the nine-hole course at Kahuku, is $20 per person, and it's a walking-only course.

The reservation system is the same for all municipal courses: call ☎ 296-2000 and key information into the recorded system as prompted. The earliest bookings are taken just three days in advance for visitors and one week in advance for resident golfers.

The only municipal course near Waikiki is the Ala Wai Golf Course, which lays claim to being the 'busiest in the world.' Local golfers who are allowed to book earlier in the week usually take all the starting times, leaving none for visitors. However, visiting golfers who don't mind a wait may show up at the Ala Wai window and get on the waiting list; as long as the entire golfing party waits at the course, they'll usually get you on before the day is over. If you come without clubs, you can rent them for about $20 at the 18-hole courses and for $10 at Kahuku.

The following is a list of Oahu's municipal courses:

Ala Wai Golf Course
(☎ 733-7387) on Kapahulu Ave, inland of the Ala Wai Canal near Waikiki; 18 holes, par 70

Ewa Villages Golf Course
(☎ 681-0220) 91-1760 Park Row St, Ewa; 18 holes, par 72

Kahuku Golf Course
(☎ 293-5842) South Golf Course Rd, Kahuku; 9 holes, par 35, no carts

Pali Golf Course
(☎ 266-7612) 45-050 Kamehameha Hwy, Kaneohe; 18 holes, par 72

Ted Makalena Golf Course
(☎ 675-6052) Waipio Point Access Rd, Waipahu; 18 holes, par 71

West Loch Golf Course
(☎ 675-6076), 91-1126 Okupe St, Ewa Beach; 18 holes, par 71

Nonmunicipal Courses

The courses that follow are the resort courses, public courses or semi-private courses that are open to the public. As a general rule, resort courses and public courses are open to visitors without restrictions, whereas semi-private courses usually restrict nonmembers to a certain number of slots or to off-peak times when their members are less likely to be playing.

Not listed are the private golf courses that are open only to members and their guests or the military courses that are open only to US military personnel and their dependents.

The rates given are the full normal rate, but there are often generous discounts if you're staying at one of the resort hotels affiliated with a course or if you simply tee off at other than prime time. Many courses have twilight rates, and despite the name that doesn't always mean late-day golfing. At Makaha Valley Country Club, for instance, if you tee off before 11 am, the fee is $95 but if you wait until after 11 am, it drops to $55.

Bayview Golf Links
(☎ 247-0451) 45-285 Kaneohe Bay Drive, Kaneohe; public, 18 holes, par 60, greens fee $62 including cart

Hawaii Country Club
(☎ 621-5654) 94-1211 Kunia Rd, Kunia; public, 18 holes, par 72, greens fee $65 including cart

Hawaii Kai Championship Golf Course
(☎ 395-2358) 8902 Kalanianaole Hwy, Honolulu; public, 18 holes, par 72, greens fee $90 including cart

Hawaii Kai Executive Golf Course
(☎ 395-2358) 8902 Kalanianaole Hwy, Honolulu; public, 18 holes, par 54, greens fee $29

Hawaii Prince Golf Club
(☎ 944-4567) 91-1200 Fort Weaver Rd, Ewa Beach; resort, 27 holes, par 72, greens fee $135 including cart

Kapolei Golf Course
(☎ 674-2227) 91-701 Farrington Hwy, Kapolei; public, 18 holes, par 72, greens fee $70/90 on weekdays/weekends including cart

Koolau Golf Course
(☎ 236-4653) 45-550 Kionaole Rd, Kaneohe; semi-private, 18 holes, par 72, greens fee $125 including cart

Ko Olina Golf Club
(☎ 676-5300) 92-1220 Aliinui Drive, Ewa Beach; resort, 18 holes, par 72, greens fee $145 including cart

Links at Kuilima
(☎ 293-8574) Turtle Bay Hilton, Kahuku; resort, 18 holes, par 72, greens fee $125 including cart

Luana Hills Country Club
(☎ 262-2139) 770 Auloa Rd, Kailua; semi-private, 18 holes, par 72, greens fee $80

Makaha Golf Club
(☎ 695-9511) 84-626 Makaha Valley Rd, Makaha; resort, 18 holes, par 72, greens fee $125 including cart

Makaha Valley Country Club
(☎ 695-9578) 84-627 Makaha Valley Rd, Makaha; public, 18 holes, par 71, greens fee $95 including cart

Mililani Golf Club
(☎ 623-2222) 95-176 Kuahelani Ave, Mililani; semi-private, 18 holes, par 72, greens fee $95 including cart

Moanalua Golf Club
(☎ 839-2311) 1250 Ala Aolani St, Honolulu; semi-private, nine holes, par 36, greens fee $20

New Ewa Beach Golf Club
(☎ 689-8351) 91-050 Fort Weaver Rd, Ewa Beach; semi-private, 18 holes, par 72, greens fee $135 including cart

Olomana Golf Links
(☎ 259-7926) 41-1801 Kalanianaole Hwy, Waimanalo; semi-private, 18 holes, par 72, greens fee $80 including cart

Pearl Country Club
(☎ 487-3802) 98-535 Kaonohi St, Aiea; semi-private, 18 holes, par 72, greens fee $90 including cart

Turtle Bay County Club
(☎ 293-8574) Turtle Bay Hilton, Kahuku; resort, nine holes, par 72, greens fee $50 including cart

Waikele Golf Club
(☎ 676-9000) 94-200 Paioa Place, Waipahu; semi-private, 18 holes, par 72, greens fee $108 including cart

TENNIS

Oahu has 181 county tennis courts throughout the island. If you're staying in Waikiki, the most convenient locations are the 10 lighted courts at Ala Moana Beach Park; the 10 unlighted courts at the Diamond Head Tennis Center, at the Diamond Head end of Kapiolani Park (see Waikiki map); and the

Some of Oahu's most interesting residents live under the sea.

CASEY & ASTRID WITTE MAHANEY

The acrobatic *Octopus cyanea*

ANDREW SALLMON

A colorful Picasso triggerfish

CASEY & ASTRID WITTE MAHANEY

Bluestripe butterflyfish swims by

CASEY & ASTRID WITTE MAHANEY

RON DALQUIST

The coral reefs in Hanauma Bay offer some of Oahu's best snorkeling.

LEE FOSTER

Sailing off Waikiki

CASEY & ASTRID WITTE MAHANEY

Snorkeling here is like swimming in an aquarium.

Windsurfing on the windward coast

Sunset Beach Park on Oahu's North Shore

Fashion statement at Sunset Beach Park

Got fish? Hawaiian monk seal

Pincushion seastar at Mahaka Caverns

A large school of bluestripe snapper

four lighted Kapiolani Park courts, opposite the Waikiki Aquarium (see Waikiki map). Court time at these county facilities is free and on a first-come, first-served basis.

The county tennis courts do not rent tennis rackets, but Planet Surf (☎ 924-9050), 159 Kaiulani Ave in Waikiki, rents rackets for $5 a day, $20 a week.

With real estate at a premium, few Waikiki hotels have the room for tennis courts. The Ilikai Hotel (☎ 944-6300), 1777 Ala Moana Blvd, and the Pacific Beach Hotel (☎ 922-1233), 2490 Kalakaua Ave, each have two courts and charge $5 per hour per person for hotel guests, $8 for nonguests; rackets can be rented for $4.

Outside Waikiki, the Turtle Bay Hilton in Kahuku (☎ 293-8811) charges $12 per person per day, with one-hour playing time guaranteed; rackets rent for $8 a day. The resort has a pro shop and gives lessons.

CYCLING

Cycling is gradually becoming more mainstream on Oahu. The county is currently piecing together its first bicycle master plan, which calls for adding nearly a hundred miles of bike lanes, including a route that will link Diamond Head and Aloha Tower, though the implementation is still years away.

In the meantime, the county has published a free 'Bike Oahu' map that shows which roads are suitable for novice and experienced cyclists. The county also has installed bike racks on its public buses, making it easy to head out one way by bike and return by bus.

Although cycling along roads isn't a problem – other than traffic and the shortage of bike lanes – getting off the beaten path is a bit more complicated, because access to public forests and trails is limited.

On densely populated Oahu, mountain bikers are often pitted against hikers, and access issues are still in the formative stage. For instance, bikes have been banned from the off-road Tantalus trails, Honolulu's main forest trail network, because tire tracks were causing trail erosion. Although the Tantalus trails are currently closed to cyclists all year, the government has batted around the possibility of opening them in the dry summer months but keeping them closed to cyclists in the rainier winter season. In the meantime, the paved Tantalus Drive, which is also open to vehicle travel, remains a popular biking route.

One popular forest trail that is open to mountain bikers is the Maunawili Trail, a scenic 10-mile trek that connects the mountain crest at the Nuuanu Pali Lookout with Waimanalo on the windward coast. For details, see Maunawili Trail in the Pali Hwy section of the Windward Coast chapter.

The nonprofit Hawaii Bicycling League (☎ 735-5756), 3442 Waialae Ave, No 1, Honolulu, HI 96812, holds bike rides around Oahu nearly every Saturday and Sunday, ranging from 10-mile jaunts to 60-mile treks. Some outings are geared strictly to road travel and others include off-road sites. Rides are free and open to the public; the main requisite is that helmets be worn. Visit their website (www.hbl.org).

For information on getting around Oahu by bike, including bicycle rentals and where to pick up cycle maps, see the Bicycle section in the Getting Around chapter.

RUNNING

Islanders are big on jogging. In fact, it's estimated that Honolulu has more joggers per capita than any other city in the world. Kapiolani Park and Ala Moana Park are two favorite jogging spots. There's also a 4.8-mile run around Diamond Head crater that's a well-beaten track.

Oahu has about 70 road races each year, from 1-mile fun runs and 5-mile jogs to competitive marathons, biathlons and triathlons. For an annual schedule of running events with times, dates and contact addresses, write to the Department of Parks & Recreation, City & County of Honolulu, 650 S King St, Honolulu, HI 96813 or view the schedule at www.co.honolulu.hi.us/parks/programs/marathon.htm on the Web.

Oahu's best-known race is the Honolulu Marathon, which in recent years has mushroomed into the second largest marathon in the USA. Held in mid-December, it's an open-entry event, with an estimated half of

The Honolulu Marathon is the second-largest marathon in the USA.

the 27,000 entrants being first-time marathon runners. For information, send a self-addressed, stamped envelope to Honolulu Marathon Association, 3435 Waialae Ave, No 208, Honolulu, HI 96816. Those writing from overseas are asked to include two international response postage coupons. You can also download an entry form from www .honolulumarathon.org on the Web.

The Department of Parks & Recreation holds a Honolulu Marathon Clinic 7:30 am most Sundays at the Kapiolani Park Bandstand. It's free and open to everyone from beginners to seasoned marathon runners. Participants join groups of their own speed.

The comprehensive, bimonthly magazine *Hawaii Race* (☎/fax 922-4222, mjaffe@aloha .net), 3442 Waialae Ave, suite 6, Honolulu, HI 96816, includes upcoming race schedules for all of Hawaii, as well as qualification details and actual entry forms for the major races. A subscription costs $18 a year; a single sample copy will usually be sent free on request.

HORSEBACK RIDING

While there's no horseback riding offered in the Honolulu area, there are a couple of options on the windward side of the island.

Correa Trails (☎ 259-9005), 41-050 Kalanianaole Hwy in Waimanalo, offers one-hour guided trail rides along the Koolau Mountains, with scenic views of the ocean. The $50 fee includes free transportation to and from Waikiki. There are rides four times a day, every day except Monday.

Kualoa Ranch (☎ 237-8515), opposite Kualoa Regional Park, has 40-minute trail rides for $28 and 1½-hour rides for $45.

The Turtle Bay Hilton (☎ 293-8811) in Kahuku has 45-minute trail rides for $35 and 1½-hour sunset rides for $65.

SKYDIVING & GLIDER RIDES

Skydiving and glider rides, including those listed here, are offered at the Dillingham Airfield in Mokuleia on the North Shore. Sometimes there are discounted deals, so always ask about specials and promotions.

For around $200, Skydive Hawaii (☎ 945-0222) will attach you to the hips and shoulders of a skydiver so you can jump together from a plane at 13,000 feet, freefall for a minute and finish off with 10 to 15 minutes of canopy ride. The whole process, including some basic instruction, takes about 1½ hours. Participants must be at least 18 years of age and weigh less than 200 pounds. Arrangements can also be made to take up experienced skydivers for solo jumps. Planes take off daily, weather permitting.

Glider Rides (☎ 677-3404) offers 20-minute flights on an engineless piloted glider craft, which is towed by an airplane and then released to slowly glide back to earth. Flights leave daily between 10:30 am and 5 pm, weather permitting. The cost is $100 for one person or $120 for two.

Soar Hawaii (☎ 637-3147) offers 30-minute glider rides for $120 and a 40-minute ride for $130. The cost is the same for either one or two people – though a single person can often negotiate $20 or so off the rate. For thrill seekers, they also offer acrobatic rides that feature barrel rolls, spirals and wingovers.

CRUISES

Numerous sunset sails, dinner cruises and party boats leave daily from Kewalo Basin, just west of Ala Moana Park. Rates range from $20 to $100, with dinner cruises averaging about $50. Many provide transport to and from Waikiki and advertise various come-ons and specials; check the free tourist magazines for the latest offers.

A handful of catamarans depart from Waikiki Beach, including the *Manu Kai* (☎ 946-7490), which docks behind the Duke Kahanamoku statue and charges $10 for one-hour sails. The *Mai Ta'i* catamaran (☎ 922-5665), which departs from the beach in front of the Sheraton Waikiki, offers 1½-hour sails for $20, longer sunset sails for $30.

Royal Hawaiian Cruises (☎ 848-6360) runs two-hour whale-watching cruises from January to April aboard the *Navatek I*, a sleek, high-tech catamaran designed to minimize rolling. There's a morning cruise at 8:30 am that costs $39 for adults and $24 for children ages three to 11. The boat leaves from Pier 6, near the Aloha Tower.

Atlantis Submarines (☎ 973-9811) has a 65-foot, 48-passenger sightseeing submarine that descends to a depth of 100 feet. The tour lasts 1¾ hours, including boat transport to and from the sub. About 45 minutes are spent cruising beneath the surface around a ship and two planes that were deliberately sunk to create a dive site. Tours leave from Hilton Hawaiian Village on the hour from 8 am to 4 pm daily and cost $89 for adults, though if you book the 2 pm trip, there's a $59 special. The cost for children 12 and younger is $39 for all trips.

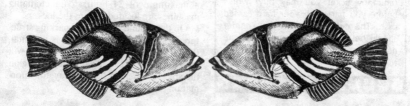

Getting There & Away

AIR

Honolulu is a major Pacific hub and an intermediate stop on many flights between the US mainland and Asia, Australia, New Zealand and the South Pacific. Passengers on any of these routes are usually allowed to make a stopover in Honolulu.

Honolulu International Airport

Honolulu International is a modern airport that's recently completed an extensive upgrade and expansion. Although it's a busy place, it's not particularly difficult to get around.

The airport has all the expected services, including fast-food restaurants, lounges, newsstands, sundry shops, lei stands, gift shops, duty-free shops, a medical clinic with

---

Warning

The information in this chapter is particularly vulnerable to change. Prices for international travel are volatile, routes are introduced and canceled, schedules change, special deals come and go, and rules and visa requirements are amended. Airlines and governments seem to take a perverse pleasure in making price structures and regulations as complicated as possible. In addition, the travel industry is highly competitive and there are many hidden costs and benefits.

The upshot of this is that you should get quotes and advice from as many airlines and travel agents as possible, and make sure you understand how a fare (and any ticket you may buy) works before you part with your hard-earned cash. The details given in this chapter should be regarded as pointers and are not a substitute for your own careful, up-to-date research.

✿✿✿✿✿✿✿✿✿✿✿✿✿✿

---

a nurse on duty 24 hours a day and a mini-hotel for naps and showers.

There's a visitor information booth, car rental counters and hotel/condo courtesy phones in the baggage claim area. You can also pick up *This Week Oahu*, *Spotlight's Oahu Gold* and other free tourist magazines from nearby racks.

If you arrive early for a flight and are looking for something to do, the Pacific Aerospace Museum ($3) in the main departure lobby has multimedia displays on aviation and is open 9 am to 6 pm daily.

Money Thomas Cook has foreign exchange booths spread around the airport, including in the international arrival area (open 5:30 am until the last foreign flight arrives) and in the central departure lobby next to the barber shop (open 8:30 am to 4:30 pm). On the opposite side of the same barber shop are American Express and Bank of Hawaii ATMs that give cash advances on major credit cards and cash withdrawals for ATM cards using the Cirrus and Plus systems. Because Thomas Cook adds on some hefty transaction fees, using the ATM may be a more economical option.

If you're in no hurry, you can avoid needling transaction fees by going to the Bank of Hawaii on the ground level of the terminal, across the street from baggage claim D. It's open 8:30 am to 4 pm Monday to Thursday and to 6 pm on Friday.

Baggage Storage There are coin-operated lockers in front of gates 13, 14 and 24 that cost 50¢ per hour, or $3 per 24 hours, up to a maximum of 24 hours; coin changing machines are located next to the lockers.

On the ground floor of the parking structure, opposite the main overseas terminal, there is a baggage storage service that will hold items for $3 to $10 a day, depending on the size. It's open 24 hours a day; for information call ☎ 836-6547.

Intra-Airport Shuttle The free Wiki Wiki Shuttle connects the more distant parts of the airport by linking the main terminals with the inter-island terminals. It can be picked up streetside in front of the main lobby (on the upper level) and in front of the inter-island gates. The hours of operation for the shuttle service are 6 am to 10:30 pm daily.

Airlines

The following airlines have scheduled flights to Honolulu International Airport: Air Canada, Air New Zealand, All Nippon Airlines, Aloha Airlines, America West Airlines, American Airlines, Canadian Airlines, China Airlines, Continental Airlines, Delta Air Lines, Garuda Indonesia, Hawaiian Airlines, Japan Airlines, Korean Air, Northwest Airlines, Philippine Airlines, Qantas Airways, Singapore Airlines, TWA and United Airlines.

See the toll-free directory at the back of the book for the phone numbers for these airlines.

Buying Tickets

There are numerous airlines that fly to Hawaii and a variety of fares are available. Rather than just walking into the nearest travel agent or airline office, it pays to do a bit of research and shopping around first.

You might want to start by perusing the travel sections of magazines and large newspapers, like the *New York Times*, the *San Francisco Chronicle* and the *Los Angeles Times* in the USA; the *Sydney Morning Herald* or Melbourne's *Age* in Australia; and *Time Out* or *TNT* in the UK.

Airfares are constantly in flux. Fares vary with the season you travel, the day of the week you fly, your length of stay and the flexibility the ticket provides for flight changes and refunds. Still, nothing determines fares

Air Travel Glossary

Baggage Allowance This will be written on your ticket. For international travelers, it's usually one 20kg item to go in the hold, plus one item of hand luggage. With most US airlines, however, passengers are allowed to check in two bags, each weighing up to 70lbs. Note that airlines are becoming very strict about the size of carry-on luggage.

Bucket Shops These are unbonded travel agencies specializing in discounted airline tickets.

Bumped Just because you have a confirmed seat doesn't mean you're going to get on the plane (see Overbooking).

Cancellation Penalties If you have to cancel or change a discounted ticket, there are often heavy penalties involved; insurance can sometimes be taken out against these penalties. Some airlines impose penalties on regular tickets as well, particularly against 'no-show' passengers.

Check-In Airlines ask you to check in a certain amount of time ahead of the flight departure (usually one to two hours). If you fail to check in on time and the flight is overbooked, the airline can cancel your booking and give your seat to somebody else.

Confirmation Having a ticket written out with the flight and date you want doesn't necessarily mean you have a seat until the agent has checked with the airline that your status is 'OK' or confirmed. Meanwhile, you could just be 'on request.'

Electronic Ticket If you're flying from the US mainland to Hawaii, it's possible to book your flight with an electronic ticket (also called E-ticket or ticketless travel). Essentially, you get a receipt, but no ticket, from your airline or travel agent; you merely show your identification at the ticket counter to get your boarding pass. One big advantage is that it is impossible to lose your ticket.

ITX An ITX, or 'independent inclusive tour excursion,' is often available on tickets to popular holiday destinations. Officially, it's a package deal combined with hotel accommodations, but many agents will sell you one of these for the flight only and give you phony hotel vouchers in the unlikely event that you're challenged at the airport.

Lost Tickets If you lose your airline ticket, an airline will usually treat it like a traveler's check and, after inquiries, issue you another one, though there may be a fee involved. Legally, however, an airline is entitled to treat it like cash and if you lose it, then it's gone forever. Take good care of your tickets.

No-Shows No-shows are passengers who fail to show up for their flight. Full-fare passengers who fail to turn up are sometimes entitled to travel on a later flight. The rest are penalized (see Cancellation Penalties).

Air Travel Glossary

On Request This is an unconfirmed booking for a flight.

Onward Tickets An entry requirement for many countries is that you have a ticket out of the country. If you're unsure of your next move, the easiest solution is to buy the cheapest onward ticket to a neighboring country or a ticket from a reliable airline that can later be refunded if you do not use it.

Open Jaw Tickets These are return tickets where you fly out to one place and return from another. If available, this can save you backtracking to your arrival point.

Overbooking Airlines hate to fly empty seats, and because every flight has some passengers who fail to show up, airlines often book more passengers than they have seats. Usually excess passengers make up for the no-shows, but occasionally somebody gets bumped. Who is it most likely to be? The passengers who check in late.

Point-to-Point Tickets These are discount tickets that can be purchased on some routes in return for passengers waiving their rights to a stopover.

Reconfirmation With some airlines, it's necessary to reconfirm your reservation at least 72 hours prior to the departure time of an onward or return flight. If you don't do this, the airline can delete your name from the passenger list and you could lose your seat.

Restrictions Discounted tickets often have various restrictions on them – such as advance payment, minimum and maximum periods you must be away (eg, a minimum of one week or a maximum of six months), and penalties for changing the tickets.

Round-the-World Tickets RTW tickets give you a limited period (usually a year) in which to circumnavigate the globe. You can go anywhere the carrying airlines go, as long as you don't backtrack. The number of stopovers or total number of separate flights is decided before you set off and they usually cost more than a basic return flight.

Standby This is a discounted ticket that allows you to fly only if there is a seat free at the last moment. Standby fares are usually available only on domestic routes, and they are largely a thing of the past in the USA.

Travel Periods Ticket prices vary with the time of year. There is a low (off-peak) season and a high (peak) season, and often a low-shoulder season and a high-shoulder season as well. Usually, the fare depends on your outward flight – if you depart in the high season and return in the low season, you pay the high-season fare.

more than business, and when things are slow, regardless of the season, airlines typically drop fares to fill the empty seats.

The airlines each have their own requirements and restrictions, which also seem to be constantly changing. For the latest deals, browse travel services on the Internet, visit a knowledgeable travel agent or simply start calling the different airlines and compare ticket prices.

When you call, it's important to ask for the lowest fare, since that's not always the first one the agent will quote you. Each flight has only a limited number of seats available at the cheapest fares. When you make reservations, the agents will generally tell you the best fare that's still available on the date you give them, which may or may not be the cheapest fare that the airline is currently offering. If you make reservations far enough in advance and are a little flexible with dates, you'll usually do better.

In addition to a straightforward roundtrip ticket, a stop in Hawaii can also be part of a Round-the-World or Circle Pacific ticket. See those sections, below, for additional information.

Round-the-World Tickets Round-the-World (RTW) tickets, which allow you to fly on the combined routes of two or more airlines, can be an economical way to circle the globe.

RTW tickets are valid for one year and you must travel in one general direction without backtracking. Although most airlines restrict the number of sectors that can be flown within the USA and Canada to four, and a few heavily traveled routes are sometimes blacked out, stopovers are otherwise generally unlimited on most airlines. However, in recent years some airlines have been capping the number of free stopovers and charging a fee for additional stops.

In most cases a 14-day advance purchase is required. After the ticket is purchased, dates can usually be changed without penalty and tickets can be rewritten to add or delete stops for $25 to $75 each, depending upon the carrier.

There's an almost endless variety of possible airline and destination combinations. Because of Honolulu's central Pacific location, Hawaii can be included on most RTW tickets. As a general rule, travel solely in the Northern Hemisphere will be notably cheaper than travel that includes destinations in the Southern Hemisphere.

British Airways and Qantas Airways offer a couple of RTW tickets that allow you to combine routes covering the South and Central Pacific regions, Asia and Europe. One version, the One World Explorer, is based on the number of continents you visit, requires traveling to a minimum of three continents and allows three stops in each continent visited; extra stops can be added for an additional US$100 each. The One World Explorer costs US$2800 in the USA, A$2599 in Australia and £860 in the UK. A second version is the Global Explorer, which is based instead on the total miles flown, allowing 28,500 miles of travel. The Global Explorer, which allows six free stops (additional stops can be added for US$83 each), costs US$3089 in the USA, A$2949 in Australia and £999 in the UK. Because Qantas has a code-sharing partnership with American Airlines (which means you can book a flight through Qantas, such as New York-Los Angeles, using a Qantas ticket coupon, but you'll actually fly with American), these RTW tickets also allow some travel within the USA.

As another example, Continental Airlines offers standard RTW tickets that allow unlimited stops for one set fare, linking up with either Malaysia Airlines, Singapore Airlines or Thai Airways for US$2650. With these airlines, an itinerary could take you from the US mainland to Honolulu, Guam and Bali or Manila. From there, one possible route would be to continue through Hong Kong, Saigon, Calcutta, Delhi, Istanbul, Rome and Paris before returning back to North America.

Circle Pacific Tickets There are a number of tickets that allow wide-ranging travel within the Pacific Rim area, including a stop in Hawaii.

OVERSEAS AIR ROUTES

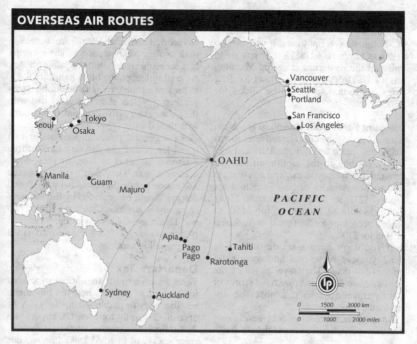

The best known, though not the best value, is the Circle Pacific ticket, whereby two airlines link up to allow stopovers along their combined Pacific Rim routes. Rather than simply flying from Point A to Point B, these tickets allow you to swing through much of the Pacific and eastern Asia, taking in a variety of destinations – as long as you keep traveling in the same circular direction.

Circle Pacific routes generally cost about US$2789 when purchased in the USA and A$3385 when purchased in Australia. Circle Pacific fares include four stopovers, with the option of adding additional stops at US$50 each. There's typically a seven-day advance purchase requirement and a maximum allowable stay of six months.

The routes and airline combinations are numerous, and your itinerary can be selected from scores of potential destinations. For example, a Qantas-United ticket could take you from Los Angeles to Honolulu, on to Tokyo, south to Singapore, followed by Sydney and then back to Los Angeles.

There are other variations to Circle Pacific tickets, including some with more attractive fares. Air New Zealand, in conjunction with Singapore Airlines, offers a Pacific Escapade fare that allows unlimited stops as long as you don't travel more than 22,000 miles, and it's about 10% cheaper than the regular Circle Pacific fares.

If you're coming from the USA and don't want to go all the way to Asia, Air New Zealand also offers a Coral Explorer fare that allows travel from Los Angeles to New Zealand, Australia and a number of South Pacific islands, with a return via Honolulu. The base price ranges from US$1050 to US$1600, depending on the season, with two stops included in the fare (additional stops cost US$150 each).

Another interesting option, the Circle Micronesia pass with Continental Airlines, departs from Los Angeles or San Francisco and combines Honolulu with the islands of Micronesia. The price depends on how much of Micronesia you opt to see. If you only go as far as Guam, it's US$1230; if you go to Palau, at the westernmost end of Micronesia, it's US$1650. The pass allows for four stops; additional stops can be added for US$50 each.

Discount Fares from Honolulu Honolulu is a good place to get discounted fares to virtually any place around the Pacific. Fares vary according to the month, airline and demand, but often you can find a roundtrip fare to Los Angeles or San Francisco for around $275; to Tokyo for $400; to Hong Kong, Manila or Singapore for $550; to Saigon or Sydney for $650; and to Auckland or Bali for $700.

If you don't have a set destination in mind, you can sometimes find some great on-the-spot deals. The travel pages of the Sunday *Honolulu Advertiser* have scores of ads by travel agencies that advertise discounted overseas fares.

Some of the more significant travel agencies that specialize in discount tickets are:

Cheap Tickets
   (☎ 947-3717, 800-377-1000, www.cheaptickets
   .com) Kapiolani Blvd at Atkinson Drive, and
   at 2615 S King St, suite 100, both in Honolulu

King's Travel
   (☎ 593-4481, 800-801-4481, www.kingstravel
   .com) Imperial Plaza Bldg, 725 Kapiolani Blvd,
   Honolulu

Panda Travel
   (☎ 734-1961) 1017 Kapahulu Ave, Honolulu

Travelers with Special Needs

If you have special needs of any sort – you require a vegetarian diet, are taking a baby or have a medical condition that warrants special consideration – you should let the airline know as soon as possible so they can make arrangements accordingly. Remind them when you reconfirm your reservation and again when you check in at the airport. It may also be worth calling several airlines before you book your ticket to find out how each of them handles your particular needs.

Most international airports, including Honolulu International Airport, will provide an escorted cart or wheelchair from check-in desk to plane when needed, and have ramps, lifts, accessible toilets and reachable phones. Aircraft toilets, on the other hand, are likely to present a problem for some disabled passengers; travelers should discuss this with the airline at an early stage and, if necessary, with their doctor.

As a general rule, children under two travel for 10% of the standard fare (or free on some airlines) as long as they don't occupy a seat. They don't get a baggage allowance either. 'Skycots,' baby food and diapers should be provided by the airline if requested in advance. Children between two and 12 can usually occupy a seat for half to two-thirds of the full fare, and do get a baggage allowance.

Departure Tax

Taxes for US airports are normally included in the price of tickets when you buy them, whether they're purchased in the USA or abroad. Generally, for each US airport you fly into, including connections and stopovers, there's a tax of $1 to $3 tacked on to your ticket price.

Also added to the ticket price are a $6 airport departure tax on all passengers bound for a foreign destination and a $6.50 North American Free Trade Agreement (NAFTA) tax on all passengers entering the USA from a foreign country.

There are no additional departure taxes to pay when leaving Hawaii.

US Mainland

There's a lot of competition amongst airlines flying to Honolulu from the major mainland cities, and at any given time, any one of the airlines could have the cheapest fare. The toll-free directory at the back of the book lists the phone numbers for the airlines mentioned in this section.

Typically, the lowest roundtrip fares from the US mainland to Honolulu are about $600 to $850 from the East Coast and $275 to $450 from the West Coast. For those flying from the East Coast, there are times when it may be cheaper to buy two separate tickets – one to the West Coast with a low-fare carrier such as Southwest Airlines, and then a separate ticket to Honolulu.

Although conditions vary, the cheapest fares are generally for midweek flights and have advance purchase requirements and other restrictions. They are usually nonrefundable and unchangeable, at least on the outbound flight (although most airlines make allowances for medical emergencies).

The following airlines fly to Honolulu from both the East and the West Coasts: American Airlines, Continental Airlines, Delta Air Lines, Northwest Airlines, TWA and United Airlines.

In addition, Hawaiian Airlines flies nonstop to Honolulu from Seattle, Portland, San Francisco and Los Angeles. Depending on the season and current promotional fares, a roundtrip ticket from Portland or Seattle is usually around $450. The standard fares from Los Angeles and San Francisco are also in the $450 range, though Hawaiian commonly offers discounted fares from those cities for about $300.

As we go to press, the other inter-island carrier, Aloha Airlines, is planning to initiate its first-ever service to the mainland, with daily flights between Honolulu and Oakland, California.

Flight time to Honolulu is about 5½ hours from the West Coast, 11 hours from the East Coast.

Canada
Both Air Canada and Canadian Airlines offer flights to Honolulu from Vancouver and from other Canadian cities via Vancouver. The cheapest roundtrip fares to Honolulu are around C$550 (US$349) from Vancouver, C$675 (US$429) from Calgary or Edmonton and C$1000 (US$635) from Toronto. These fares are for midweek travel, generally allow a maximum stay of either 30 or 60 days and have a 14-day advance purchase requirement.

Australia
Qantas flies to Honolulu from Sydney or Melbourne (via Sydney, but with no change

of plane), with roundtrip fares ranging from A$999 (US$631) up to A$1479 (US$934), depending on the season. These tickets require a minimum stay of four days and a maximum stay of 60 days. There are currently no US carriers providing service between Australia and Honolulu, though United and Continental both have done so in the past.

New Zealand
Air New Zealand has Auckland-Honolulu roundtrip fares for NZ$1449 (US$772). These tickets, which have to be purchased at least seven days in advance, allow stays of up to six months: one free stopover is allowed and others are permitted for an additional NZ$100 per stop. The one-way fare, which also allows a free stopover in Fiji, is NZ$1079 (US$575).

South Pacific Islands
For travel from Fiji, Air New Zealand has a one-way fare from Nadi to Honolulu for F$994 (US$478) and a six-month excursion ticket, with no advance purchase requirement, for F$1346 (US$681).

For travel from other South Pacific islands, Hawaiian Airlines flies to Honolulu from Tahiti and American Samoa. From American Samoa, the one-way fare is US$403, with

Agricultural Inspection

All luggage and carry-on bags leaving Hawaii for the US mainland are checked by an agricultural inspector using an X-ray machine. You cannot take out gardenia, jade vine or roses, even in leis, although most other fresh flowers and foliage are permitted. You can bring home pineapples and coconuts, but most other fresh fruits and vegetables are banned. Other things not allowed to enter mainland states include plants in soil, fresh coffee berries, cactus and sugarcane.

Seeds, fruits and plants that have been certified and labeled for export aren't a problem.

no advance purchase required, and the roundtrip fare starts at US$578, with a 21-day advance purchase. From Tahiti to Honolulu the standard one-way fare is a steep US$1014, but there's a seven-day 'Shopper's Special' excursion ticket with a seven-day advance purchase requirement that costs US$685.

Air New Zealand flies to Honolulu from Tonga, the Cook Islands and Western Samoa. The lowest roundtrip fare from Tonga to Honolulu costs T$1159 (US$729), requires a seven-day advance purchase and allows a stay of up to 45 days. A one-way ticket costs T$667 (US$420).

From Rarotonga on the Cook Islands, Air New Zealand's cheapest roundtrip fare to Honolulu is NZ$1319 (US$703), requires a seven-day advance purchase and allows a stay of up to one year; the one-way fare costs NZ$1049 (US$559), with a two-week advance purchase.

From Apia in Western Samoa, Air New Zealand's roundtrip fare to Honolulu is WS$1396 (US$469) and has no advance purchase requirement and a 90-day maximum stay. The one-way fare, which also has no advance purchase requirement, is WS$969 (US$326).

Micronesia

Continental Airlines has nonstop flights from Guam to Honolulu with roundtrip fares from US$850.

A more exciting way to get from Guam, however, would be Continental's island hopper, which stops en route at the Micronesian islands of Chuuk, Pohnpei, Kosrae and Majuro before reaching Honolulu. A one-way ticket with free unlimited stopovers is US$717 and there is no advance purchase requirement. If you're coming from Asia, this is a good alternative to a nonstop transpacific flight and a great way to see some of the Pacific's most remote islands without having to spend a lot of money.

Europe

The most common route to Hawaii from Europe is west via New York, Chicago or Los Angeles. If you're interested in heading east with stops in Asia, it may be cheaper to get a Round-the-World ticket (see earlier section by that name) instead of returning the same way.

American Airlines has a roundtrip fare from London to Honolulu for US$1200 that allows a stay of up to 60 days. American's cheapest roundtrip fare from Paris to Honolulu is US$900 and allows a stay of up to three months. From Frankfurt to Honolulu the lowest fare is US$950 for a stay of up to 21 days. All of the fares above are for travel between Monday and Thursday.

United Airlines, Delta Air Lines and Continental Airlines have similarly priced service to Honolulu from a number of European cities.

You can usually beat the published airline fares at bucket shops and other travel agencies specializing in discount tickets. London is arguably the world's headquarters for bucket shops, and they are well advertised. Two good, reliable agents for cheap tickets in the UK are Trailfinders (☎ 020-7937-5400), 215 Kensington High St, London, and STA Travel (☎ 020-7361-6262), 117 Euston Rd, London.

Japan

Fares in this section are in yen; there are approximately 120 yen to one US dollar.

Japan Airlines flies to Honolulu from Tokyo, Osaka, Nagoya, Fukuoka and Sapporo. Excursion fares vary a bit with the departing city and the season, but, except at busier holiday periods, they're generally about ¥140,000 for a ticket valid for three months. The one-way fare from Tokyo is ¥149,700.

Two American carriers, Continental Airlines and Northwest Airlines, also have flights to Honolulu from Japan, with ticket prices that are competitive with those of Japan Airlines.

An interesting alternative, if you're only going one way, is to fly from Japan to Guam (¥72,950) and then pick up a Continental Airlines ticket that allows you to island-hop through much of Micronesia on your way to Honolulu – for less than the cost of a direct one-way Japan-Honolulu ticket.

Southeast Asia

There are numerous airlines that fly directly to Hawaii from Southeast Asia. The fares given here are standard published fares, though bucket shops in places such as Bangkok and Singapore should be able to come up with much better deals. Also, if you're traveling to the USA from Southeast Asia, tickets to the West Coast are not that much more than tickets to Hawaii, and many allow a free stopover in Honolulu.

Northwest Airlines flies to Honolulu from Hong Kong, Bangkok, Manila, Seoul and Singapore. Thai Airlines, Korean Air and Philippine Airlines have numerous flights between Southeast Asian cities and Honolulu. Although there are some seasonal variations, the standard roundtrip fares are about US$1100 from Manila, US$1200 from Seoul and Bangkok, US$1500 from Hong Kong and US$1800 from Singapore.

Central & South America

Most of the flights to Hawaii from Central and South America go via Houston or Los Angeles, though a few of those from the eastern cities go via New York.

United Airlines has flights from numerous cities in Mexico and Central America, including San José, Guatemala City, Mexico City, Guadalajara and Cancún. Their lowest roundtrip fare from Mexico City to Honolulu is US$850, which allows a maximum stay of 30 days.

Within Hawaii

There are frequent flights between Honolulu and the Neighbor Islands of Maui, Kauai, the Big Island, Molokai and Lanai.

The two main carriers, Hawaiian Airlines (☎ 838-1555, 800-367-5320) and Aloha Airlines (☎ 484-1111, 800-367-5250), both have a standard one-way fare of $93 for flights between Honolulu and the major airports of Lihue (on Kauai), Kahului (on Maui) and Kona and Hilo (both on the Big Island). Roundtrip fares are double the one-way fares. Hawaiian Airlines and Island Air (☎ 484-2222, 800-323-3345), an Aloha Airlines affiliate, fly to the islands of Molokai and Lanai for the same fares.

However, you can save a bundle by using discount coupons rather than full-fare tickets. The coupons don't have advance purchase requirements, and you can make reservations ahead of time before buying them.

Both Hawaiian Airlines and Aloha Airlines sell coupon booklets containing six tickets good for inter-island flights between any two destinations they serve. The booklets cost around $330 when purchased from the airlines at the airport ticket counter. These tickets can be used by any number of people and on any flight without restrictions You can also buy individual coupons from discount travel agents for around $50.

In addition, if you have a MasterCard or Visa credit card, you can purchase Hawaiian Airlines coupons for $55.50 per ticket from Bank of Hawaii ATMs, one of which is located in the inter-island terminal at the Honolulu Airport (across from Burger King); others are located around Hawaii at the ubiquitous 7-Eleven stores. Unlike coupon books, you can buy just a single ticket when you use an ATM. You will need to use your PIN number along with your credit card (it's a credit card transaction).

Aloha Airlines offers American Automobile Association (AAA) members a 25% discount on the standard tickets on its inter-island flights. The discount is available to members and those traveling with them.

There are also other schemes that come up from time to time, so always ask the airline agent what promotional fares are being offered when you call to make reservations.

SEA

In recent years, a handful of cruise ships have begun offering tours that include Hawaii. Many of these trips are referred to as 'repositioning tours,' since they typically visit Hawaii during April, May, September and October on ships that are otherwise used in Alaska during the summer and in the Caribbean during the winter.

Most of these cruises last 10 to 12 days and have fares that start at around $150 a day per person, based on double occupancy, though discounts and promotions can bring that price down. Airfare to and from the departure point is extra.

Princess Cruises (☎ 800-568-3262) generally offers cruises that go between Honolulu and Tahiti, or between Honolulu and Vancouver, Canada. Both Royal Caribbean Cruise Line (☎ 800-327-6700) and Holland America Cruise Line (☎ 800-426-0327) typically depart for Honolulu from Ensenada, Mexico or from Vancouver. Norwegian Cruise Line (☎ 800-327-7030) most commonly goes between Honolulu and Kiribati. Most of the cruises include stopovers in Maui, Kauai and the Big Island.

Because US federal law bans foreign-flagged ships from offering cruises that carry passengers solely between US ports, a foreign port is included on all trips. Curiously, the only cruise ship in the USA that currently flies a US flag is the *Independence*,

which sails solely within the Hawaiian Islands. See the Getting Around chapter for information on the *Independence* cruise.

ORGANIZED TOURS

There are a slew of package tours available to Hawaii. The basic ones just include airfare and accommodations, and others include car rentals, sightseeing tours and all sorts of recreational activities. If you're interested, travel agents can help you sort through the various packages.

For those with limited time, package tours can be the cheapest way to go. Costs vary, but one-week tours with airfare and no-frills hotel accommodations usually start around $500 from the US West Coast, $800 from the US East Coast, based on double occupancy. If you want to stay somewhere fancy, the price can easily climb to double that.

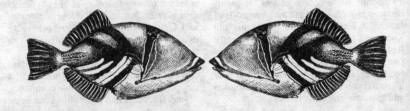

Getting Around

Oahu is an easy island to get around, whether you're traveling by public bus or private car.

Compared to mainland urban centers, Oahu's traffic is generally manageable, although in Honolulu it can get quite jammed during rush hour – weekdays from 7 to 9 am and 3 to 6 pm. Expect heavy traffic in both directions on the H-1 Fwy during this time, as well as on the Pali and Likelike highways headed towards Honolulu in the morning and away from Honolulu in the late afternoon. If you're going to the airport during rush hour, give yourself plenty of extra time.

TO/FROM THE AIRPORT

From the airport you can get to Waikiki by local bus, by airport shuttle services, by taxi or by rental car. A taxi to Waikiki from the airport will cost about $20. The main car rental agencies have booths or courtesy phones in the airport baggage claim area.

The easiest way to drive to Waikiki from the airport is to take Hwy 92, which starts out as Nimitz Hwy and turns into Ala Moana Blvd, leading directly into Waikiki. Although this route hits more local traffic, it's hard to get lost on it.

If you're into life in the fast lane, connect instead with the H-1 Fwy heading east.

On the return to the airport from Waikiki, beware of the poorly marked interchange where H-1 and Hwy 78 split; if you're not in the right-hand lane at that point, you could easily end up on Hwy 78. It takes about 20 minutes to get from Waikiki to the airport via H-1 *if* you don't hit traffic.

Public Bus

Travel time between the airport and the far end of Waikiki on city bus Nos 19 and 20 is about an hour; the fare is $1. The bus stops at the roadside median on the 2nd level, in front of the airline counters. There are two stops; it's best to wait for the bus at the first one, which is in front of Lobby 4. Luggage is limited to what you can hold on your lap or

store under your seat, the latter space comparable to the space under an airline seat.

Shuttle Bus

Two private companies, Super Shuttle (☎ 841-2928, 877-247-8737) and Airport Express (☎ 949-5249), offer shuttle service between the airport and Waikiki hotels. The ride averages 45 minutes, but can be more or less depending on how many passengers are dropped off before reaching your hotel. Catch these buses at the roadside median on the ground level, in front of the baggage claim areas; there's a courtesy phone near the tourist information booth.

The charge is $6 one way or $10 roundtrip for adults; children ages 6 to 12 pay half-price and those under 6 travel free. You don't need a reservation from the airport to Waikiki, but you do need to call at least a few hours in advance for the return van to the airport. Shuttles operate 6 am to 10 pm.

BUS

Oahu's public bus system, called TheBus, is extensive and easy to use. TheBus has about 80 routes, which collectively cover most of Oahu. You can take the bus to watch windsurfers at Kailua or surfers at Sunset Beach, visit Chinatown or the Bishop Museum, snorkel at Hanauma Bay or hike Diamond Head.

Some of the island's prime viewpoints are beyond reach, however. For instance, TheBus doesn't stop at the Nuuanu Pali Lookout, go up to the Tantalus green belt or run as far as Kaena Point.

Buses stop only at marked bus stops. Each bus route can have a few different destinations. The destination is written on the front of the bus next to the number. Buses generally keep the same number when inbound and outbound. For instance, bus No 8 can take you either into the heart of Waikiki or away from it towards Ala Moana – so take note of both the number and the written destination before you jump on.

Getting Oriented

Almost all visitors to Oahu land at Honolulu International Airport, the only commercial airport on the island. The airport is on the western outskirts of the Honolulu district, 9 miles west of Waikiki.

The H-1 Fwy, the main south-shore freeway, is the key to getting around the island. H-1 connects with Hwy 72, which runs around the southeast coast; with the Pali (61) and Likelike (63) highways, which go to the windward coast; with Hwy 93, which leads up the leeward Waianae Coast; and with H-2, Hwys 99 and 750, which run through the center of the island on the way to the North Shore.

Incidentally, H-1 is a US *interstate* freeway – an amusing designation for a road on an island state in the middle of the Pacific.

Directions on Oahu are often given by using landmarks. If someone tells you to go 'Ewa' (an area west of Honolulu) or 'Diamond Head' (east of Waikiki), it simply means to head in that direction. Two other commonly used directional terms that you can expect to hear are *mauka*, meaning inland side, and *makai*, meaning ocean side.

If you're in doubt, ask the bus driver. They're used to disoriented visitors, and most drivers are patient and helpful.

Overall, the buses are in excellent condition – if anything, they're a bit too modern. Newer buses are air-conditioned, with sealed windows and climate-control that sometimes seems so out of 'control' that drivers wear jackets to ward off the cold! Currently, about half of the buses are equipped with wheelchair lifts and many have bike racks that cyclists can use for free.

Although TheBus is convenient enough, this isn't Tokyo – if you set your watch by the bus here, you'll come up with Hawaiian Time. In addition to not getting hung up on schedules, buses can sometimes bottleneck, with one packed bus after another passing right by crowded bus stops. Waiting for the

bus anywhere between Ala Moana and Waikiki on a Saturday night can be a particularly memorable experience.

Still, TheBus usually gets you where you want to go, and as long as you don't try to cut your travel time too close or schedule too much in one day, it's a great deal.

Cost

The one-way fare for all rides is $1 for adults, 50¢ for children ages six to 18. Children under the age of six ride free. You can use either coins or $1 bills; bus drivers don't make change.

Transfers, which have a time limit stamped on them, are given free when more than one bus is required to get to a destination. If needed, ask for one when you board.

Visitor passes, valid for unlimited rides over four consecutive days, cost $10 and can be purchased at any of the ubiquitous ABC Stores.

Monthly bus passes, valid for unlimited rides in a calendar month, cost $25 and can be purchased at satellite city halls, 7-Eleven convenience stores and Foodland and Star supermarkets.

Seniors (65 years and older) and disabled people of any age can buy a $20 bus pass that is valid for unlimited rides during a two-year period. Senior passes are issued at satellite city halls upon presentation of an identification card with a birth date.

For most visitors, the most convenient satellite city hall will be the one at the Ala Moana Center (☎ 973-2600), at 1450 Ala Moana Blvd, Honolulu. It is open 9 am to 5:30 pm weekdays and 8 am to 4 pm on Saurday. For information on other satellite city hall locations and hours, call ☎ 527-6695.

Schedules & Information

Bus schedules vary with the route; many operate from about 6 am to 8 pm, though some main routes continue until around midnight. TheBus has a great telephone service. As long as you know where you are and where you want to go, anytime between 5:30 am and 10 pm you can call ☎ 848-5555, and they'll tell you not only which bus to catch, but also when the next one will be there. This same number also has a TDD service for the hearing impaired and can provide information on which buses are wheelchair accessible.

You can get printed timetables for individual routes free from any satellite city hall, including the one at the Ala Moana Center. Timetables can also be found in the downtown Honolulu library and a few places in Waikiki, including the Waikiki Beach police station, the International Marketplace food court and the McDonald's at the Waikiki Tower hotel.

When you pick up the timetables, be sure to grab one of the free schematic route maps, a handy brochure that maps out routes for the entire island and shows the corresponding bus numbers.

In addition, local convenience shops and bookstores sell commercial bus maps and schedules for around $4 to $5. These maps focus a bit more attention on reaching the main tourist destinations from Waikiki. A good, free alternative is *VIP – Visitor Information Publication Oahu*, a glossy fold-out map that not only shows bus routes but also maps out bus stop locations in some of the more touristed areas such as Waikiki, downtown Honolulu and Kailua. The VIP map, which is sponsored by advertisers, can be picked up at the airport tourist information booths.

Common Routes

Bus Nos 8, 19, 20 and 58 run between Waikiki and the Ala Moana Center, Honolulu's central transfer point. There's usually a bus every 10 minutes or less. From Ala Moana you can connect with a broad network of buses to points around the island.

Bus Nos 2, 19 and 20 will take you between Waikiki and downtown Honolulu.

Bus No 4 runs between Waikiki and the University of Hawaii.

CAR

The minimum age for visitors to drive in Hawaii is 18, though car rental companies usually have higher age restrictions. If you're younger than age 25, you should call the car rental agencies in advance to check their policies regarding restrictions and surcharges. Dollar is generally one of the more flexible agencies for renting cars to people who are under 25.

Other than the age requirement, you can legally drive in the state as long as you have a valid driver's license issued by a country that is party to the United Nations Conference on Road & Motor Transport – which covers virtually everyone.

However, car rental companies will generally accept valid foreign driver's licenses only if they're in English. Otherwise, most will require renters to show an international driver's license along with their home license.

Driving Times

Although actual driving time may vary depending upon traffic conditions, the average driving times and distances from Waikiki to points of interest around Oahu are as follows:

destination	mileage	time
USS *Arizona* Memorial	12 miles	30 minutes
Haleiwa	29 miles	50 minutes
Hanauma Bay	11 miles	25 minutes
Honolulu Airport	9 miles	20 minutes
Kaena Point State Park	43 miles	75 minutes
Kailua	14 miles	25 minutes
Laie	34 miles	60 minutes
Makaha Beach	36 miles	60 minutes
Nuuanu Pali Lookout	11 miles	20 minutes
Sea Life Park	16 miles	35 minutes
Sunset Beach	37 miles	65 minutes
Waimea	34 miles	60 minutes
Waipahu	16 miles	30 minutes

Road Rules

Driving is on the right-hand side of the road, as it is in the rest of the USA.

Drivers at a red light can make a right turn after coming to a full stop and yielding to oncoming traffic, unless there's a sign at the intersection prohibiting the turn.

In Hawaii drivers and front-seat passengers are required to wear seat belts. State law also strictly requires the use of child

Circle-Island Route

It's possible to make a nice day excursion circling the island by bus, beginning at the Ala Moana Center. The No 52 Wahiawa-Circle Island bus goes clockwise up Hwy 99 to Haleiwa and along the North Shore. At the Turtle Bay Hilton, on the northern tip of Oahu, it switches signs to No 55 and comes down the windward coast to Kaneohe and down the Pali Hwy back to Ala Moana. The No 55 Kaneohe-Circle Island bus does the same route in reverse. If you take this route nonstop, it takes about four hours and costs just $1.

For a shorter excursion from Waikiki, you can make a loop around southeast Oahu by taking bus No 58 to Sea Life Park and then bus No 57 up to Kailua and back into Honolulu.

Because you'll need to change buses, ask the driver for a transfer when you first board. Transfers have time limits and aren't meant to be used for stopovers, but you can usually grab a quick break at Ala Moana. If your transfer expires while you're exploring, you'll need to pay a new $1 fare when you reboard the bus.

---

safety seats for children ages three and younger, while four-year-olds must either be in a safety seat or secured by a seat belt. Most of the car rental companies rent child safety seats for around $5 a day, but they don't always have them on hand so it's advisable to reserve one in advance.

Speed limits are posted and enforced. If you are stopped for speeding, expect to get a ticket, as the police rarely just give warnings.

Rental

Car rentals are readily available at the airport and in Waikiki. With most companies, the weekly rate is significantly cheaper per day than the straight daily rate. The daily rate for a small car such as a Geo Metro or Ford Escort, with unlimited mileage, ranges from around $25 to $45, while typical weekly rates are $150 to $200.

You are usually required to keep the car for a minimum of five or six days in order to get the weekly rate.

Rates vary a bit from company to company, and also within each company, depending on season, time of booking and current promotional fares. If you belong to an automobile club, a frequent-flyer program or a travel club, you'll often be eligible for some sort of discount with at least one of the rental agencies, so always ask.

One thing to note when renting a car is that rates for mid-size and full-size cars are often only a few dollars more per week; because some promotional discounts exclude the economy-size cars, at times the lowest rate available may actually be for a larger car.

At any given time, any one of the rental companies could be offering the best deal, so you can save money by taking a little time to shop around. Be sure to ask the agent for the cheapest rate, as the first quote given is not always the lowest.

It's a good idea to make reservations in advance, and with most companies there's no cancellation penalty if you change your mind. Walking up to the counter without a reservation will not only subject you to higher rates, but during busy periods it's not uncommon for cars to be rented out altogether.

On daily rentals, most cars are rented on a 24-hour basis, so you could get two days' use by renting at midday and driving around all afternoon, then heading out to explore somewhere else the next morning before the car is due back. Most companies even allow an hour's grace period.

Rental rates generally include unlimited mileage, though if you drop off the car at a location that is different from where you picked it up, there's usually a drop-off fee.

Having a major credit card greatly simplifies the rental process. Without one, some agents simply will not rent vehicles, and others will require prepayment by cash or traveler's checks, as well as a deposit (often around $300). Some do an employment verification and credit check; others don't do background checks, but they reserve the right for the station manager to decide whether to rent to you or not. If you intend to rent a car without a credit card, it's wise to make your plans well in advance.

Most car rental agencies typically request the name and phone number of the place where you're staying. Be aware that many car rental companies are loath to rent to people who list a campground as their address on the island, and a few specifically add 'No Camping Permitted' to their rental contracts.

The following are international companies operating in Honolulu; their cars can be booked from offices around the world. The telephone numbers listed are the Oahu numbers, followed by toll-free numbers in the USA.

Alamo	☎ 833-4585, 800-327-9633
Avis	☎ 834-5536, 800-831-8000
Budget	☎ 537-3600, 800-527-7000
Dollar	☎ 831-2330, 800-367-7006
Hertz	☎ 831-3500, 800-654-3131
National	☎ 831-3800, 800-227-7368

Budget, National, Hertz, Avis and Dollar all have rental cars available at Honolulu International Airport. Alamo has its operations about a mile outside the airport, on the corner of Nimitz Hwy and Ohohia St.

All things being equal, try to rent from a company with its lot inside the airport – not only is it more convenient but, more importantly, on the way back to the airport all the highway signs lead to the in-airport car returns. Having to drive around looking for a car rental agency lot outside the airport can cost you valuable time when you're trying to catch a flight.

In addition to their airport facilities, most of the international companies have multiple branch locations in Waikiki – many in the lobbies of larger hotels. When you make your reservation, keep in mind that the best rates sometimes aren't offered at the smaller branch offices, so even if you're already in Waikiki, it might be worth your while to catch a bus to the airport and pick your car up there – especially for longer rentals or if you're planning on keeping the car until you fly out of Oahu.

Insurance

As for car insurance, rental companies in Hawaii have liability insurance that covers people and property you might hit while driving a rental vehicle. Damage to the rental vehicle itself is not covered, unless you accept the collision damage waiver (CDW) option offered by the rental agency. This added coverage is typically an additional $15 to $17 a day.

The CDW is not really insurance per se, but rather a guarantee that the rental company won't hold you liable for any damages to their car (though even then there are exceptions). If you decline the CDW, you will usually be held liable for any damages up to the full value of the car. If damages do occur and you find yourself in a dispute with the rental company, you can call the state Department of Commerce & Consumer Affairs at ☎ 587-1234 (key in 7222 for recorded information on your legal rights).

If you have collision coverage on your vehicle at home, it might cover damages to car rentals in Hawaii. Check with your insurance company before your trip.

Some credit cards, including most 'gold cards' issued by Visa and MasterCard, offer you reimbursement coverage for collision damages if you rent the car with their credit card and decline the CDW. If your credit card doesn't offer this service, it may be worth changing to one that does. Be aware, however, that most collision coverage provided by a credit card isn't valid for rentals of more than 15 days or for exotic models, jeeps, vans and 4WD vehicles.

Moped

Mopeds are another transportation option, though perhaps a bit daunting for the uninitiated: You have to contend with Honolulu's heavy traffic, which presents a challenge to those unaccustomed to such conditions or to those who don't have sufficient moped experience.

State law requires mopeds to be ridden by one person only and prohibits their use on sidewalks and on freeways. Mopeds must always be driven in single file and may not be driven at speeds in excess of 30mph. In

Hawaii, all mopeds are limited to a maximum 2 horsepower, 50cc. To drive a moped, you must have a valid driver's license. Hawaii residents can drive mopeds at age 15, but those with an out-of-state driver's license must be at least 18 years old.

Blue Sky Rentals (☎ 947-0101), on the ground floor of Inn on the Park Hotel, 1920 Ala Moana Blvd (see Waikiki map), is a good Waikiki spot to rent a moped. The rates, which include tax, are $20 from 8 am to 6 pm, $25 for 24 hours and $105 for a week.

Diamond Head Mopeds (☎ 921-2899), at the corner of Lewers St and Kuhio Ave, also rents mopeds at similar rates (see Waikiki map for location).

Parking

Parking can be a challenge in Honolulu's busiest areas. In Waikiki, most hotels charge $8 to $15 a day for guest parking in their garages. However, if you're willing to go a little out of your way, you can save money.

At the west end of Waikiki, there's a public parking lot at the Ala Wai Yacht Harbor that has free parking for up to a maximum of 24 hours. At the east end of Waikiki, the zoo parking lot on Kapahulu Ave has meters that cost just 25¢ an hour with a four-hour parking limit.

In downtown Honolulu, there's metered parking along Punchbowl St and on Hale-kauwila St opposite the federal building. There are also a limited number of metered spaces in the basement of the state office building on the corner of Beretania and Punchbowl Sts. Both downtown Honolulu and the adjacent Chinatown area also have parking garages that charge by the hour.

Outside of Waikiki and Honolulu, parking is generally free and, with the exception of a few popular beaches, finding a space is seldom a problem.

TAXI

Taxis have meters and charge a flag-down fee of $2 to start, and from there fares increase in 25¢ increments at a rate of $2 per mile. There's an extra charge of 35¢ for each suitcase or backpack.

Taxis are readily available at the airport and larger hotels but are otherwise generally hard to find. To phone for one, try Sida (☎ 836-0011), Charley's (☎ 955-2211), Americabs (☎ 591-8830) or City Taxi (☎ 524-2121). If you're at a phone booth without coins, you can reach City Taxi toll free by calling ☎ 800-359-2121.

BICYCLE

It's possible to cycle your way around Oahu, but there's a lot of traffic to contend with, especially in the greater Honolulu area. Hawaii has been slow to adopt cycle-friendly policies – a few new road projects now include cycle lanes, but such lanes are still relatively rare.

In Waikiki, the best main roads for cyclists are the one-way streets of canalside Ala Wai Blvd and beachside Kalakaua Ave, both of which have minimal cross-traffic.

The State Department of Transportation publishes a free 'Bike Oahu' map with possible routes, divided into those for novice cyclists, those for experienced cyclists and routes that are not bicycle-friendly. In Waikiki, two places to look for the map are the HVCB visitor information center (see the Local Tourist Offices section in the Facts for the Visitor chapter) and Blue Sky Rentals (see the Moped section earlier in this chapter); you can also request a map from the Bicycle Coordinator at the City & County of Honolulu (☎ 527-5044).

If you want to take your bike out of town and want the option of taking the bus for part of the journey, a number of public buses have been equipped with racks that can carry two bicycles. To use the bike rack, first tell the bus driver you will be loading your bike, then secure your bicycle onto the fold-down rack, board the bus and pay the regular fare.

Not all routes have buses with cycle racks, but many of the long-distance routes do, including the Pearl Harbor bus (No 3), the Beach Bus to Hanauma Bay (No 22), the Makaha bus up the Waianae Coast (No

51), both of the Circle Island buses that cover the North Shore and the windward coast (Nos 52 and 55) and the Waimanalo and Sea Life Park buses along southeast Oahu (Nos 57 and 58). For other routes, call TheBus (☎ 848-5555) to determine if a rack-equipped bus is scheduled on the route you plan to take.

The state of Hawaii does not require cyclists to wear helmets, but they are recommended, and some bicycle rental shops, including Blue Sky Rentals, provide them free of charge.

For information on bike riding with a group, see the Cycling section in the Activities chapter.

Rental

Planet Surf (☎ 924-9050), 159 Kaiulani Ave, Waikiki, and opposite Pupukea Beach Park in Waimea, rents bikes from $10 a day. Blue Sky Rentals (☎ 947-0101), 1920 Ala Moana Blvd, Waikiki, has mountain bikes, road bikes and hybrids from $15 for an 8 am to 6 pm rental, $20 for a 24-hour period.

There are a few other rental places in Waikiki that rent bicycles at similar rates; try Diamond Head Mopeds (☎ 921-2899), 408 Lewers St, and Coconut Cruisers (☎ 926-1526), on Koa Ave near Uluniu Ave.

HITCHHIKING

Hitchhiking is uncommon in Hawaii, and results are mixed at best. Hitchhikers should consider each situation carefully before getting in cars, and women should be especially wary of hitching alone.

Hitchhiking is never entirely safe anywhere in the world, and Lonely Planet does not recommend it.

ORGANIZED TOURS

In addition to the following tours, information on guided cycling and hiking tours can be found in the Activities chapter.

Bus Tours

Because Honolulu has such a good public bus system, extensive self-touring, even without a rental car, is a viable option. However,

waiting for buses and walking between the bus stops and the sights does take time, and you can undoubtedly pack much more into a day by joining an organized tour.

Conventional sightseeing tours by van or bus are offered by E Noa Tours (☎ 591-2561), Polynesian Adventure Tours (☎ 833-3000) and Roberts Hawaii (☎ 539-9400).

These companies offer several different tours. Polynesian Adventure Tours, for example, has a half-day Honolulu city tour that includes the main downtown sights, Punchbowl crater and the USS *Arizona* Memorial. They also have another half-day tour of southeast Oahu that takes in Diamond Head, Hanauma Bay, Sandy Beach, Nuuanu Pali Lookout, Queen Emma Summer Palace and Tantalus; each tour costs $22 for adults, $18 for children.

The mainstay for the tour companies, however, are full-day (roughly 8:30 am to 5:30 pm) circle-island tours that average $55 for adults, $25 for children. A typical tour starts out with a visit to Diamond Head crater and a drive past the southeast Oahu sights; goes up the windward coast, taking in the Byodo-In temple in Kaneohe and the Mormon Temple in Laie; circles back along the North Shore, stopping at Sunset Beach and Waimea Valley Adventure Park; and then drives past the pineapple fields of central Oahu on the return to Waikiki. Some tours also include a visit to the Polynesian Cultural Center in Laie.

A good alternative island tour is offered by Alala EcoAdventures, which is geared for those who want to actually take a dip at the beach and explore some of the sights more thoroughly. The tour typically begins with a drive through Waikiki, stopping at Diamond Head and then touring the southeast side of the island, including Hanauma Bay and Makapuu Beach Park. They also visit the pineapple fields of central Oahu and spend time at Haleiwa and Sunset Beach.

The tour is offered a few times a week, lasts all day (generally 10 am to 9 pm), costs just $25 and is booked through Hostelling International Honolulu (☎ 946-0591).

Waikiki Trolley

The Waikiki Trolley is an open-air, trolley-style bus that begins in Waikiki. Its main route, the 'red line,' is geared for tourists following a beaten path around Honolulu's main shopping and sightseeing attractions. There are about two dozen stops, including the Honolulu Zoo, Waikiki Aquarium, Ala Moana Center, Honolulu Academy of Arts, Iolani Palace, Hawaii Maritime Center, Aloha Tower, Bishop Museum, Chinatown and the Ward Centre.

There's also a 'blue line,' which goes east from Waikiki and has a more limited route, stopping at the Honolulu Zoo, Waikiki Aquarium, Hanauma Bay, Halona Blowhole and Sea Life Park. Narration is provided en route and passengers can get off at any stop and pick up the next trolley.

Both lines depart daily from the Royal Hawaiian Shopping Center in Waikiki; the red line leaves every 20 minutes and the blue line leaves hourly, between 8:30 am and 6:30 pm. One-day passes cost $18 for adults and $8 for children for a single line; $30 for adults and $10 for children for both lines. Multi-day passes are also available.

The trolley is convenient if you're sticking solely to its predetermined routes, but it's a pricey alternative to the public bus, which is fairly frequent along these routes and offers a four-day pass for only $10 (see the Bus section earlier in this chapter).

Walking Tours

There are a handful of educational and cultural groups that offer insightful walking tours of Honolulu. The most popular – and the only ones operating on a fixed weekly schedule – are the tours of Chinatown offered by the Chinese Chamber of Commerce and the Hawaii Heritage Center. For details on these two tours, see the Chinatown section of the Honolulu chapter.

More esoteric, and less frequent, are the downtown Honolulu tours that are led by guides from Kapiolani Community College. These have varied historical themes – from queens of old Hawaii to the crime beat of the 1920s. The cost is $25 and the tours typically last two hours, with advance registra-

tion required. Schedules are available from the Office of Continuing Education (☎ 734-9211), Kapiolani Community College, 4403 Diamond Head Rd, Honolulu, HI 96816.

The Mission Houses Museum in Honolulu also offers a two-hour guided walk of the downtown area. The tour is peppered with historical commentary. It costs just $7; call ☎ 531-0481 for more details and the current schedule.

Tours to the Neighbor Islands

Overnighters If you want to visit another island but only have a day or two to spare, it might be worth looking into 'overnighters,' which are handy mini-packaged tours to the Neighbor Islands that include roundtrip airfare, car rental and hotel accommodations. Rates depend on the accommodations you select, with a one-night package typically starting at $130 per person, based on double occupancy. You can add additional days for a fee, usually about $60 per person.

The largest tour companies specializing in overnighters are: Roberts Hawaii (☎ 523-9323 on Oahu, 800-899-9323 from the mainland) and Pleasant Island Holidays (☎ 922-1515).

Cruises American Hawaii Cruises (☎ 800-765-7000), 2100 Nimitz Hwy, Honolulu, HI 96819, operates the cruise ship *Independence*, which makes a seven-day tour around Hawaii. Each Saturday all year round, the ship leaves Honolulu and visits Kauai, Maui and the Big Island before returning to Honolulu.

Cruise rates start at $1400 for the least-expensive inside cabin and go up to $3550 for an outside suite. Fares are per person, based on double occupancy, and there's an additional $85 for port charges.

Although more modest than the ultramodern mammoths that cruise the Caribbean, the *Independence* is a full-fledged cruise ship, 682 feet long, with lavish buffet meals, swimming pools and the like. It carries a crew of 325 and 1021 passengers.

For information on short cruises that usually stay close to Oahu's shores, see the Activities chapter.

Honolulu

Highlights

- Touring gracious Iolani Palace, home of Hawaii's last monarchs
- Strolling among the lofty trees and rare tropical plants in Foster Botanical Garden
- Enjoying a steaming bowl of noodle soup in one of Chinatown's many eateries
- Spending the day browsing in one of Honolulu's fascinating museums
- Hiking in the lush green Tantalus area

Honolulu is the only major city in Hawaii. It has a population of nearly 400,000 and is the state's center of business, culture and politics. It's been the capital of Hawaii since 1845.

Home to people from throughout the Pacific, Honolulu is a city composed of minorities, without an ethnic majority. Honolulu's ethnic diversity can be seen on almost every corner – the sushi shop next door to the Vietnamese bakery, the Catholic church around the block from the Chinese Buddhist temple and the rainbow of schoolchildren waiting for the bus.

Honolulu offers a wide range of things to see and do. It boasts a lovely city beach, some good museums, elegant public gardens and an abundance of good restaurants. By and large, it's an easy city to explore. The largest concentration of historical and cultural sights are clustered in downtown Honolulu and adjacent Chinatown, which are well suited for getting about on foot.

Because of heavy traffic and tight parking in downtown Honolulu and Chinatown during the week, it's best to take advantage of the city's excellent public bus system, though traffic is seldom a problem in the evening or on the weekends. Lots of city bus routes converge downtown – so many that

Hotel St, which begins downtown and crosses Chinatown, is restricted to bus traffic only. See the Getting Around sections for each neighborhood for details.

Information

The following information pertains to locations in downtown Honolulu and Chinatown. For information on places in Waikiki, see the Waikiki chapter.

Money There is a downtown branch of the Bank of Hawaii at 111 S King St. It's open 7:30 am to 3 pm Monday to Thursday, 7:30 am to 4:30 pm Friday. In Chinatown, the Bank of Hawaii, 101 N King St, is open 8:30 am to 4 pm Monday to Thursday, 8:30 am to 6 pm on Friday and 9 am to noon on Saturday.

Post & Communications The downtown branch of the Honolulu post office is on the Richards St side of the Old Federal Building. It's open 8 am to 4:30 pm weekdays. A small post office in the Chinatown Cultural Plaza is open from 9 am to 4 pm Monday to Friday and 9 am to noon on Saturday.

You can go online and check email at Kinko's (☎ 528-7171), 1050 Bishop St, which is open 24 hours a day and charges 20¢ a minute. You can also try your luck at using one of the online computers at the public library – officially you need a library card to do so, but they're sometimes relaxed on the policy when it's not busy. The main library is in downtown Honolulu, next to Iolani Palace.

For additional information on post and communications, see the Facts for the Visitor chapter, earlier in this book.

Airline Offices A number of airlines have ticket offices in the downtown Honolulu area. Within a two-minute walk of the intersection of Bishop and S Hotel Sts, you'll find

United Airlines, Northwest Airlines, Delta Air Lines, Aloha Airlines and Hawaiian Airlines. See the Toll-Free Numbers directory at the back of this book for the 800 numbers of the major airlines.

DOWNTOWN HONOLULU (MAP 2)

Downtown Honolulu is a hodgepodge of past and present, with both sleek high-rises and stately Victorian-era buildings. Architecturally, the area has some striking juxtapositions – there's a 19th-century royal palace, a modernistic state capitol, a coral-block New England missionary church and a Spanish-style city hall all within sight of one another.

In addition to sightseeing, you can attend a Friday noon band concert on the palace lawn, lounge in the courtyard of Hawaii's central library or take in the sweeping view of the city from the top of the Aloha Tower.

Walking Tour

Downtown Honolulu is ideal for strolling, with its most handsome buildings within easy walking distance of each other. You could make a quick tour in a couple of hours, but if you're up for more leisurely exploration, it's possible to spend the better part of a day poking around (details on each sight follow this section).

A good starting place for a walking tour is **Iolani Palace**, the area's pivotal spot, both historically and geographically. If time permits, joining a guided tour of Iolani Palace offers a glimpse into Hawaii's royal past. In any case, you are free to stroll around the palace grounds. Behind the palace, you will find a **statue of Queen Liliuokalani**. From here, you can continue to the **state capitol**. Enter the capitol through the rear of the building and exit on the Beretania St side, which is opposite the **war memorial**.

After turning left up Beretania St, you'll pass Washington Place and **St Andrew's Cathedral**. In the lobby of the **State Office Tower**, directly opposite the cathedral, you'll find a tile mural depicting Hawaiian royalty. From there, walk down Richards St past **No 1 Capitol District**, which houses more state

government offices; the **Alii Place Building**, which has a Hawaiiana mural above the entrance; and the attractive **YWCA** and **Hawaiian Electric Company** buildings.

If you care to make the walk longer, turn right on Merchant St to see the historic buildings that house some of Hawaii's largest corporations and the skyscrapers that have sprung up around them. The loftiest and most notable high-rise is the new **First Hawaiian Center**, which houses an art gallery.

Otherwise, turn left down Merchant St, where you'll see the **Old Federal Building**, **Aliiolani Hale** and the **statue of Kamehameha the Great**, before making another left on Mililani St and an immediate right on S King St, which will bring you to the historic **Kawaiahao Church** and the **Mission Houses Museum**.

As you make your way back to Iolani Palace, you can visit two more period buildings on Punchbowl St: **Honolulu Hale** (City Hall) and the **Hawaii State Library**.

Iolani Palace

Iolani Palace is the only royal palace in the USA. It was the official residence of King Kalakaua and Queen Kapiolani from 1882 to 1891 and of Queen Liliuokalani, Kalakaua's sister and successor, for two years after that.

Following the overthrow of the Hawaiian kingdom in 1893, the palace became the capitol – first for the republic, then for the territory and later for the state of Hawaii.

It wasn't until 1969 that the current state capitol was built and the legislators moved out of their cramped palace quarters. The senate had been meeting in the palace dining room and the house of representatives in the throne room. By the time they left, Iolani Palace was in shambles, the grand koa staircase was termite-ridden and the Douglas fir floors pitted and gouged.

After extensive renovations topping $7 million, the palace was largely restored to its former glory, and in 1978, it opened as a museum. Today, visitors must wear booties over their shoes to protect the highly polished wooden floors.

The banyan tree between Iolani Palace and the capitol was planted by Queen Kapiolani.

Iolani Palace was modern for its day. Every bedroom had its own full bath with hot and cold running water, copper-lined tubs, a flushing toilet and a bidet. According to the palace tour leaders, electric lights replaced the palace gas lamps a full four years before the White House in Washington, DC, got electricity.

The **throne room**, decorated in red and gold, features the original thrones of the king and queen and a *kapu* stick made of the long, spiral, ivory tusk of a narwhal. In addition to celebrations full of pomp and pageantry, the throne room was used by King Kalakaua for dancing his favorite western dances – the polka, the waltz and the Virginia reel, which he danced into the wee hours of the morning.

Not all the events that took place there were joyous. Two years after she was dethroned, Queen Liliuokalani was brought back to the palace and tried for treason in the throne room. In a move calculated to humiliate the Hawaiian people, she spent nine months as a prisoner in Iolani Palace, her former home.

Guided tours of the palace leave every 15 minutes from 9 am to 2:15 pm Tuesday to Saturday and cost $8 for adults, $3 for children ages five to 12. Children younger than five are not admitted. The admission price includes a 15-minute video, shown in the barracks, on palace history. The tours themselves last 45 minutes. Sometimes you can join a tour on the spot, but it's advisable to make advance reservations by phoning ☎ 522-0832. The palace is wheelchair accessible.

The **palace grounds** have a lengthy history. Before Iolani Palace was built, there was a simpler house on these grounds that was used by King Kamehameha III, who ruled for 30 years (1825-54). In ancient times it was the site of a *heiau* (temple).

The palace ticket window and a gift shop are in the former **barracks** of the Royal Household Guards, a building that looks oddly like the uppermost layer of a medieval fort that's been sliced off and plopped on the ground.

The **domed pavilion** on the grounds was originally built for the coronation of King Kalakaua in 1883 and is still used for the inauguration of governors and for concerts by the Royal Hawaiian Band.

The **grassy mound** surrounded by a wrought iron fence was the site of a royal tomb until 1865, when the remains of King Kamehameha II and Queen Kamamalu (who both died of measles in England in 1824) were moved to the Royal Mausoleum in Nuuanu. The huge **banyan tree** between the palace and the state capitol is thought to have been planted by Queen Kapiolani.

For more on Hawaii's royalty, see the History section in the Facts about Oahu chapter.

State Capitol

Hawaii's state capitol is not your standard gold-domed building. Built in the 1960s, it was a grandiose attempt at a 'theme' design.

Its two central legislative chambers are cone-shaped to represent volcanoes; the rotunda is open to let gentle trade winds blow through; the supporting columns represent palm trees; and the whole structure is encircled by a large pool symbolizing the ocean surrounding Hawaii.

Unfortunately, the building not only symbolizes the elements, but it has been quite effective in drawing them in. The pool tends to collect brackish water; rain pouring into the rotunda necessitated the sealing of many of the skylights; and Tadashi Sato's 'Aquarius' floor mosaic, meant to show the changing colors and patterns of Hawaii's seas, got so weathered it had to be reconstructed. After two decades of trying unsuccessfully to deal with all of the problems on a piecemeal basis, the state put the facility through a thorough renovation (completed in 1997). Visitors are free to walk through the rotunda and peer through viewing windows into the two legislative chambers.

In front of the capitol is a **statue of Father Damien**, the Belgian priest who in 1873 volunteered to work among the lepers of Molokai. He died of the disease 16 years later at age 49. The stylized sculpture was created by Venezuelan artist Marisol Escubar.

In the back of the capitol, the **Queen Liliuokalani statue** depicts Hawaii's last queen. It faces Washington Place, Liliuokalani's home and place of exile for more than 20 years. The bronze statue holds the Hawaiian constitution that Queen Liliuokalani wrote in 1893 (it would have restored the monarchy's powers, but US businessmen, in reaction to it, declared the monarchy overthrown); 'Aloha Oe,' a popular hymn that she composed; and 'Kumulipo,' the Hawaiian chant of creation. The statue is often draped with leis of hibiscus or maile.

Directly opposite the state capitol is a **sculptured eternal torch** – a war memorial dedicated to soldiers who died in WWII. It sits between two underground garage entrances on Beretania St.

Washington Place

Washington Place, the governor's official residence, is a large colonial-style building surrounded by stately trees, built in 1846 by US sea captain John Dominis. The captain's son, also named John, became the governor of Oahu and married the Hawaiian princess who later became Queen Liliuokalani. After the queen was dethroned, she lived at Washington Place in exile until her death in 1917.

A plaque near the sidewalk on the left side of Washington Place is inscribed with the words to 'Aloha Oe,' the anthem composed by Queen Liliuokalani.

The large tree in front of the house on the right side of the walkway is a pili nut tree, recognizable by the buttresslike roots extending from the base of its trunk. In Southeast Asia the nuts of these trees are used to produce oil.

St Andrew's Cathedral

King Kamehameha IV, who reigned from 1855 to 1863, was attracted by the royal trappings of the Church of England and decided to build his own cathedral in Hawaii. He and his consort, Queen Emma, founded the Anglican Church of Hawaii in 1858.

The cathedral's cornerstone was finally laid in 1867 by King Kamehameha V. Kamehameha IV had died four years earlier on St Andrew's Day – hence the church's name.

St Andrew's is on the corner of Alakea and Beretania Sts. The architecture is French Gothic, and materials for the cathedral were shipped in pieces from England. Its most striking feature is the impressive window of handblown stained glass that forms the western facade and reaches from the floor to the eaves. In the right section of the glass you can see the Reverend Thomas Staley, the first bishop sent to Hawaii by Queen Victoria, alongside Kamehameha IV and Queen Emma.

Richard St Buildings

The elegant five-story building on Richards St opposite the state capitol houses the offices of the state legislature. This building, called **No 1 Capital District**, has something of the appearance of a Spanish mission, with courtyards and ceramic tile walls and floors. Built in 1928, it served as the YMCA Armed Services building for more than five decades.

Also noteworthy is the three-story **YWCA** at 1040 Richards St. Built in 1927, it's the work of Julia Morgan, the renowned architect who designed the William Randolph Hearst San Simeon estate in California.

Farther down Richard St, at the corner of King St, is the **Hawaiian Electric Company**'s four-story administration building. The building is of Spanish colonial architecture and has an arched entryway and ornate period lamps hanging from hand-painted ceilings. The entrance leads to the customer-service department, so it's fine to walk in and take a look.

Diagonally opposite, on the corner of Richards and Merchant Sts, is the **Old Federal Building**, another interesting edifice with Spanish colonial features. Completed in 1922, it holds a post office and customs house.

Aliiolani Hale

Aliiolani Hale (House of Heavenly Kings) was the first major government building constructed by the Hawaiian monarchy. The building has housed the Hawaii Supreme Court since its construction in 1874 and was once also home to the state legislature. The building has a distinctive clock tower, graceful stairwells and a stained-glass skylight. Aliiolani Hale was designed by Australian architect Thomas Rowe to be a royal palace, although it was never used as such.

It was on the steps of Aliiolani Hale, in January 1893, that Sanford Dole proclaimed the establishment of a provisional government and the overthrow of the Hawaiian monarchy.

The **statue of Kamehameha the Great** stands in front of Aliiolani Hale, opposite Iolani Palace. On June 11, which is a state holiday honoring Kamehameha, the statue is ceremoniously draped with layer upon layer of 12-foot leis.

The Kamehameha statue was cast in 1880 in Florence, Italy, by American sculptor Thomas Gould. The current statue is actually a recast, as the original statue was lost at sea near the Falkland Islands. The sunken statue, which was recovered from the ocean floor after the second version was dedicated in 1883, eventually completed its trip to Hawaii. Rather than exchange the statues, the original was sent to Kohala, the Big Island birthplace of Kamehameha, where it now stands.

Kawaiahao Church

Oahu's oldest church, on the corner of Punchbowl and King Sts, was built on the site where the first missionaries constructed a thatched house of worship shortly after their arrival in 1820. The original church was an impressive structure that measured 54 feet by 22 feet and seated 300 people on *lauhala* mats.

Still, thatch wasn't quite what the missionaries had in mind. They wanted a western-style building, so they designed a typical New England-style Congregational church with simple Gothic influences.

Built between 1838 and 1842, the church is made of 14,000 hefty coral slabs, many weighing more than 1000lb. Hawaiian divers chiseled the huge blocks of coral out of Honolulu's underwater reef.

The clock tower was donated by Kamehameha III, and the clock, built in Boston and installed in 1850, still keeps accurate time. The interior of the church is breezy and cool. The rear seats, marked by *kahili* (feather) staffs and velvet padding, were for royalty and are still reserved for descendants of royalty today. The church is usually open to visitors 8 am to 4 pm.

The **tomb of King Lunalilo**, the successor to Kamehameha V, is on the church grounds at the main entrance. Lunalilo ruled for only one year before his death in 1874 at the age of 39.

At the rear of the church is a **cemetery** where many of the early missionaries are buried, along with other important westerners of the day, including the infamous Sanford Dole. Dole played a key role in overthrowing Queen Liliuokalani, and he went on to become the first territorial governor.

Mission Houses Museum

Three of the original buildings of the Sandwich Islands Mission headquarters still stand: the Frame House (built in 1821), the Chamberlain House (1831) and the Printing Office (1841). They're open to the public as the Mission Houses Museum, 553 S King St. The houses are authentically furnished with handmade quilts on all the beds, settees in the parlor and iron cooking pots in the big stone fireplaces.

The first missionaries packed more than their bags when they left Boston – they actually brought a prefabricated wooden house, now called the **Frame House**, around the Horn with them. Designed to withstand cold New England winter winds, the house's small windows block out Honolulu's cooling trade winds instead, keeping the two-story house hot and stuffy. It is the oldest wooden structure in Hawaii.

The coral-block **Chamberlain House** was the early mission storeroom, a necessity as Honolulu had few shops in those days. Upstairs are hoop barrels, wooden crates packed with dishes and a big desk with pigeonhole dividers and the quill pen Levi Chamberlain used to work on accounts. Levi was the person appointed by the mission to buy, store and dole out supplies to the missionary families, who each had an allowance. His account books show that in the early missionary years, 25¢ would buy either 1 gallon of oil, one penknife or two slates.

The **Printing Office** housed the lead-type press that was used to print the Bible in the Hawaiian language.

The Mission Houses Museum (☎ 531-0481) is open 9 am to 4 pm Tuesday to Saturday. Admission is $6 for adults and $2 for children (children younger than six are admitted for free). Although you can explore the visitor center and the Chamberlain House on your own, the Printing Office and Frame House can only be seen with a guide. Guided tours, which last an hour, are usually given at 9:30 and 11 am and 1 and 2:30 pm, but the schedule can vary, so it's a good idea to call ahead.

Honolulu Hale

City Hall, also known as Honolulu Hale, is largely of Spanish mission design, with a tiled roof, decorative balconies, arches and pillars. Built in 1927, it bears the initials of CW Dickey, Honolulu's most famous architect of the day. The building, which is on the National Register of Historic Places, has frescoes by Einar Peterson and an open-air courtyard that's sometimes used for concerts and art exhibits.

Hawaii State Library

The central branch of the statewide library system, on the corner of King and Punchbowl Sts, is in a beautifully restored early-20th-century building with a grand column facade. Its collection of over half a million titles is the state's best and includes comprehensive Hawaii and Pacific sections.

The library (☎ 586-3500) is open 9 am to 5 pm on Monday, Friday and Saturday; 9 am to 8 pm on Tuesday and Thursday; and 10 am to 5 pm on Wednesday.

Next door, the **Hawaii State Archives** is the repository for official government documents and an extensive photo collection. It's open to the public for research 8 am to 4:30 pm weekdays.

First Hawaiian Center

The new 30-story First Hawaiian Center, Hawaii's tallest building and the headquarters of the First Hawaiian Bank, occupies the block surrounded by King, Bishop, Merchant and Alakea streets.

The building contains a quality gallery, operated in conjunction with the Contemporary Museum, that features changing exhibits of modern Hawaiian art. The gallery is open free to the public 8:30 am to 4 pm Monday to Thursday and 8:30 am to 6 pm on Friday.

The building itself has some notable features, including a four-story-high glass wall containing 195 prisms that was designed by New York glass artist Jamie Carpenter. Also worth a look is *Enchanting Garden,* a flowing-water sculpture created by Satoru Abe (it is near the King St entrance).

Other Historic Buildings

The **old Honolulu Police Station** (1931), on the corner of Bethel and Merchant Sts, has beautiful interior ceramic tile work in earthen tones on its counters and walls. It now houses the state departments of housing and finance. Also worth a look is the old **Honolulu Publishing Building** across the street.

The four-story **Alexander & Baldwin Building**, on the corner of Bishop and Queen Sts, was built in 1929. Tropical fruit and the Chinese characters for prosperity and long life are carved into the columns at the Bishop St entrance. Inside the portico are interesting ceramic tile murals of Hawaiian fish. Samuel Alexander and Henry Baldwin, both sons of missionaries, vaulted to prominence in the sugar industry and created one of Hawaii's 'Big Five' controlling corporations. The other four – Theo Davies, Castle & Cooke, Amfac and C Brewer – all built their headquarters within a few blocks of here.

The four-story, 70-year-old **Dillingham Building**, on the corner of Bishop and Queen Sts, is built in the Italian Renaissance style, with arches, marble walls, elaborate elevator doors and an arty brick floor. This period building is mirrored in the reflective glass of the adjacent 30-story Grosvenor Center – a true study in contrasts.

Aloha Tower

Built in 1926 at the edge of the downtown district, the 10-story Aloha Tower is a Honolulu landmark that for years was the city's tallest building. In the days when tourists traveled by ship, this icon of pre-war Hawaii – with its four-sided clock tower inscribed with the word 'Aloha' – greeted all arriving passengers. Today visiting cruise ships still disembark at the terminal beneath the tower.

Take a look at the interior of the cruise ship terminal, which has wall-to-wall murals depicting early-20th-century Honolulu life. The scenes include hula dancers, Hawaiian kids diving off the pier and mainland passengers disembarking from one of the San Francisco-to-Honolulu ships that docked here during that era.

The Aloha Tower's top-floor observation deck offers a sweeping 360° view of Honolulu's large commercial harbor and downtown area. An elevator zips visitors to the top from 9 am to sunset daily. It's not the most scenic angle on the city, but it's interesting nonetheless, and there's no admission charge.

In addition to the cruise ship terminal and the tower itself, the complex holds the Aloha Tower Marketplace, a shopping center with nearly 100 kiosks, stores and eateries. Fittingly, some of the shops specialize in Hawaiiana items, and most of the places to eat have harbor views. For information on these restaurants, see the Places to Eat section later in this chapter.

Aloha Tower is at Pier 9, off Ala Moana Blvd at the harbor end of Fort St. From Waikiki it can be reached by public bus Nos 19 and 20.

You can also get to Aloha Tower by a trolley-style bus that's marked 'Aloha Tower Marketplace.' The trolley (☎ 528-5700) runs between Waikiki and the Aloha Tower every 20 minutes 9 am to 9 pm daily and costs $2 each way. Stops include the Hilton Hawaiian Village, the Waikiki police station on Kalakaua Ave and the Waikiki Surf hotel on Kuhio Ave.

By car from Waikiki, simply head west on Ala Moana Blvd. There's parking directly in front of Aloha Tower Marketplace and southeast of the Hawaii Maritime Center at Pier 6. During peak hours on weekdays, both lots charge $4 for up to three hours and $1 per 20 minutes thereafter; have your ticket validated at a shop or restaurant and the fee is reduced to $2 for the first three hours. There's a flat rate of just $2 all day on weekends and after 4:30 pm on weekdays.

Hawaii Maritime Center

The Hawaii Maritime Center (☎ 536-6373) is on Honolulu Harbor's Pier 7, on the Diamond Head side of the Aloha Tower. The center has a maritime museum and is home to the *Falls of Clyde*, said to be the world's last four-masted, four-rigged ship. The berth for the double-hulled sailing canoe *Hokulea* is also here.

The main museum has an interesting mishmash of maritime displays and artifacts, including a good whaling-era exhibition and model replicas of ships. There's a reproduction of a Matson liner stateroom and some interesting old photos of Waikiki in the days when just the Royal Hawaiian and the Moana hotels shared the shore with Diamond Head. Both hotels belonged to Matson, which spearheaded tourism in Hawaii. Ironically, it sold out to the Sheraton hotel chain in 1959, just before the jet age and statehood launched sleepy tourism into a booming industry.

The 266-foot iron-hulled *Falls of Clyde*, built in Glasgow, Scotland, in 1878, is permanently on display. In 1899, Matson Navigation bought the ship and added a deckhouse, and the *Falls* began carrying sugar and passengers between Hilo and San Francisco. It was later converted into an oil tanker and eventually stripped down to a barge.

After being abandoned in Ketchikan, Alaska, where it had been relegated to the lowly function of a floating oil storage tank, the *Falls* was towed to Seattle. A group of Hawaiians raised funds to rescue the ship in 1963, just before it was scheduled to be sunk to create a breakwater off Vancouver. With the aid of the Bishop Museum, the *Falls* was eventually brought to Honolulu and restored. It is now registered as a National Historic Landmark. Visitors can stroll the deck and walk down into the cargo holds.

The 60-foot *Hokulea* was constructed to resemble the type of ship used by Polynesians in their migrations. It has made a number of voyages from Hawaii to the South Pacific, retracing the routes of the early Polynesian seafarers and using age-old methods of navigation, most notably wave patterns and the position of the stars. When in port, the canoe is docked beside the museum.

The Hawaii Maritime Center is open 8:30 am to 5 pm daily. Admission, which includes boarding the *Falls*, costs $7.50 for adults, $4.50 for children ages six to 17 and free for children under six.

To get there, take bus No 19 or 20 from Waikiki. By car, it's off Ala Moana Blvd, about a mile northwest of Ward Warehouse. There's free parking for museum visitors on Richards St, just east of the museum.

Fort St Mall

Fort St is a pedestrian shopping mall lined with an ever-growing number of high-rises. Although the mall is not interesting in itself, if you are downtown, it is a reasonable place to eat. It is not as good as Chinatown, but it is a few blocks closer to downtown Honolulu.

Hawaii Pacific University, a small but expanding private school, has much of its campus at the north end of the mall.

The **Cathedral of Our Lady of Peace**, the center of the Roman Catholic Church in Hawaii, is at the Beretania St end of the Fort St Mall. Built of coral blocks in 1843, it's older and more ornate than St Andrew's Cathedral.

Father Damien, who later served Molokai's leprosy colony, was ordained at the cathedral in 1864.

Getting Around

If you're heading to the Iolani Palace area from Waikiki, the bus No 2 is the most frequent and convenient bus. If you're going directly to Aloha Tower Marketplace or the Hawaii Maritime Center from Waikiki, take bus No 19 or 20 or the Aloha Tower trolley (see the Aloha Tower section for more details). For additional information on the bus system, see the Bus section in the Getting Around chapter.

If you drive, there's metered parking along Punchbowl St and on Halekauwila St opposite the Prince Kuhio Federal Building. There are also a limited number of metered spaces in the basement of the state office building on the corner of Beretania and Punchbowl Sts.

CHINATOWN (MAP 2)

A visit to Chinatown is a bit like a journey to Asia – although it's predominantly Chinese, it has Vietnamese, Thai and Filipino influences as well.

Chinatown is busy and colorful. It has a lively market that could be right off a back street in Hong Kong; fire-breathing dragons coil around the red pillars outside the Bank of Hawaii; and good, cheap ethnic restaurants abound. You can get a tattoo, consult with a herbalist, munch on moon cakes or slurp a steaming bowl of Vietnamese soup. There are temples, shrines, noodle factories, antique shops and art galleries to explore.

On Chinatown's northern boundary is a former royal estate that now encompasses the Foster Botanical Garden, the city's finest botanical garden. It offers a pleasant contrast to the buzz of activity found in the markets and along the busy streets.

Walking Tour

Chinatown is one of the most intriguing quarters of the city for sauntering about. This is best done in the daytime, not only because that's when the markets and shops are open, but also because Chinatown has seen a rise in nighttime youth gang activity. More detailed descriptions of most of the places mentioned here follow this section.

Chinatown is a fun place to poke around on your own. Although you could start a walking tour at virtually any street corner, a good spot to begin a rough loop route is in front of the **Hawaii Theatre** on the corner of Bethel and Pauahi Sts. From there proceed up Pauahi St and make a left on **Nuuanu Ave**, which has a handful of historic buildings.

Then turn right onto N Hotel St, toward the center of Chinatown. In contrast to the creeping gentrification that marks the downtown edge of Chinatown, N Hotel St still bears witness to Honolulu's seamier side. Here you'll find darkened doorways advertising 'video peeps' for 25¢ and bawdy nightspots with names like Risqué Theatre and Club Hubba Hubba.

At **Maunakea St**, turn left and you're in the heart of Chinatown, with its herbalists, noodle shops and the bustling **Oahu Market**. At the intersection of N King and River Sts, there are some excellent neighborhood restaurants where you could stop for a quick bite to eat. Continue walking northeast along **River St**, which turns into a pedestrian

mall, passes more restaurants and a couple of religious sites and then terminates opposite the entrance of the **Foster Botanical Garden**.

After touring the gardens and the nearby **Kuan Yin Temple**, you could reenter the main Chinatown district by heading back on Maunakea St. At the intersection of Maunakea and N Beretania, you'll find rows of small lei shops where lei makers deftly string flowers and heady fragrances fill the air. (Note: If you're planning on taking a lei home as a souvenir, be aware that there are agricultural restrictions against taking gardenia, jade vine or roses out of the state, even in leis. However, most other fresh flowers and foliage are okay.)

In addition to exploring on your own, two organizations offer weekly Chinatown walking tours. Keep in mind, however, that it can feel a bit touristy being led around in a group. Still, the guides provide a commentary with historical insights, and they often take you to a few places you're unlikely to walk into otherwise.

The Hawaii Heritage Center (☎ 521-2749) leads walking tours of Chinatown from 9:30 to 11:30 am on Friday for $5. Reservations are not taken; meet on the sidewalk in front of Ramsay Galleries at 1128 Smith St.

The Chinese Chamber of Commerce (☎ 533-3181) leads walking tours of Chinatown from 9:30 am to noon on Tuesday for $5. Meet at the chamber office, 42 N King St.

Hawaii Theatre

The neoclassical Hawaii Theatre (☎ 528-0506), 1130 Bethel St, first opened in 1922 with silent films playing to the tunes of a pipe organ. Dubbed the 'Pride of the Pacific,' it ran continuous shows during WWII, but the development of mall cinemas in the 1970s was its undoing.

After closing in 1984, the theater's future looked dim, even though it was on the National Register of Historic Places. So theater buffs came to the rescue, forming a nonprofit group and purchasing the property from the Bishop Estate. They raised enough money from donations and grants

The Big Fire

Around 1860, Chinese immigrants who had worked off their sugarcane plantation contracts began settling in Chinatown and opening up small businesses.

In December 1899 the bubonic plague broke out in the area. The 7000 Chinese, Hawaiians and Japanese who made the crowded neighborhood their home were cordoned off and forbidden to leave. As more plague cases arose, the board of health decided to conduct controlled burns of infected homes.

On January 20, 1900, the fire brigade set fire to a building on the corner of Beretania St and Nuuanu Ave. The wind suddenly picked up, and the fire spread out of control, racing toward the waterfront. To make matters worse, police guards stationed inside the plague area attempted to stop quarantined residents from fleeing. Nearly 40 acres of Chinatown burned to the ground.

Not everyone thought the fire was accidental. Just the year before, Chinese immigration into Hawaii was halted by the US annexation of the islands, and Chinatown itself was prime real estate on the edge of the burgeoning downtown district. Despite the adverse climate, the residents of Chinatown held their own and a new Chinatown arose from the ashes.

In the 1940s, thousands of American GIs walked the streets of Chinatown before being shipped off to Iwo Jima and Guadalcanal. Many spent their last days of freedom in Chinatown's 'body houses,' pool halls and tattoo parlors.

to undertake an extensive multimillion-dollar restoration.

The 1400-seat theater has a lovely interior, with trompe-l'oeil mosaics and bas-relief depicting scenes from Shakespearean plays. It reopened in 1996 for dance, drama and music performances and is now one of the leading entertainment venues in Honolulu.

One-hour guided tours, emphasizing the theater's history, art and architecture, are offered on the first and third Tuesday of every month at 11 am and 2 pm; there's a $5 fee to join the tour.

Nuuanu Ave

The **Chinatown Police Station**, on the corner of N Hotel St and Nuuanu Ave in the Perry Block Building (circa 1888), has enough 1920s atmosphere to resemble a set from *The Untouchables*.

Just down the street is the **Pantheon Bar**, now abandoned but noteworthy as the oldest watering hole in Honolulu and a favorite of sailors in days past.

Across the street, **Lai Fong Department Store**, 1118 Nuuanu Ave, sells antiques, knickknacks and old postcards of Hawaii dating back to the first half of the 20th century. Even walking into the store itself is a bit like stepping back into the 1940s. Lai Fong's, which has been in the same family for 70 years, also sells Chinese silks and brocades by the yard and makes silk dresses to order.

There are two noteworthy **art galleries** on this street. At 1164 Nuuanu Ave, you'll find the gallery of Pegge Hopper, whose prints of voluptuous Hawaiian women adorn many a wall in the islands. Sisu Gallery, next door at 1160 Nuuanu Ave, features avant-garde exhibits ranging from photo art to sculpture.

Incidentally, the **granite-block sidewalks** along Nuuanu Ave were made from the discarded ballasts of ships that brought tea from China in the 19th century.

Maunakea St

On the corner of N Hotel and Maunakea Sts is **Wo Fat**, a former restaurant with a facade that resembles a Chinese temple. Although its glory days have faded, it stands as one of Chinatown's oldest buildings, erected just after the fire of 1900.

If you're up for a snack, **Shung Chong Yuein**, 1027 Maunakea St, sells delicious moon cakes, almond cookies and other pastries at reasonable prices. This is the place to buy dried and sugared foods – everything

[Continued on page 129]

Honolulu Map Section

NED FRIARY

MAP 1 GREATER HONOLULU

To Pearl Harbor

Salt Lake

Hia Aloha Park

Moanalua Gardens

Fort Shafter Army Reservation

Kalihi Valley Park

Halsey Terrace Naval Housing

Puuloa Rd

78

Kuhio Park

Kalihi St

Lunalilo Fwy

63

Nimitz Hwy

Kamehameha Park

1 ■
2 ▼ ■ 3
Ualena St 4 5 6
Koapaka St
Aolele St

Lagoon Drive

7 ■

Keehi Lagoon Park

90

N King St

8

9 ▼

H1

Lanakila Park

Dillingham Blvd

Nimitz Hwy

Honolulu Community College

Vineyard Blvd

Honolulu International Airport

Sand Island Access Rd

Kapalama Military Reservation

92

Kapalama Basin

Iwilei Rd

Pacific St

Beret Par

N Beretania St

Aala Park

CHINA TOWN

Keehi Lagoon

Kalihi Channel

Kalihi Channel

Sand Island

Honolulu Harbor

10

Restaurant Row

Sand Island State Recreation Area

Kakaako Waterfront State Park

Mamala Bay

PLACES TO STAY
1 Holiday Inn
3 Best Western Plaza Hotel
5 Nimitz Shower Tree
7 Pacific Marina Inn

PLACES TO EAT
4 Nimitz Mart
9 Helena's Hawaiian Foods
12 Hale Vietnam
13 3660 On The Rise

OTHER
2 Gas Station
6 Alamo Car Rental
8 Bishop Museum
10 Aloha Tower
11 Movie Museum

0   1   2 km
0   .5   1 mile

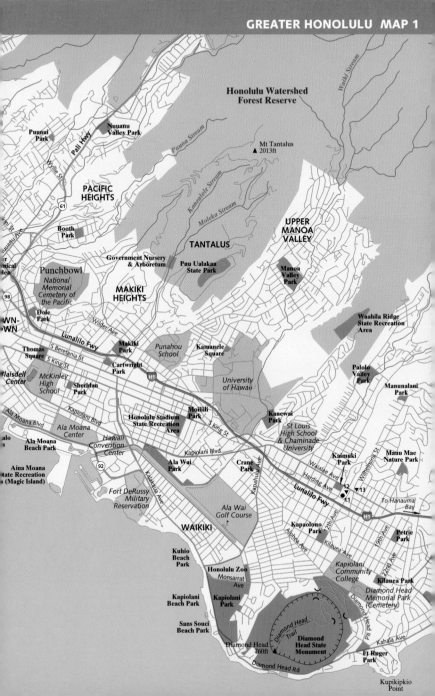

Honolulu Watershed
Forest Reserve

Weliki Stream

Puunui
Park

Nuuanu
Valley Park

Pali Hwy

Pauna Stream

Mt Tantalus
▲ 2013ft

61

PACIFIC
HEIGHTS

Kaneaiole Stream

Moleka Stream

UPPER
MANOA
VALLEY

Booth
Park

Government Nursery
& Arboretum

TANTALUS

Nuuanu Ave

Puu Ualakaa
State Park

Manoa
Valley
Park

mical
ch

Punchbowl

98

National
Memorial
Cemetery of
the Pacific

MAKIKI
HEIGHTS

Waahila Ridge
State Recreation
Area

Dole
Park

Wilder Ave

Punahou
School

Kamanele
Square

Palolo
Valley
Park

WN-
WN

Lunalilo Fwy

S Beretania St

Makiki
Park

Manunalani
Park

Thomas
Square

S King St

Cartwright
Park

University
of Hawaii

Kanewai
Park

Maau Mae
Nature Park

laisdell
Center

McKinley
High
School

Sheridan
Park

H1

St Louis
High School
& Chaminade
University

alo

Kapiolani Blvd

Honolulu Stadium
State Recreation
Area

Moiliili
Park

S King St

Ala Moana Blvd

Ala Moana
Center

Ala Moana
Beach Park

Hawaii
Convention
Center

Kapiolani Blvd

Crane
Park

Kaimuki
Park

Harding Ave

Waialae Ave

Whitmore St

Aina Moana
ate Recreation
a (Magic Island)

92

Ala Wai
Park

Kapahulu Ave

Lunalilo Fwy

▼12
●
▲11

▼13

Kalakaua Ave

Fort DeRussy
Military
Reservation

Ala Wai Golf Course

H1

To Hanauma
Bay

WAIKIKI

Kapaolono
Park

12th Ave

Kilauea Ave

19th Ave

22nd Ave

Petrie
Park

Kuhio
Beach
Park

Honolulu Zoo

Monsarrat
Ave

Aloha Ave

Kapiolani
Community
College

Kilauea Park

Kapiolani
Beach Park

Kapiolani
Park

Diamond Head
Memorial Park
(Cemetery)

Diamond Head Rd

Kahala Ave

Sans Souci
Beach Park

Diamond Head
Trail

Diamond
Head State
Monument

Diamond Head
760ft

Ft Ruger
Park

Diamond Head Rd

Kupikipkio
Point

MAP 2 DOWNTOWN HONOLULU & CHINATOWN

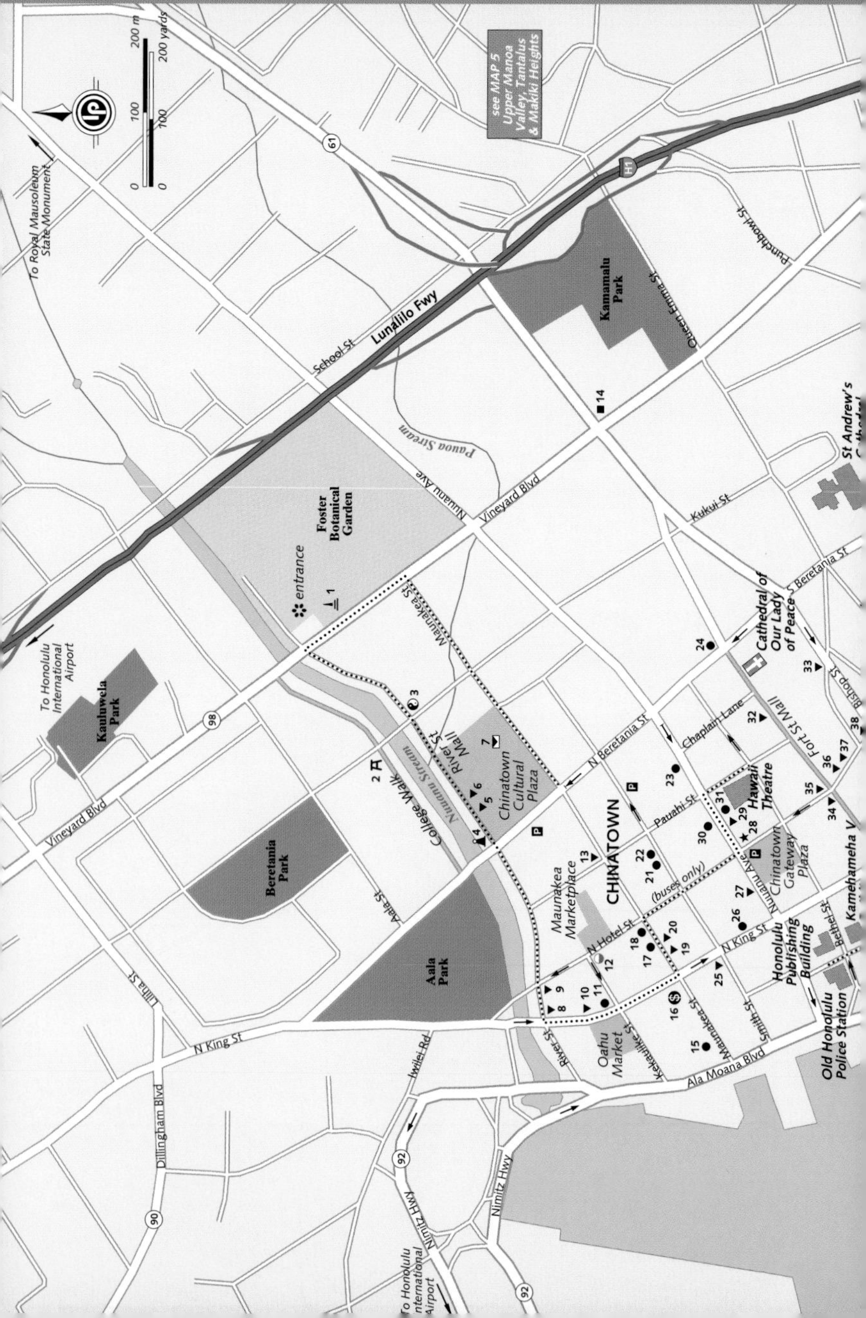

see MAP 5
Upper Manoa
Valley, Tantalus
& Makiki Heights

To Royal Mausoleum
State Monument

200 m
200 yards
100
100
0
0

61

School St

Lunalilo Fwy

Nuuanu Ave

Pauoa Stream

Kamamalu
Park

Vineyard Blvd

Kukui St

Pauoa Stream

Nuuanu St

Punchbowl St

St Andrew's
Cathedral

Foster
Botanical
Garden

entrance

♣ 1

Kanuwela
Park

To Honolulu
International
Airport

98

Vineyard Blvd

Beretania
Park

Maunakea St

2 🏛

College Walk

Nuuanu Stream

River St Mall

3

7

Chinatown
Cultural
Plaza

5

6

4

Berelania St

Cathedral of
Our Lady
of Peace

24

Beretania St

33

Chaplain Lane

N Beretania St

23

Pauahi St

Fort St Mall

Bishop St

Hawaii
Theatre

37

29 ★ 31

28

30

Maunakea
Marketplace

3

22

21

Nuuanu Ave

Chinatown
Gateway
Plaza

36

35

34

38

Kukui St

CHINATOWN

18

12

17

20

19

N Hotel St

(buses only)

26

27

Honolulu
Publishing
Building

Kamehameha V

Aala
Park

Aala St

River St

8 9

11

10

16 $

N King St

25

N King St

Oahu
Market

15

Maunakea St

Smith St

Ala Moana Blvd

Old Honolulu
Police Station

Bethel St

Lilha St

Dillingham Blvd

Iwilei Rd

N King St

To Honolulu
International
Airport
Nimitz Hwy

90

92

Nimitz Hwy

92

14

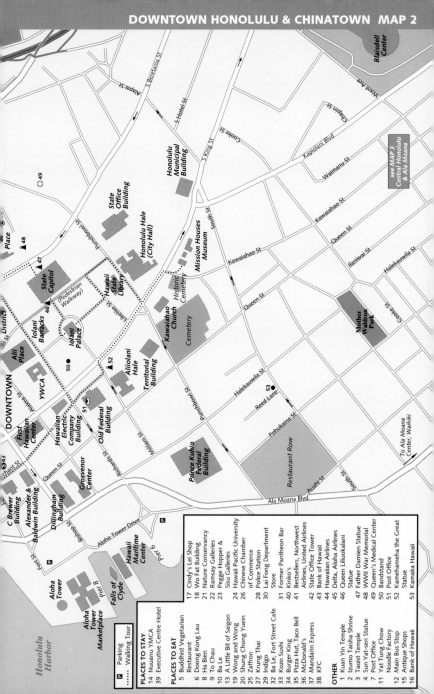

Blaisdell
Center

see MAP 3
Central Honolulu
& Ala Moana

Honolulu
Municipal
Building

State Office
Building

Honolulu Hale
(City Hall)

State
Capitol

(Pedestrian)
Walkway

Hawaii State
Library

Mission Houses
Museum

Iolani
Barracks

State
District

Iolani
Palace

Historic
Cemetery

Kawaiahao
Church

Aliiolani
Hale

Cemetery

Alii
Place

Territorial
Building

DOWNTOWN

YWCA

Mother
Waldron
Park

First
Hawaiian
Center

Hawaiian
Electric
Company
Building

Old Federal
Building

Reed Lane

C Brewer
Building

Grosvenor
Center

Prince Kuhio
Federal
Building

Restaurant Row

Alexander &
Baldwin Building

Dillingham
Building

To Ala Moana
Center, Waikiki

Ala Moana Blvd

Aloha
Tower

Hawaii
Maritime
Center

Aloha
Tower
Marketplace

Falls of
Clyde

Pier 8

Honolulu Harbor

P Parking
····· Walking Tour

PLACES TO STAY
14 Nuuanu YMCA
39 Executive Centre Hotel

PLACES TO EAT
5 Buddhist Vegetarian
    Restaurant
6 Doong Kong Lau
8 Ha Bien
9 To Chau
10 Ba Le
13 A Little Bit of Saigon
19 Wong and Wong
20 Shung Chong Yuein
25 Zaffron
27 Krung Thai
29 Indigo
32 Ba Le, Fort Street Cafe
33 Kozo Sushi
34 Burger King
35 Pizza Hut, Taco Bell
36 McDonald's
37 Mandarin Express
38 KFC

17 Cindy's Lei Shop
18 Wo Fat Building
21 Nature Conservancy
22 Ramsay Galleries
23 Pegge Hopper &
    Sisu Galleries
24 Hawaii Pacific University
26 Chinese Chamber
    of Commerce
28 Police Station
30 Lai Fong Department
    Store
31 Former Pantheon Bar
40 Kinko's
41 Bestsellers, Northwest
    Airlines, United Airlines
42 State Office Tower
43 Bank of Hawaii
44 Hawaiian Airlines
45 Delta, Aloha Airlines
46 Queen Liliuokalani
    Statue
47 Father Damien Statue
48 WWII War Memorial
49 Queen's Medical Center
50 Bandstand
51 Post Office
52 Kamehameha the Great
    Statue
53 Kamaka Hawaii

OTHER
1 Kuan Yin Temple
2 Izumo Taisha Shrine
3 Taoist Temple
4 Sun Yat-sen Statue
7 Post Office
11 Yat Tung Chow
    Noodle Factory
12 Main Bus Stop
15 Antique Shops
16 Bank of Hawaii

MAP 3 CENTRAL HONOLULU & ALA MOANA

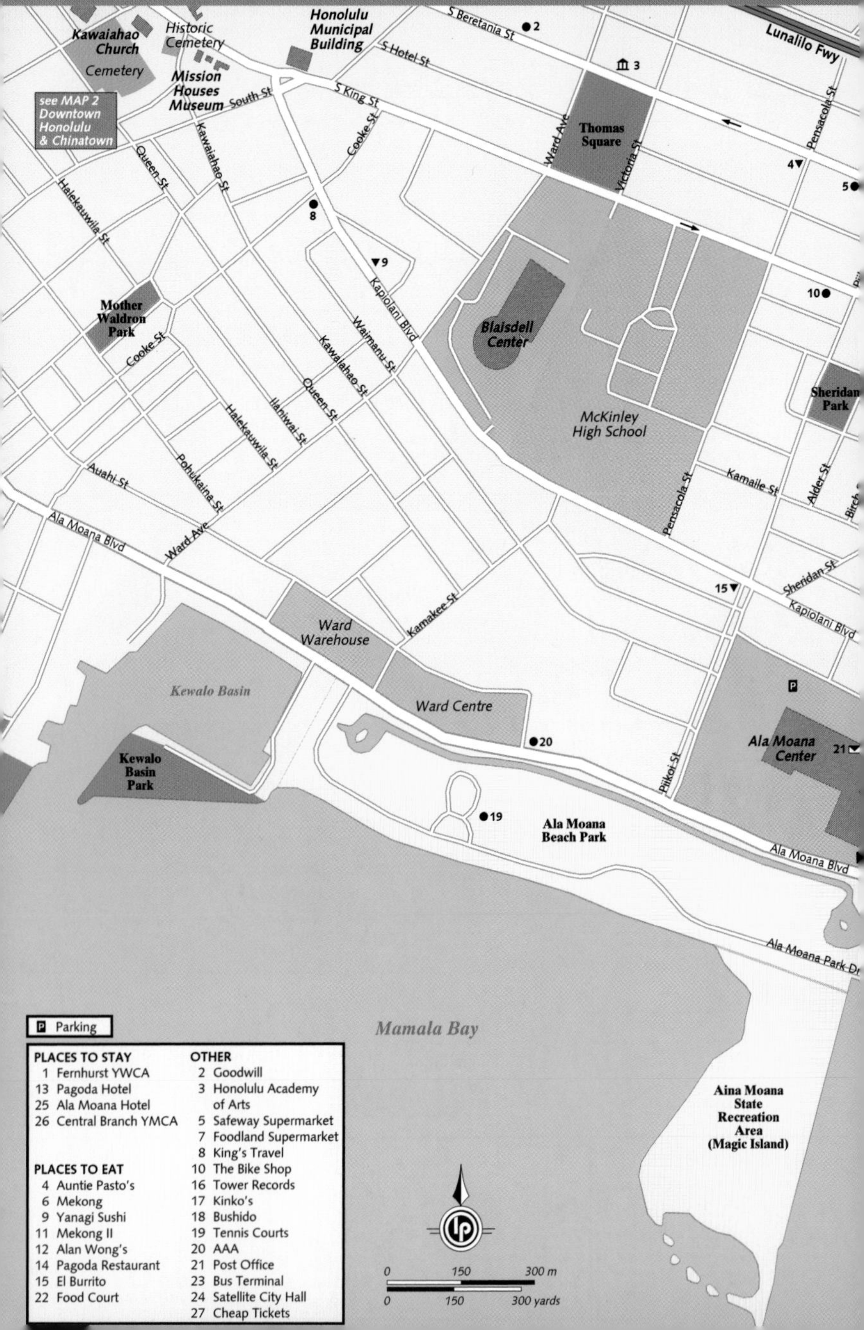

Kawaiahao Church

Cemetery

Historic Cemetery

Honolulu Municipal Building

Mission Houses Museum

see MAP 2 Downtown Honolulu & Chinatown

S Beretania St ● 2

S Hotel St

🏛 3

Lunalilo Fwy

S King St

South St

Kawaiahao St

Queen St

Halekauwila St

Cooke St

● 8

▼ 9

Kapiolani Blvd

Waimanu St

Kawaiahao St

Ward Ave

Thomas Square

Victoria St

Pensacola St

4 ▼

5 ●

10 ●

Blaisdell Center

Mother Waldron Park

Cooke St

Halekauwila St

Ilaniwai St

Queen St

McKinley High School

Sheridan Park

Kamaile St

Alder St

Birch

Auahi St

Ward Ave

Pohukaina St

Ala Moana Blvd

Pensacola St

Sheridan St

15 ▼

Kapiolani Blvd

Ward Warehouse

Kamakee St

Kewalo Basin

Ward Centre

● 20

P

Ala Moana Center

21 ▼

Kewalo Basin Park

Ala Moana Beach Park

Piikoi St

● 19

Ala Moana Blvd

Ala Moana Blvd

Ala Moana Park Dr

Mamala Bay

Aina Moana State Recreation Area (Magic Island)

P Parking

PLACES TO STAY
1 Fernhurst YWCA
13 Pagoda Hotel
25 Ala Moana Hotel
26 Central Branch YMCA

PLACES TO EAT
4 Auntie Pasto's
6 Mekong
9 Yanagi Sushi
11 Mekong II
12 Alan Wong's
14 Pagoda Restaurant
15 El Burrito
22 Food Court

OTHER
2 Goodwill
3 Honolulu Academy
   of Arts
5 Safeway Supermarket
7 Foodland Supermarket
8 King's Travel
10 The Bike Shop
16 Tower Records
17 Kinko's
18 Bushido
19 Tennis Courts
20 AAA
21 Post Office
23 Bus Terminal
24 Satellite City Hall
27 Cheap Tickets

0   150   300 m
0   150   300 yards

LP

Lunalilo St

to MAP 5
Upper Manoa
Valley, Tantalus
& Makiki Heights

Makiki St

Punahou St

1

Punahou
School

Makiki
Park

Wilder Ave

Matlock Ave

Cartwright
Park

Dole St

Kinau St

Lunalilo Fwy

Artesian Way

6 ▼

S Beretania St

H1

7 ●

Young St

S King St

Bingham St

Coyne St

Punahou St

S Beretania St

Elm St

▼11

Artesian St

McCully St

Young St

Rycroft St

S King St

see MAP 4
University Area

13 ■

14 ▼

12 ▼

Kalakaua Ave

Algaroba St

Waiola St

16 ●

Citron St

Honolulu
Stadium
State
Recreation
Area

17 ●

Kaheka St

Date St

Keeaumoku St

18 ●

Kalauokalani Way

Fern St

#3

Hauoli St

Pumehana St

24 ●

P

Kona St

27 ●

Kapiolani Blvd

McCully St

Lime St

Wiliwili St

25 ■

Hawaii
Convention
Center

26 ■

Atkinson Drive

Iolani St

Hoawa St

Isenberg St

Ala Wai Canal

Ala Wai Blvd

Kalakaua Ave

Ala Wai Blvd

Ala Wai
Park

92

Hobron Lane

Hobron Lane

Ena Rd

see Waikiki map
(Waikiki chapter)

Niu St

Pau St

Ala Wai
Yacht
Harbor

Ala Moana Blvd

Keoniana St

Kuamoo St

Namahana St

Olohana St

Kalaimoku St

Kuhio Ave

Launiu

Kaiolu St

Lewers St

WAIKIKI

Kalia Rd

Fort DeRussy
Military
Reservation

Hilton
Lagoon

Maluhia Rd

To Waikiki Beaches,
Diamond Head

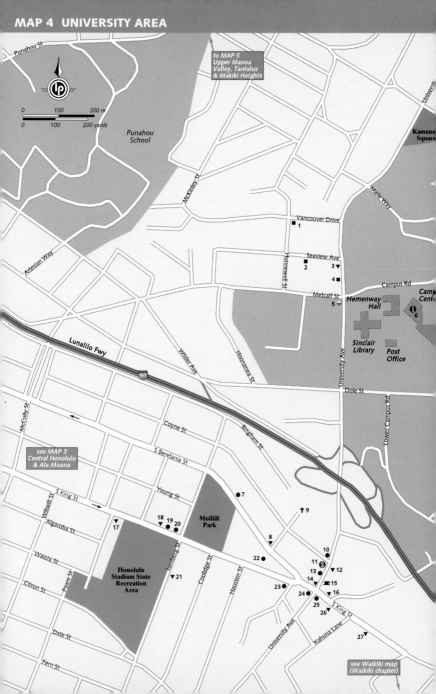

MAP 4 UNIVERSITY AREA

PLACES TO STAY
1 Manoa Valley Inn
2 Hostelling International Honolulu
4 Atherton YMCA

PLACES TO EAT
3 Coffeeline
8 Yakiniku Camellia
12 Ba Le
14 Ezogiku Noodle Cafe
16 Chan's Gourmet Buffet
17 Chiang Mai
18 India Bazaar, Kozo Sushi
21 Maple Garden
26 Diem
27 Longboard Cafe

OTHER
5 Bus Stop
6 Campus Information
7 Anna Bannanas
9 Church of the Crossroads
10 Varsity Twins
11 Bank of Hawaii
13 Rainbow Books & Records
15 Coffee Cove Online
19 Quilts Hawaii
20 Hula Supply Center
22 Star Market
23 Down to Earth Natural Foods
24 Kinko's
25 Cheap Tickets

'o Manoa Valley

Manoa Stream

Maile Way

Hamilton Library

Kennedy Theatre

East-West Center

East-West Rd

Burns Hall

University of Hawaii

Cooke Field

Kahanamoku Pool

Rainbow Stadium

Kanewai Park

Kalele Rd

Manoa Stream

Dole St

To Hanauma Bay

Old Waialae Rd

Palolo Stream

St Louis Drive

St Louis High School & Chaminade University of Honolulu

MAP 5 UPPER MANOA VALLEY, TANTALUS & MAKIKI HEIGHTS

Honolulu Watershed
Forest Reserve

To Kailua

Nuuanu Pali Drive

Waolani Stream

Queen Emma
Summer Palace

Nuuanu
Valley
Park

Nuuanu Stream

Puunui
Park

Wyllie St

Pali Hwy

61

Waolani Stream

Hsu Yin
Temple

Kawananakoa
Place

Royal Mausoleum
State Monument

PACIFIC
HEIGHTS

Pauoa Stream

Tantalus Drive

Nuuanu Ave

Kuakini St

Kawananakoa
Park

Pauoa Rd

Booth
Park

Kaneha Stream

Makiki Forest
Baseyard

Auwaiolimo
Park

Auwaiolimu St

Papakolea
Park

Tantalus Drive

Government
Nursery &
Arboretum

To Honolulu
International
Airport

Puowaina Drive

MAKIKI
HEIGHTS

Mott-Smith Drive

Makiki Heights Drive

Round Te...
Drive

Kamamalu
Park

Punchbowl

National Memorial
Cemetery of the Pacific

Contemporary
Museum

Makiki Heights Drive

see MAP 2
Downtown
Honolulu
& Chinatown

H1

Queen's
Medical
Center

98

Wilder Ave

Keeaumoku St

Makiki St

Honolulu Siddha
Meditation Center

DOWN-
TOWN

Lunalilo Fwy

To Waikiki

0   .5   1km
0   .25   .5 miles

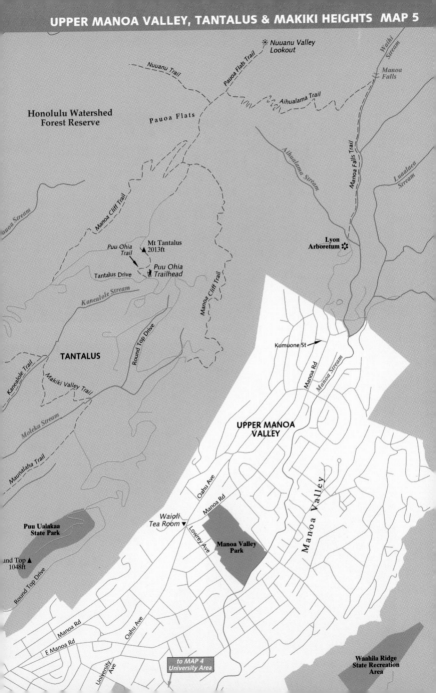

Nuuanu Trail

Pauoa Flats Trail

✳ Nuuanu Valley
Lookout

Waihi Stream

⇥ Manoa
Falls

Aihualama Trail

Pauoa Flats

**Honolulu Watershed
Forest Reserve**

Aihualama Stream

Manoa Falls Trail

Luaalaea Stream

Manoa Cliff Trail

_____ Stream

Mt Tantalus
2013ft

Puu Ohia Trail

**Lyon
Arboretum** ❀

Puu Ohia
Trailhead

Tantalus Drive

Manoa Cliff Trail

Kanealole Stream

Kumuone St

Round Top Drive

Manoa Rd

Manoa Stream

TANTALUS

Kanealole Trail

Makiki Valley Trail

Moleka Stream

**UPPER MANOA
VALLEY**

M a n o a   V a l l e y

Maunalaha Trail

Oahu Ave

Manoa Rd

Waioli
Tea Room ▼

Lowrey Ave

**Manoa Valley
Park**

**Puu Ualakaa
State Park**

...nd Top ▲
1048ft

Round Top Drive

Manoa Rd

E Manoa Rd

Oahu Ave

University Ave

to MAP 4
University Area

**Waahila Ridge
State Recreation
Area**

LEE FOSTER

Diamond Head, the crown jewel of the Waikiki landscape

NED FRIARY

Kites ready for takeoff at Kapiolani Park

LEE FOSTER

Royal Hawaiian Hotel, a Waikiki landmark

Formerly a swamp, Waikiki Beach is Hawaii's most popular tourist destination.

Concrete canyon Honolulu style: Bishop St

The Aloha Tower, keeping time since 1926

Chinatown has many lei shops.

For a permanent souvenir, consider a tattoo.

Crack seed, usually dried fruits or seeds, is a popular snack in the islands.

The fish stops here, Honolulu Market.

A statue of Sun Yat-sen stands on River St.

Built to divert streams that once flowed into Waikiki, the Ala Wai Canal is perfect for canoe practice.

The Hsu Yin Temple, Honolulu, reaches skyward.

The grace of a Japanese tea ceremony, Waikiki

The war god Kukailimoku, Bishop Museum

[Continued from page 128]
from candied ginger and pineapple to candied squash and lotus root. They also sell boiled peanuts that are quite good if you can resist comparing them to roasted peanuts.

Across the street is **Cindy's Lei Shop**, a friendly place with leis made of maile, lantern ilima and Micronesian ginger as well as the more common orchids and plumeria. Prices won't break the bank, as they start at just $3.50 for a lei of tuberose flowers.

Oahu Market
The focal point of Chinatown is the Oahu Market, on the corner of Kekaulike St and N King St. It has been a Honolulu institution since 1904.

There are stalls jammed with everything one could need for preparing a Chinese meal: pig heads, gingerroot, fresh octopus, quail eggs, slabs of tuna, jasmine rice, long beans and salted jellyfish.

In 1984, the tenants organized and purchased the market themselves to save it from falling into the hands of developers. Today, it gets a lot of competition from the bustling new Mauna Kea Marketplace.

River St Pedestrian Mall
The River St pedestrian mall, beside the Nuuanu Stream, is a place where old men play mahjong and checkers at outdoor tables. Eat-in and take-out restaurants line the street, including a couple of Chinese options and the peculiarly named Kent's Drive In, a hole-in-the-wall eatery serving plate lunches on a *pedestrian* walkway.

A statue of Chinese revolutionary leader Sun Yat-sen stands at the N Beretania St end of the mall.

Chinatown Cultural Plaza
This plaza, covering the better part of a block, is bordered by N Beretania St, Maunakea and River Sts.

The modern complex doesn't have the character of Chinatown's older shops, but inside it's still quintessential Chinatown, with tailors, acupuncturists and calligraphers alongside travel agents, restaurants and a Chinese news press. There's also a small produce and meat market. In a small courtyard, elderly Chinese light incense and leave mangoes at a statue of Kuan Yin.

Taoist Temple
Organized in 1889, the Lum Sai Ho Tong Society was one of more than 100 societies started by Chinese immigrants in Hawaii to help preserve their cultural identity. This one was for the Lum clan, which hails from an area west of the Yellow River. At one time the society had more than 4000 members, and even now there are nearly a thousand Lums in the Honolulu phone book.

The society's Taoist temple, on the corner of River and Kukui Sts, honors the goddess Tin Hau, a Lum child who rescued her father from drowning and was later deified as a result. Many Chinese claim to see her apparition when they travel by boat. The elaborate altar inside the temple is open for viewing when the street-level door is unlocked, which is typically 8:30 am to 2 pm daily.

Izumo Taisha Shrine
The Izumo Taisha Shrine, across the river from the Taoist temple on Kukui St, is a small wooden Shinto shrine built by Japanese immigrants in 1923. During WWII, the property was confiscated by the city of Honolulu and wasn't returned to its congregation until 1962.

Incidentally, the 100lb sacks of rice that sit near the altar symbolize good health, and ringing the bell placed at the shrine entrance is considered an act of purification for those who come to pray.

Foster Botanical Garden
Foster Botanical Garden, at the northern end of Chinatown, is an impressive 14-acre collection of tropical plants. Its entrance is on Vineyard Blvd, opposite the end of River St.

The garden took root in 1850, when German botanist William Hillebrand purchased 5 acres of land from Queen Kalama and planted the trees that now tower in the center of the property. Captain Thomas Foster bought the property in 1867 and continued planting the grounds. In the 1930s, the tropical garden was bequeathed to the city of Honolulu, and it is now a city park.

The garden is laid out according to plant groups, including sections of palms, orchids, plumeria and poisonous plants. Stroll through the Economic Garden to see how nutmeg, allspice and cinnamon grow. In this section, there are also other herbs and spices, a vanilla vine and a black pepper vine that climbs 40 feet up a gold tree.

The herb garden was the site of the first Japanese language school in Oahu. Many Japanese immigrants sent their children here to learn how to read Japanese, hoping to maintain their cultural identity and the option of someday returning to Japan. During the bombing of Pearl Harbor a stray artillery shell exploded in a room full of students. A memorial marks the site.

At the other end of the park, the wild orchid garden makes a good place for close-up photography. Unfortunately, this side of the garden is skirted by the H-1 Fwy, which detracts from an otherwise peaceful stroll.

Foster Botanical Garden holds many extraordinary plants. For instance, the garden's East African *Gigasiphon macrosiphon*, a tree with white flowers that open in the evening, is thought to be extinct in the wild. The tree is so rare that it doesn't have a common name.

The native Hawaiian loulu palm, taken long ago from Oahu's upper Nuuanu Valley, may also be extinct in the wild. The garden's chicle tree, New Zealand kauri tree and Egyptian doum palm are all reputed to be the largest of their kind in the USA. Oddities include the cannonball tree, the sausage tree and the double coconut palm that's capable of producing a 50-lb nut.

Foster Garden is open 9 am to 4 pm daily. Admission costs $5 for those ages 13 and older, $1 for children. Trees are labeled, and a free self-guided tour booklet is available at the entrance.

The Friends of Foster Garden provides volunteer guides who lead hour-long walking tours at 1 pm weekdays. Call ☎ 522-7066 for reservations.

Herbs & Noodles

Chinatown's herbalists act as both physicians and pharmacists, and the walls in their shops are lined with small wooden drawers, each filled with a different herb. The herbalists will size you up, feel your pulse and ask you to describe your ailments so they can determine which of the many drawers to open and which herbs and flowers to mix and wrap up for you to take home and boil together. The objective is to balance yin and yang forces. You can find herbalists at the Chinese Cultural Plaza and along N King and Maunakea Sts.

NED FRIARY

There are also half a dozen noodle factories in Chinatown. If you look inside, you'll see clouds of white flour hanging in the air and thin sheets of dough running around rollers and emerging as noodles. One easy-to-find shop is Yat Tung Chow Noodle Factory, 150 N King St, next to Ba Le, which makes noodles in nine sizes, from skinny golden thread to fat *udon*.

Kuan Yin Temple

The Kuan Yin Temple, on Vineyard Blvd near the entrance of Foster Garden, is a bright red Buddhist temple with a green ceramic-tile roof. The ornate interior is richly carved and filled with the sweet, pervasive smell of burning incense.

The temple is dedicated to Kuan Yin Bodhisattva, goddess of mercy, whose statue is the largest in the prayer hall. Devotees burn paper 'money' for prosperity and good luck. Offerings of fresh flowers, oranges and other fruit are placed at the altar. The pomelo, the large citrus fruit that is often stacked pyramid-style at the altar, is considered a symbol of fertility because of its many seeds.

Honolulu's multiethnic Buddhist community worships at the temple, and respectful visitors are welcome.

Getting Around

From Waikiki, to get to Chinatown by car, take Ala Moana Blvd and turn at Smith St or Bethel St. Or take Beretania St and head *makai* (toward the sea) down Nuuanu Ave or Maunakea St. N Hotel St is open to bus traffic only.

Chinatown is full of one-way streets, traffic is tight and it can be difficult to find a parking space. Your best bet for metered parking ($1 an hour, three-hour limit) is the lot off Smith St between Pauahi and Beretania Sts. There are parking garages charging comparable rates at the Chinatown Gateway Plaza on Nuuanu Ave and in the Hale Pauahi complex on N Beretania St (just north of Maunakea St).

Avoid parking hassles by taking the bus. From Waikiki, take bus No 2 to Hotel St and the center of Chinatown, or bus No 20 to River St on the western edge of Chinatown.

CENTRAL HONOLULU & ALA MOANA (MAP 3)

Ala Moana means 'Path to the Sea.' Ala Moana Blvd (Hwy 92) connects the Nimitz Hwy and the airport with downtown Honolulu and continues into Waikiki. Ala Moana is also the name of the area west of Waikiki Beach, which includes Honolulu's largest beach park and a huge shopping center.

Ala Moana Center

The Ala Moana Center is Hawaii's biggest shopping center, with some 200 shops. When outer islanders fly to Honolulu to shop, they go to Ala Moana. Tourists wanting to spend the day at a mall usually head there too. Ala Moana Center is Honolulu's major bus transfer point and tens of thousands of passengers transit through daily, so even if you weren't planning to go to the center, you're likely to end up there.

Ala Moana has a Sears, Liberty House, Neiman Marcus, JC Penney, Longs Drugs, Foodland supermarket and Shirokiya, a department store with a Japanese food market. You'll also find local color at the Crack Seed Center, where you can scoop from jars full of pickled mangoes, rock candy, salty red ginger, cuttlefish and banzai mix.

There are also airline offices, a couple of banks, a travel agency and a good food court with dozens of ethnic fast-food stalls.

On the inland side of the center, near Sears, is a post office open 8:30 am to 5 pm Monday to Friday, 8:30 am to 4:15 pm on Saturday. Also on the ground level, but at the opposite end of the row, is a satellite city hall where you can get bus schedules and county camping permits.

To get to the Ala Moana Center from Waikiki by car, simply head west on Ala Moana Blvd. Bus Nos 8, 19, 20 and 58 connect Waikiki with the Ala Moana Center.

Ala Moana Beach Park

Ala Moana Beach Park, opposite the Ala Moana Center, is a fine city park with much less hustle and bustle than Waikiki. The park is fronted by a broad, golden-sand beach, nearly a mile long, that's buffered from the traffic noise of Ala Moana Blvd by a spacious, grassy area with shade trees.

This is where Honolulu residents go to jog after work, play volleyball and enjoy weekend picnics. The park has full beach facilities, several softball fields and tennis courts, and free parking. It's a very popular park, yet big enough that it never feels crowded.

Ala Moana is a safe place to swim and is a good spot for distance swimmers. However, at low tide the deep channel that runs the length of the beach can be a hazard to poor swimmers who don't realize it's there, because it drops off suddenly to overhead depths. If you want to measure laps, it's 500m between the lifeguard tower at the Waikiki end and the post in the water that is midway between the third and fourth lifeguard towers.

The 43-acre peninsula jutting from the east side of the park is the **Aina Moana State Recreation Area**, more commonly known as Magic Island. During the school year, you can often find high school outrigger canoe teams practicing here in the late afternoon. There's a nice walk around the perimeter of Magic Island, and sunsets can be picturesque, with sailboats pulling in and out of the adjoining Ala Wai Yacht Harbor. This is also a hot summer surf spot.

To get to the beach park by car from Waikiki, take Ala Moana Blvd west. If you're taking the bus from Waikiki, Nos 8 and 20 stop on Ala Moana Blvd opposite the beach park.

Honolulu Academy of Arts

The Honolulu Academy of Arts (☎ 532-8700), 900 S Beretania St, is an exceptional museum, with permanent Asian, European, American and Pacific art collections with works ranging from ancient times to the present.

Just to the right of the front door is a room with paintings by Matisse, Cézanne, Gauguin, van Gogh and Picasso. In the middle of the room there is an inviting place to sit and take it all in.

The museum is open and airy and has numerous small galleries that enclose six garden courtyards. The Spanish Court has a small fountain surrounded by Greek and Roman sculptures and Egyptian reliefs dating back to 2500 BC.

There are sculptures and miniature figurines from India, jade and bronze objects from ancient China and Madonna-and-child oil paintings from 14th-century Italy, as well changing exhibits.

The Hawaiian section is small but choice, with feather leis, tapa beaters, poi pounders and koa calabashes. The adjacent collection from Papua New Guinea, Micronesia and the South Pacific includes ancestor figures, war clubs and masks.

The museum is open 10 am to 4:30 pm Tuesday to Saturday and 1 to 5 pm on Sunday. Admission is $5 for adults, $3 for senior citizens and students, free for children 12 and younger. There is also a theater, gift shop, library and lunch cafe.

The museum is off the tourist track and seldom crowded. Bus No 2 from Waikiki stops out front. Behind the museum there's street-side metered parking as well as a parking lot that charges just $1 with museum validation.

UNIVERSITY AREA (MAP 4)

The University of Hawaii (UH) at Manoa, the central campus of the statewide university system, is east of downtown Honolulu and 2 miles north of Waikiki.

The university has strong programs in astronomy, geophysics, marine sciences and Hawaiian and Pacific studies, and the campus attracts students from islands throughout the Pacific. It has a total enrollment of approximately 17,000 students and offers degrees in 88 fields of study.

Manoa Garden restaurant in Hemenway Hall is a student gathering spot. The hall and the Campus Center are behind Sinclair Library, which fronts University Ave opposite the bus stop.

At the east side of the University of Hawaii campus is the **East-West Center**, 1777 East-West Rd, a federally funded educational institution established in 1960 by the US Congress.

The center's stated goal is the promotion of mutual understanding among the people of Asia, the Pacific and the USA. Some 2000 researchers and graduate students work and study at the center, examining development policy, the environment and other Pacific issues.

Changing exhibits on Asian art and culture are displayed in **Burns Hall**, on the corner of Dole St and East-West Rd. It's open 8 am to 5 pm on weekdays; admission is free. The center occasionally has other

University Information

UH Tours The Information Center (☎ 956-7235) in the Campus Center provides campus maps and answers questions. Free one-hour walking tours of the campus, emphasizing history and architecture, leave from the Campus Center at 2 pm on Monday, Wednesday and Friday; to join a tour, simply arrive 10 minutes before the tour begins.

Newspaper *Ka Leo O Hawaii*, the student newspaper, lists lectures, music performances and other campus happenings. Pick it up for free at the university libraries and other places around campus.

Attending University For information on undergraduate studies at the University of Hawaii, contact the Admissions & Records Office (☎ 956-8975), 2600 Campus Rd, Room 001, Honolulu, HI 96822; for information on graduate studies, contact the Graduate Division (☎ 956-8544), Spalding Hall, 2540 Maile Way, Room 354, Honolulu, HI 96822.

The summer session consists primarily of two six-week terms. Tuition is $392 per credit for nonresidents and $122 per credit for residents. For the summer catalog, contact the Summer Session (☎ 956-7221), 2500 Dole St, Krauss Building, Room 1001, Honolulu, HI 96822.

There are also shorter, noncredit recreation and craft classes organized through Campus Leisure Programs (☎ 956-6468). These classes are open to the general public. Most classes, such as beginning hula, lei making, slack-key guitar and ceramics, meet once or twice a week and cost around $50 for a month-long session. Of particular interest to short-term visitors are the outdoor programs, such as hiking outings ($10) and sailing classes ($100).

multicultural programs open to the public, such as music concerts or scholastic seminars. For current happenings, call the center at ☎ 944-7111.

Bus No 4 runs between the university and Waikiki, bus No 6 between the university and Ala Moana.

UPPER MANOA VALLEY (MAP 5)

The Upper Manoa Valley, *mauka* (toward the mountains) of the university, ends at forest reserve land in the hills above Honolulu. The road up the valley runs through a well-to-do residential neighborhood before reaching the trailhead to Manoa Falls and the Lyon Arboretum.

Manoa Falls Trail

The trail to Manoa Falls is a beautiful hike, especially for one so close to the city. The trail runs for three-quarters of a mile above a rocky streambed before ending at the falls. It takes about 30 minutes to reach the falls.

Surrounded by lush, damp vegetation and moss-covered stones and tree trunks, you get the feeling you are walking through a thick rain forest a long way from civilization. The sounds are purely natural: the chirping of birds and the rush of the stream and waterfall.

There are all sorts of trees along the path, including tall *Eucalyptus robusta*, with its soft, spongy, reddish bark; flowering orange African tulip trees; and other lofty varieties. When the wind blows through the trees, they creak like wooden doors in old houses. Many of them were planted by the nearby Lyon Arboretum, which at one time held a lease on the property.

Wild purple orchids and red ginger grow near the falls, adding a colorful element to the tranquil scene. The falls are steep and drop about 100 feet into a small shallow pool. The pool is not deep enough for swimming, and occasional falling rocks make swimming inadvisable anyway.

It's an easy hike, with just a 400-foot gain in elevation. The trail is usually a bit muddy, but not too bad if it hasn't been raining lately. Be careful not to trip over exposed tree roots – they're potential ankle breakers, especially if you're moving at a quick pace. The packed clay can be slippery in some steep places, so take your time, pick up a walking stick and enjoy the trail.

Aihualama Trail

About 75 feet before Manoa Falls, an inconspicuous trail starts to the left of the chain-link fence. This is the Aihualama Trail, well worth a little 15-minute side trip. Just a short way up, you'll get a broad view of Manoa Valley.

After walking for about five minutes, you'll enter a bamboo forest with some massive old banyan trees. When the wind blows, the forest releases eerie crackling sounds. It sounds enchanted or spooky, depending on your mood.

You can return to the Manoa Falls Trail or go on for another mile to Pauoa Flats, where the trail connects with the Puu Ohia-Pauoa Trail in the Tantalus area. See the Tantalus & Makiki Heights section for more trail information.

Lyon Arboretum

If you want to identify trees and plants you've seen along the trail to Manoa Falls, the Lyon Arboretum, 3860 Manoa Rd, is a great place to visit after your hike.

Dr Harold Lyon, after whom the arboretum is named, is credited with introducing 10,000 exotic trees and plants to Hawaii. Approximately half of these are represented in this 193-acre arboretum, which is under the auspices of the University of Hawaii.

This is not a landscaped tropical flower garden, but a mature and largely wooded arboretum where related species are clustered in a seminatural state.

Among the plants in the Hawaiian ethnobotanical garden are mountain apple, breadfruit and *taro*; *ko*, the sugarcane brought by early Polynesian settlers; the *kukui*, which was used to produce lantern oil; and *ti*, which was used for medicinal purposes during ancient times and for moonshine after westerners arrived.

The arboretum also has herbs and spices and cashew, cacao, papaya, betel nut, macadamia nut, jackfruit and calabash trees, as well as greenhouses and classrooms.

A good choice among the arboretum's many short trails is the 20-minute walk up to **Inspiration Point**, which offers a view of the hills that enclose the valley. En route you'll encounter wonderful scents, inviting stone benches and lots of birdsong. The path loops through ferns, bromeliads and magnolias and passes by tall trees, including a bo tree, a species that is a descendant of the tree Gautama Buddha sat under when he received enlightenment.

The arboretum is open from 9 am to 3 pm Monday to Saturday. A $1 donation is appreciated. Free guided tours (☎ 988-0465 for reservations) are given at 1 pm on the first Friday and third Wednesday of each month and at 10 am on the third Saturday of the month.

The reception center has a book and gift shop as well as helpful staff members who will provide a map of the garden and information on the arboretum's organized hikes, workshops and children's programs.

Getting There & Away

From Ala Moana Center take the No 5 Manoa Valley bus to the end of the line, which is at the junction of Manoa Rd and Kumuone St. From there, it's a 10-minute walk to the end of Manoa Rd, where the Manoa Falls Trail begins. Lyon Arboretum is at the end of the short drive just to the left of the trailhead.

The taro plant grows in the Lyon Arboretum.

To reach this area by car, simply drive to the end of Manoa Rd. There's room to park at the trailhead, but it's not a very secure place, so don't leave anything valuable in the car. Lyon Arboretum has a parking area adjacent to its gardens, but it's reserved for arboretum visitors only.

TANTALUS & MAKIKI HEIGHTS (MAP 5)

Just 2 miles from downtown Honolulu, a narrow switchback road cuts its way up the lush green forest reserve land of Tantalus and the Makiki Valley. The road climbs almost to the top of 2013-foot Mt Tantalus, with swank, mountainside homes tucked in along the way.

Although the road is one continuous loop, the western side is called Tantalus Drive and the eastern side Round Top Drive. The 8½-mile circuit is Honolulu's finest scenic drive, offering splendid views of the city below.

The route is winding, narrow and steep, but it's well paved. Among the profusion of dense tropical growth, bamboo, ginger, elephant-ear taro and fragrant eucalyptus trees are easily identified. Vines climb and twist to the top of telephone poles.

A network of hiking trails runs between Tantalus Drive and Round Top Drive and throughout the forest reserve, with numerous trailheads off both roads. The trails are seldom crowded, which seems amazing considering how accessible they are. Perhaps because the drive itself is so nice, the only walking most people do is between their car and the scenic lookouts.

The Makiki Heights area below the forest reserve is one of the most exclusive residential areas in Honolulu and the site of a museum of contemporary art. There's bus service as far as Makiki Heights, but none around the Tantalus-Round Top loop drive.

Puu Ualakaa State Park

From Puu Ualakaa State Park you can see an incredible panorama of all Honolulu. The park entrance is 2½ miles up Round Top Drive, which is off Makiki St. From the entrance, it's half a mile in to the lookout; bear to the left when the road forks.

> ### Rolling Sweet Potatoes
>
> This park gets its name, Puu Ualakaa (Rolling Sweet Potato Hill), from an old harvesting technique: In olden times, the slopes were planted with sweet potatoes. It is said that at harvest time they were dug up and rolled down the hill for easy gathering. The hill's other name, Round Top, dates to more recent times.

The sweeping view from the lookout extends from Kahala and Diamond Head on the far left, across Waikiki and downtown Honolulu, to the Waianae Range on the far right. To the southeast is the University of Hawaii at Manoa, easily recognizable by its sports stadium; to the southwest you can see clearly into the green mound of Punchbowl Crater; the airport is visible on the edge of the coast and Pearl Harbor beyond that.

Although the best time for taking photos is generally during the day, this is also a fine place to watch evening settle over the city. Arrive at least 30 minutes before sunset to see the hills before they're in the shadows.

The park gates are locked from 6:45 pm (7:45 pm in summer) to 7 am. For taking in the view at night (or anytime), there are a couple of scenic roadside pull-offs before the park. There's no bus service to this park.

Contemporary Museum

The Contemporary Museum (☎ 526-0232), 2411 Makiki Heights Drive, is a delightful modern art museum occupying an estate with 3½ acres of wooded gardens.

The estate house was constructed in 1925 for Mrs Charles Montague Cooke, whose other former home is the present site of the Honolulu Academy of Arts.

You enter the museum through bronze gates into a covered courtyard with an arrangement of parabolic mirrors that reflect the view hundreds of times over.

Inside, the galleries feature quality exhibits of paintings, sculpture and other contemporary artwork by both national and international artists. A newer building on the lawn holds the museum's most prized piece, a vivid environmental installation by David Hockney based on his sets for *L'Enfant et les Sortilèges*, Ravel's 1925 opera. There's also a cafe that serves lunch and afternoon desserts.

The museum is open 10 am to 4 pm Tuesday to Saturday and noon to 4 pm on Sunday. Admission is $5 for adults and $3 for students and senior citizens; it's free for children 12 and under. Docent-led tours are conducted at 1:30 pm and are included in the price of admission. If you happen to come by on the third Thursday of the month, admission is free. Visit the museum's website (www.tcmhi.org) for a preview.

The museum, near the intersection of Mott-Smith Drive and Makiki Heights Drive, can be reached on the No 15 bus from downtown Honolulu.

Meditation Center

The Honolulu Siddha Meditation Center, (☎ 942-8887), 1925 Makiki St, operated by followers of Gurumayi Chidvilasananda, has various events that are open to interested visitors, including an orientation program, videos of Gurumayi, chanting and meditation sessions.

As a general rule, Wednesday and Saturday evenings are the main program nights. In addition, there are sometimes group meals and workshops that are open to the public; call for information on upcoming activities and to arrange a visit.

Makiki Valley Loop Trail

Three of the Tantalus area hiking trails – Maunalaha Trail, Makiki Valley Trail and Kanealole Trail – can be combined to make the Makiki Valley Loop Trail, a popular 2½-mile hike.

The loop goes through a lush and varied tropical forest that begins and ends in Hawaii's first state nursery and arboretum. In this nursery, hundreds of thousands of trees were grown to replace the sandalwood forests that were leveled in Makiki Valley and elsewhere in Hawaii in the 19th century.

The **Maunalaha Trail** begins at the rest rooms below the parking lot of the Makiki Forest baseyard. It crosses a bridge, passes taro patches and climbs up the east ridge of Makiki Valley, passing Norfolk pine, bamboo and fragrant allspice and eucalyptus trees. There are some good views along the way.

After three-quarters of a mile, you'll come to a four-way junction, where you'll take the left fork and continue on the **Makiki Valley Trail**. The trail goes through small gulches and across gentle streams with patches of ginger. Near the Moleka Stream crossing, there are mountain apple trees (related to allspice and guava) that flower in the spring and bear fruit in the summer. Yellow guava and strawberry guava also grow along the trail. There are some fine views of the city below.

The **Kanealole Trail** begins as you cross Kanealole Stream and then follows the stream back to the baseyard, three-quarters of a mile away. The trail leads down through a field of Job's tears; the beadlike bracts of the female flowers of this tall grass are often used for leis.

Kanealole Trail is usually muddy, so wear shoes with good traction and pick up a walking stick. Halfway down there's a grove of nonnative mahogany trees.

Getting There & Away To get to the Makiki Forest baseyard, turn left off Makiki St and go half a mile up Makiki Heights Drive. Where the road makes a sharp bend, proceed straight ahead through a green gate into the Makiki Forest Recreation Area and continue until you reach the baseyard. There's a parking lot on the right, just before the office.

You can also take the No 15 bus that runs between downtown and Pacific Heights. Get off near the intersection of Mott-Smith Drive and Makiki Heights Drive and walk down Makiki Heights Drive to the baseyard. It's a mile-long walk between the bus stop and the trailhead.

An alternative is to hike just the Makiki Valley Trail. You can reach it by going up Tantalus Drive 2 miles from its intersection with Makiki Heights Drive. As you come around a sharp curve, look for the wooden post marking the trailhead on the right. You can take this route in as far as you want and backtrack out or link up with other trails along the way.

Puu Ohia Trail

The Puu Ohia Trail, in conjunction with the Pauoa Flats Trail, leads up to a lookout with a view of the Nuuanu reservoir and valley. It's nearly 2 miles one way and makes a hardy hike.

The trailhead is at the very top of Tantalus Drive, 3.6 miles up from its intersection with Makiki Heights Drive. There's a large turnoff opposite the trailhead where you can park.

The Puu Ohia Trail begins with reinforced log steps and leads past ginger, lush bamboo groves and lots of eucalyptus, a fast-growing tree that was planted to protect the watershed. About a half mile up, the trail reaches the top of 2013-foot Mt Tantalus (Puu Ohia).

From Mt Tantalus, the trail leads to a service road. Continue on the road to its end, where there's a Hawaiian Telephone building. The trail picks up again behind the left side of the building.

Continue down the trail until it reaches the Manoa Cliff Trail and go left. Walk on for a short distance until you come to another intersection, where you'll turn right onto the **Pauoa Flats Trail**.

The trail leads down into Pauoa Flats and on to the lookout. The flats area can be muddy; be careful not to trip on exposed tree roots.

You'll pass two trailheads before reaching the lookout. The first is **Nuuanu Trail**, on the left, which runs three-quarters of a mile along the western side of Upper Pauoa Valley and offers broad views of Honolulu and the Waianae Range.

The second is **Aihualama Trail**, a bit farther along on the right, which takes you 1¼ miles through tranquil bamboo groves and past huge old banyan trees to Manoa Falls. If you follow this route, you can hike down the Manoa Falls Trail, a distance of about a mile,

to the end of Manoa Rd and from there catch a bus back to town (see the Upper Manoa Valley section for bus details).

ELSEWHERE IN HONOLULU
Bishop Museum

The Bishop Museum (Map 1; ☎ 847-3511), 1525 Bernice St, is considered by many to be the best Polynesian anthropological museum in the world.

One side of the main gallery, the **Hawaiian Hall**, has three floors of exhibits that cover the cultural history of Hawaii. The 1st floor, dedicated primarily to Hawaii before westerners arrived, has a full-sized pili-grass thatched house and numerous other displays, including carved temple images, calabashes and shark-toothed war clubs.

One of the museum's most impressive holdings is a feather cloak that was worn by Kamehameha the Great. It was created entirely of the yellow feathers of the now-extinct mamo, a predominately black bird with a yellow upper tail. Eighty thousand mamos were caught, plucked and released to create this single cloak. To get a sense of just how few feathers each bird had available for sacrifice, look at the nearby taxidermic mamo, to the left of the Queen Liliuokalani exhibit.

The 2nd floor is dedicated to the varied influences of 19th-century Hawaii. Here you will find traditional tapa cloth robes, missionary-inspired quilt work and barter items that Yankee traders brought to the islands; there's also a small whaling exhibit.

The top floor has displays on the various ethnic groups that comprise present-day Hawaii. Like Hawaii itself, it has a bit of everything, including samurai armor, Portuguese festival costumes, Taoist fortune-telling sticks and a Hawaiian ukulele made of two coconut shell halves.

In the Hawaiian Hall lobby, craftspeople demonstrate Hawaiian quilting, lauhala weaving, lei making and other traditional crafts; the demonstrations are held 9 am to 2:30 pm Monday to Friday. A Hawaiian music and dance performance is given at 11 am and 2 pm daily. Guided tours depart from the hall at 10 am and noon weekdays.

Preserving Pacific Island History

Bishop Museum is well respected, not only for its collections, but for the ethnological research it spearheaded throughout the Pacific. Beginning in the 1920s, supported by mainland philanthropy and Ivy League scholars, the museum organized teams of archaeologists and anthropologists and sent them to record the native cultures of the Pacific Islands before they were forever lost.

RON DALQUIST

The most renowned of the researchers was Kenneth Emory, who was born in Boston but spent his early years in Hawaii, where he became fluent in the Hawaiian language. His knowledge of Hawaiian gave him the linguistic underpinnings to understand all Polynesian dialects. For five decades, he sailed on schooners and mail boats to the far corners of the Pacific, collecting film footage of native dancers, recording their songs, measuring their temples (both buildings and skulls!) and transcribing their folklore.

Emory's treatises are the most important (and sometimes the only) anthropological documentation of many Pacific Island cultures, from Lanai to Tuamotu. He was affiliated with the museum until his death at age 94 in 1992.

The **Polynesian Hall** contains masks from Melanesia, stick charts from Micronesia and weapons and musical instruments from across Polynesia.

The **Kahili Room**, a small gallery on the 1st floor of the main hall, is dedicated to Hawaiian royalty. It houses the horse carriage used by Queen Liliuokalani and a display of kahili, the feathered staffs used at official events such as coronations and royal funerals.

The museum also has a modern wing, called the **Castle Building**, with interactive natural history displays that children will enjoy. Here one can listen to dolphins, look at life through the eyes of a frog or enter a reconstructed lava tube – unfortunately, exhibits have been known to be marked 'out of order.'

The Bishop Museum is open 9 am to 5 pm daily. Admission is $14.95 for adults, $11.95 for children ages four to 17, free for children under age four. For a preview, visit the museum's website (www.bishop.hawaii.org).

The museum is also home to Oahu's only planetarium, but it is temporarily closed while the antiquated facility is replaced with a new, state-of-the-art planetarium that is expected to be completed in the year 2001.

The gift shop off the lobby sells many books on the Pacific that are not easily found elsewhere, as well as some quality Hawaiiana crafts and souvenirs. There's also a snack shop open to 4 pm.

To get to the Bishop Museum by bus from Waikiki or downtown Honolulu, take the No 2 School St bus to Kapalama St, walk toward the ocean and turn right on Bernice St. By car, take exit 20B off H-1, go inland on Houghtailing St and turn left on Bernice St.

Moanalua

In olden times Moanalua (Map 1) was a stopover for people traveling between Honolulu and Ewa, as well as a vacation spot for Hawaiian royalty. In 1884, Princess Pauahi Bishop willed the valley to Samuel M Damon, and it's now privately owned by his estate.

Moanalua Gardens Moanalua Gardens, maintained by the Damon Estate, is a large, grassy park with grand shade trees. The park is the site of King Kamehameha V's gingerbread-trimmed summer cottage, which overlooks a taro pond. Beyond it, a Chinese-style hall is fronted by carp ponds and stands of golden-stemmed bamboo. The center of the park has a grassy stage where the Prince Lot Hula Festival is held on the third Saturday in July.

This is not a must-see spot, except during the festival, but it is a pleasant place to stroll if you happen to be passing by. To get there, take the Puuloa Rd/Tripler Hospital exit off Hwy 78 and then make an immediate right turn into the gardens.

Moanalua Trail The trail up Moanalua Valley, once paved with cobblestone, is now a gravel and dirt road. It's a dry area, and there is only partial shade along the trail. There are both indigenous and nonnative plants, and lots of birds. Seven stone bridges remain along the path in various stages of disrepair.

The nonprofit Moanalua Gardens Foundation (☎ 839-5334), 1352 Pineapple Place, Honolulu, HI 96819, works to preserve Moanalua Valley in its natural state. Their efforts to raise public awareness of the valley's history and environmental uniqueness helped defeat plans that would have routed the new H-3 Fwy through Moanalua Valley.

The foundation gives interpretive walks into Moanalua Valley at least one Sunday each month. The easy 5-mile walks begin at 9 am, finish around 1 pm and cost $3. Reservations can be made in advance. If you want to hike the trail on your own, the Damon Estate requests that you first call ahead for permission to enter.

If you follow the road all the way in, it's about 4 miles. Numbered posts along the first half of the trail correspond to a self-guided brochure available for $5 from the foundation's office; add $4 for shipping to order it by mail.

To get to the trailhead, take the Moanalua Valley/Red Hill exit off Hwy 78 (one exit past Moanalua Gardens). Stay to the right and then follow the sign for Moanalua Valley, uphill 1½ miles on Ala Aolani St to where the road ends at a parking lot. There are rest rooms and drinking water in the little park at the trailhead.

Sand Island State Recreation Area

Sand Island (Map 1) is a 500-acre island on the western side of Honolulu Harbor. About a third of the island has been set aside as a state recreation area.

The park is heavily used by locals who camp, fish and picnic there on weekends, but it has little appeal to the casual visitor. Camping is free by permit and is limited to five nights per month. For information on applying for a camping permit, see Camping under Accommodations in the Facts for the Visitor chapter at the front of the book.

Sand Island is not reached from the downtown area, but via the Sand Island Access Rd, a few miles west of the island, off the Nimitz Hwy (Hwy 92). The access road to the park travels 2½ miles through an industrial area with a wastewater treatment plant, oil tanks, scrap metal yards and the like. The airport is directly across the lagoon, and Sand Island is on the flight path.

The park has showers, rest rooms and a sandy beach, which, while cleaner than it's been in years past, is still far from pristine.

Punchbowl

Punchbowl (Map 5) is the bowl-shaped remnant of a long-extinct volcanic crater. At an elevation of 500 feet, it sits a mile north of the downtown district and offers a fine view of the city, out to Diamond Head and the Pacific beyond.

The early Hawaiians called the crater *Puowaina*, the 'hill of human sacrifices.' It's believed there was a heiau at the crater and that the slain bodies of kapu breakers, those who deviated from the practice of the taboos that strictly regulated all social interaction, were brought to Punchbowl to be cremated upon the heiau altar.

Today it's the site of the 115-acre National Memorial Cemetery of the Pacific. The remains of Hawaiians sacrificed to appease the gods now share the crater floor with the bodies of more than 25,000 soldiers, more than half of whom were killed in the Pacific during WWII.

The remains of Ernie Pyle, the distinguished war correspondent who covered both world wars and was hit by machine gun fire on Ie Shima during the final days of WWII, lie in section D, grave 109. Five stones to the left, at grave D-1, lies astronaut Ellison Onizuka, the Big Island native who perished in the 1986 Challenger space shuttle disaster. Their resting places are marked with the same style of flat granite stone that marks each of the cemetery's graves.

A huge memorial at the rear of the cemetery has eight marble courts representing different Pacific regions. The memorial is inscribed with the names of the 26,289 Americans missing in action from WWII and the Korean War. Two additional half courts have the names of 2489 soldiers missing from the Vietnam War.

For a good view of the city, walk to the lookout, 10 minutes south of the memorial.

The cemetery is open 8 am to 5:30 pm October through February and from 8 am to 6:30 pm March through September.

If you're driving to Punchbowl, take the H-1 to the Pali Hwy. There's a marked exit as you start up the Pali Hwy; watch closely, because it comes up quickly. From there, drive slowly and follow the signs as you wind through a series of narrow streets on the short route up to the cemetery. Its entrance is off Puowaina Drive.

By bus, take a No 2 from Waikiki to downtown Honolulu and get off at Beretania and Alapai Sts, where you transfer to bus No 15. Ask the driver where to get off. It's about a 15-minute walk to Punchbowl from the bus stop.

Queen Emma Summer Palace

On the north side of Honolulu is the Queen Emma Summer Palace (Map 5; ☎ 595-3167), a former residence of Queen Emma, the consort of Kamehameha IV.

Emma, who was three-quarters royal Hawaiian and a quarter English, was the granddaughter of the captured sailor John Young. He became a friend and adviser of Kamehameha the Great. The house is also known as Hanaiakamalama, the name of John Young's home in Kawaihae on the Big Island, where he served as governor. The name means 'the foster child of the moon.'

The Youngs left the home to Queen Emma, who often slipped away from her formal downtown home to this cooler retreat. It's a bit like an old Southern plantation mansion, with a column porch, high ceilings and louvered windows to catch the breeze.

The home was forgotten after Queen Emma's death in 1885 and was scheduled to be razed in 1915 when the estate was turned into a public park. At the last minute, the Daughters of Hawaii, a women's group founded by the descendants of missionaries, rescued the house from the wrecker's ball, and they have since run it as a museum.

The house is furnished similarly to how it looked in Queen Emma's day, decorated largely with period furniture collected from five of Emma's homes. Some of the more interesting pieces are a cathedral-shaped koa cabinet made in Berlin and filled with a set of china from Queen Victoria; feather cloaks and capes; and Emma's necklace of tiger claws, a gift from the maharaja of India.

It's open 9 am to 4 pm daily except holidays. Admission is $5 for adults and $1 for children under age 12.

There's a gift shop at the rear of the palace, and it sells Hawaiiana books and native crafts such as koa bracelets and bowls made from native woods; it's open the same hours as the museum.

The Queen Emma Summer Palace is on the Pali Hwy (Hwy 61) at the 2-mile marker. By bus, take the No 4 Nuuanu Dowsett, which runs about every 15 minutes from Waikiki. Be sure to let the bus driver know in advance that you want to go to the Queen Emma Summer Palace so you don't miss the stop.

Royal Mausoleum State Monument

The Royal Mausoleum (Map 5) contains the remains of Kings Kamehameha II, III, IV and V, as well as King David Kalakaua and Queen Liliuokalani, Hawaii's last reigning

HAWAII STATE ARCHIVES

King Kalakaua is buried in the Royal Mausoleum.

monarchs. Conspicuously absent are the remains of Kamehameha the Great, the last king to be buried in secret in accordance with Hawaii's old religion.

The original mausoleum building, which is usually locked, is now a chapel; the caskets are in nearby crypts. Other gravestones honor Kamehameha I's British confidante John Young and American Charles Reed Bishop, husband of Bernice Pauahi Bishop.

The Royal Mausoleum, at 2261 Nuuanu Ave (just before the avenue meets the Pali Hwy), is open 8 am to 4:30 pm weekdays. There's no admission charge. You can take the same No 4 Nuuanu Dowsett bus from Waikiki that serves the Queen Emma Summer Palace.

Just across Nuuanu Ave from the mausoleum, on Kawananakoa Place, is **Hsu Yin Temple**, a Buddhist temple that's worth a quick look if you're visiting the mausoleum. At the altar are the standard offerings of oranges and burning incense, and prints on the walls depict Buddha's life story.

PLACES TO STAY
Near the Airport
Budget For long layovers or midnight flights, there are two inexpensive places where you can catnap or just take a shower.

The more appealing option is *Sleep & Shower* (☎ 836-3044, fax 834-8985, Terminal Box 42, Honolulu, HI 96819), between lobbies five and six right in the airport's main terminal. It has 17 small, private rooms, each with a single bed and its own bathroom. The place is clean, modern and relatively quiet, although there is some vibration from the shuttle bus that runs overhead. Overnight (eight-hour) stays, including shower, cost $30; a two-hour daytime nap and shower costs $17.50; it is $5 for each additional hours. Only one person is allowed to stay in each room. There are also five dorm beds at the side of the lobby that cost $19 overnight, with shower, but they're best suited for heavy sleepers, because this is in a semi-open part of the lobby.

If you want to shower only, the cost is $7.50, with towels, shampoo and shaving cream provided. It's open 24 hours. Reservations are taken for the overnight stays, except in the dorm, and MasterCard and Visa are accepted.

The other establishment is *Nimitz Shower Tree (Map 1; ☎ 833-1411, 3085 N Nimitz Hwy)*, which occupies a converted warehouse in an industrial area not far from the airport hotels. The facilities are basic: the private 'roomettes' are rows of little cubicles with louvered doors and an open wall at the top, so it's a bit like being in a dorm. The cost is $24 to $33 for an overnight sleep, including shower. You can also go there just to take a shower ($7.50). It's open 24 hours. They also rent out rooms by the week for $110, which attracts a fair number of local boarders.

Mid-Range If you have some dire need for a hotel near Honolulu International Airport, there are three hotels outside the airport, but they're along a busy highway and beneath flight paths. All three hotels provide free 24-hour transport to and from the airport, which is about 10 minutes away.

The most comfortable option is the *Best Western Plaza Hotel-Honolulu Airport (Map 1; ☎ 836-3636, 800-528-1234, fax 834-7406, 3253 N Nimitz Hwy, Honolulu, HI 96819)*, a modern hotel with 274 pleasant rooms, each with a king or two double beds, TV and refrigerator. The only drawback is the noise from the heavy traffic on the

HONOLULU

nearby highway that has an overpass adjacent to the front of the hotel – ask for a rear room. Rack rates are $97, but there's often a 'manager's special' for $85; nonsmoking rooms are available. The hotel has a pool, lounge and restaurant. Within walking distance is the Nimitz Mart center, which has a handful of fast-food places, including a Ba Le Vietnamese cafe, a Subway Sandwiches shop and a Cajoe's Roasted Chicken.

Holiday Inn-Honolulu Airport (Map 1; ☎ 836-0661, 800-800-3477, fax 833-1738, 3401 N Nimitz Hwy, Honolulu, HI 96819), on the corner of Rodgers Blvd, has 308 rooms and a standard rate of $112. The rooms are on the small side and relatively bland, but this four-story hotel has typical Holiday Inn amenities, including a lounge, pool and restaurant. Guests have a choice of a king or two double beds; nonsmoking rooms are available. There's commonly a promotional rate, dubbed the 'manager's special,' that discounts the standard rate by about 20%.

Pacific Marina Inn (Map 1; ☎ 836-1131, fax 833-0851, 2628 Waiwai Loop, Honolulu, HI 96819) is a mile farther east in an industrial area, but on the plus side, it has the least traffic noise. This three-decker motel has small, straightforward rooms for $88, but there's usually an 'airport special' of $55 to $65; you can call them using the courtesy phone in the baggage claim area of the airport. The rooms have air-con, TVs and phones, and there's a pool on the grounds.

Elsewhere in Honolulu

Budget *Hostelling International Honolulu (Map 4; ☎ 946-0591, fax 946-5904, 2323A Seaview Ave, Honolulu, HI 96822)* is a small hostel in a quiet residential neighborhood near the University of Hawaii. There are seven dorm rooms with bunk beds that can accommodate up to 42 travelers, with men and women in separate dorms. Rates are $12.50 for HI members and $15.50 for nonmembers. There are also two rooms for couples that cost an extra $10 per room.

If you're not a Hostelling International (HI) member, there's a three-night maximum stay. HI membership is sold on site; the cost is $25 for Americans, $18 for foreign visitors. Credit cards are accepted. Office hours are 8 am to noon and 4 pm to midnight. There are a TV lounge, common-use kitchen, laundry room, lockers and bulletin boards with useful information for new arrivals.

From the Ala Moana Center, catch bus No 6 or 18 (University or Woodlawn), get off at the corner of University Ave and Metcalf St and walk one block uphill to Seaview Ave. By car, take exit 24B off the H-1 Fwy, go mauka (inland) on University Ave and turn left at Seaview Ave.

During the school year the *Atherton YMCA (Map 4; ☎ 946-0253, fax 941-7802, 1810 University Ave, Honolulu, HI 96822)* operates as a dorm for full-time University of Hawaii students only. During summer holidays (mid-May to mid-August) it is usually open on a space-available basis to nonstudents, although some years it's full with students. Rates are $20 per day for a room with a bed, dresser, desk and chair; there's also a $25 processing fee. Reservations are made by application, which is available by mail or fax. The Y is directly opposite the university.

Fernhurst YWCA (Map 3; ☎ 941-2231, fax 949-0266, fernywca@gte.net, 1566 Wilder Ave, Honolulu, HI 96822) has rooms for women only in a three-story building about a mile from the university. There are 60 rooms, each intended for two guests, with two single beds, two lockable closets, two dressers and a desk. Two rooms share one bathroom. The cost is $25 per person. If you get a room to yourself, which is easier during the low season, it costs $5 more. Rates include breakfast and dinner, except on weekends and holidays; there are limited kitchen facilities on each floor.

Payment is required in advance; guests must be YWCA members (if you're not a member elsewhere, you can purchase a membership there for $30 a year). It costs an additional $20 to rent linen, or you can bring your own. Although the Y accepts tourists, most guests are local, because Fernhurst provides transitional housing for women in need. There's a laundry room, TV room and a garden courtyard with a small pool. Fernhurst is at the intersection of Wilder Ave and Punahou St on the No 4 and 5 bus lines.

The **Nuuanu YMCA** *(Map 2; ☎ 536-3556, 1441 Pali Hwy, Honolulu, HI 96813)*, at the intersection of Pali Hwy and Vineyard Blvd, has mostly long-term tenants but rents some rooms for $25 a day, $143 a week. Accommodations are for men only. Rooms are small and spartan, with louvered windows, a single bed and a small metal desk and chair. Bathrooms are shared. Guests have access to a TV lounge, the weight room and pool.

The **Central Branch YMCA** *(Map 3; ☎ 941-3344, fax 941-8821, 401 Atkinson Drive, Honolulu, HI 96814)*, on the east side of the Ala Moana Center, is the most conveniently located of the YMCAs. There are 114 rooms in all. The rooms with shared bath, which are available to men only, are small and simple and resemble those in a student dorm, with a desk, a single bed, a lamp, a chair and linoleum floors. The cost is $29 for a single, or for $40 they'll put in a rollaway bed and two people can share the room.

Rooms with private bath, which are a bit nicer but still small and basic, are open to both men and women and cost $36.50/51.50 for singles/doubles. All rooms have phones that guests can use to make free local calls. Guests receive YMCA privileges, including free use of the sauna, pool, gym and handball courts. There are coin laundry facilities, a TV lounge and a coffee shop. Credit cards are accepted.

Mid-Range The **Pagoda Hotel** *(Map 3; ☎ 941-6611, 800-367-6060, fax 955-5067, reservations@hthcorp.com, 1525 Rycroft St, Honolulu, HI 96814)*, north of the Ala Moana Center, has two sections. The rooms in the hotel itself, where you'll find the front desk and central lobby, are quiet and have the expected amenities, including air-con, TV, phone and refrigerator. There are also studios with kitchenettes in a nearby apartment complex, but they can feel a bit too removed from the main hotel – especially if you're checking in at night.

The hotel rooms cost $90 and the studios cost $95. Children under 18 occupying the same room as their parents stay free. There's nothing distinguished about this hotel other than a restaurant with a carp pond, but it is one way to avoid jumping into the Waikiki scene. The hotel maintains a website (www .pagodahotel.com).

Top End **Manoa Valley Inn** *(Map 4; ☎ 947-6019, 800-535-0085, fax 946-6168, marc@ aloha.net, 2001 Vancouver Drive, Honolulu, HI 96822)*, on a quiet side street near the University of Hawaii, is an authentically restored Victorian inn that's on the National Register of Historic Places. The inn's common areas and the eight guest rooms are furnished with antiques, and there are complimentary evening wine, a parlor and a billiard room. Rates, which include continental breakfast, are $99 for rooms with shared bath and $140 to $190 for rooms with private bath. The inn is managed by Marc Resorts.

The 1169-room **Ala Moana Hotel** *(Map 3; ☎ 955-4811, 800-367-6025, fax 944-6839, 410 Atkinson Drive, Honolulu, HI 96814)* looms above the Ala Moana Center, just beyond Waikiki. The rooms, which resemble those of a chain hotel, have TV, phones, air-con, small refrigerators and room safes. Rates start at $125 for lower-floor city-view rooms and climb to $225 for 'concierge' ocean-view rooms on the 29th to 35th floors. West of Waikiki, the hotel is a popular place for airline crews staying overnight.

The **Executive Centre Hotel** *(Map 2; ☎ 539-3000, 800-949-3932, fax 523-1088, 1088 Bishop St, Honolulu, HI 96813)* is Honolulu's only downtown hotel. Geared for businesspeople, it has 116 suites, each large and comfortable with modern amenities that include three phones, private voice mail, two TVs, a refrigerator, room safe and whirlpool bath. As the hotel is on the upper floors of a high-rise, most of the rooms have fine city views. There's a heated lap pool and a fitness center, as well as a business center with desks, computers, secretarial services and laptop rentals.

Rates, which include a continental breakfast and the morning newspaper, range from $170 for a mountain view to $195 for an executive ocean-view suite, the latter with kitchen facilities and a washer/dryer. If you're on business, the hotel's corporate rates begin at $121; otherwise there are periodic promotions and discounts, including 50% off for members of the Entertainment travel club.

PLACES TO EAT

Honolulu has an incredible variety of restaurants that mirror the city's multiethnic composition, and if you know where to look, it can also be quite cheap. The key is to get out of the tourist areas and eat where the locals do.

Downtown Honolulu (Map 2)

Restaurant Row The Restaurant Row, a rather sterile complex on the corner of Ala Moana Blvd and Punchbowl St, caters primarily to the downtown business crowd. There are a **Burger King**, a **Subway Sandwiches**, a **Bad Ass Coffee Co**, a **pizzeria**, an **ice cream shop** and several restaurants.

Payao (☎ 521-3511), a Thai eatery related to the popular university-area Chiang Mai restaurant, has an extensive menu, with vegetarian selections for around $7, curries, beef, chicken and noodle dishes for around $8 and seafood dishes for a bit more. It's open 11 am to 2 pm Monday to Saturday and 5 to 9:30 pm nightly.

Island Salsa (☎ 536-4777) takes its name from its salsa table, where customers can select from freshly made sauces ranging from the tame to the fire-eater. Although there's no lard in the food, in other ways it's near-authentic Mexican fare. Two tacos or a hefty burrito, with either tofu, grilled vegetable or chicken filling, cost $8 to $9, and combo plates with black beans and rice cost $12. It's open 11 am to 11 pm daily.

The best top-end choice at Restaurant Row is **Sunset Grill** (☎ 521-4409), which features grilled fresh fish and meats from around $20 at dinner and salads, calamari and sandwiches for half that price at lunch. It also periodically runs an all-you-can-eat ribs deal ($10.95), starting at 5 pm and going until the ribs run out. In addition to good food, the restaurant boasts an extensive wine list – including numerous selections by the glass. It's open 11 am to 11 pm weekdays and 5 pm to at least 10 pm on weekends.

There's also a branch of **Ruth's Chris Steak House** (☎ 599-3860), a pricey chain restaurant offering quality à la carte steaks for around $25; add $5 for a baked potato or salad. It's open 5 to 10 pm nightly.

Aloha Tower Marketplace The Aloha Tower Marketplace, the waterfront shopping complex and cruise ship terminal immediately west of the downtown district, is easily recognized by its landmark clock tower.

Gordon Biersch Brewery Restaurant (☎ 599-4877), seaside on the marketplace's 1st floor, is one of the most popular spots to go in Honolulu for a drink. Hawaii's first and most successful microbrewery restaurant, it features its own German-style lagers made according to Germany's centuries-old purity laws. The food is also very good: typical Hawaiian *pupus* and creative salads, sandwiches and pizzas are available for under $10, and hot pastas, Louisiana seafood gumbo or New York steaks run from $10 to $20. It's open 10:30 am to 10 pm daily (to 11 pm on weekends). There's live entertainment Wednesday through Saturday night.

Although it overlooks the parking lot and not the water, **Chai's Island Bistro** (☎ 585-0011) also attracts a crowd. A spin-off of the popular Singha Thai restaurant in Waikiki, it features Pacific Rim cuisine, with appetizers such as crispy duck *lumpia*, ahi tempura and organic salads for less than $10. Lunch entrees range from chicken satay for $11 to brandy-glazed lamb chops for $20; at dinner the same entrees jump $5. It's open 11 am to 4 pm on weekdays and 4 to 10 pm nightly.

If you favor a view over food, the Aloha Tower Marketplace has two waterfront restaurants opposite each other on the 2nd floor. The **Rodeo Cantina** (☎ 545-1200) serves lunchtime Mexican combination plates with black beans and rice, for $7 to $10, and dinnertime plates for a couple of dollars more. The **Big Island Steak House** (☎ 537-4446) has lunchtime grilled sandwiches for around $9 and steaks from $12; at dinner, steaks and prime rib cost $15 to $21.

The **Food Lanai**, also on the 2nd floor, has a water-view food court and nearly a

For Vegetarians

Honolulu doesn't have many entirely vegetarian restaurants, but there are a couple.

One establishment worth recommending is **Buddhist Vegetarian Restaurant** (Map 2; ☎ 532-8218) on the River St mall in Chinatown. It offers creative vegetarian Chinese food, including mock meat and seafood dishes.

In the University of Hawaii area, you'll find a vegetarian deli inside **Down to Earth Natural Foods** (Map 4; 2525 S King St) with inexpensive hot and cold take-out fare. For vegetarian Indian food there's **India Bazaar** (Map 4; ☎ 949-4840) in a little shopping center at 2320 S King St. **Coffeeline** (Map 4; ☎ 947-1615), a little cafe opposite the university, at the corner of University and Seaview Aves, serves up vegan soups, salads and simple vegetarian dishes.

In addition, there are many restaurants throughout Honolulu that have extensive vegetarian selections on their menus. Most Thai restaurants, including those listed in this book, have at least a page of vegetarian offerings, as do a number of Chinese and Vietnamese restaurants.

For a quick snack, Honolulu's ubiquitous **Ba Le** chain makes a tasty vegetarian sandwich of diced Asian vegetables on a crispy baguette for a mere $2. At the other end of the gastronomic scale, there's **Alan Wong's** (Map 3; ☎ 949-2526, 1857 S King St), one of Honolulu's top gourmet restaurants, which offers a three-course vegetarian dinner every night for $45.

The Vegetarian Society of Hawaii, a nonprofit organization that aims to educate people about the benefits of vegetarianism, sponsors social activities such as lectures, picnics and dining outings. Call ☎ 944-8344 for information about upcoming events.

dozen fast-food stalls selling soup, salad, udon, pizza and plate lunches – most for around $6. It's open 7 am to 9 pm daily (to 6 pm on Sunday).

Fort St Mall The Fort St Mall, a pedestrian street on the edge of the downtown district, has a number of cheap restaurants within walking distance of Iolani Palace. It's convenient for downtown workers and sightseers, but certainly not a draw if you're elsewhere around town.

Taco Bell, *McDonald's*, *Burger King*, *KFC* and *Pizza Hut* are all near the intersection of Hotel St and Fort St Mall.

A good option is **Ba Le** (1154 Fort St Mall), a branch of the Chinatown restaurant. It serves inexpensive Vietnamese sandwiches, shrimp rolls, green papaya salads and French coffees. There are plenty of vegetarian options and the highest-priced item, a seafood sandwich, is just $4. It's open 7 am to 7 pm weekdays and 8:30 am to 4 pm on Saturday.

Adjacent to Ba Le is the **Fort Street Cafe** (1152 Fort St Mall), a popular student hangout with plate lunches, Vietnamese pho

soups and various saimin dishes for around $5. It's open 7 am to 7 pm weekdays and 7 am to 4 pm on Saturday.

For Chinese fast food, there's **Mandarin Express** (116 S Hotel St). Although the food is served from steamer trays, it's usually fresh at mealtimes, and you can eat heartily for around $5; after 3 pm there's a 20% discount. It's open 9 am to 6 pm weekdays only.

Kozo Sushi (1150 Bishop St), a block south of the Fort St Mall, has good inexpensive sushi for takeout. It's open 9 am to 5 pm Monday to Thursday, to 5:30 pm on Friday.

Chinatown (Map 2)

For a quintessentially local dining option, head to the food court in the **Maunakea Marketplace** on N Hotel St. Here you'll find about 20 stalls with mom-and-pop vendors dishing out home-style Chinese, Thai, Vietnamese, Korean and Filipino food. You can get a solid meal for $5 and chow down at tiny wooden tables crowded into the central walkway. It's open from around 7 am to 3:30 pm daily.

Ba Le (150 N King St) is another good place for a quick, inexpensive bite. Crispy baguettes cost 40¢ and vegetarian sandwiches – a tangy combo of crunchy carrots, daikon and cilantro – are $2; a sandwich with meat is $3. For a caffeine jolt, there's sweet, strong French coffee with milk for $1.75 – hot or cold. They also make good croissants, shrimp rolls and tropical tapioca puddings. It's open 6 am to 5 pm daily (to 3 pm on Sunday).

Krung Thai (☎ 599-4803, 1028 Nuuanu Ave) is a little, good-value Thai eatery on the edge of Chinatown. Lunch, the only meal served, is geared to the business community's 30-minute lunch breaks, with food ready in steamer trays. You can choose from a dozen hot dishes such as chicken *Panang*, beef eggplant and vegetarian curry. One item costs $4, two items $4.89, and all are served with rice or noodles. It's open 10:30 am to 2:30 pm weekdays. There are tables in a rear courtyard where you can sit and enjoy your meal.

A favorite Chinatown eatery is the Vietnamese restaurant *To Chau* (☎ 533-4549, 1007 River St), where the specialty is pho, a delicious soup of beef broth, rice noodles, thin slices of beef and a garnish of cilantro and green onion. It comes with a second plate of fresh basil, mung bean sprouts and slices of hot chile pepper. It's a bargain at just $3.85 for a regular bowl or $5.20 for an extra-large one.

The shrimp rolls with spicy peanut sauce ($3) are a good choice, and the restaurant also serves rice and noodle dishes, but just about everybody comes for the soup. To Chau is open 8 am to 2:30 pm daily. It's so popular that even at 10 am you may have to line up outside the door for one of the 16 tables. It's well worth the wait.

Ha Bien (☎ 531-1185, 198 N King St), next door to To Chau, is another popular Vietnamese restaurant with good, inexpensive food. Although Ha Bien specializes in noodle and rice dishes, the menu also includes spring rolls, soups and crêpes. Most dishes cost $5 to $6. It's open 8 am to 4 pm on weekdays, to 3:30 pm on weekends.

You can also find an assortment of small Vietnamese restaurants on Maunakea St near its intersection with Pauahi St, including *A Little Bit of Saigon* (☎ 528-3663, 1160 Maunakea St), which serves a decent pho for $5, good fried tofu or chicken noodle dishes for $7 and various combination plates for under $10. It's open 10 am to 10 pm daily.

The service can be a bit abrupt at *Wong and Wong* (☎ 521-4492, 1023 Maunakea St), but this popular Chinese eatery offers good, reasonably priced Cantonese food. Most items on the extensive menu, including a tasty crispy chicken, are priced $5 to $8. It's open 10:30 am to 11 pm daily.

Doong Kong Lau (☎ 531-8833), in the Chinatown Cultural Center on the River St pedestrian mall, has standard Chinese fare, including some Hakka regional dishes. Vegetable, poultry and pork dishes cost $6 to $7, while seafood plates are a few dollars more. Generous lunch specials are available for around $5. It's open 9:30 am to 8:30 pm daily.

Immediately west of Doong Kong Lau on the River St mall is the *Buddhist Vegetarian Restaurant* (☎ 532-8218), in the Chinatown Cultural Plaza. This health-oriented Chinese dining spot offers some incongruously named dishes such as vegetarian duck, and sweet-and-sour vegetarian pork, that creatively use tofu and wheat gluten to duplicate the flavors and textures of meat and seafood. Nonetheless, the restaurant is 100% vegetarian. The food is good and the menu is not only imaginative but extensive as well, with most dishes priced $7 to $10.

There's also a dim sum menu available at lunch. It's open 10:30 am to 2 pm and 5:30 to 9 pm daily except Wednesday.

Zaffron (☎ 533-6635, 69 N King St), at the southwest side of Chinatown, is a small, family-run Indian restaurant that offers six different plate lunches priced at $7 each. The choices include vegetarian dishes, tandoori chicken and meat or fish curries. Each plate lunch includes *chole*, *aloo sabiz*, rice and nan. Lunch is served 11 am to 2:30 pm Monday to Saturday. It's also open 6 to 9:30 pm on Friday and Saturday, at which time there's a buffet dinner for $12.50.

For upmarket dining, there's *Indigo* (☎ 521-2900, 1121 Nuuanu Ave), which has a relaxed, open-air courtyard and very good contemporary Asian-Pacific cuisine. Located on the Chinatown-downtown border, behind the Hawaii Theatre, Indigo is a favorite dinner spot for theatergoers.

A special treat here is the creative dim sum appetizers, such as tempura ahi rolls and goat cheese wontons. Dinner features duck, steak and fish dishes for $17 to $20. The gourmet pizzas ($8.50) that come in vegetarian, Peking duck and spicy chicken varieties are popular at lunch. It's open 11:30 am to 2 pm Tuesday to Friday and 5:30 to 9:30 pm Tuesday to Saturday.

Central Honolulu & Ala Moana (Map 3)

Central Honolulu has two well-stocked supermarkets: *Foodland (1460 S Beretania St)* and *Safeway (1121 S Beretania St)*.

Auntie Pasto's (☎ 523-8855, 1099 S Beretania St) has good Italian food at honest prices. Pasta with tomato sauce costs $5.50, $7 with fresh vegetables in butter and garlic and $8 with pesto sauce. The Parmesan cheese is freshly grated and the Italian bread is served warm. Although it's off the tourist track, this popular spot attracts a crowd and you may have to wait for a table – particularly on the weekend. It's open 11 am to 10:30 pm Monday to Friday and 4 to 10:45 pm on Saturday and Sunday.

El Burrito (☎ 596-8225, 550 Piikoi St), near the Ala Moana Center, could be a neighborhood restaurant on a back street in Mexico City. This hole-in-the-wall squeezes in about a dozen tables and serves Honolulu's most authentic Mexican food. Two tamales, enchiladas or chiles rellenos with rice and beans average $9. It's open 11 am to 8 pm Monday to Thursday, to 9 pm on Friday and Saturday. Expect lines at dinnertime, especially on the weekend.

The *Garden Cafe (☎ 532-8734, 900 S Beretania St)*, a courtyard restaurant inside the Honolulu Academy of Arts, offers a chance to dine in support of the arts. The menu is mostly sandwiches, soups and salads for around $8 to $11. It's open 11:30 am to 1 pm Tuesday to Saturday. Reservations are suggested, particularly if there's a special exhibit taking place at the museum.

Mekong (☎ 591-8841, 1295 S Beretania St) is not only home to the original Keo's (a small Honolulu chain), but it still has the original Thai chef. It also has a menu similar to its upmarket spin-off, but in this tiny eatery, posters replace the artwork, you bring your own booze and prices are about a third less. The tasty spring rolls come with lettuce, mint leaves and peanut sauce and cost $6, and most beef, chicken and vegetarian main dishes are a dollar more. Nothing on the menu is more than $10.

It's open 11 am to 2 pm on weekdays and 5 to 9:30 pm nightly. Parking is available in the lot at the west side of the building, next to the florist. There's also a *Mekong II (☎ 941-6184, 1726 S King St)*, which has essentially the same menu.

The *Pagoda Restaurant (☎ 941-6611, 1525 Rycroft St)*, at the Pagoda Hotel, serves just average food but offers a pleasant setting bordering a carp pond. The breakfast menu (6:30 to 10:30 am) is extensive, with many choices for around $5. There's a lunch buffet of Japanese and American dishes for $11 that's served 11 am to 2 pm weekdays. There's also a nightly dinner buffet ($17 to $19) served 4:30 to 9:30 pm. It features an array of dishes including prime rib, Alaskan snow crab, sashimi, tempura, a salad bar and a dessert bar.

Yanagi Sushi (☎ 537-1525, 762 Kapiolani Blvd) is one of Honolulu's most popular places for moderately priced sushi. It's open 11 am to 2 pm and 5:30 pm to 2 am daily (to 10 pm on Sunday).

Alan Wong's (☎ 949-2526, 1857 S King St) is one of Hawaii's top restaurants – a high-energy place specializing in upmarket Hawaii Regional cuisine. Chef Wong, who won accolades at the Big Island's exclusive Mauna Lani Resort before striking out on his own, features a creative menu with an emphasis on fresh local ingredients.

Appetizers, such as sashimi, tempura ahi or duck salad, cost $7.50 to $10, and entrees average $30 for spicy seafood paella, beef tenderloin with Kona lobster or ginger-crusted onaga. Each night there's also a five-course 'tasting menu' for $65 and a three-course vegetarian menu for $45. Alan

Wong's is a little east of the university area and is open 5 to 10 pm nightly; reservations are usually essential.

Ala Moana Center This shopping center's food court, called *Makai Market*, is a circus, with neon signs, hundreds of tiny tables crowded together and nearly 50 fast-food stands. There's something for everyone, from salads to daiquiris, ice cream to pizza, and Chinese, Japanese, Korean, Hawaiian, Filipino, Thai and Mexican specialties.

If you have the munchies, this is a good place to stop when you're between buses. It's like window-shopping – you can walk through, preview the food and select what you want. The food court is on the ocean side of the Ala Moana Center's ground floor. It's open 8 am to 9 pm Monday to Saturday and 9 am to 6 pm on Sunday.

Panda Express has good, MSG-free Mandarin and Szechuan food, with dishes like spicy chicken, broccoli beef and eggplant with garlic sauce. Combination plates with fried rice or chow mein and two entrees are $5, three entrees $6. The food is fresh, and you can pick what looks best from the steamer trays.

Yummy Korean BBQ is a similar concept, with Korean selections that include rice and a number of tasty pickled veggies and kimchis, with plates from $5.50 to $7.

Patti's Chinese Kitchen is a big-volume restaurant with a few dozen dishes to choose from. It costs $5 for two selections, $6 for three selections, including rice or noodles. If you really want to indulge, you can get a whole roast duck for $11. There's also a limited selection of dim sum and desserts, such as almond cookies and *haupia*.

Naniwa Ya Ramen dishes up steaming bowls of authentic Japanese ramen noodles for around $6 and has *gyoza*, a tasty grilled dumpling that goes great with beer, for $3.

Cactus Jack's offers tacos, tostadas or fajitas with rice and beans for around $6. At nearby *Little Cafe Siam*, two tasty skewers of chicken satay in peanut sauce cost $2.25, and at *Sbarro* a big slice of pizza costs around $3.

Paradise Bakery & Café makes nice muffins and bagels and the nearby *Twisted Pretzel* sells fresh pretzels and the locally popular *malasada,* a Portuguese-style fried doughnut that's served warm.

Also in the Ala Moana Center is a *Foodland* supermarket that's open 7 am to 11 pm daily. There are also *McDonald's, Pizza Hut, Häagen-Dazs* and *Dunkin' Donuts* fast-food chains; their hours are the same as the food court's.

Ward Centre Ward Centre, a shopping complex at 1200 Ala Moana Blvd, has a couple of coffee shops and delis, a branch of *Keo's* Thai restaurant and about a dozen other dining spots.

Mocha Java/Crepe Fever, on the center's ground level, is a popular hangout serving good fresh fruit smoothies, coffees, crêpes, omelettes, sandwiches, desserts and other light dishes. It's open 7 am to 9 pm Monday to Saturday and 8 am to 4 pm on Sunday.

You'll find a slightly more expensive espresso bar inside *Borders* bookstore at the opposite end of the complex – it closes 30 minutes before the bookstore, which is open 9 am to at least 11 pm daily (9 pm on Sunday).

Bernard's New York Deli (☎ 594-3354), at the street-level northwest corner of the center, offers authentic Jewish deli fare, including bagels, cheese blintzes, deli sandwiches on rye and smoked lox with matzo brei. Nothing on its extensive menu costs more than $10. On weekends until 11:30 am there's a breakfast buffet for $8. The deli is open 6:30 am to 9 pm except on Sunday when it closes early.

Scoozee's (☎ 597-1777), also on the ground level, is a trendy nouveau-Italian cafe with good pastas, pizzas and calzones for $10 and sandwiches for a tad less. It's open 11 am to 10 pm Sunday through Thursday and to 11 pm on Friday and Saturday.

The food is a bit too Americanized at *Compadres* (☎ 591-8307), but this busy Mexican restaurant still draws a crowd and wins plenty of local awards. Combination plates with rice and beans average $10 to

$15. It's on the center's upper level and is open 11 am to 11 pm on weekdays, to midnight on Friday and Saturday and until 10 pm on Sunday.

The *Brew Moon* (☎ 593-0088), a stylish, high-energy place, is a branch of a small Boston-based chain of microbreweries. It specializes in ales, ranging from a low calorie 'moonlight' brew to the copper-colored 'Hawaii 5' malt; a 20oz sampler with five different ales costs $5.50, a single brew $4.75. Brew Moon serves a wide variety of snacks, including nachos, *poke* and shrimp rolls for around $8; burgers and sandwiches with fries are also in that price range. Meals such as jambalaya chicken or ginger sesame stir-fry are around $10 at lunch and $15 at dinner. It's open 11 am to 1 am daily.

At the top end is *A Pacific Cafe Oahu* (☎ 593-0035), a branch of Jean-Marie Josselin's well-regarded Pacific Rim restaurant on Kauai. The menu features calamari tempura, fresh fish carpaccio and similar appetizers for around $10. Entrees, such as blackened ahi with hearts of palm or rack of lamb, average $25. The lunch menu has similar but smaller servings for prices that are about 40% less. It's on the center's upper level and is open 11:30 am to 2 pm weekdays and 5:30 to 9 pm daily.

Ward Warehouse The Ward Warehouse, on the corner of Ala Moana Blvd and Ward Ave, is a shopping complex adjacent to the Ward Centre. Both centers have free garage parking and can be reached by bus Nos 8, 19 and 20.

The three restaurants are on the upper level and have harbor views, so be sure to ask for a window table when you make your reservations.

For cheap eats, the *Old Spaghetti Factory* (☎ 591-2513) is hard to beat. This family-style restaurant has an elaborate decor, chock-full of antiques, heavy woods, Tiffany stained glass – even an old streetcar. At lunch (11:30 am to 2 pm weekdays), you can order spaghetti with tomato sauce for $3.75, with clam sauce for $4.65 or with meatballs for $5.85. All meals come with bread and a

simple green salad. Dishes are about a dollar more at dinner, which is served 5 to 10 pm weekdays, 11:30 am to 10:30 pm Saturday and 4 to 9:30 pm on Sunday. The food itself is not special, but the price is right and the decor is interesting.

Kincaid's Fish, Chop & Steak House (☎ 591-2005) is a pleasant place serving good, moderately priced seafood and steaks. A favorite lunch spot for downtown business-people, the restaurant offers lunch entrees that include such things as spicy Cajun fettuccine for $10, seared ahi Caesar salad or oven-roasted garlic prawns for $13 and grilled ahi with pineapple salsa for $15. At dinner, fresh fish entrees and steaks are priced from $17 to $24. It's open 11 am to 5 pm for lunch and 5 to 10 pm for dinner daily.

Stuart Anderson's (☎ 591-9292), a chain steak house, has lunches in the $8 to $10 range and dinners for about double that. The lunch menu is served 11 am to 4 pm Monday to Saturday. Dinner is served 4 pm to at least 10 pm Monday to Saturday and noon to 9:30 pm on Sunday.

In addition to the restaurants, there are a few food stalls on the ground floor that sell $6 plate lunches: *Korean BBQ Express*, has Korean fare; *L&L Drive-Inn* is a chain with local dishes; and *Dairy Queen*, a chain with generic fast food. Also at ground level is *Coffee Works*, a little cafe that sells coffee, espresso, scones and bagels.

University Area (Map 4)

Not surprisingly, the area around the University of Hawaii at Manoa supports an interesting collection of reasonably priced ethnic restaurants, coffee shops and health food stores. The following places are all within a 10-minute walk of the three-way intersection of King St, Beretania St and University Ave.

Coffeeline (☎ 947-1615), at the corner of University and Seaview Aves, is a student hangout serving coffees and vegetarian meals. Vegan soup costs $2.50; omelets, sandwiches and salads are around $4; and a few hot dishes, such as spinach lasagna, cost $5.

It's open 7 am to 4 pm weekdays and 7 am to noon on Saturday.

Ezogiku Noodle Cafe *(1010 University Ave)*, on the corner of Beretania St, serves up ramen for $6.50, *gyoza* for $3.75 and a handful of other dishes, including curries and fried rice. While it's nothing memorable, it is on par with similar fast-food noodle shops in Japan. It's open 11 am to 11 pm daily.

Across the street, a branch of the Vietnamese restaurant **Ba Le** *(1091 University Ave)* sells good inexpensive French rolls, croissants and sandwiches. A tasty vegetarian sandwich costs $2, and a roast beef version goes for $4.

Down to Earth Natural Foods *(2525 S King St)* is a large natural foods supermarket with everything from Indian chapatis to local organic produce and a dozen varieties of granola sold in bulk. It's a great place to shop, and the healthier yogurts and wholegrain breads that some of Honolulu's more with-it supermarkets sell are substantially cheaper here. It's open 7:30 am to 10 pm daily. The store also has a vegetarian deli with a salad bar and hot dishes such as vegan chow fun or vegetable curry for $5 a pound. There's a conventional grocery store, **Star Market**, across the street.

Diem *(☎ 941-8657, 2633 S King St)*, near the corner of University Ave, is a small Vietnamese restaurant with $5 lunch specials served until 3 pm daily. Dinner specials that include an entree, salad, rice and appetizer cost $9. Diem is open 11 am to 3 pm and 5 to at least 9 pm daily.

Chan's Gourmet Buffet *(☎ 949-1188, 2600 S King St)* is a long-established Chinese restaurant that has thrown away its menu and switched to buffet meals. It now caters to students and other value-oriented diners with a generous $6 lunch buffet (10:30 am to 4 pm Sunday to Friday) of about 50 items, mostly Chinese food but also some Japanese and American dishes. At dinner (4:30 to 10:30 pm daily) the price goes up to $8 but seafood dishes are added to the buffet. On Saturday there's a dim sum brunch (9 am to 4 pm) for $9.

India Bazaar *(☎ 949-4840)*, in a little shopping center at 2320 S King St, is a small cafe selling inexpensive Indian food. There's a vegetarian *thali* that includes spiced rice and three curry items for $6 and a chicken thali for $7. Side orders of *papadams*, chapatis and *raita* cost less than $1. It's open 11 to 9 pm Monday to Saturday.

In the same complex is a branch of **Kozo Sushi** *(☎ 973-5666)*, a local chain that specializes in good, inexpensive sushi. An excellent choice is the California *maki*, a crab and avocado sushi roll that comes eight pieces to the set for $3.50. Although it's mostly take-out, the shop has a couple of tables where you can sit and eat. It's open 9 am to 7 pm daily (to 6 pm on Sunday).

Maple Garden *(☎ 941-6641, 909 Isenberg St)*, around the corner from S King St, is a popular local Szechuan restaurant with good food at reasonable prices. Vegetarian entrees, which include a delicious eggplant in hot garlic sauce, average $6.50, while most meat dishes are about a dollar more. If you like duck, they make a tasty smoked Szechuan version for $8.25. At lunch there are a couple of multi-item plate specials that include hot-and-sour soup and an almond tofu dessert, for just $6. It's open 11 am to 2 pm and 5:30 to 10 pm daily.

Chiang Mai *(☎ 941-1151, 2239 S King St)* serves northern Thai food, including a wonderful sticky rice. There are two dozen vegetarian dishes and a range of meat dishes for around $7. It's open 11 am to 2 pm weekdays and 5:30 to 10 pm nightly.

Yakiniku Camellia *(☎ 946-7595, 2494 S Beretania St)* has a tasty all-you-can-cook Korean lunch buffet for $9.95 from 11 am to 3 pm. It's quality food, and if you've worked up an appetite, it's a fine deal. The mainstay of the menu is pieces of chicken, pork and beef that you select from a refrigerated cabinet and grill at your table. Accompanying this are 18 marinated side dishes, miso and seaweed soups, simple vegetable salads and a few fresh fruits. The mung bean and watercress dishes tossed with sesame seeds are sweet and mild. When selecting kimchis, keep in mind that the redder they are, the hotter they are. Dinner, from 3 to 10 pm, costs $15.75 and offers essentially the same fare with the addition of sashimi. Everything in this restaurant is authentic, right down to the vending machine that sells newspapers from Korea.

The *Longboard Cafe* (☎ 951-6435, 2671 S King St) is a little dinner restaurant specializing in good Eurasian food. Appetizers include stuffed chicken wings for $4 and a nice Thai chicken salad for $7. Main dishes, which average $10 to $15, range from Thai curries to chicken masala and scampi. It's open 5 to 9:30 pm daily.

Elsewhere in Honolulu

Although it's well off the beaten path, *Hale Vietnam* (Map 1; ☎ 735-7581, 1140 12th Ave), in the Kaimuki area, is a top-notch local favorite with delicious Vietnamese food at moderate prices. A nice starter are the temple rolls ($4.25), a combination of fresh basil, mint, tofu and yam rolled in rice paper. The yellow curries are excellent and cost around $9 for vegetarian, beef or chicken dishes. The extensive menu also features pho soups ($6) and a good variety of vegetarian and seafood dishes. It's open 11 am to 10 pm daily.

Helena's Hawaiian Foods (Map 1; ☎ 845-8044, 1364 N King St) is a friendly, family-run operation that's been serving good, inexpensive Hawaiian food since 1946. It's a thoroughly local eatery, with 10 simple Formica-top tables and a mix of vinyl chairs and stools. The elderly women who run the restaurant make a delicious kalua pig; also notable are the pipikaula and the lomi salmon.

Helena's is a survivor, and walking in the door is a bit like stepping 50 years back in time. Nearly everything on the à la carte menu is less than $2.50, and complete meals with poi (fresh, day-old or sour) or rice are $5.50 to $9. It's open 11 am to 7:30 pm Tuesday to Friday only.

For a trendy restaurant with a loyal Honolulu following, try *3660 On the Rise* (Map 1; ☎ 737-1177, 3660 Waialae Ave). It features 'Euro-Island' cuisine, blending continental and island flavors. Starters such as escargot, ahi poke spring rolls or local barbecued prawns cost around $10. Main dishes average $20 and include Hawaiian-style seafood

steamed in ti leaf, roast duck in mango salsa and Black Angus garlic steak.

It's closed on Monday but otherwise open for dinner 5:30 to at least 9 pm. Reservations are suggested. The restaurant is out of the way, 3 miles northeast of Waikiki, on Waialae Ave between 12th and 13th Aves.

A distinctive choice is the Salvation Army's *Waioli Tea Room* (Map 5; ☎ 988-5800, 2950 Manoa Rd) in Manoa Valley, between the University of Hawaii and the Lyon Arboretum. It has various open-air dining rooms looking out onto gardens. In one of the gardens is the restored grass hut that author Robert Louis Stevenson stayed in during his retreat at Waikiki Beach; the cottage was dismantled and moved to this site in 1926. Another area has a chapel that's a popular wedding spot.

The main event here is the afternoon high tea, which is served on the veranda at 2:30 pm on Sunday. At $16, it's not cheap, but it's an elegant affair with fine china, a dozen-plus teas and a good selection of homemade scones and pastries. You can also get breakfast here, with waffles and omelets, as well as lunchtime sandwiches, such as chicken curry with mango chutney, and specialty salads like fresh ahi on island greens. Most menu items are priced around $10.

It's open for meals 8 am to 4 pm daily. For the high tea, reservations are required and usually need to be made at least a day in advance.

For a genteel treat, try the *Contemporary Cafe* (Map 5; ☎ 523-3362, 2411 Makiki Heights Drive), which has a pleasant lawn setting in the Contemporary Museum in Makiki Valley. There are always healthy salads, such as grilled chicken Caesar, Greek salad with shrimp or soba noodles with baked tofu, for around $10. Sandwiches, served with tortilla chips and hummus, include grilled vegetables on focaccia or a Gardenburger for $8.50 and chicken or fresh fish sandwiches for a tad more.

Lunch is served 11 am to 2 pm Tuesday to Saturday and noon to 2 pm on Sunday. Desserts and beverages are available until 3 pm. Reservations are recommended. It's not necessary to pay museum admission if you're just having lunch – simply let the staff person at the door know that you're there for the cafe.

ENTERTAINMENT
Honolulu has a lively entertainment scene. The best updated listings are in the free *Honolulu Weekly*, which is easily found throughout the city, and the TGIF insert in the Friday edition of the *Honolulu Advertiser*.

Theater & Concerts
Honolulu has a symphony, an opera company, ballet troupes, chamber orchestras and numerous community theater groups.

The impeccably restored *Hawaii Theatre* (Map 2; ☎ 528-0506, 1130 Bethel St) is a popular venue for dance, music and theater. Performances range from top contemporary Hawaiian musicians such as Hapa and Hookena to modern dance pieces and film festivals.

The *Blaisdell Center* (Map 3; ☎ 591-2211, 777 Ward Ave) presents concerts, Broadway shows and family events, such as the Honolulu Symphony, the Ice Capades, the American Ballet Theatre, the Brothers Cazimero and occasional big-name rock musicians.

The *Academy Theatre* (Map 3; ☎ 532-8768, 900 S Beretania St), at the Honolulu Academy of Arts, and to a lesser degree, the *East-West Center* (Map 4; ☎ 944-7111), adjacent to the University of Hawaii, both present multicultural theater and concerts, such as performances of Chinese opera and recitals of Japanese koto music.

There are more than a dozen theater companies on Oahu, performing everything from Broadway musicals to David Mamet satires and pidgin fairy tales. For a schedule of current theater productions, see the entertainment section of the Honolulu newspapers.

The *Aloha Stadium* (☎ 486-9300), on the western outskirts of Honolulu (see Pearl Harbor Area map), has the island's largest audience capacity and is the location for some of the biggest concerts, such as those by Celine Dion, the Rolling Stones and Janet Jackson.

Music & Dancing
The *Pier Bar* (Map 2; ☎ 536-2166), at the Aloha Tower Marketplace, has live music 7 pm to 2 am Tuesday to Saturday, featuring swing, alternative music and top-name contemporary Hawaiian musicians such as Willie K and Henry Kapono. There's no cover on Tuesday, when it's usually Hawaiian music; other nights there's typically a $3 cover.

Also at the Aloha Tower Marketplace, the *Gordon Biersch Brewery Restaurant* (Map 2; ☎ 599-4877), a popular waterfront microbrewery, has live contemporary Hawaiian, alternative rock and soft rock 8:30 pm to midnight on Thursday, Friday and Saturday. There's no cover charge.

Rumours (Map 3; ☎ 955-4811, 410 Atkinson Drive) at the Ala Moana Hotel, has dancing to recorded music 9 pm to 4 am on weekends, with top 40 music on Friday and '70s to '90s music on Saturday. On Sunday, there's ballroom dancing 5 to 9 pm and Top 40 music 9 pm to midnight. The cover is $5 and you must be at least 21 years old to be admitted.

Anna Bannanas (Map 4; ☎ 946-5190, 2440 S Beretania St), not far from the university, features blues, rock and reggae bands from 9:30 pm to 2 am Thursday to Sunday. There's usually a cover charge of $4.

Cinemas
Honolulu has several movie theaters showing first-run feature films, including *Restaurant Row 9 Cinemas* (Map 2; ☎ 526-4171), a nine-screen multiplex at Restaurant Row, and the *Varsity Twins* (Map 4; ☎ 296-1818), a two-screen cinema on University Ave near the University of Hawaii. Both offer matinee showings for $4.

To see progressive movies, there's the *Academy Theatre* (Map 3; ☎ 532-8768, 900 S Beretania St) at the Honolulu Academy of Arts. It showcases American independent cinema, foreign films and avant-garde shorts. Tickets cost $5.

The *Movie Museum* (Map 1; ☎ 735-8771, 3566 Harding Ave) is a fun place for film buffs to watch classic oldies, such as Humphrey Bogart and Lauren Bacall flicks, in a theater with just 18 comfy lounge chairs. Movies show at 8 pm Thursday to Monday, as well as in the afternoon on Saturday and Sunday. Admission is $5; reservations are recommended.

Free Entertainment

The *Royal Hawaiian Band* performs from 12:15 to 1:15 pm on Friday (except during August) on the lawn of the Iolani Palace (Map 2).

In the *Ala Moana Center* (Map 3), a courtyard area called Centerstage is the venue for free performances by high school choirs, gospel groups, ballet troupes, local bands and the like. There's something happening almost daily – look for the schedule in the Ala Moana Center's free shopping magazine.

The *Mayor's Office of Culture & Arts* sponsors numerous free performances, art exhibits and musical events, ranging from street musicians in city parks to band concerts in various locales around Honolulu. Call ☎ 527-5666 for information on current events.

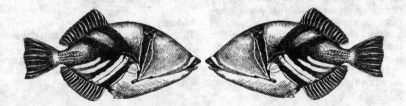

Waikiki

Waikiki, the largest tourist destination in Hawaii, has a long, attractive white-sand beach that's lined with high-rise hotels and set against a backdrop of scenic Diamond Head.

Crowded with package tourists from both Japan and North America, Waikiki has 25,000 permanent residents and some 65,000 visitors on any given day, all in an area roughly 1½ miles long and half a mile wide. It boasts 33,000 hotel rooms, 450 restaurants, 350 bars and clubs, and more shops than you'd want to count.

Waikiki has plenty of activities that make for good fun, such as the Kodak Hula Show, outrigger canoe rides and sunning on the beach. Like any city scene, the deeper you dig, the more you'll find. For example, you can join in a Japanese tea ceremony, take a surfing lesson from one of the aging beach-boys or listen to a free Sunday concert by the Royal Hawaiian Band in Kapiolani Park.

Although the beaches are packed during the day, at night most of the action is along the streets, where window-shoppers, time-share touts and street-corner prostitutes all go about their business. A variety of live music, from mellow Hawaiian to rock, wafts from clubs and hotel lounges.

Waikiki Beach has wonderful orange sunsets, with the sun picturesquely dropping down between cruising sailboats. The beach is also quite romantic to stroll along at night, enhanced by the dramatic city skyline and the soothing sounds of the surf lapping at the shore, and it's dark enough to enjoy the star-filled sky.

ORIENTATION

Waikiki is bounded on two sides by the Ala Wai Canal, on another by the ocean and on the fourth by the expansive Kapiolani Park.

There are three parallel roads through Waikiki: Kalakaua Ave, the beach road named after King David Kalakaua; Kuhio Ave, the main drag for Waikiki's buses, which is named after Prince Jonah Kuhio Kalanianaole; and Ala Wai Blvd, which borders the Ala Wai Canal.

City buses are not allowed on Kalakaua Ave, and trucks are prohibited at midday. Traffic on this four-lane road is one-way, so it's relatively smooth for driving. However, pedestrians need to be cautious, as cars tend to zoom by at a fairly fast clip.

INFORMATION
Tourist Offices

The Hawaii Visitors and Convention Bureau has its visitor information office (☎ 924-0266) in the Royal Hawaiian Shopping Center, 2201 Kalakaua Ave, Suite A401A (Building A, 4th floor), at the Lewers St end of the center. It has racks of brochures and general tourist literature, and is open 8 am to 5 pm weekdays.

Free tourist magazines, such as *This Week Oahu*, *Spotlight's Oahu Gold* and *Guide to Oahu*, can readily be found on street corners and in hotel lobbies throughout Waikiki.

Money

There's a Bank of Hawaii at 2220 Kalakaua Ave and a First Hawaiian Bank at 2181 Kalakaua Ave. Both banks are open 8:30 am to 4 pm Monday to Thursday and 8:30 am to 6 pm Friday.

There are numerous ATMs around Waikiki that accept major bank and credit cards. Those at Food Pantry, 2370 Kuhio Ave, and at the nearby 7-Eleven convenience store, 2299 Kuhio Ave, are both accessible 24 hours a day.

Post

The main Waikiki post office, 330 Saratoga Rd, is open 8 am to 4:30 pm weekdays, except Wednesday, when it's open 8 am to 6 pm. The post office's Saturday hours are 9 am to noon.

From Swamp to Resort

A little more than a century ago, Waikiki was almost entirely wetlands. It had more than 50 acres of fishponds, as well as extensive taro patches and rice paddies. Fed by mountain streams from the upland Manoa and Makiki Valleys, Waikiki was one of Oahu's most fertile and productive areas.

Waikiki's narrow beachfront was soon replaced with private gingerbread-trimmed cottages that were built by Honolulu's more well-to-do citizens.

Author Robert Louis Stevenson, who frequented Waikiki in those days, wrote:

If anyone desires such old-fashioned things as lovely scenery, quiet, pure air, clear sea water, heavenly sunsets hung out before his eyes over the Pacific and the distant hills of Waianae, I recommend him to Waikiki Beach.

Tourism took root in 1901, when the Moana opened its doors as Waikiki's first real hotel. A tram line was constructed to connect Waikiki to downtown Honolulu, and city folk crowded aboard for outings to the beach. Tiring quickly of the pesky mosquitoes that thrived in the wetlands, these early beachgoers petitioned to have Waikiki's 'swamps' brought under control.

In 1922 the Ala Wai Canal was dug to divert the streams that flowed into Waikiki. Old Hawaii lost out, as farmers had the water drained out from under them. Coral rubble was used to fill the ponds, creating what was to become Hawaii's most valuable piece of real estate. Water buffaloes were replaced by tourists.

Waikiki's second hotel, the Royal Hawaiian, was completed in 1927 and became the crown jewel of the Matson Navigation Company.

The Royal was the land component for cruises on the *Malolo*, one of the premier luxury ships of the day. The $7.5 million ship, built while the $2 million hotel was under construction, carried 650 passengers from San Francisco to Honolulu each fortnight. The Pink Palace, as the Royal Hawaiian was nicknamed, opened with an extravagant $10-a-plate dinner.

Hotel guests ranged from the Rockefellers to Charlie Chaplin, from Babe Ruth to royalty. Some of the guests brought dozens of trunks, their servants and even their Rolls Royces.

The Depression, however, put a damper on things, and WWII saw the Royal Hawaiian turned into a 'rest and relaxation' center for servicemen.

In 1950, Waikiki had only 1400 hotel rooms, and surfers could drive their cars to the beach and park right on the sand. In the 1960s tourism took over in earnest. By 1968, Waikiki had some 13,000 hotel rooms, and in the following two decades, that number more than doubled.

The lack of available land finally halted the boom of new hotels. In a desperate attempt to squeeze in one more high-rise, St Augustine's Church, standing on the last speck of undeveloped property along busy Kalakaua Ave, was nearly sold in 1989 to a Tokyo developer for $45 million. It took a community uproar and a petition to the Vatican to nullify the deal.

There's a branch post office at the Hilton Hawaiian Village, 2005 Kalia Rd, that's open 8 am to noon and 1 to 4 pm Monday to Saturday.

Bookstores
Waldenbooks (☎ 922-4154), which has a good collection of Hawaiiana books, travel guides and paperback fiction, is at the Waikiki Shopping Plaza, 2270 Kalakaua Ave.

Libraries
The Waikiki-Kapahulu Public Library, 400 Kapahulu Ave, is open 10 am to 5 pm Monday, Thursday, Friday and Saturday and 10 am to 8 pm Tuesday and Wednesday. It's a relatively small library, but it does subscribe to the daily Honolulu newspapers as well as the *New York Times* and the *Wall Street Journal*.

Laundry
Many Waikiki accommodations have on-site laundry facilities. If yours doesn't, there are public coin laundries open 6:30 am to 10 pm daily at the Waikiki West hotel, 2330 Kuhio Ave; the Waikiki Coral Seas hotel, 250 Lewers St; and the Outrigger Waikiki, 2335 Kalakaua Ave.

Film & Photography
Fox Photo, with Waikiki branches in the Royal Hawaiian Shopping Center (☎ 926-2960) and in the Sheraton Moana hotel (☎ 922-4340), does one-hour photo processing. To buy film and to have slides processed, Longs Drugs is a good choice. It offers pro-

cessing by Kodak and Fuji. Slides generally take two to three days, prints a day or two, and the cost is cheaper than at camera shops. Although there are no branches in Waikiki, there's a Longs Drugs (☎ 946-6905) on the upper level of the Ala Moana Center.

Parking
Parking cheaply in Waikiki can be a challenge. Many of the hotels charge $8 to $15 a day for guest parking in their garages.

At the west end of Waikiki, the best bet is the public parking lot at the end of the Ala Wai Yacht Harbor, which has free parking up to a maximum of 24 hours.

At the east end of Waikiki, the zoo parking lot on Kapahulu Ave has meters that cost just 25¢ an hour with a four-hour parking limit. If you like taking chances, you can try your luck parking overnight at the zoo; however, if you don't move out early enough in the morning, you may be greeted with the sight of a police officer placing a $25 ticket on your window.

Note: Hawaii is notorious for rip-offs of rental vehicles, so do not leave valuables in the car.

Airline Offices
Most airline offices are at the Ala Moana Center or in downtown Honolulu. However, United Airlines (☎ 800-241-6522) has a Waikiki office at 2316 Kalakaua Ave, and Korean Air (☎ 923-1896) is on the same block, at 2350 Kalakaua Ave.

Emergency
Dial ☎ 911 for all police, fire and medical emergency services.

Doctors On Call (☎ 971-6000), 2222 Kalakaua Ave, Room 212, has a 24-hour clinic with X-ray and lab facilities. The charge for an office-visit is approximately $85 to $150. They'll also make house calls, though this is apt to run more than twice the office visit cost. Doctors On Call also operates smaller branch clinics, with more typical business hours, at the Hilton Hawaiian Village (☎ 973-5252), the Royal Hawaiian Hotel (☎ 923-4499) and the Hyatt Regency Waikiki (☎ 971-8001).

WARNING
REMOVE ALL
VALUABLES FROM
YOUR VEHICLE

STATE OF HAWAII
DEPARTMENT OF LAND &
NATURAL RESOURCES

NED FRIARY

Dangers & Annoyances

There's been a clampdown on the hustlers who used to push time-shares and other con deals from every other street corner in Waikiki. They're not totally gone – there are just fewer of them (and some have meta-morphosed into 'activity centers'). If you see a sign touting car rentals for $5 a day, you've probably found one.

Time-share salespeople will offer you all sorts of deals, from free luaus to sunset cruises, if you'll just come to hear their 'no obligation' pitch. *Caveat emptor.*

For information on ocean safety, see the Dangers & Annoyances section in the Facts for the Visitor chapter.

WALKING TOUR

It's possible to make an interesting two- to three-hour walking tour of Waikiki by com-bining a stroll along the beach with a walk along Kalakaua Ave. Most of the sights mentioned here are described in greater detail in the sections that follow.

You can walk the full length of Waikiki along the sand and the sea wall. Although the beach walk gets crowded at midday, at other times it's usually less packed than the sidewalks along Kalakaua Ave.

A good place to begin the walk is the **Kapahulu Groin**, near the northern border of **Kapiolani Park**, where you can observe Waikiki's top boogie-boarding action. As you continue west along the beach, you can stop for a swim, watch surfers ride the off-shore breaks and take a look at some of the seaside hotels.

After you reach the Halekulani Hotel, continue to the **US Army Museum** at the Fort DeRussy Military Reservation and then head up Beach Walk to Kalakaua Ave, where you'll turn right. On the corner of Lewers St and Kalakaua Ave is the **First Hawaiian Bank**, the interior of which has notable Hawaiiana murals by the fresco artist Jean Charlot. A free brochure describ-ing the murals is available from the bank's information desk.

As you continue down Kalakaua Ave, you can take in the historic **Royal Hawaiian** and **Moana** hotels, visit the **Oceanarium** at the

Pacific Beach Hotel and take a look at the **Damien Museum** behind St Augustine's Church. Upon returning to Kapahulu Groin, you might want to visit the **Honolulu Zoo** and, if you still have time, stroll around Kapi-olani Park and see the **Waikiki Aquarium**.

BEACHES

The 2-mile stretch of white sand that runs from the Hilton Hawaiian Village to Kapi-olani Park is commonly called Waikiki Beach, although different sections along the way have their own characteristics and names.

In the early morning the beach belongs to walkers and joggers, and it's surprisingly quiet. Strolling down the beach toward Diamond Head at sunrise can actually be a meditative experience.

By midmorning it looks like a normal resort beach, with boogie-board and surf-board concessionaires setting up shop and catamarans pulling up on the beach offering $15 sails. By noon it is packed, and the chal-lenge is to walk down the beach without stepping on anyone.

Waikiki Beach is good for swimming, boogie boarding, surfing, sailing and other beach activities most of the year. Between May and September, summer swells can make the water a little rough for swimming, but they also make it the best season for surfing. Because of all the activity, Waikiki beaches simply aren't that good for snorkel-ing; the best of them is Sans Souci.

There are lifeguards and showers at many places along the beach.

Kahanamoku Beach

Fronting the Hilton Hawaiian Village, Kahanamoku Beach is the westernmost section of Waikiki. The beach is named for Duke Kahanamoku, a surfer and swimmer who won an Olympic gold medal in the 100m freestyle in 1912 and went on to become a Hawaiian celebrity.

Kahanamoku Beach is protected by a breakwater at one end and a pier at the other, with a coral reef running between the two. It's a calm swimming area with a sandy bottom that slopes gradually.

Borrowed Sands

Most of Waikiki's beautiful white sands are not its own. Tons of sand have been barged in over the years, much of it from Papohaku Beach on the island of Molokai.

As the beachfront developed, landowners haphazardly constructed sea walls and offshore barriers to protect their properties. In the process they blocked the natural forces of sand accretion, and erosion has long been a serious problem at Waikiki.

Sections of the beach are still being replenished with imported sand, although much of it ends up washing into the ocean, where it fills channels and depressions and alters the surf breaks.

❀❀❀❀❀❀❀❀❀❀❀❀❀

Fort DeRussy Beach

One of the least crowded Waikiki beaches, Fort DeRussy Beach borders 1800 feet of the Fort DeRussy Military Reservation. It is a public beach, as are all beaches in Hawaii; the federal government provides lifeguards and there are showers and other facilities, including arbor picnic shelters. In addition, you'll find an inviting grassy lawn that has a bit of sparse shade from palm trees, providing an alternative to frying on the sand.

The water is usually calm and good for swimming. When conditions are right, you can windsurf, boogie board and board surf as well. There are two beach huts, open daily, where you can rent windsurfing equipment, boogie boards, kayaks and snorkel sets.

Gray's Beach

Gray's Beach, the local name for the beach near the Halekulani Hotel, was named for a boarding house called Gray's-by-the-Sea that stood on the site in the 1920s. On the same stretch of beach was the original Halekulani, a lovely low-rise mansion that was converted into a hotel in the 1930s. In the 1980s, the mansion gave way to the present high-rise hotel.

Because the sea wall in front of the Halekulani Hotel is so close to the waterline, the beach fronting the hotel is often totally submerged by the surf.

The section of Gray's Beach that is between the Halekulani Hotel and the Royal Hawaiian Hotel varies in width from season to season. The waters off the beach are shallow and calm, offering good conditions for swimming.

Central Waikiki Beach

The area from the Royal Hawaiian Hotel to the Waikiki Beach Center is the busiest section of the whole beach and has a nice spread of sand for sunbathing.

Most of the beach has a shallow bottom with a gradual slope. There's pretty good swimming here, but there's also a lot of activity, with catamarans, surfers and plenty of other swimmers in the water. Keep your eyes open.

Offshore are Waikiki's best-known surf breaks – Queen's Surf and Canoe's Surf.

Waikiki Beach Center The Waikiki Beach Center, just opposite the Hyatt Regency Waikiki, has rest rooms, showers, a police station, surfboard lockers and rental concession stands.

The **Wizard Stones of Kapaemahu** – four boulders on the Diamond Head side of the police station – are said to contain the secrets and healing powers of four Tahitian sorcerers named Kapaemahu, Kinohi, Kapuni and Kahaloa, who visited Oahu in ancient times. Before returning to Tahiti, they transferred their powers to these stones.

Just west of the stones is a bronze **statue of Duke Kahanamoku** (1890-1968), Hawaii's most decorated athlete, standing with one of his longboards. Considered the 'father of modern surfing,' Duke, who made his home in Waikiki, gave surfing demonstrations on beaches around the world from Sydney, Australia, to Rockaway Beach, New York. Many local surfers took issue with the placement of the statue, which has Duke standing with his back to the sea – a position they say he never would have taken in real life. In response the city moved the statue as far from the ocean and as close to the sidewalk as possible.

Star Beach Boys, a beachside concession stand, rents surfboards and boogie boards by the hour, gives surfing lessons and offers inexpensive outrigger canoe rides. See Surfing in the Activities chapter for details.

Kuhio Beach Park

Kuhio Beach Park is marked on its east end by Kapahulu Groin. It is a walled storm drain with a walkway on top of it. The walkway juts out into the ocean from the end of Kapahulu Ave.

A low breakwater sea wall runs about 1300 feet out from Kapahulu Groin, paralleling the beach. This breakwater was built to control sand erosion, and in the process, two nearly enclosed swimming pools were formed. Local kids walk out on the breakwater, which is called 'The Wall,' but it can be dangerous to the uninitiated due to a slippery surface and breaking surf.

The pool closest to Kapahulu Groin is best for swimming, with the water near the breakwater reaching overhead depths. However, because circulation is limited, the water gets murky with a noticeable film of suntan oil. The 'Watch Out Deep Holes' sign refers to holes in the pool's sandy bottom that can be created by swirling currents. Those who can't swim should be cautious in the deeper areas of the pool, because the holes can take you by surprise.

The park, incidentally, is named after the distinguished Hawaiian statesman Prince Kuhio, who maintained his residence on this beach. His house was torn down in 1936, 14 years after his death, in order to expand the beach.

Between the old-timers who gather each afternoon to play chess and cribbage at Kuhio's sidewalk pavilions and the kids boogie boarding off the Groin, this section of the beach has as much local color as tourist influence.

The city has recently approved a controversial plan to remove one lane of Kalakaua Ave along this area and bring in more sand to extend Kuhio Beach Park a few more feet. If they follow through with the plans, expect plenty of noise and disruption during the project.

Kapahulu Groin Kapahulu Groin is one of Waikiki's hottest boogie-boarding spots. If the surf's right, you can find a few dozen boogie boarders, mostly teenage boys, riding the waves. The kids ride straight for the Groin's cement wall and then veer away at the last moment, drawing 'oohs' and 'ahs' from the tourists who gather to watch them.

Kapahulu Groin is also a great place to catch Oahu's spectacular sunsets.

Kapiolani Beach Park

Kapiolani Beach Park starts at Kapahulu Groin and extends to the Natatorium, past the Waikiki Aquarium.

Queen's Surf is the name given to the wide midsection of Kapiolani Beach. The stretch in front of the pavilion is a beach popular with the gay community. It's a pretty good area for swimming and has a sandy bottom. The section of beach between Queen's Surf and Kapahulu Groin is shallow and has a lot of broken coral.

Kapiolani Beach Park is a relaxed place with little of the frenzied activity found in front of the central strip of Waikiki hotels. It's a popular weekend picnicking spot for local families, and children splash in the water as parents line up the barbecue grills.

There's a big grassy field that's good for spreading out a beach towel and unpacking a picnic basket. Free parking is available near the beach along Kalakaua Ave. There are rest rooms and showers in the Queen's Surf pavilion. The surfing area offshore is called Public's.

Natatorium The Natatorium, at the Diamond Head end of Kapiolani Beach, is a 100m-long saltwater swimming pool built after WWI as a memorial for soldiers who died in that war. There were once hopes of hosting an Olympics on Oahu, with this pool as the focal point. In the end, Olympic competitions were never held here, but two Olympic gold medalists – Johnny Weissmuller and Duke Kahanamoku – both trained in this tide-fed pool.

The Natatorium, which is on the National Register of Historic Places, has long been closed and in disrepair, but after years of debate, the city recently allocated $11 million to restore the facility.

Sans Souci Beach
Down by the New Otani Kaimana Beach Hotel, Sans Souci is a nice little sandy beach away from the main tourist scene. It has outdoor showers and a lifeguard station.

Many residents come to Sans Souci for daily swims. A shallow coral reef close to shore makes for calm, protected waters and provides reasonably good snorkeling. More coral can be found by following the Kapua Channel as it cuts through the reef, but beware of currents that can pick up in the channel. Check conditions with the lifeguard before venturing out.

HISTORIC HOTELS
Waikiki's two historic hotels, the Royal Hawaiian and the Moana (now the Sheraton Moana Surfrider), both retain their period character and are worth a visit. These beachside hotels, which are on the National Register of Historic Places, are a couple of blocks from each other on Kalakaua Ave.

With its pink turrets and Moorish/Spanish architecture, the Royal Hawaiian Hotel is a throwback to the era when Rudolph Valentino was *the* romantic idol and travel to Hawaii was by luxury liner. Inside, the hotel is lovely and airy, with high ceilings and chandeliers and everything in rose colors.

The hotel was originally on a 20-acre coconut grove, but over the years the grounds have been chipped away by a huge shopping center on one side and a high-rise mega-hotel on the other. Still, the small garden at the rear is filled with birdsong – a rare sound in most of Waikiki.

The Sheraton Moana Surfrider, which has undergone a splendid restoration, has the aura of an old plantation inn. On the 2nd floor, just up the stairs from the lobby, there's a display of memorabilia from the early hotel days, with scripts from the 'Hawaii Calls' radio show, period photographs and a short video. At 11 am and 5:15 pm daily, visitors can join hour-long historical tours of the hotel that leave from the

concierge desk; tours are free to the public, and reservations are not necessary.

For information on staying in these hotels, see the Places to Stay section, later in this chapter.

FORT DeRUSSY
Fort DeRussy Military Reservation is a US Army post used mainly as a recreation center for the armed forces. This large chunk of Waikiki real estate was acquired by the US Army a few years after Hawaii was annexed to the USA. Prior to that, it was swampy marshland and a favorite duck-hunting spot for Hawaiian royalty.

The Hale Koa Hotel on the property is open only to military personnel, but there's public access to the beach and the adjacent military museum. The section of Fort DeRussy between Kalia Rd and Kalakaua Ave has public footpaths that provide a shortcut between the two roads.

US Army Museum of Hawaii
Battery Randolph, a reinforced concrete building built in 1911 as a coastal artillery battery, houses the army museum at Fort DeRussy. It once held two 14-inch diameter disappearing guns that had an 11-mile range and were designed to recoil back into the concrete walls for reloading after each firing. A 55-ton lead counterweight would then return the carriage to position. When the guns were fired, the entire neighborhood shook. To get a sense of how huge these guns were, go up to the roof, where you'll see one of the 7-inch replacements – despite being half the size of the original, it still has a formidable presence.

In addition to the guns and a collection of WWII tanks, there are detailed exhibits with dioramas, scale models and period photos on military history as it relates to Hawaii.

The battery houses a wide collection of weapons, including a few of the shark-tooth clubs and flintlock pistols that Kamehameha the Great employed to take control of the island chain two centuries ago (see the History section in the Facts about Oahu

[Continued on page 161]

A classic Hawaiian sunset

Fragrant leis are an island tradition.

Muumuus in motion at the Kodak Hula Show in Waikiki

WAIKIKI

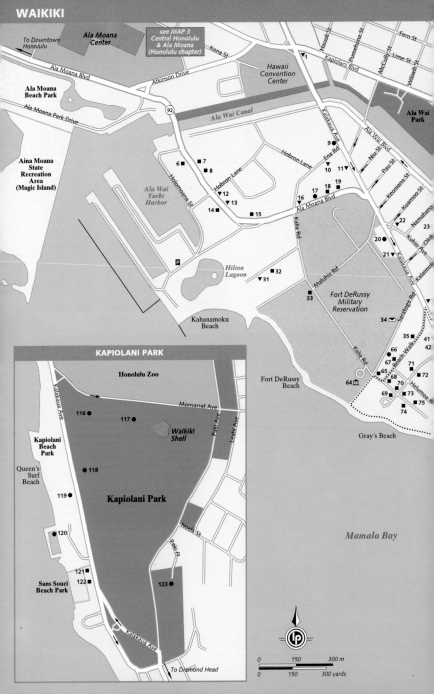

To Downtown Honolulu

Ala Moana Center

see MAP 3
Central Honolulu
& Ala Moana
(Honolulu chapter)

Hawaii Convention Center

Ala Moana Blvd

Atkinson Drive

Kona St

Kalakaua Ave

Kapiolani Blvd

Hauoli St
Pumehana St
McCully St
Fern St
Lime St
Wiliwili St

Ala Moana Beach Park

Ala Moana Park Drive

92

Ala Wai Canal

Ala Wai Blvd

Ala Wai Park

Aina Moana State Recreation Area (Magic Island)

Ala Wai Yacht Harbor

Hobron Lane

Holomoana St

Hobron Lane

6 ■ ■ 7
■ 8

9 ●

Ena Rd

10 ▼ 11 ▼

Niu St
Pau St
Kaiolu St
Koʻo St

Ala Wai Blvd

22 ▼

23

Kuhio Ave

Kuamoo St

Keoniana St

Namahana St

▼ 12
■ 13

14 ■

■ 15

Kalia Rd

Ala Moana Blvd

16 ● 17 ■ 18 ■
19 ■

20 ●

21 ▼

Kalakaua Ave
Kaiamoku

P

Hilton Lagoon

■ 32
▼ 31

Maluhia Rd

Fort DeRussy Military Reservation

33 ■

34 ✉

35 ■

41 ■
42

66 ●
67 ●
65 ● 68 ■
69 ● 70 ■
74 ■

71 ■
72 ■
73 ■
75 ■

Saratoga Rd

Beach Walk

Helumoa Rd

Kahanamoku Beach

Kalia Rd

Fort DeRussy Beach

64 🏛

Gray's Beach

Mamala Bay

KAPIOLANI PARK

Honolulu Zoo

Monsarrat Ave

Kalakaua Ave

116 ●

117 ●

Waikiki Shell

Paki Ave

Leahi Ave

Kapiolani Beach Park

Queen's Surf Beach

118 ●

119 ●

Kapiolani Park

120 ●

Noela St

Paki Pl

121 ■
122 ■

123 ●

Sans Souci Beach Park

Kalakaua Ave

To Diamond Head

0   150   300 m
0   150   300 yards

Honolulu Stadium
State Recreation Area

Date St
Citron St
Coolidge St
Kalhuna Lane
S King St
To Airport
Palolo Stream
Waialae Ave

Hoawa St
Isenberg St
Hausten St
University Ave
to MAP 4
University Area
(Honolulu chapter)
H1

Kamoku St
Date St
Kapiolani Blvd
2

3 ▼
4

Kaimuki Ave
Crane
Park

5 ▼

Kapahulu Ave

Ala Wai
Park

Manoa-Palolo Drainage Canal

Winam Ave

Kaiulu St
27

26
Aloha Drive
30
29

Lewers St
Manuku St
Seaside Ave
48
47
49
50
51

Nohonani St
Nahua St
Walina St
54
56
57
58
59
55 ▼
60
61

Kanekapolei St
Cleghorn St

Ala Wai Canal

Date St
Hunter St
62 ▼
Williams St
63 ▼

Mooheau
Ave
Hoolulu St

Royal Hawaiian Way
Waikiki
Shopping
Plaza
46

Duke's Lane
52
53

International
Market
Place
78

↑ Ala Wai Golf Course

Martha
St

▼ 115

Herbert St

Royal
Hawaiian
Shopping
Center
77

79
80
81
91
88
89
90
92
93
94
95
82
87
85
86
83
84

Kalaula St
Kaiulani Ave
Prince Edward St
Koa Ave
Uluniu Ave

Central Waikiki
Beach

96
97
98
100
99
108
109
110
111

Kuhio Ave
Liliuokalani Ave
Kealohilani Ave
Ohua Ave
Kuhio Ave
Paoakalani Ave
Lemon Rd
Cartwright Rd
101
107
106
105
104
103
102
Kuhio
Beach
Park

Pualani Way
Ainakea Way
Wai Nani Way
Ala Wai Blvd

114
113
112

Castle St
Brokaw St
Kanaina Ave
Campbell Ave

Kapahulu Ave
Leahi Ave
Paki Ave

Kapahulu
Groin

K Entrance

Kapahulu Ave
Honolulu Zoo

see Kapiolani Park
inset map

Kapiolani
Beach
Park

Kalakaua Ave
Kapiolani Park
Monsarrat Ave
Kanaina Ave

P Parking
⋯ Walking Tour

WAIKIKI

PLACES TO STAY

6 Hawaii Prince Hotel
7 Hawaii Polo Inn
8 Ala Moana Towers
14 The Ilikai
15 Holiday Inn Waikiki
18 Island Hostel
19 Doubletree Alana Waikiki Hotel
23 Royal Garden at Waikiki
25 Hotel Honolulu
27 Coconut Plaza Hotel
28 Waikiki Malia
29 Waikiki Surf
30 Waikiki Surf East
32 Hilton Hawaiian Village
33 Hale Koa Hotel
35 The Breakers
48 Hawaiian Seaside Hostel
49 Ohana Surf
50 Ilima Hotel
51 Hawaiian King Hotel
60 Aloha Surf Hotel
61 Waikiki Sand Villa Hotel
65 Waikiki Royal Islander
67 Hale Pua Nui
68 Waikiki Edgewater
69 Outrigger Reef Hotel
70 Waikiki Tower
71 Waikiki Coral Seas
72 Waikiki Reef Towers
73 Imperial of Waikiki
74 Halekulani Hotel
75 Waikiki Parc Hotel
76 Sheraton Waikiki
77 Royal Hawaiian Hotel
79 Outrigger Waikiki
81 Sheraton Princess Kaiulani
83 Sheraton Moana Surfrider
87 Hyatt Regency Waikiki
89 Hostelling International Waikiki
90 Waikiki Prince Hotel
92 InterClub Hostel Waikiki
93 Pacific Monarch
94 Royal Grove Hotel
95 Banana Bungalow Waikiki Beach
96 Waikiki Circle Hotel
97 Waikiki Resort Hotel
98 Pacific Beach Hotel

101 Hawaiian Regent
102 Hawaiian Waikiki Beach Hotel
103 Waikiki Grand
104 Queen Kapiolani Hotel
105 Polynesian Hostel Beachclub
106 Waikiki Beachside Hotel
108 Ocean Resort Hotel Waikiki
109 Waikiki Sunset
121 New Otani Kaimana Beach Hotel
122 Colony Surf Hotel

PLACES TO EAT

1 Hard Rock Cafe
3 Coffee Haven
4 KC Drive Inn
5 Leonard's
6 Prince Court, Takanawa, Hakone
10 Pho Tri
11 Eggs 'n Things
12 Starbucks, McDonald's
13 Dynasty
16 California Pizza Kitchen, Singha Thai
21 Kyo-ya
22 Keo's
23 Cascada
31 Bali, Golden Dragon
32 Bali
36 Tenteko Mai
37 Curry House Coco Ichibanya
39 Kyotaru
40 Moose McGillycuddy's
41 Planet Hollywood
55 Fatty's Chinese Kitchen
56 Patisserie
57 Chili's
58 Food Pantry
59 Perry's Smorgy
62 New Kapahulu Chop Suey
63 Ono Hawaiian Food
68 Patisserie
69 Shore Bird Beach Broiler
71 Perry's Smorgy
74 La Mer, Orchids
75 Parc Cafe
77 Surf Room
79 Duke's Canoe Club
80 Häagen-Dazs
83 Banyan Veranda

88 Tanaka of Tokyo
98 Oceanarium Restaurant
99 Cheeseburger in Paradise
107 Ezogiku
112 Sam Choy's Diamond Head Restaurant
113 Rainbow Drive-In
115 Irifune's
122 David Paul's Diamond Head Grill

OTHER

2 Foodland
9 Wave Waikiki
17 Blue Sky Rentals
20 24-hour Gas Station
24 Island Treasures Antiques
26 Diamond Head Mopeds
34 Waikiki Post Office
38 In-Between
42 First Hawaiian Bank
43 Hawaii Visitors & Convention Bureau
44 Bank of Hawaii
45 Doctors On Call
46 Waikiki Theatres/IMAX
47 Angles Waikiki, Fusion Waikiki
52 7-Eleven
53 Waikiki Town Center
54 Scruples
64 US Army Museum of Hawaii
66 Urasenke Tea Ceremony
78 Liberty House, United Airlines
82 Budget & Hertz Offices
84 Board Rentals
85 Waikiki Beach Center, Police
86 Wizard Stones, Duke Kahanamoku Statue
91 Planet Surf
100 St Augustine's Church, Damien Museum
103 Hula's Bar & Lei Stand
110 Waikiki Community Center
111 Waikiki-Kapahulu Library
114 Bailey's Antique Shop
116 Kapiolani Bandstand
117 Kodak Hula Show
118 Tennis Courts
119 Waikiki Aquarium
120 Natatorium
123 Diamond Head Tennis Center

If you like sharks, visit the Hunters on the Reef exhibit at the Waikiki Aquarium.

[Continued from page 160]
chapter for more information on Kamehameha). Despite the small, but interesting, nod to native Hawaiian history, the bulk of the exhibits, not surprisingly, concentrate on the US military presence in Hawaii, beginning in 1898 with the Philippine-bound army troops that used Oahu as a way station.

The WWII exhibits are extensive and include displays you might not expect in a military museum, such as coverage of the unfounded suspicions and hardships faced by Hawaii's Japanese-Americans during this time period. Other exhibits concentrate on the Korean and Vietnam wars. The site also has a theater with films outlining current-day projects in Hawaii and Micronesia by the Army Corps of Engineers.

The museum is open 10 am to 4:15 pm Tuesday through Sunday; closed Christmas and New Year's Day. Admission is free.

KAPIOLANI PARK

The nearly 200-acre Kapiolani Park, at the Diamond Head end of Waikiki, was a gift from King Kalakaua to the people of Honolulu in 1877. Hawaii's first public park, it was dedicated to Kalakaua's wife, Queen Kapiolani.

In its early days, horse racing and band concerts were the park's biggest attractions. Although the racetrack is gone, the concerts continue, and Kapiolani Park is still the venue for a wide range of community activities.

The park contains the Waikiki Aquarium, the Honolulu Zoo, Kapiolani Beach Park, the Waikiki Shell, the Kodak Hula Show grounds and the Kapiolani Bandstand.

The Royal Hawaiian Band presents free afternoon concerts nearly every Sunday at the Kapiolani Bandstand. Dance competitions, Hawaiian music concerts and other activities take place at the bandstand throughout the year.

The Waikiki Shell is an outdoor amphitheater where symphony, jazz and rock concerts take place. For current information on performances, check the papers or call the Blaisdell Center (☎ 591-2211).

Kapiolani Park also has sports fields, tennis courts, tall banyan trees and expansive lawns that are ideal for kite flying. It's a pleasant park, and despite all the activities that go on, it's large enough to also have a lot of quiet space.

Waikiki Aquarium

This interesting aquarium (☎ 923-9741), 2777 Kalakaua Ave, dates to 1904 and recently underwent a $3 million makeover. The aquarium has interactive displays, a mini-theater and a viewing gallery, where visitors can sit and look through a 14-foot window at circling reef sharks.

The Waikiki Aquarium is a great place to identify colorful coral and fish you've seen while snorkeling or diving. Tanks re-create various Hawaiian reef habitats, including those found in a surge zone, a sheltered reef, a deep reef and an ancient reef. There are rare Hawaiian fish with names like the bearded armorhead and the sling-jawed wrasse, along with black-tip sharks, moray

WAIKIKI

eels and flash-back cuttlefish wavering with pulses of light.

In addition to Hawaiian marine life, you'll find various exhibits on other Pacific ecosystems. In 1985 the aquarium was the first to breed the Palauan chambered nautilus in captivity. A few of these sea creatures, with their unique spiral chambered shells, are on display. There are also some giant clams from Palau; less than an inch long when acquired in 1982, they now measure over 2 feet and rank as the largest in the USA.

The aquarium has a touch tank for children, a green sea turtle and three Hawaiian monk seals.

It's open 9 am to 5 pm daily, although entry is not allowed after 4:30 pm. Admission is $6 for adults, $4 for seniors over 60 and students with ID, $2.50 for children ages 13 to 17, and free for children 12 and younger. Take a look at their website (www.mic.hawaii.edu/aquarium) for a preview before you visit.

Honolulu Zoo

The Honolulu Zoo (☎ 971-7171), at the northern end of Kapiolani Park, underwent extensive renovations that upgraded it into a respectable city zoo, with some 300 species spread across 42 acres. The highlight is the nicely naturalized African Savanna section, which has lions, cheetahs, white rhinos, giraffes, zebras, hippos and monkeys. There's also an interesting reptile section and a small petting zoo that allows children to see animals up close.

The zoo's tropical bird section not only covers the usual colorful exotics, such as toucans and flamingoes, but also displays a number of Hawaiian natives, such as the Hawaiian stilt, the Hawaiian gallinule, the Hawaiian goose *(nene)* and the *apapane* (a bright red forest bird).

In front of the zoo there's a large banyan tree that is home to hundreds of white pigeons – escapees from a small group brought to the zoo in the 1940s.

The zoo is open 9 am to 4:30 pm daily, except Christmas and New Year's Day. Admission is $6 for adults, $1 for children ages six to 12 and free for children younger than six.

Kodak Hula Show

The Kodak Hula Show (☎ 627-3300), off Monsarrat Ave near the Waikiki Shell, is a staged photo opportunity of hula dancers, ti-leaf skirts and ukuleles. The musicians are a group of older ladies who performed at the Royal Hawaiian Hotel in days gone by.

This is the scene shown on classic postcards where dancers hold up letters forming the words 'Hawaii' and 'Aloha.' The whole thing is quite touristy and heavily nostalgic, but it's entertaining and it's free.

Kodak has been hosting this show since 1939. The benches are set up stadium-style around a grassy stage area, with the sun at your back. The idea is for everyone to shoot a lot of film – and it works. Even though Kodak no longer monopolizes the film market, the tradition continues.

Shows are held 10 to 11:15 am Tuesday, Wednesday and Thursday. Make an effort to be on time, because once the show starts, latecomers are only admitted between acts.

LEE FOSTER

The Kodak Hula Show is a Waikiki tradition.

OTHER WAIKIKI SIGHTS

The **Oceanarium**, in the Pacific Beach Hotel, 2490 Kalakaua Ave, is an three-story, 280,000-gallon aquarium that forms the backdrop for two of the hotel's restaurants. Even if you're not dining in one of them, you can view the aquarium quite easily from the lobby. Divers enter the Oceanarium to feed the tropical fish at noon and 1, 6:30 and 8:15 pm daily.

St Augustine's Church, off Kalakaua Ave and Ohua Ave, is a quiet little sanctuary in the midst of the hotel district. In the rear of the church, a second building houses the modest **Damien Museum**, honoring Father Damien, the Belgian priest famed for his work at the leprosy colony on Molokai. It has a video presentation on the colony, some interesting historical photos and a few of Damien's personal possessions.

As a fitting tribute to Father Damien's life, the building also houses a lunchtime soup kitchen. Museum hours are 9 am to 3 pm weekdays; entry is free.

Every day at dawn, people walk and jog along the **Ala Wai Canal**, which forms the northern boundary of Waikiki. Late in the afternoon, outrigger canoe teams paddle up and down Ala Wai Canal and out to the Ala Wai Yacht Harbor, offering photo opportunities for the passersby.

PLACES TO STAY

Waikiki's main beachfront strip, Kalakaua Ave, is lined with high-rise hotels with $150-plus rooms. As is the norm in resort areas, most of these hotels cater to package tourists, driving the prices up for individual travelers.

Better values are generally found at the smaller places on the backstreets, with the prices dropping proportionally as you get farther from the beach. There are hotels in the Kuhio Ave area and up near the Ala Wai Canal that are as nice as some of the beachfront hotels, at half the price. If you don't mind walking 10 minutes to the beach, you can save yourself a bundle.

Places to Stay – Budget

Hostels In addition to the one Hostelling International hostel, there are a number of private businesses providing hostel-style dormitory accommodations around Waikiki. They all cater to backpackers and draw a fairly international crowd. There are no curfews or other restrictions, except that some of these places, in an effort to avoid taking on local boarders, may require travelers to show a passport or an onward ticket.

Most of the hostels are small scale, but the newest place to jump into the fray, the Banana Bungalow, is a large operation, with a capacity nearly as large as all the other private hostels combined. Whether there will now be enough business to keep all of these hostels in business remains to be seen. And just how the additional competition will play out – whether the smaller places will compete by improving, or take the opposite route and cut back on spending – is another unknown. It is reasonable, however, to expect changes to some of the places that follow.

Hawaiian Seaside Hostel (☎ 924-3306, fax 923-2110, reservations@hawaiianseaside .com, 419 Seaside Ave, Honolulu, HI 96815) occupies an aging two-story apartment building set back in an alley off Seaside Ave. The place is run down and the mattresses are seasoned, but it has a travelers' atmosphere and cheap rates. Small dorm rooms with six bunk beds cost $12 per bed, while semiprivate rooms that hold only two people cost $15 per person. Discounts, equivalent to roughly one night free, are available on weekly stays.

There's an open-air courtyard with a pool table, cable TV and a common kitchen; limited water-sports equipment can be borrowed for free. The hostel has three computers with fast Internet connections ($3 per 30 minutes) available for guests. It's about a 10-minute walk from Waikiki Beach. Visit the hostel's website (www.hawaiianseaside .com) for additional information.

InterClub Hostel Waikiki (☎ 924-2636, fax 922-3993, 2413 Kuhio Ave, Honolulu, HI 96815) is a well-established, private hostel that recently scaled back its capacity. Bunk beds are arranged five to eight to a room; each room has its own refrigerator and bathroom. Dorm beds cost $15. The hostel also has a few simple private rooms for $45, with linoleum floors, refrigerators, balconies and private baths.

There's a lounge and TV room, a washer/dryer and lockers. One drawback is that the building is right on heavily trafficked Kuhio Ave, so it may be noisy for light sleepers. To stay at InterClub, you need a passport or an onward ticket out of Hawaii.

The **Waikiki Beachside Hotel** (☎ 923-9566, fax 923-7525, hokondo@aol.com, 2556 Lemon Rd, Suite B101, Honolulu, HI 96815) is a small condo complex that's been converted into hostel-style accommodations. It has dorm beds from $15 to $18 and private rooms for around $55. The units each have a refrigerator, stove and private bath. It's not fancy, but it has a higher standard of cleanliness than most of the other small hostels. Visit their website (www.waikiki-hotel.com/beachside) for additional information.

The **Banana Bungalow Waikiki Beach** (☎ 924-5074, 888-246-7835, fax 924-4119, hires@bananabungalow.com, 2463 Kuhio Ave, Honolulu, HI 96815) is hands down the most modern and cushy hostel in Hawaii. It occupies a 12-story building on Kuhio Ave, convenient to the bus and about a five-minute walk from the beach. Run by a small mainland chain, the place is a cross between a hostel and a hotel, with about 25 rooms containing six to eight dorm beds that are priced at $16 per person. There are also 35 private rooms, with one king or two twin beds, priced from $60; taxes are included in the rates. MasterCard and Visa are accepted.

All rooms, whether dorm or private, have a bathroom, balcony, phone, cable TV and air-con. There's a choice of coed or same-sex dorms. Guests have use of kitchen facilities, a big-screen TV and a coin laundry. Computers with Internet access are available at the rate of $1 per 10 minutes. Inexpensive barbecues are held three nights a week, and there's a daily tour to Hanauma Bay, Pearl Harbor or a hiking destination for $7 or less. Snorkel gear, boogie boards, surfboards and mopeds can be rented on-site at reasonable rates.

Free transportation is provided from the airport; transportation back to the airport is $4. Visit their website (www.bananabungalow.com) for additional information.

Hostelling International Waikiki (☎ 926-8313, fax 922-3798, 2417 Prince Edward St, Honolulu, HI 96815) is a 60-bed hostel on a backstreet a few short blocks from Waikiki Beach. Like many of Waikiki's hostels, it's in an older low-rise apartment complex, and the units are converted for hostel use mainly by adding extra beds – often in what used to be the living room.

Dorm beds cost $16, tax included. There are also four rooms for couples, with small refrigerators and private bathrooms, priced at $40. There's a maximum stay of seven nights and a $3 surcharge if you're not a Hostelling International (HI) member; HI membership can be purchased on-site for $25 for Americans, $18 for foreign visitors.

Office hours are 7 am to 3 am. Unlike most other HI hostels, there's no dormitory lockout or curfew, and a group kitchen is accessible throughout the day. Four parking spaces are available at $5 a day. Reservations can be made by phone or fax with a credit card; MasterCard, Visa and American Express are accepted. Occasionally, you can get a bed as a walk-in, but at busy times reservations are often necessary two to three weeks in advance.

On the western end of Waikiki is **Island Hostel** (☎/fax 942-8748, 1946 Ala Moana Blvd, Honolulu, HI 96815), which has about 20 studio rooms in Hawaiian Colony, an apartment building that's been tidied up after years of neglect. All of the rooms have TV, hot plates and a bathroom. The dorm beds are in older rooms that can feel a bit confined, but there are only four people to a room, and they're a notch above some of the competition. The cost for a dorm bed is $16.50, tax included; there's a small discount for weekly stays.

Nearly half of the rooms in the hostel are private (most with one single and one double bed, though at least one has bunk beds) and many have been upgraded with new tile floors and fresh paint. The renovated private rooms cost $55, and older private rooms cost $50; prices for private rooms fluctuate a bit with the season, and if things are slow, you might be able to work out a better deal.

Although it's a bit farther from the beach than other hostels, it's still within walking distance and, on the plus side, the beach at this end of Waikiki is less crowded. Credit cards are accepted.

A short walk from the beach is the *Polynesian Hostel Beachclub* (☎ 922-1340, 877-504-2924, fax 923-4146, reservation@hostelhawaii .com, 2584 Lemon Rd, Honolulu, HI 96815), which occupies a small three-story apartment complex on a side street behind the Queen Kapiolani Hotel. There are a variety of sleeping arrangements. You can get a bunk bed in a small dorm (four to six people) for $16.75, tax included; a bedroom in a two-bedroom apartment at $32/38 for singles/doubles; or a fully private studio with a kitchen for $50 a double. Each apartment has its own bathroom, but only the studios have private kitchens.

There's a common room with a full kitchen, a laundry area and occasional activities. Parking is available for $5. The drawback is the noise – particularly the garbage trucks that make their rounds on Lemon Rd around dawn. Visit their website for a preview (www.hostelhawaii.com).

Hotels The *Waikiki Prince Hotel* (☎ 922-1544, fax 924-3712, 2431 Prince Edward St, Honolulu, HI 96815) is a decent low-end value with 24 units in a six-story building next door to Hostelling International Waikiki. The rooms are simple but clean and have air-con, TV and private bath. There are small double rooms for $40 and larger rooms with kitchenettes for $55. In the low season, the seventh night is free. There's no pool, but it's just a couple of minutes' walk to the beach.

So many retirees return each winter to the 85-room *Royal Grove Hotel* (☎ 923-7691, fax 922-7508, rghawaiii@gte.net, 151 Uluniu Ave, Honolulu, HI 96815) that it can be a challenge to get a room in the high season without advance reservations. In the oldest wing there are small rooms for $43 that have no air-con and are streetside and exposed to traffic noise. The main wing has $57 rooms that are straightforward but perfectly adequate, with air-con and lanais. Both types of rooms have a double and two single beds, TV, kitchenette and private bath. This is an older, no-frills hotel, but unlike other places in this category, it has a small pool.

Hale Pua Nui (☎ 923-9693, fax 923-9678, 228 Beach Walk, Honolulu, HI 96815) is an older four-story building with 22 studio apartments. It's strictly a budget place and the rooms are worn, but each has two twin beds, a kitchenette, fan, air-con, TV and phone – and the beach is but a five-minute walk away. Rates are $45/57 in the low/high season, and there are discounts for stays of two weeks or more. When things are slow, guests are divided between locals and tourists, but in winter, it is packed with visitors, particularly Canadians.

Hawaii Polo Inn (☎ 949-0061, 800-669-7719, fax 949-4906, 1696 Ala Moana Blvd, Honolulu, HI 96815), a member of the Marc Resorts chain, is at the westernmost end of Waikiki. The 66 motel-style rooms are lined up in rows, with their entrances off a long outdoor corridor. The rooms have been renovated, but they're still straightforward. All have small refrigerators, coffeemakers, phones and TVs; some have lanais, although generally the lanai area is at the expense of room space.

The published rates start at $98/109 in the low/high season, but when things are slow, they will commonly offer a discounted rate of $55 to $65, which is certainly a good deal. There are also discounted auto-club and senior rates. Request a room in back to minimize the traffic noise that comes from busy Ala Moana Blvd.

The *Waikiki Sand Villa Hotel* (☎ 922-4744, 800-247-1903, fax 923-2541, 2375 Ala Wai Blvd, Honolulu, HI 96815) is on the Ala Wai Canal, a 10-minute walk from Waikiki Beach. The 223 rooms are compact and rather ordinary but have TV, refrigerators, air-con, room safes, bathtubs and small lanais, some with views across the golf course toward Manoa Valley. Ask for one of the corner units, which have the best views.

Standard rooms, which are on the lower floors, cost $74/85 in the low/high season, while upper floors are about $10 more. Most rooms have both a double and a twin bed, and children younger than 12 stay free. There are also poolside studios with kitchenettes that can sleep up to four people for $133/148. Rates include a simple continental breakfast.

Rooms can be booked from overseas by calling ☎ 1800-127-756 in Australia, 0800-440-712 in New Zealand and 0031-11-2858 in Japan.

The nearby **Aloha Surf Hotel** (☎ 923-0222, 800-423-4514, fax 924-7160, 444 Kanekapolei St, Honolulu, HI 96815) should only be considered as a last option, as rooms are overdue for renovation. Rooms are also on the small side and lack refrigerators – an amenity you can usually expect at this price. All 202 rooms have air-con, TV, phones and room safes. Standard rooms on the two lower floors cost $76/86 in the low/high season. Higher-floor rooms with lanais cost $10 more. There's a swimming pool.

Places to Stay – Mid-Range

Hotel Honolulu (☎ 926-2766, 800-426-2766, fax 922-3326, hotelhnl@lava.net, 376 Kaiolu St, Honolulu, HI 96815), a quiet oasis set back from busy Kuhio Ave, is Waikiki's only gay hotel. It has the character of an unhurried inn, with helpful management and lots of hanging ferns. The 19 main units are decorated with flair, each with its own theme ('Samurai,' 'Deco Deco,' 'Norma Jean,' etc), and are large and comfortable, with lanais, kitchens, ceiling fans and air-con. Studios cost $89 to $99, one-bedroom units cost $109 to $119.

There are also five smaller, nontheme studios in an adjacent building for $75. Coffee is free, and there's a deck but no pool.

The 451-room **Ocean Resort Hotel Waikiki** (☎ 922-3861, 800-367-2317, fax 924-1982, 175 Paoakalani Ave, Honolulu, HI 96815), a former Quality Inn, hosts a fair number of people on low-end package tours. Nonetheless, the rooms have the same amenities as more-expensive hotels, with air-con, cable TV, phones, refrigerators and room safes. Nonsmoking rooms are available on request, and there are two pools. The published rate for standard rooms is $93/103 in the low/high season, and larger rooms on higher floors cost $125/135. When things are slow, they sometimes offer walk-in rates that drop as low as $55 for either size of room.

Ilima Hotel (☎ 923-1877, 800-367-5172, fax 924-8371, mail@ilima.com, 445 Nohonani St, Honolulu, HI 96815) is a smaller hotel in a less hurried section of Waikiki, about a 10-minute walk from the beach. All 99 units are roomy and bright, with large lanais, two double beds, tasteful rattan furnishings, cable TV with HBO and kitchens with a stove, microwave and full-size refrigerator. The staff is friendly, the lobby has interesting Hawaiiana murals, and there's a small heated pool and fitness room. Popular with business travelers and other return visitors, the Ilima offers free local phone calls and free parking, which is a rarity in Waikiki.

The rates vary according to the floor, although the rooms themselves are the same. High-season rates start at $102/107 for singles/doubles in studios on the 4th floor and rise to $122/127 for studios on the 10th to 16th floors. There are also some one- and two-bedroom suites for $152 and $197, respectively. All rates are $12 less from April to mid-December. Visit their website (www.ilima.com) for additional information.

Patrick Winston owns 14 pleasant units in the **Hawaiian King Hotel** (☎ 922-3894, 800-545-1948 (daytime), winston@iav.com, 417 Nohonani St, Suite 409, Honolulu, HI 96815). Each has one bedroom with either a queen or two twin beds, a living room, TV, phone, air-con, ceiling fans, a lanai and a kitchen with microwave, refrigerator and hot plate. Many also have an oven, some have a washer/dryer and all have thoughtful touches. Although it's an older complex, a lot of money has gone into these units and they have a spiffy decor that's on par with pricier places. There's a courtyard pool.

Rates are $109 to $119 in the high season and $20 less in the low season; there are also some unrenovated rooms that are cheaper at $65/85 in the low/high season. Ask about discounts, as Patrick can sometimes fill last-minute vacancies at lower rates. There's a four-day minimum stay.

The Breakers (☎ 923-3181, 800-426-0494, fax 923-7174, 250 Beach Walk, Honolulu, HI 96815) is a friendly, older low-rise hotel with 64 units surrounding the courtyard pool. Although some of the units are a bit worn, they are otherwise comfortable. The regular rooms each have a double bed, a single bed and a kitchenette. The cost is $91 on the ground floor (without a lanai) or $97 on the 2nd floor (with a lanai).

There are also large suites that have a separate bedroom with a queen bed, a living room that resembles a studio with two twin beds, a full kitchen and a table for four; these cost $130 for two people, $146 for four. All rooms have air-con, TVs, room safes and phones. Avoid the rooms closest to Saratoga Rd, which has lots of traffic.

A member of Castle Resorts & Hotels, the 313-room *Queen Kapiolani Hotel* (☎ 922-1941, 800-533-6970, fax 922-2694, 150 Kapahulu Ave, Honolulu, HI 96815) is a 19-story hotel at the quieter Diamond Head end of Waikiki. This older hotel has an aging regal theme: chandeliers, high ceilings and faded paintings of Hawaiian royalty. Standard rooms cost $107/120 in the low/high season.

The standard rooms vary greatly in size, with some very pleasant and others so small they can barely hold a bed. The simplest way to avoid a closet-size space is to request a room with two twin beds instead of a single queen. Also, be sure to get a room without interconnecting doors, which can act like a sound tunnel to the next room. Some of the ocean-view rooms, which cost $40 more, have lanais with fine, unobstructed views of Diamond Head.

The 20-story *Waikiki Resort Hotel* (☎ 922-4911, 800-367-5116, fax 922-9468, 2460 Koa Ave, Honolulu, HI 96815) is a Korean-owned hotel with a Korean restaurant. Not surprisingly, it has many Korean guests on package tours. Its clean, modern rooms have mini-refrigerators, TVs, phones, air-con, room safes and lanais. The regular rates begin at $108; a room/car deal is available for an additional $10.

The 200-room *Holiday Inn Waikiki* (☎ 955-1111, 888-992-4545, fax 947-1799, 1830 Ala Moana Blvd, Honolulu, HI 96815) is a recommendable mid-range hotel at the western end of Waikiki. Rooms are modern and comfortable, with either two double beds or one king bed, a desk, room safe, TV, refrigerator, coffeemaker and a bathroom

with a tub and hair dryer. Some also have lanais. Rates depend on the floor and range from $117 to $130, but there are numerous discounts, including an ongoing promotion called 'Great Rates' that takes 15% off.

There's a pool and deck, and the beach is about a 10-minute walk away. Unlike most hotels on busy Ala Moana Blvd, the Holiday Inn is set back from the road, so it tends to be noticeably quieter. The hotel maintains a website (www.holiday-inn-waikiki.com).

An interesting, little-known option is *Imperial of Waikiki* (☎ 923-1827, 800-347-2582, fax 923-7848, 205 Lewers St, Honolulu, HI 96815), a pleasant all-suite time-share that rents out unfilled rooms on a space-available basis. It's a good value, especially considering it's directly opposite the Hale-kulani, Waikiki's most exclusive hotel, and just a two-minute walk from the beach.

A studio with a double pull-down bed, a queen sofa bed, toaster, coffeemaker, microwave and refrigerator costs $99 for up to two people. A small one-bedroom suite with a kitchenette, a queen bed in the bedroom and a pull-down bed and queen sofa bed in the living room costs $119 for up to four people. There are also roomier one-bedroom suites with two baths and full kitchens for $20 more, and well-equipped two-bedroom, two-bath units for $189 for up to five people.

There's a pool and a 24-hour front desk. All prices are $10 less in the low season.

The *Coconut Plaza Hotel* (☎ 923-8828, 800-882-9696, fax 923-3473, 450 Lewers St, Honolulu, HI 96815) is a quiet 80-room hotel near Ala Wai Blvd. Rooms have contemporary decor and are comfortable enough, though they're on the small side. Rooms with refrigerators, microwaves, TV, air-con and lanais cost $110, and those that also include a two-burner stove go for $160. There are various promotions, including senior (age 50-plus) discounts, that lower these rates. A simple complimentary continental breakfast is included. The hotel maintains a website (www.coconutplaza.com).

Waikiki Circle Hotel (☎ 923-1571, 800-922-7866, fax 926-8024, 2464 Kalakaua Ave, Honolulu, HI 96815), booked through the

Aston chain, is a small hotel with a good central location opposite the beach. It has 104 rooms on 13 floors, all with lanais, two double beds, room safes, phones, TVs and air-con. The hotel is older but has been renovated and the rooms are comfortable. This circular building has a back room on each floor that's called 'city view' and costs $120; although you can't see the ocean, these are farther from the road and quieter. Each floor also has two rooms with partial ocean views for $135 and five rooms with unobstructed ocean views for $150.

All rates are $20 more from Christmas through March and in July and August. Request one of the upper-floor rooms, which have the same rates but better views.

The *Royal Garden at Waikiki* (☎ 943-0202, 800-367-5666, fax 946-8777, 440 Olohana St, Honolulu, HI 96815) is a midsize hotel with 220 comfortable rooms. The rooms vary in decor, but all have air-con, TV, room safes, phones, bathrooms with tubs, a wet bar with refrigerator and a private lanai. Rates begin at $130 for the standard rooms, which are on the lower floors. A complimentary continental breakfast is included. The Royal Garden has an elegant marble lobby, two swimming pools and an exercise room.

Pacific Monarch (☎ 923-9805, 800-922-7866, fax 924-3220, 142 Uluniu Ave, Honolulu, HI 96815) is a 34-story condominium hotel. Although some of the 216 units are a bit lackluster, they're otherwise adequate. The studios are roomy, each with a table, desk, double bed, sofa bed, small refrigerator and two-burner hot plate. The one-bedroom units have a small bedroom and a living space with a full kitchen, a dining table for four, a sofa bed and a large lanai. The complex has a rooftop pool and Jacuzzi.

Aston, a large chain specializing in condos, is the rental agent for more than half of the units, with low- and high-season rates at $125/145 for a studio and $160/180 for a one-bedroom unit. Up to four people can stay at these rates. Ask about promotions, as this property sometimes has rates as low as $85, at which time it's a more attractive option.

Waikiki Grand (☎ 923-1511, 800-535-0085, fax 923-4708, marc@aloha.net, 134 Kapahulu Ave, Honolulu, HI 96815) is a 173-room hotel opposite the zoo. The rooms are rather small and ordinary, but they have the standard amenities: TV, phone, air-con, mini-refrigerator and coffeemaker. The hotel has a pool. The rack rates listed in the hotel brochure are a pricey $129 for a standard room or $149 for a room with a kitchenette, but there are sometimes hefty discounts. The hotel is a member of the Marc Resorts chain.

The *Doubletree Alana Waikiki Hotel* (☎ 941-7275, 800-367-6070, fax 949-0996, 1956 Ala Moana Blvd, Honolulu, HI 96815) is a 313-room hotel on the west side of Waikiki. The rooms are modern with mini-bars, coffeemakers, TV, phones, room safes and little lanais. The outdoor pool is heated, and there are good restaurants within easy walking distance.

The regular published rates begin at a pricey $185 for a room with a city view and $210 for a room with an ocean view, but there are a number of discounts. For example, sometimes a 'holiday rate' is available, and the same rooms drop to $105 for the city view, $125 for the ocean view. There's also a $123 corporate rate for businesspeople that includes parking. This hotel chain maintains a website (www.doubletree.com) with additional information.

The *New Otani Kaimana Beach Hotel* (☎ 923-1555, 800-356-8264, fax 922-9404, kaimana@pixi.com, 2863 Kalakaua Ave, Honolulu, HI 96815) is right on Sans Souci Beach on the quieter Diamond Head side of Waikiki. Popular with return visitors, it's a pleasantly low-key place with 125 units. Room rates start at $125/140 in the low/high season; studios with kitchenettes start at $150/165. All have air-con, TV, refrigerators and lanais.

Waikiki Sunset (☎ 922-0511, 800-922-7866, fax 923-8580, 229 Paoakalani, Honolulu, HI 96815) is a 435-unit condominium complex handled by Aston. The one-bedroom units each have a lanai as well as a large living room with a full kitchen. Rates for rooms on lower floors are $180/205 in the low/high season. Ask about special promo-

Outrigger canoe

tions (even in the high season, there's often a 'property special' for $138), AAA rates and travel-club discounts. If you're able to get a discounted rate on one of the better-furnished units, it's a reasonable value.

The 817-room *Hale Koa Hotel* (☎ 955-0555, 800-367-6027, fax 800-425-3329, reservations@halekoa.com, 2055 Kalia Rd, Honolulu, HI 96815), on Fort DeRussy Beach, is reserved for US military personnel (both active and retired) and their families. Rates, which vary by floor and by the guest's rank, begin around $60 a night. This is a modern, 1st-class hotel with a fitness center, three swimming pools and an array of activities available for guests. Visit their website (www.halekoa.com).

Outrigger Hotels Over the years, the *Outrigger (Box 88559, Honolulu, HI 96830)* chain has snapped up and renovated many of Waikiki's mid-range hotels; at last count it had 21. Overall, it's a well-run and fairly good-value chain, although there's a wide range in both price and quality. At any rate, with one phone call, you can check on the availability of 25% of the hotel rooms in Waikiki!

To book rooms at any Outrigger, you can call ☎ 303-369-7777 or fax 303-369-9403. Outrigger also has the following toll-free numbers: ☎ 800-688-7444 and fax 800-622-4852 from the USA and Canada; ☎ 1-800-688-74443 and fax 1-800-622-48522 from Australia, New Zealand, Hong Kong and the United Kingdom; ☎ 0800-181-8598 from Germany; and ☎ 1-800-688-74443 from Japan. Additional toll-free numbers, via AT&T USA Direct 800 service, are available from many other countries – the local AT&T representative can provide the access number.

Outrigger's email address is reservations@outrigger.com, and www.outrigger.com is the website.

Ask about any promotional deals when making your reservations – currently these include a 'Free Ride' program, which provides a free Budget rental car when you book at the regular room rate; a 'First Night Free' on stays of six nights; and a 20% 'Island Hopper' discount on stays of seven consecutive nights at any combination of the chain's Waikiki and Neighbor Island hotels. Travelers aged 50 and older are entitled to a discount of 20% (25% for AARP/CARP members). In addition, some Outrigger hotels, including the low-end Coral Seas and the high-end Outrigger Reef, offer 50% discounts to members of the Encore and Entertainment travel clubs.

All Outrigger rooms have air-con, phones, cable TVs, room safes and coffeemakers; and most also have refrigerators. Nonsmoking rooms are available, and children younger than 18 stay free.

Note that Outrigger is planning to regroup its low-end properties under the label Ohana Hotels, but they'll remain under the same Outrigger umbrella, and reservation details should remain the same. The 303-room *Waikiki Surf* (☎ 923-7671, 2200 Kuhio Ave, Honolulu, HI 96815) was recently renovated and is one of Outrigger's better deals in the Kuhio area. Standard hotel rooms cost $90 and are small but otherwise quite pleasant; each has a mini-refrigerator, lanai and either one queen or two twin beds. The kitchenette units are a good value, as they cost just $5 more and are roomier, with a king or two

WAIKIKI

double beds, a larger refrigerator and either a two-burner hot plate or a microwave. There are also one-bedroom units for up to four people for $140.

If preparing your own meals is a consideration, the **Waikiki Surf East** (☎ 923-7671, *422 Royal Hawaiian Ave, Honolulu, HI 96815*), a block north of the Waikiki Surf, is a recommendable place, with kitchenettes in all its 102 units. Both the studios and one-bedroom units are large, and most have a sofa bed, as well as a regular king or two double beds. Prices are the same for up to four people: $100 for the studios and $140 for the one-bedroom units. The accommodations are superior to many higher-priced Outriggers – the lower price simply reflects the distance from the beach and the fact that the hotel is a converted apartment building with no restaurant or other lobby facilities.

The recently renovated **Ohana Surf** (☎ 922-5777, *2280 Kuhio Ave, Honolulu, HI 96815*) has 251 pleasant rooms, each with a lanai, refrigerator and two-burner stove. Rates are $90 on the lower floors and $100 on the higher floors, the latter less prone to catch the drone of traffic on busy Kuhio Ave. Although it's a couple of blocks inland, the rooms are otherwise on par with many beachside hotels charging nearly twice the price.

Waikiki Malia (☎ 923-7621, *2211 Kuhio Ave, Honolulu, HI 96815*) is a 328-room high-rise hotel opposite the Waikiki Surf. Rooms are comfortable, each with a mini-refrigerator, tiny one-chair lanai and, in most cases, two double beds. Some of the rooms are wheelchair accessible. Ask for an upper-floor room on the back side, as they're the quietest. All rooms, regardless of the floor, have the same rate of $105. There are also one-bedroom suites for $145. The hotel has a rooftop tennis court and a 24-hour coffee shop.

A curious mid-range option is the **Ala Moana Towers** (☎ 942-7722, *1700 Ala Moana Blvd, Honolulu, HI 96815*), a tall, thin high-rise hotel at the western end of Waikiki. Set back a little from Ala Moana Blvd, there's some buffer from traffic noise, and with only four units per floor, this narrow 40-story

complex is less bustling than most Waikiki hotels. The rooms are a bit compact, but pleasant, and have kitchenettes with a microwave, refrigerator, oven and hot plates. Request one of the upper floors, as these have a splendid view of either the yacht harbor or the city. The rate is $100 for a city view and $120 for a ocean view. There's a fun glass-walled outdoor elevator.

There are a number of Outrigger hotels closer to the water, including the 109-room **Waikiki Coral Seas** (☎ 923-3881, *250 Lewers St, Honolulu, HI 96815*), a small hotel popular with return guests. Although Outrigger gives the property its low-end economy rating, the rooms are comfortable and adequately furnished with either one queen or two double beds, and there's even a lanai. Regular rooms cost $90, kitchenette units $100 and one-bedroom units $130.

Just a stone's throw from the beach is the 184-room **Waikiki Edgewater** (☎ 922-6424, *2168 Kalia Rd, Honolulu, HI 96815*). It's an older property with simple but sufficient rooms, each with a small refrigerator and either two twins or a queen bed. Rates are $90 for a standard room and $100 for a kitchenette. Ask for one of the rear rooms, as they tend to be quieter.

The **Waikiki Royal Islander** (☎ 922-1961, *2164 Kalia Rd, Honolulu, HI 96815*) is a smaller hotel with 100 rooms, a friendly staff and a good location just across from Fort DeRussy Beach. The rooms in this 12-story hotel are on the small side, but are pleasant and have all the standard amenities. The best rooms for ocean views are the upper-floor corner ones, all of which end in the numbers 01. The only drawback is that the hotel is on a busy intersection, so roadside rooms on the lower floors can be noisy. Rates are $90 to $115, depending upon the view.

The 439-room **Waikiki Tower** (☎ 922-6424, *200 Lewers St, Honolulu, HI 96815*) is a high-rise hotel a few minutes' walk from the beach. The rooms are comfortable, with a lanai, small refrigerator and either two doubles or a king bed. The cheapest rates are for rooms from the 12th floor down, which cost $115. Rooms on floors 14 and above are essentially the same but cost $15 more. There are also kitchenette rooms with a microwave from $120.

A tad farther from the beach is the 479-room **Waikiki Reef Towers** (☎ 924-8844, 227 Lewers St, Honolulu, HI 96815), which also has rooms that are comfortable and well equipped. The regular rooms begin at $105, and roomy kitchenette units with microwaves and an extra sofa bed cost $120.

Right on the beach, the 885-room **Outrigger Reef Hotel** (☎ 923-3111, 2169 Kalia Rd, Honolulu, HI 96815) underwent a $50 million renovation. As might be expected, the rooms are spiffy, albeit without much character, and have the usual 1st-class amenities. Wheelchair-accessible rooms are available, and some floors are designated for nonsmokers only. Rates, which are the same year round, range from $160 for a nonview room to $325 for an oceanfront room.

The chain's other beachfront hotel, the 530-room **Outrigger Waikiki** (☎ 923-0711, 2335 Kalakaua Ave, Honolulu, HI 96815), was also renovated, and it offers modern amenities and rates that rise with the view. Rooms begin at $175 for the lower floors and climb to $350 for an ocean view. Set on a prime stretch of sand, there's lots of activity here, from beach events to seaside dining.

Places to Stay – Top End

The following hotels all have standard 1st-class amenities and in-house restaurants. All are on the ocean or across the street from it and have swimming pools.

A good-value top-end hotel is the 298-room **Waikiki Parc Hotel** (☎ 921-7272, 800-422-0450, fax 923-1336, 2233 Helumoa Rd, Honolulu, HI 96815), which is across the street from its more upmarket sister, the Halekulani. The hotel has a pleasantly understated elegance. Rooms are average in size, but have nice touches, such as ceramic-tile floors, shuttered lanai doors and bathtubs.

Standard rooms cost $175, and the upper-level ocean-view rooms top out at $270. If you book in the mid-range, request the 8th floor, which has larger lanais. The hotel often runs promotional rates such as the 'Park and Sunrise' deal that includes breakfast and free parking for $146; a room and car

package for $158; and a 25% room-rate discount for those over 55 years of age.

Overseas reservation numbers are the same as those listed for the Halekulani Hotel (later in this section). The hotel also maintains a website (www.waikikiparc.com).

The **Pacific Beach Hotel** (☎ 922-1233, 800-367-6060, fax 922-0129, 2490 Kalakaua Ave, Honolulu, HI 96815) is a high-rise hotel with 831 rooms. The accommodations, although not distinguished, are pleasant, with comfortable beds, TVs, phones, room safes, mini-refrigerators, lanais and bathrooms with tubs. Room rates range from $180 to $300.

Nonsmoking rooms are available. There are tennis courts and a fitness center, and the hotel has an impressive three-story aquarium filled with tropical fish.

The **Hawaiian Regent** (☎ 922-6611, 800-367-5370, fax 921-5222, hwnrgnt@aloha.net, 2552 Kalakaua Ave, Honolulu, HI 96815) is one of Waikiki's largest hotels, with 1346 rooms in a huge mazelike complex. However, rooms are quite ordinary for the money, with rates ranging from $165 to $270.

The 713-room **Hawaiian Waikiki Beach Hotel** (☎ 922-2511, 800-877-7666, fax 923-3656, 2570 Kalakaua Ave, Honolulu, HI 96815) looks almost like a reflection of the larger Hawaiian Regent across the street, and the rooms are comparable but less expensive. Prices start at $120. The best value is the Mauka Tower, an annex off to the side of the main building, where the rates are at the low end and the rooms are larger and quieter than in the main hotel.

The **Sheraton** (☎ 800-325-3535 from the USA and Canada, ☎ 008-07-3535 from Australia and ☎ 1-120-003535 from Japan) pretty much owns a little stretch of the beach, boasting 4400 rooms in its four Waikiki hotels. Sheraton maintains a website (www.sheraton-hawaii.com).

The 1150-room **Sheraton Princess Kaiulani** (☎ 922-5811, fax 923-9912, 120 Kaiulani Ave, Honolulu, HI 96815) is the Sheraton's least expensive Waikiki property. Rates begin at $160. One of Waikiki's older hotels, it was built in the 1950s by Matson Navigation to help turn Waikiki into a middle-class destination, and from the outside it looks rather like an apartment complex. However, the interior is more appealing, and the rooms are modern. It's in the busy heart of Waikiki across the street from the beach.

The 793-room *Sheraton Moana Surfrider* (☎ 922-3111, fax 923-0308, 2365 Kalakaua Ave, Honolulu, HI 96815) is a special place for those fond of colonial hotels. Built in 1901, the Moana was Hawaii's first beachfront hotel. It's undergone a $50 million historic restoration, authentic right down to the carved columns on the porte cochere. Despite the fact that modern wings (the 'Surfrider' section) have been attached to the main hotel's flanks, the Moana has survived with much of its original character intact.

The lobby is open and airy with high plantation-like ceilings, reading chairs and Hawaiian artwork. The rooms in the original building were closely restored to their early-19th-century appearance. The furnishings on each floor are made from a different wood, for example, koa on the 5th and cherry on the 6th, and TVs and refrigerators are discreetly hidden behind armoire doors.

Rates in the historic wing range from $265 for city views to $405 for ocean views.

The pink, Moorish-style *Royal Hawaiian Hotel* (☎ 923-7311, fax 923-8999, 2259 Kalakaua Ave, Honolulu, HI 96815), now a Sheraton property, was Waikiki's first luxury hotel. Despite being overshadowed by highrises, it's still a beautiful building, cool and airy, and loaded with charm. The historic section maintains a classic appeal, with some of the rooms having quiet garden views. This section is easier to book too, as most guests prefer the modern high-rise wing with its ocean views.

Character comes at a price: rates begin at a steep $305 in the historic wing, $535 in the high-rise tower.

Sheraton Waikiki (☎ 922-4422, fax 922-9567, 2255 Kalakaua Ave, Honolulu, HI 96815) is the 1850-room mega-hotel that looms over the Royal Hawaiian Hotel. The bustling lobby resembles an exclusive Tokyo shopping center, lined with expensive jewelry stores and boutiques with French names and designer labels. The hotel has central elevators that deposit guests at some of the longest corridors in Hawaii.

Rates range from $250 for a city view to $465 for a luxury ocean-view unit.

The Ilikai (☎ 949-3811, 800-245-4524, fax 947-4523, 1777 Ala Moana Blvd, Honolulu, HI 96815), a member of the Nikko chain, overlooks the Ala Wai Yacht Harbor. This twin-tower hotel houses 800 rooms, most of which are good-sized and have a lanai. A couple of floors are equipped for business travelers and have in-room fax machines and modem capabilities.

Rates begin at $230, but if you're paying this kind of money, it's best to opt for an ocean-view room, as these have fine sunset views across the yacht harbor, tend to be quieter than streetfront rooms and cost only $20 more. Visit their website for more information (www.ilikaihotel.com).

The nearby *Hawaii Prince Hotel* (☎ 946-0811, 800-321-6248, fax 946-0811, 100 Holomoana St, Honolulu, HI 96815), managed by a Japanese chain, is more upscale than the Ilikai. An ultramodern high-rise that overlooks the yacht harbor, it has 521 sleek rooms, each boasting an ocean view. There's a business center with computers, copiers and secretarial services; a fitness center; and free shuttle service around Waikiki, which can be useful, as there's no beach in this neighborhood.

The regular rates begin at $260, but there are ongoing promotions, including a room and car package or a room and breakfast for two, that cost $210. The hotel can be booked from overseas through either the Prince or Westin hotel networks. Westin also maintains a website (www.westin.com).

The beachfront *Hilton Hawaiian Village* (☎ 949-4321, 800-445-8667, fax 947-7898, 2005 Kalia Rd, Honolulu, HI 96815) is Hawaii's largest hotel, with 2545 rooms and a new wing in the making. The ultimate in mass tourism, it's practically a package-tour city unto itself – all self-contained for people who never want to leave the hotel grounds. It's quite a busy place, right down to the roped-off lines at the front desk, which resembles an airline check-in counter. The Hilton is on a nice beach, has some good restaurants and offers free entertainment, including Friday-night fireworks.

The rooms are modern and comfortable, with rates starting at $210 for a garden view, $325 for an ocean view.

Hyatt Regency Waikiki (☎ 923-1234, 800-233-1234, fax 923-7839, 2424 Kalakaua Ave, Honolulu, HI 96815) has twin 40-story towers with 1230 rooms. There's a maximum of 18 rooms per floor, so it's quieter and feels more exclusive than other hotels its size. Rooms are pleasantly decorated with rattan furnishings and cost $240 to $400, depending on the view. Between the towers there's a large atrium with cascading waterfalls and tropical plants. Hyatt maintains a website (www.hyatt.com).

The *Colony Surf Hotel (☎ 924-3111, 888-924-7873, fax 923-2249, 2895 Kalakaua Ave, Honolulu, HI 96815)* is right on Sans Souci Beach, on the quieter Diamond Head side of Waikiki. New owners purchased this classic boutique-style hotel a couple of years ago and virtually rebuilt it from the ground up. The renovated hotel wing has 50 contemporary rooms that have an agreeable, low-key elegance.

Rooms cost $255 with a Diamond Head view and $295 with an ocean view. There's also an older condominium wing at the side of the hotel that has spacious 900-sq-foot seaside units starting at $255 for the lower floors and rising to around $295 for the best ocean-view units. Visit the hotel's website (www.colonysurf.com) for more information.

The *Halekulani Hotel (☎ 923-2311, 800-367-2343, fax 926-8004, 2199 Kalia Rd, Honolulu, HI 96815)* is considered Waikiki's premier hotel. The 456 rooms, which are pleasantly subdued rather than posh, have large balconies, marble vanities, deep soaking tubs and little touches like bathrobes and fresh flowers. Rooms with garden views cost $295, while those fronting the ocean are $425. Suites start at $700. The Halekulani can be booked through Prima Reservations System: ☎ 800-676-106 in Australia, 0-800-181-535 in England, 05-90-8573 in France and 0-130-844278 in Germany. Visit their website (www.halekulani.com) for more information.

PLACES TO EAT

Waikiki has no shortage of places to eat, although the vast majority of the cheaper ones are easy to pass up. Generally, the best inexpensive food is found outside Waikiki, where most Honolulu residents live and eat. Waikiki's top-end restaurants, on the other hand, are some of the island's best, though they can quickly burn a hole in your wallet.

Places to Eat – Budget

For inexpensive bakery items, try the *Patisserie (2330 Kuhio Ave)*, beside the Waikiki West hotel, or its other branch in the lobby of the Waikiki Edgewater hotel *(2168 Kalia Rd)*. Both are open from at least 6:30 am to 9 pm daily and sell reasonably priced pastries, croissants, bread and coffee. If you want to eat in, there's a small sit-down area where you can get standard breakfast items, sandwiches and deli salads.

Fatty's Chinese Kitchen (2345 Kuhio Ave) is a hole-in-the-wall eatery in an alley on the west side of the Miramar hotel. It serves some of the cheapest food to be found in these parts, with rice or chow mein plus one hot entree for only $3.50. Add $1 for each additional entree. Despite the low cost, the food is good – on par with Chinese restaurants elsewhere that charge twice the price. The atmosphere is purely local, with a dozen stools lining a long bar and the cook on the other side chopping away. Fatty's is open 10:30 am to 10:30 pm daily.

At the northwest corner of the *International Market Place (2330 Kalakaua Ave)* there's a food court with about two dozen stalls selling cinnamon buns, shave ice, frozen yogurt, pizza, sandwiches and various plate lunches, including Korean, Chinese, Mexican and Greek – nothing really notable, but it is cheap.

There's a *Häagen-Dazs* ice cream shop on Kalakaua Ave, just east of the International Market Place.

Moose McGillycuddy's *(310 Lewers St)* serves 20 different omelettes for $4.95 each, but the best deal is the early-bird special (7:30 to 8:30 am) of two eggs, bacon and toast for $1.99. The restaurant also has an extensive menu of burgers, sandwiches, Mexican food, salads and drinks at moderate prices. It's open for meals 7:30 am to 9:30 pm daily, with breakfast served until 11 am. There's music and dancing nightly until at least 2 am.

Breakfast Ideas

Signs draped from buildings advertising breakfast specials for $2 to $4 are commonplace around Waikiki. **Eggs 'n Things** *(1911 Kalakaua Ave)* and **Moose McGilly-cuddy's** *(310 Lewers St)* both have perennial breakfast specials.

Food Pantry *(2370 Kuhio Ave)* has a doughnut counter, and the **Patisserie** *(2330 Kuhio Ave, 2168 Kalia Rd)* has a full bakery serving pastries, as well as a few inexpensive egg dishes. Bagels, scones and a large selection of coffee drinks are available at **Starbucks** *(1178 Ala Moana Blvd)*, in the Discovery Bay Center.

Fast-food chains such as **Jack in the Box**, **McDonald's** and **Burger King** offer their quick, cheap breakfasts from just about every other corner. If you're really hungry and not too demanding about quality, the $5 all-you-can-eat breakfast buffet at **Perry's Smorgy** *(250 Lewers St, 2380 Kuhio Ave)* is a good deal.

For $10 to $20, you can try one of the all-you-can-eat breakfast buffets that many of the larger hotels offer, but few are worth the money. A couple of noteworthy exceptions, both with beachfront dining, are the simple, but adequate, breakfast buffet for $7 at the **Shore Bird Beach Broiler** *(2169 Kalia Rd)* in the Outrigger Reef Hotel (7:30 to 11 am daily) and the more elaborate spread for $10 at **Duke's Canoe Club** *(2335 Kalakaua Ave)* in the Outrigger Waikiki Hotel (7 to 10:30 am daily).

❀❀❀❀❀❀❀❀❀❀❀❀

Tenteko Mai *(2126 Kalakaua Ave)* is an unpretentious little place with good authentic Japanese ramen for $7.50. It also has tasty *gyoza*, which is a grilled garlic-and-pork-filled dumpling, for $4 a half dozen. The scene feels like a neighborhood eatery in Tokyo, with seating at stools around a U-shaped bar and fellow diners chatting away in Japanese. It's open 11 am to midnight daily.

A bit cheaper, but also a notch down in quality, is the nearby **Curry House Coco Ichibanya** *(2136 Kalakaua Ave)*, which has Japanese-style curry-rice dishes for $5 to $7. It's open 11 am to midnight daily.

The two **Perry's Smorgy** restaurants *(2380 Kuhio Ave)*, at the corner of Kanekapolei St, and in the Waikiki Coral Seas hotel *(250 Lewers St)*, offer inexpensive all-you-can-eat buffets. Breakfast (7 to 11 am) includes pancakes, eggs, ham, coffee and fresh pineapple, papaya and melon. It's a tourist crowd, and the food is cafeteria quality, but it's hard to beat the $4.99 price. Lunch, which includes a reasonable fruit and salad bar, as well as simple hot dishes such as fried chicken, is served 11:30 am to 2:30 pm and costs $5.99. Dinner (5 to 9 pm) adds a round of beef and costs $8.99. If it's convenient, opt for the Kuhio Ave location, as it has a surprisingly pleasant gardenlike setting.

Eggs 'n Things *(1911 Kalakaua Ave)* is a bustling all-nighter, open 11 pm to 2 pm daily. It specializes in breakfast fare, with a variety of waffles, pancakes, crepes and omelettes priced from $5 to $8, though the most popular deal is the 'Early Riser' special of three pancakes and two eggs that's offered from 5 to 9 am for just $3.

Also at the west side of Waikiki is **Pho Tri** *(478 Ena Rd)*, which specializes in *pho*, a Vietnamese noodle soup spiced with fresh green basil. A large bowl of chicken or beef pho costs $6, as do various rice plates. It's open 10 am to 10 pm daily.

Ezogiku *(2546 Lemon Rd)*, a little hole-in-the-wall noodle shop entered off of Paoakalani Ave, is part of a Tokyo chain eatery. The food is not distinguished, but the prices are reasonable, with ramen from

$6.50 and gyoza for $3.75. It's open 11 am to midnight daily.

American fast-food chains are well represented in Waikiki: there are three *Burger King*, four *McDonald's* and six *Jack in the Box* restaurants (the latter open 24 hours). In addition to the usual menus, they add some island touches, such as passion fruit juice, *saimin* (noodle soup) and Portuguese sausage. All three chains usually have discount coupons in the free tourist magazines.

Kapahulu Ave The run of neighborhood ethnic restaurants on Kapahulu Ave makes a nice alternative to dining in Waikiki proper. Kapahulu Ave starts in Waikiki, near the zoo, and runs up to the H-1 Fwy.

Ono Hawaiian Food (☎ 737-2275, 726 Kapahulu Ave) is *the* place in the greater Waikiki area to get Hawaiian food served Hawaiian-style. It's a simple diner, but at dinnertime people line up on the sidewalk waiting to get in. Either a *kalua* pig plate or a *laulau* plate (pork or beef with salted fish and taro leaves) costs $7.75. Both come with *lomi* (marinated raw salmon), *pipikaula* (beef jerky), *haupia* (coconut custard) and your choice of rice or *poi* (taro root paste). Or, if you prefer, there's an à la carte menu – either way, you can eat your fill of traditional Hawaiian fare for less than $10. It's open 11 am to 7:30 pm Monday to Saturday.

New Kapahulu Chop Suey (☎ 734-4953, 730 Kapahulu Ave) serves big plates of Chinese food. The combination special lunch plate costs just $4.15, the special dinner $5, and a score of other dishes are priced less than $6. Although it's certainly not gourmet, it's a lot of food for the money. It's open 11 am to 9 pm daily.

Irifune's (☎ 737-1141, 563 Kapahulu Ave) is a funky little joint decorated with Japanese country kitsch, and it serves tasty MSG-free food. Alcohol is not served, but you can bring in beer from the nearby liquor store. The gyoza for $3.50 is good, as is the garlic tofu with vegetables at $9. There are combination dinners for around $10 that include tempura and options such as *tataki ahi*, a delicious fresh tuna that's seared lightly on the outside, sashimi-like inside, and served with a tangy sauce. Lunch specials start at $7.50.

Although few tourists come up this way, the restaurant is popular with locals. You might have to wait 30 minutes to be seated at dinner, but it's well worth it. Irifune's is open 11:30 am to 1:30 pm and 5:30 to 9:30 pm Tuesday to Saturday.

Leonard's (☎ 737-5591, 933 Kapahulu Ave), a Portuguese bakery about half a mile north of Irifune's, is known throughout Honolulu for its *malasadas*, a type of sweet fried dough, rolled in sugar and served warm – like a doughnut without the hole. The cost is just 55¢ each, and the bakery also sells a few other pastries, such as tasty cinnamon raisin snails, for less than $1. It's open 6 am to 9 pm daily (to 10 pm on Friday and Saturday).

Coffee Haven (☎ 732-2090, sip@coffee-haven.com, 1026 Kapahulu Ave), a bit farther up the road, is a friendly little Internet cafe that makes a pleasant breakfast stop, even if you don't need to check your email. It has coffee, scones, salads and sandwiches, as well as delicious homemade cherry and apple pies for $1.85 a slice. Internet access costs $4 an hour on Macs, $6 an hour on PCs, with a 50¢ minimum.

KC Drive Inn (☎ 737-5581, 1029 Kapahulu Ave), near the freeway, features Ono Ono malts (a combination of chocolate and peanut butter that tastes like a liquified Reese's Peanut Butter Cup) for $2.50 and waffle dogs (a hot dog wrapped in a waffle) for $2, as well as inexpensive breakfast fare, plate lunches, burgers and saimin for either eat-in or takeout. Open 6 am to at least 11:30 pm daily, it's been a local favorite since the 1930s.

If you're on foot, *Rainbow Drive-In* (☎ 737-0177), at the intersection of Kapahulu and Kanaina Aves, is much closer to central Waikiki, has similar fast food and just as much of a local following. It's open 7:30 am to 9 pm daily.

See also the listing for *Sam Choy's Diamond Head Restaurant* (Places to Eat – Top End), in the same Kapahulu neighborhood but with higher prices.

WAIKIKI

Grocery Stores

The best place to get groceries in Waikiki is the **Food Pantry** (2370 Kuhio Ave), which is open 24 hours a day. Its prices are higher than those of the chain supermarkets, which are all outside Waikiki, but lower than those of the smaller convenience stores. Food Pantry, like most grocery stores in Hawaii, accepts credit cards.

Beyond Waikiki, the easiest supermarket to get to without a car is the **Foodland** at the Ala Moana Center, as virtually all buses stop at the center. If you have a car, there's a **Foodland** north of Waikiki, near the eastern intersection of King and Kapiolani Sts.

❀❀❀❀❀❀❀❀❀❀❀❀❀

Places to Eat – Mid-Range

A recommendable place to eat is the **Shore Bird Beach Broiler** (☎ 922-2887, 2169 Kalia Rd), at the Outrigger Reef Hotel, which has a casual beachfront location, open-air dining and reasonable prices. At one end of the dining room, there's a big common grill where you cook your own order; mahimahi, sirloin steak or teriyaki chicken cost $13. Meals come with an all-you-can-eat buffet bar that includes salad, chili, rice and fresh fruit. The buffet bar without a main entree costs just $8. Dinner is served 4:30 to 10 pm nightly; get seated before 6 pm and you can enjoy the sunset and take advantage of cheaper early-bird prices as well.

It's a busy place, so unless you get there early, expect to wait for a table – however, this is scarcely a hardship, as you can hang out on the beach in the meantime. Shore Bird also has a breakfast buffet from 7:30 to 11 am daily for $7. Look for coupons in the free tourist magazines and knock a dollar off all meal prices.

Duke's Canoe Club (☎ 922-2268, 2335 Kalakaua Ave), at the Outrigger Waikiki hotel, also has a nice waterfront view. The restaurant takes its name from the late surfing king Duke Kahanamoku and the outrigger canoe club that was on the beach here in earlier days. While it's a big operation,

the food is good for the money. From 7 to 10:30 am there's a breakfast buffet with cereal, omelettes to order, fresh fruit and pastries for $10, or you can pay $8 and select from just the cold dishes.

At lunch, 11:30 am to 2:30 pm, there's a buffet with a salad bar and hot dishes such as chicken, mahimahi and pork for $10. At dinner, 5 to 10 pm, various fresh fish dishes cost $20, and chicken and steak meals are priced from $15. All dinners come with a full salad bar that includes cold pasta dishes, greens, fruit and muffins. There's also a children's menu with burgers, chicken or spaghetti for $5.

The Honolulu branch of the **Hard Rock Cafe** (☎ 955-7383, 1837 Kapiolani Blvd) is just over the Ala Wai Canal, on the outer edge of Waikiki. The place is enlivened by loud rock music and decorated with old surfboards and a 1959 Cadillac 'woody' wagon hanging precariously above the bar. Hard Rock serves good burgers and fries for around $8 and other all-American food, including barbecued ribs and milkshakes, but it's the atmosphere as much as the food that draws the crowd. It's open 11:30 am to 11 pm daily (to 11:30 pm on weekends).

Competing for a similar audience is **Planet Hollywood** (☎ 924-7877, 2155 Kalakaua Ave), which has a flashy celluloid motif, with Hollywood memorabilia lining the walls and flicks playing on big-screen TVs. Part of the attraction is the hope, however seldom realized, of catching a glimpse of one of the restaurant's Hollywood shareholders, such as Arnold Schwarzenegger or Whoopi Goldberg.

Sandwiches, burgers and thin-crust pizzas cost around $10, and pastas and fajitas average $13. There's also a $4 children's menu that includes pizza, pasta and burgers and fries. It's open 11:30 am to 11 pm daily; the bar stays open until midnight.

Cheeseburger in Paradise (☎ 923-3731, 2500 Kalakaua Ave) is the latest theme eatery – this one boasting a tropical motif. It's open air, and some of the tables look out (across Kalakaua Ave) at the beach. It features decent sandwiches, including Black Angus burgers, Cajun chicken and vegetarian Gardenburgers, for $7 to $10. There are also similarly priced salads. It's open 8 am to midnight daily; there's entertainment 7 to 10 pm nightly.

Chili's (☎ 922-9697, 2350 Kuhio Ave) is a popular Tex-Mex chain restaurant from the mainland that serves soft tacos with rice and beans or burgers with fries for around $8, grilled chicken for $10 and baby back ribs for $18. It also has decent salads. It's open from 11 am to 11 pm daily.

The ***Oceanarium Restaurant*** (☎ 922-1233, 2490 Kalakaua Ave), in the Pacific Beach Hotel, has standard fare with anything but standard views, as the dining room wraps around an impressive three-story aquarium filled with colorful tropical fish. At breakfast, there are waffles or French toast for $7 or a full buffet for $13. At lunch, sandwiches average $8, and at dinner, meals begin at $16. The more expensive ***Neptune's Garden*** (☎ 922-1233), a seafood restaurant in the same hotel, also has views of the aquarium.

A fun place to dine is ***Tanaka of Tokyo*** (☎ 922-4702, 2250 Kalakaua Ave), in the Waikiki Shopping Plaza, or in King's Village (☎ 922-4233, 131 Kaliulani Ave). Both restaurants have about 20 U-shaped teppanyaki tables, each with a central grill that's presided over by a chef with 'flying knives,' who cooks and serves the meals to the diners at his table. Meals are set courses that include salad, miso soup, rice, shrimp appetizer and dessert. The dinner price, which is determined by the entree selected, ranges from $18 for chicken to $36 for lobster tail. Lunch is priced $10 to $15. Look in the free tourist magazines for coupons that are good for half off one meal when two people dine together. Both restaurants are open 11:30 am to 2 pm on weekdays and 5:30 to 10 pm nightly.

California Pizza Kitchen (☎ 955-5161, 1910 Ala Moana Blvd) serves tasty thin-crust pizza cooked in a wood-fired brick oven. One-person pizzas range from $8 for a traditional tomato and cheese to $10 for more intriguing creations, such as the tandoori chicken pizza, which comes with mango chutney. This mainland chain restaurant also has a variety of pasta dishes, both traditional

and exotic, for $8 to $12 and good green salads, with generous half-order portions for $5. It's open 11:30 am to 10 pm Monday to Thursday, 11:30 am to 11 pm Friday and Saturday, and noon to 10 pm Sunday.

In the same building, ***Singha Thai*** (☎ 941-2893, 1910 Ala Moana Blvd) has award-winning Thai food and a troupe of Thai dancers that performs from 7 to 9 pm nightly. For starters, the grilled-beef salad and the hot-and-sour *tom yum* soup are tasty house specialties that cost $8 each. Entrees, such as spicy chicken shiitake-mushroom stir-fry and various curry and noodle dishes, average $14. It's open for dinner only, 4 to 11 pm nightly.

Keo's (☎ 943-1444, 2028 Kuhio Ave), Waikiki's other top-rated Thai restaurant, has similarly good food and slightly cheaper prices. The one drawback is that its new location, roadside on busy Kuhio Ave, can be noisy. Nonetheless, Keo's, which has long been a favorite with visiting celebs ranging from Jimmy Carter to Keanu Reeves, continues to have a loyal following. Owner Keo Sananikone liberally spices the dishes with organically grown herbs from local farms. House specialties include various curries, Evil Jungle Prince (a spicy dish with basil and coconut milk), spring rolls and green papaya salad. Main dishes can be ordered in vegetarian ($10), chicken ($11) or shrimp ($13) versions. It's open from 5 pm nightly.

Kyotaru (☎ 924-3663, 2154 Kalakaua Ave) is a popular Japanese restaurant that specializes in sushi. The prices are moderate, and takeout is available. There are dozens of varieties to choose from, including *kamigata* sushi (Osaka-style), *edomae* sushi (Tokyo-style) and California-style sushi, including a tasty rolled version with shrimp and avocado. If you order in, you can get various sushi combination meals, with tempura, yakitori or noodles, for $12 to $20. Takeout is available daily 10 am to 9:30 pm, and restaurant service is available 11 am to 3 pm and 5 to 9:30 pm.

Dynasty (☎ 947-3771, 1178 Ala Moana Blvd), in the Discovery Bay Center, is a large Chinese restaurant with a substantial menu of à la carte dishes for around $10.

The best deals are the lunch specials, which include spring rolls, fried rice and a choice of four main dishes for $7.50; or the dinner specials, which feature hot-and-sour soup, spring rolls, fried rice, a choice of lemon chicken or sweet-and-sour pork and almond tofu dessert for $13.50. Lunch is served 11 am to 2 pm, dinner 5:30 to 10 pm.

Places to Eat – Top End

Reservations are always a good idea at any of the top-end restaurants. The best place for fine Chinese dining is the *Golden Dragon* (☎ 946-5336, 2005 Kalia Rd), in the Hilton Hawaiian Village, which has both excellent food and a good ocean view. Although the varied menu has some expensive specialties, there are many dishes, including oyster beef and a deliciously crispy lemon chicken, that are priced around $15. There's also an early-bird special until 7 pm Tuesday to Thursday for $19.50. It includes wonton soup, fried rice, sweet-and-sour pork and General Tsao chicken – a dish seasoned with hot chilies. It's open for dinner only, 6 to 9 pm Tuesday to Sunday.

Sam Choy's Diamond Head Restaurant (☎ 732-8645, 449 Kapahulu Ave), on the outskirts of Waikiki, about half a mile beyond the zoo, offers Hawaii Regional cuisine in a contemporary setting. Unlike many other restaurateurs specializing in such fare, Choy serves guests hearty portions that include both soup and salad with all entrees. Among the favorite choices here are the seafood *laulau* (fish steamed in ti leaves), the fresh fish with shiitake mushrooms and the oriental marinated lamb chops – all priced around $25. There are a couple of appetizers, including seared ahi sashimi, but because the entrees are so generous, most diners forgo the first course. It's open 5:30 to 9:30 pm Monday to Thursday and 5 to 10 pm Friday to Sunday.

The *Banyan Veranda* (☎ 922-3111, 2365 Kalakaua Ave), at the Sheraton Moana Surfrider, features buffets served on the hotel's historic courtyard veranda. While the food is not gourmet quality, it is good, and the setting is a gem. Every night there's a sunset buffet from 6 to 10 pm, accompanied by Hawaiian music and hula dancing until 7:30 pm and a classical pianist after that. The meal, which costs $25, features Chinese dim sum, Vietnamese summer rolls, sushi, salads, oysters on the half shell, hot fish and meat dishes and tempting desserts. All in all, it's a class act that's hard to beat.

Brunches Worth the Splurge

Waikiki's most elegant Sunday brunch buffet is served at *Orchids* (☎ 923-2311, 2199 Kalia Rd) in the Halekulani Hotel. The grand spread includes sashimi, sushi, prime rib, smoked salmon, roast suckling pig, roast turkey, an array of salads and fruits, and a decadent dessert bar. In addition, there's a fine ocean view, orchid sprays on the tables and a soothing flute and harp duo. The buffet costs $34 (more on holidays) and lasts from 9:30 am to 2:30 pm. It's best to make advance reservations, or you may encounter a long wait.

A pleasant runner-up is the Royal Hawaiian Hotel's *Surf Room* (☎ 931-7194, 2259 Kalakaua Ave), which has an alfresco beachside setting and a fine Sunday brunch spread served 11 am to 2:30 pm. It includes many seafood dishes (such as sashimi and Alaskan crab legs), a waffle and omelette station, prime rib, salads and tempting desserts. The main drawback is that at $33.50, it's nearly as pricey as Orchids, though it isn't as much of an event.

If you favor a historic colonial atmosphere over beachside dining, then there's the Sunday brunch at the *Banyan Veranda* (☎ 922-3111, 2365 Kalakaua Ave), at the Sheraton Moana Surfrider. It features a dozen salads, sashimi, oysters on the half shell, beef Wellington, eggs Benedict, apple crepes, omelette and waffle stations and a generous dessert bar. The brunch, which is accompanied by live classical music, is served 9 am to 1 pm and costs $32.50.

The *Parc Cafe* (☎ 921-7272, 2233 Helumoa Rd), in the Waikiki Parc Hotel, has buffet meals in a continental-style cafe setting. Although the Parc was once an excellent deal that attracted Honolulu residents and tourists alike, more recently the food has slipped down a notch while the prices have inched upward.

The lunch buffet (11:30 am to 2 pm) costs $16.50 Wednesday and Friday, when it features Hawaiian food; a pricey $25.50 Sunday, when it begins at 11 am and is called brunch; and $15 on other days, when it features Asian-theme salads and a wok station. The dinner buffet (5:30 to 9:30 pm) includes the catch of the day, prime rib, salads and desserts. The cost is $18 Monday to Thursday and $25.50 Friday to Sunday, when it adds sashimi and seafood dishes to the menu.

More of a treat is the upmarket *Prince Court* (☎ 956-1111, 100 Holomoana St), on the 3rd floor of the Hawaii Prince Hotel at the western end of Waikiki, which offers a view of the yacht harbor and a nice lunch buffet of Asian and western dishes. Selections include dim sum, ginger chicken, fresh seafood, salads and tempting desserts. Offered 11:30 am to 2 pm weekdays, the buffet costs $17.95. For dinner the restaurant features Pacific Rim cuisine, including a number of creative fish options, with à la carte dishes averaging $25 and a four-course menu for $60.

If you prefer solidly Japanese food, the Hawaii Prince Hotel's *Takanawa* (☎ 956-1111, 100 Holomoana St) boasts one of Oahu's finest sushi bars, with more than 30 à la carte sushi selections ($5 to $9), ranging from standards such as *maguro* (tuna) to exotic items such as *tobiko* (flying-fish roe). Takanawa also offers grilled steak and sushi combinations for $22 to $32 and a good assortment of sake and beer. It's open for dinner only, 6 to 9:30 pm nightly.

Hakone (☎ 956-1111, 100 Holomoana St), also at the Hawaii Prince Hotel, features traditional Japanese food served by kimono-clad waitresses. At lunch you can choose from five set meals costing $10 to $14 or opt for the buffet that includes a dozen varieties of sushi, a couple of hot entrees, soba noodles and salad for $17.50. At dinner,

Hakone features *teishoku*-style (fixed plate) meals, such as sashimi, tempura or fresh broiled fish, served with rice and miso soup, for around $30. It's open for lunch 11 am to 2 pm Tuesday to Friday and for dinner 6 to 9:30 pm Tuesday to Sunday.

The *Surf Room* (☎ 931-7194, 2259 Kalakaua Ave), at the Royal Hawaiian Hotel, has outdoor beachside dining, although it can be rather crowded and the food is a bit pricey. There's a $21 breakfast buffet served 6:30 to 10 am and a $23 lunch buffet served 11:30 am to 2:30 pm. The dinner menu changes nightly, with meat and seafood entrees for $25 to $30. Dinner is served 6 to 9:30 pm daily.

David Paul's Diamond Head Grill (☎ 922-3734, 2895 Kalakaua Ave), in the Colony Surf Hotel, is a swank place with splashy contemporary paintings and a wall of windows looking out to Diamond Head. Paul offers a menu similar to the one in his well-regarded Maui restaurant, with appetizers such as Kula corn chowder, Maui onion soup or Kona lobster-crab cakes for $8 to $13, and entrees, including his signature tequila shrimp, priced from $25 to $30. It's open for lunch 11:30 am to 2:30 pm weekdays and for dinner 5:30 to 10 pm nightly. There's entertainment, typically jazz, from 9 pm to midnight Tuesday to Saturday.

Orchids (☎ 923-2311, 2199 Kalia Rd), in the Halekulani Hotel, has an alfresco oceanview setting and excellent food. The menu offers both traditional items, such as rack of lamb and filet mignon, and Pacific Rim influenced dishes, such as sashimi and oriental steamed *onaga* (red snapper). Appetizers, including gravlax, shrimp spring rolls and seared ahi, cost $12 to $16, while most main courses are priced around $30. It's open for dinner 6 to 10 pm nightly.

La Mer (☎ 923-2311, 2199 Kalia Rd), in the Halekulani Hotel, is regarded by many to be Hawaii's ultimate fine-dining restaurant. It has a neoclassical French menu, with an emphasis on Provençal cuisine and a superb 2nd-floor ocean view. The dining is formal, and men are required to wear jackets (loaners are available). The four-course fixed-price dinner, which changes daily, costs $85, and the six-course version is $105. Otherwise, appetizers, such as tartare of ahi with caviar or grilled lobster salad, average $25. À la carte entrees range from $36 to $45 and include dishes such as roast duck, bouillabaisse and filet mignon. It's open 6 to 9:30 pm nightly.

Additional top-end Waikiki restaurants include *Bali* (☎ 941-2254, 2005 Kalia Rd), at the Hilton Hawaiian Village, for Hawaiian-influenced continental cuisine; *Cascada* (☎ 945-0270, 440 Olohana St), at the Royal Garden at Waikiki, for Euro-Asian specialties; and *Kyo-ya* (☎ 947-3911, 2057 Kalakaua Ave), a formal Japanese restaurant specializing in multicourse *kaiseki ryori* (a series of small dishes).

ENTERTAINMENT

Waikiki has a varied entertainment scene, and you shouldn't have any problem finding things to do. For updated schedule information for the following suggestions, check the free tourist magazines and the daily newspapers.

Hawaiiana

Waikiki has a variety of Hawaiian-style entertainment, from Polynesian shows with beating drums and hula dancers to mellow duos playing ukulele or slack-key guitar.

There's a free city-sponsored hula show at *Kuhio Beach Park* close to the Duke Kahanamoku statue at 5:30 pm every Saturday and Sunday. The performers are different each week, varying from accomplished adult dancers to troupes of young children just learning the art. All in all, it's a very pleasant scene.

From 8 to 10 pm Friday, the city also sponsors a group of musicians and hula dancers who stroll along Kalakaua Ave between the Royal Hawaiian Shopping Center and the Duke Kahanamoku statue, performing as they go.

The Keolalaulani *halau* (hula school) performs a free hula show on the 2nd floor of the *Waikiki Town Center*, a shopping center at 2301 Kuhio Ave, at 7 pm Monday, Wednesday, Friday and Saturday.

The beachside courtyard at *Duke's Canoe Club* (☎ 922-2268, 2335 Kalakaua Ave), at the Outrigger Waikiki hotel, is Waikiki's most popular venue for contemporary Hawaiian music. There's entertainment 4 to 6 pm and 10 pm to midnight daily, with the biggest names – including Kapena, Brother Noland and Henry Kapono – appearing on weekend afternoons.

At the Sheraton Moana Surfrider's *Banyan Veranda* (☎ 922-3111, 2365 Kalakaua Ave), you can listen to music beneath the same old banyan tree where 'Hawaii Calls' broadcast its nationwide radio show for four decades beginning in 1935. The performance schedule varies, but typically, there's Hawaiian music and a hula dancer from 5:30 to 7:30 pm nightly, followed by a classical pianist from 8 to 10:45 pm.

An older, genteel crowd gathers daily at the Halekulani Hotel's open-air *House Without a Key* (923-2311, 2199 Kalia Rd) for sunset cocktails, Hawaiian music and hula dancing by a former Miss Hawaii.

Luaus The *Royal Hawaiian Hotel* (☎ 923-7194) has a beachside luau from 6 to 8:30 pm Monday, with an open bar, buffet-style dinner and Polynesian show. The price is $78 for adults, or $48 for children ages 5 to 12.

See also the Entertainment section in the Facts for the Visitor chapter for other, less expensive luau shows in Oahu.

This little piggy went to the luau.

Cinemas
Waikiki Theatres (☎ 971-5133), on Seaside Ave near Kalakaua Ave, has three screens showing first-run movies.

IMAX Theatre Waikiki (☎ 923-4629, 325 Seaside Ave) shows a 40-minute movie of Hawaii's stunning vistas on a 70-foot-wide screen, with three-dimensional visual effects. It can be a fun introduction to the landscapes of the Hawaiian islands, providing much of the same effect as zooming around in a helicopter – including the sense of motion! The movie plays several times a day and costs $8.50 for adults and $6 for children aged three to 11.

Dance Clubs
Wave Waikiki (☎ 941-0424, 1877 Kalakaua Ave), with an emphasis on alternative music, is one of the area's hottest dance clubs. Hours are 9 pm to 4 am nightly, the minimum age is 21 and there's no dress code. There's typically a cover charge of about $5, though it's sometimes waived if you come in before 10 pm.

At **Moose McGillycuddy's** (☎ 923-0751, 310 Lewers St), live bands play rock 'n roll from 8 pm to at least 1 am nightly, except Sunday. There's a $3 cover charge on weekends, and you have to be 21 to get in.

Scruples (☎ 923-9530, 2310 Kuhio Ave) is a top-40, dance-music club open 8 pm to 4 am nightly. The cover charge is $5 plus a two-drink minimum, or $15 for people aged 18 to 20.

Hard Rock Cafe (☎ 955-7383, 1837 Kapiolani Blvd) frequently has live rock or ska music 11 pm to 12:30 am on weekends; there's no cover charge.

In addition, a number of the larger Waikiki hotels have nightclubs, some with dancing.

Gay & Lesbian Venues
Hula's Bar & Lei Stand (☎ 923-0669, 134 Kapahulu Ave), which has long been Waikiki's main gay venue, recently moved across town to the 2nd floor of the Waikiki Grand hotel. Open 10 am to 2 am daily, this is a popular place for gays to meet, dance and have a few drinks.

. Other gay spots in Waikiki are **Angles Waikiki** (☎ 926-9766, 2256 Kuhio Ave), a nightclub with dancing, pool and darts; **Fusion Waikiki** (☎ 924-2422, 2260 Kuhio Ave), which has DJ music and female impersonator shows; and **In-Between** (☎ 926-7060, 2155 Lauula St), west of Lewers St, a gay bar open until 2 am nightly.

Although all four of these places welcome both gay men and lesbians, Hula's and In-Between are predominantly establishments for gay men; Angles and Fusion tend to have a more mixed crowd.

Concerts
The **Waikiki Shell** in Kapiolani Park hosts both classical and contemporary music concerts. For current schedule information, call the Blaisdell Center box office (☎ 591-2211).

Tea Ceremonies
The **Urasenke Foundation of Hawaii**, (☎ 923-3059), 245 Saratoga Rd, has tea ceremony demonstrations on Wednesday and Friday, bringing a rare bit of serenity to busy Saratoga Rd. Students dressed in kimonos perform the ceremony on tatami mats in a formal tea room; for those participating, it can be a meditative experience.

It costs $2 to be served green tea and sweets, or you can watch the ceremony for free. Demonstrations take place at 10 am and 11 am; each lasts about 45 minutes. Although they're not always essential, you can make reservations by phone. Because guests leave their shoes at the door, they are asked to wear socks. The building is diagonally across the street from the Waikiki post office.

Free Entertainment
A pleasant way to pass the evening is to stroll along Waikiki Beach at sunset and sample the outdoor Hawaiian shows that take place at the beachfront hotels. You can wander along past the musicians playing at the Sheraton Moana Surfrider's **Banyan Veranda** (2365 Kalakaua Ave), watch bands performing beachside at **Duke's Canoe Club** (2335 Kalakaua Ave), see the poolside performers at the **Sheraton Waikiki** (2255 Kalakaua Ave) and so on down the line.

WAIKIKI

The ***Hilton Hawaiian Village*** *(2005 Kalia Rd)* shoots off fireworks from the beach at around 7:30 pm Friday, preceded at 6:15 pm by a torch-lighting ceremony and a hula show at the hotel pool. At 6 pm Sunday to Thursday, there's a brief torch-lighting ceremony with Hawaiian music. All events are free.

The ***Royal Hawaiian Band*** performs from 2 to 3:15 pm most Sundays, with the exception of August, at the Kapiolani Park Bandstand. It's a quintessential Hawaiian scene that caps off with the audience joining hands and singing Queen Liliuokalani's 'Aloha Oe' in Hawaiian.

The ***Royal Hawaiian Shopping Center*** (☎ 922-0588), on Kalakaua Ave, offers free events nightly in front of the shopping center's main entrance, including Polynesian 'mini-shows' and other forms of streetside entertainment.

In addition, the shopping center sponsors various daytime activities. Hula lessons are given 10 to 11 am Monday, Wednesday and Friday; lei-making lessons are 11 am to noon Monday and Wednesday; both coconut-frond weaving and Hawaiian quilting lessons are offered 9:30 to 11:30 am Tuesday and Thursday; and hour-long ukulele lessons start at 10 am Tuesday and Thursday and at 11:30 am Monday, Wednesday and Friday. All the classes are free, though supplies must be purchased for the quilting class, and it's wise to call to confirm the schedule.

Other free things to see and do in Waikiki, which are detailed earlier in this chapter, include the Kodak Hula Show in Kapiolani Park; the Damien Museum, dedicated to Father Damien; the Oceanarium, a three-story tropical fish tank at the Pacific Beach Hotel; the US Army Museum at Fort DeRussy Beach; and the daily tour of the historic Sheraton Moana hotel.

See also the Hawaiiana section for other listings.

SHOPPING

There are hundreds of shops in Waikiki vying for tourist dollars, including souvenir stalls, swimsuit and T-shirt shops, quick-stop convenience marts and fancy boutiques.

You'll never be far from one of the ubiquitous ABC discount marts, which stand on nearly every other street corner. They can be a good place to pick up vacation necessities, such as cheap beach mats, sunblock, beverages and sundry goods.

For cheap souvenirs, try the International Market Place (☎ 923-9871), in the center of Waikiki, which has scores of stalls selling everything from seashell necklaces and refrigerator magnets to T-shirts and CDs.

The Royal Hawaiian Shopping Center (☎ 922-0588), on Kalakaua Ave, is Waikiki's biggest shopping center, with a few dozen pricey clothing and jewelry shops as well as numerous gift shops, the most interesting of which is the Little Hawaiian Craft Shop (☎ 926-2662), with a range of Hawaiian-made crafts.

Liberty House (☎ 941-2345), a somewhat upmarket department store with good quality clothing, is nearby on Kalakaua Ave.

For more information on things to buy, see the Shopping section in the Facts for the Visitor chapter.

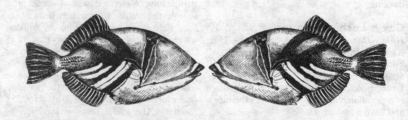

Pearl Harbor Area

Highlights

- Touring the USS *Arizona* Memorial for a sense of the tragedy that thrust the USA into WWII
- Walking the deck of the USS *Missouri*, where the formal end of WWII took place
- Learning about traditional Hawaiian medicine at Keaiwa Heiau, a temple dedicated to healing

PEARL HARBOR

On December 7, 1941, a wave of more than 350 Japanese planes attacked Pearl Harbor, home of the US Pacific Fleet. The attack, which jolted the USA into WWII, caught the US naval base totally by surprise. There had, however, been warnings, some of which were far from subtle.

At 6:40 am the USS *Ward* spotted a submarine conning tower approaching the entrance of Pearl Harbor. The *Ward* immediately attacked with its depth charges and sank what turned out to be one of five midget submarines launched by the Japanese to penetrate the harbor.

At 7:02 am a radar station on the North Shore of Oahu reported that planes were approaching. Even though they were coming from the wrong direction, they were assumed to be American planes coming from the mainland.

At 7:55 am Pearl Harbor was hit. The USS *Arizona*, hit with a 1760lb bomb, went down in a fiery inferno in just nine minutes; 1177 of its crew members, trapped inside, were killed. Twenty other US ships were sunk or damaged, along with 347 aircraft. Some 2335 US sailors lost their lives as a result of the two-hour attack.

It wasn't until 15 minutes after the bombing started that American antiaircraft guns began to shell the Japanese warplanes. The Japanese lost 29 aircraft in the attack.

USS *Arizona* Memorial

Over 1.5 million people 'remember Pearl Harbor' each year by visiting the USS *Arizona* Memorial. Operated by the National Park Service, the memorial is Hawaii's most visited attraction.

The visitor center includes a museum, a theater and a poignant offshore memorial at the site of the sunken USS *Arizona*. The park service provides a 75-minute program that includes a documentary film on the attack and a boat ride out to the memorial and back.

The 184-foot memorial, built in 1962, sits directly over the *Arizona* but does not touch the sunken ship. From the memorial, the battleship is visible 8 feet below the surface. It rests in about 40 feet of water, and even now, it oozes a gallon or two of oil each day.

The memorial contains the ship's bell, and the names of the sailors who perished onboard are inscribed on a wall. The average age of the enlisted men on the *Arizona* was just 19 years old. In the rush to recover from the attack and prepare for war, the navy decided to leave the men in the sunken ship. They remain entombed in its hull, buried at sea.

Pearl Harbor survivors, who act as volunteer historians, are sometimes available to give talks about the day of the attack. There's also a small open-air museum with interesting photos, from both Japanese and US military archives, showing Pearl Harbor before, during and after the attack. One photo is of Harvard-educated Admiral Yamamoto, the brilliant military strategist who planned the attack on Pearl Harbor – even though he

183

PEARL HARBOR AREA

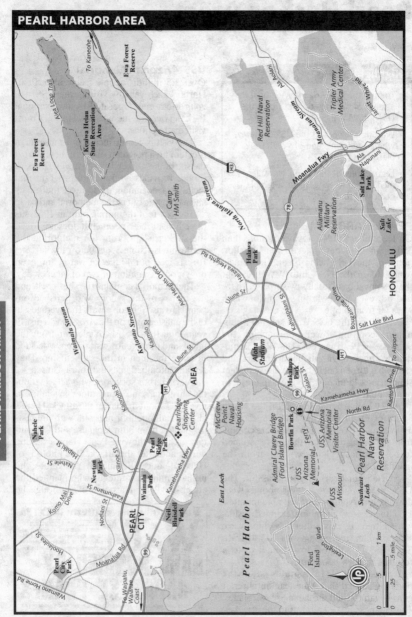

To Kaneohe

Ewa Forest Reserve

Ewa Forest Reserve

Aiea Loop Trail

Keaiwa Heiau State Recreation Area

Ewa Forest Reserve

Camp HM Smith

North Halawa Stream

Red Hill Naval Reservation

Ala Aolani

Moanalua Stream

Tripler Army Medical Center

Tripler Army White Rd

H3

Moanalua Fwy

Ala Napunani

Salt Lake Park

78

Aiamanu Military Reservation

Salt Lake

HONOLULU

Halawa Heights Rd

Halawa Park

Aiea Heights Drive

Ullune St

Bougainville Drive

Salt Lake Blvd

Waimalu Stream

Kalauao Stream

Kaamilo St

Ullune St

Kahuapaani St

Nahele Park

Kaonohi St

Ullune St

AIEA

Aloha Stadium

Makalapa Park

Kalaloa St

H1

To Airport

Nahele Park

Hapaki St

Pearl Ridge Park

Pearlridge Shopping Center

H1

99

Kamehameha Hwy

Radford Drive

Kilinoe St

McGrew Point Naval Housing

North Rd

Newton Park

Kaahumanu St

Waimalu Park

Kamehameha Hwy

Admiral Clarey Bridge (Ford Island Bridge)

Bowfin Park

USS Arizona Ferry

USS Arizona Memorial Visitor Center

Pearl Harbor Naval Reservation

Komo Mai Drive

Kaahumanu St

East Loch

USS Arizona Memorial

USS Missouri

Southeast Loch

Noelani

PEARL CITY

Neil Blaisdell Park

Hoolaulea St

99

Pearl City Park

Moanalua Rd

Pearl Harbor

Ford Island

Lexington Blvd

1 km

5 mile

To Waipahu, Waianae Coast

Waimano Home Rd

.5

.25   .5 mile

0

PEARL HARBOR AREA

personally opposed going to war with the USA. Rather than relish the victory, Yamamoto stated after the attack that he feared Japan had 'awakened a sleeping giant and filled him with a terrible resolve.'

The visitor center (☎ 422-2771; 24-hour recorded information ☎ 422-0561) is open 7:30 am to 5 pm daily, except on Thanksgiving, Christmas and New Year's Day. Weather permitting, programs run every 15 or 20 minutes from 8 am to 3 pm (from 7:45 am in summer) on a first-come, first-served basis. As soon as you arrive, pick up a ticket at the information booth (each person in the party must pick up his or her own ticket); the number printed on the ticket corresponds to the time the tour begins.

Generally, the shortest waits are in the morning, and if you arrive before the crowds, your wait may be less than half an hour; however, waits of a couple of hours are not unknown. The summer months are the busiest, with an average of 4500 people taking the tour daily; the allotment of tickets is sometimes gone by 11 am.

Admission, including the boat ride, is free, and the memorial and all its facilities are accessible to the disabled. There are also a snack bar and a shop selling souvenirs and books. The park service maintains a website about the memorial (www.nps.gov/usar).

USS *Bowfin*
Submarine Museum & Park
If you have to wait an hour or two for your USS *Arizona* Memorial tour to begin, you might want to stroll over to the adjacent USS *Bowfin* Submarine Museum & Park.

The USS *Arizona* Memorial

The park contains the moored WWII submarine the USS *Bowfin*, as well as the Pacific Submarine Museum, which traces the development of submarines from their early origins to the nuclear age.

Commissioned in May 1943, the *Bowfin* sank 44 ships in the Pacific before the end of the war. Visitors can take a self-guided tour using a 30-minute recorded cassette (included in the admission fee). Admission is $8 for adults, $3 for children ages four to 12, and includes entry to both the submarine and the museum. Children under four are not allowed on the submarine for safety reasons.

There's no charge to enter the park, view the missiles and torpedoes displayed on the grounds, look through the periscopes or inspect the Japanese *kaiten* (a suicide torpedo). The kaiten, the marine equivalent of the kamikaze pilot and his plane, was developed as a last-ditch effort to ward off invasion when the war began to close in on the Japanese homeland. A volunteer was placed in the torpedo before it was fired. He then piloted the torpedo to its target. At least one US ship, the USS *Mississinewa*, was sunk by a kaiten. It went down off Ulithi Atoll in southwestern Micronesia in November 1944.

The park and museum are open 8 am to 5 pm daily, except Thanksgiving, Christmas and New Year's Day. There is a website for the museum and park (www.aloha.net/~bowfin/surface.html).

Battleship *Missouri* Memorial
In 1998, the decommissioned USS *Missouri*, nicknamed 'Mighty Mo,' was brought to Ford Island by the nonprofit USS *Missouri* Memorial Association to add another element to Pearl Harbor's WWII sites.

The 887-foot-long ship, one of four powerful Iowa class battleships launched near the end of WWII, served as a flagship during the decisive battles of Iwo Jima and Okinawa. On September 2, 1945, the formal Japanese surrender that ended WWII took place on the battleship's deck. The *Missouri* is now docked just a few hundred yards from the sunken remains of the USS *Arizona*; together, the ships provide a unique set of historical bookends.

Lost Luster

Pearl Harbor was named for the lustrous pearl oysters that thrived in its once pristine waters. Unfortunately, during the early 19th century, foreign settlers introduced cattle to the area, and the grazing livestock so denuded the nearby uplands that the hillsides above the harbor began to erode. As a result, vast quantities of mud washed into the harbor and destroyed the oyster beds.

✿✿✿✿✿✿✿✿✿✿✿✿

Launched in 1944, the *Missouri*, with its 13-inch-thick armor plating, impressive gun turrets and 65-foot-long guns, was the last battleship ever built. In 1955, after service in the Korean War, it was placed in mothballs. Then, three decades later, it was awakened from rest during the heated Reagan-era military buildup, and after costly modernization, the *Missouri* was recommissioned in 1986. The ship made a brief appearance in the Persian Gulf War and was once again decommissioned in 1992.

Both Honolulu and San Francisco petitioned the navy to become caretakers of the historic ship. In 1996, with the Pearl Harbor connection weighing heavily in its favor, Honolulu was chosen to become Mighty Mo's permanent home.

In 1999, the USS *Missouri* opened to visitors. A tour of the ship takes approximately two hours. You can poke about the officers' quarters, visit the wardroom that now houses exhibits on the ship's history and walk the deck where General Douglas MacArthur accepted the Japanese surrender. The cost for a self-guided tour is $10; a group tour with a guide is $14; children's tickets are $4 cheaper. The battleship site (☎ 973-2494, 877-644-4896) is open 9 am to 5 pm daily. There is also a website for the memorial (www.ussmissouri.com).

It's not possible to drive directly to Ford Island, because it is an active military facility. Instead, a trolley bus shuttles visitors to the *Missouri* from Bowfin Park, where the tickets are sold. (It's also possible to buy dis-counted combination tickets to self-tour both the *Missouri* and the *Bowfin*.)

Getting There & Away

The USS *Arizona* Memorial visitor center and Bowfin Park are off Kamehameha Hwy (Hwy 99) on the Pearl Harbor Naval Base, just south of the Aloha Stadium. If you are coming from Honolulu, take H-1 west to exit 15A (Stadium/Arizona Memorial). Make sure that you follow the highway signs for the *Arizona* Memorial, and not the signs for Pearl Harbor.

The private *Arizona* Memorial Shuttle Bus (☎ 839-0911) picks up people from Waikiki hotels five times a day, with the first run at around 7 am; the last bus returns at 4:15 pm. The ride takes around 40 minutes and costs $3 one way or $5 roundtrip. Call to make arrangements.

You can get there by public bus too, but it takes longer. The No 47 Waipahu is the most direct bus line from Waikiki to the *Arizona* Memorial Visitor Center. It takes one to 1¼ hours. Bus No 20 also covers the same route, but it makes a stop at the airport, adding about 15 minutes to the travel time.

There are also private boat cruises to Pearl Harbor that leave from Kewalo Basin. These cruises cost about $25 but should be avoided, because passengers are not allowed to board the memorial.

PEARL CITY

Pearl City is the largest urban area in Hawaii, with the exception of Honolulu. It's home to about 45,000 people, including a lot of military personnel and civilians who work on the bases, but it offers little of interest to visitors.

If you're just passing through and not going to Pearl City itself, stay on H-1 and avoid the parallel Kamehameha Hwy (Hwy 99), because it is all stop-and-go traffic through blocks of fast-food restaurants and shopping malls.

Pearlridge Shopping Center is a massive shopping mall that is situated between the H-1 and the Kamehameha Hwy. On weekends, a swap meet is held a block west of the shopping center, at the drive-in theater.

KEAIWA HEIAU STATE RECREATION AREA

This park in Aiea, north of Pearl Harbor, covers 334 acres and contains an ancient medicinal temple, campgrounds, picnic facilities and a scenic hiking trail. The park is open 7 am to sunset for day visitors. As with all state parks, there are no fees.

At the park entrance is **Keaiwa Heiau**, a stone temple built in the 1600s and used by *kahuna lapaau* (healers that used plants for medicine). The kahunas used hundreds of medicinal plants and grew many on the grounds surrounding the heiau. Among those still found here are *noni*, whose pungent yellow fruits were used to treat heart disease; *kukui*, whose nuts were an effective laxative; *ulu*, whose sap was used to soothe chapped skin; and *ti* leaves that were wrapped around a sick person to break a fever. Not only did the herbs have medicinal value, but the heiau itself was considered to possess life-giving energy, and the kahuna was able to draw from the powers of both the temple and the plants.

Today, people wishing to be healed still place offerings within the heiau. The offerings reflect the multiplicity of Hawaii's cultures: rosary beads, New Age crystals and sake cups sit beside flower leis and rocks wrapped in ti leaves.

Aiea Loop Trail

The 4½-mile Aiea Loop Trail begins at the top of the park's paved loop road, next to the rest rooms, and ends at the campground, about a third of a mile below the start of the trail. The easy hike takes 2½ to three hours.

The first part of the trail goes through a eucalyptus forest and runs along the ridge. Other trees on the way include ironwood,

Norfolk Island pine, guava and native ohia lehua, which has fluffy, red flowers.

Along the trail, there are sweeping vistas of Pearl Harbor, Diamond Head and the Koolau Range. About two-thirds of the way in, the wreckage of a C-47 cargo plane that crashed in 1943 can be spotted through the foliage on the east ridge.

Camping

The park's camping area can accommodate 100 campers. Most sites have their own picnic table and barbecue grill. Sites are not crowded together, but because many of them are open, there's not a lot of privacy either.

If you're camping in winter, make sure your gear is waterproof, because it rains frequently at this 880-foot elevation, although the temperature is usually pleasant. There are rest rooms, showers, a pay phone and drinking water. Overall, it's a good choice for a campground. There's a resident caretaker by the front gate, and the gate is locked at night for security.

As with all Oahu public campgrounds, camping is not permitted on Wednesday and Thursday, and camping permits must be obtained in advance. For details, see Camping in the Accommodations section of the Facts for the Visitor chapter.

Getting There & Away

From Honolulu, head west on Hwy 78 and take the Stadium/Aiea turnoff onto Moanalua Rd. Turn right onto Aiea Heights Drive at the second traffic light. The road winds up for 2½ miles to the park.

Bus No 11 (Honolulu-Aiea Heights) serves this area, but it stops about 1¼ miles south of the park entrance, and the campsites are even farther in.

PEARL HARBOR AREA

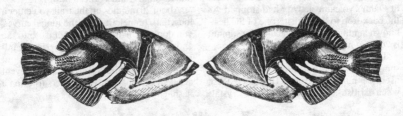

Southeast Oahu

Highlights

- Snorkeling among the colorful tropical fish of Hanauma Bay
- Climbing the Diamond Head Trail to the scenic crater summit
- Marveling at the top-notch bodysurfing action at Sandy Beach
- Taking a swim at lovely Waimanalo Beach Park

Diamond Head, Hanauma Bay and the island's most famous bodysurfing beaches are along the southeast coast, all just a 20-minute ride from Waikiki. This stretch of coast, curving around the tip of the Koolau Mountains, offers some of Oahu's most stunning scenery.

East of Diamond Head, H-1 turns into the Kalanianaole Hwy (Hwy 72) and follows the southeast coast up to Kailua. It passes the exclusive Kahala residential area, a run of shopping centers and suburban housing developments that creep up into the mountain valleys.

The highway rises and falls as it winds its way around the Koko Head area and Makapuu Point, with beautiful coastal views along the way. The area's geological formations are fascinating, with boldly stratified rocks, volcanic craters and lava sea cliffs.

DIAMOND HEAD

Diamond Head, a tuff cone and crater, was formed by a violent steam explosion deep beneath the earth's surface long after most of Oahu's volcanic activity had stopped. As the backdrop to Waikiki, it's one of the best-known landmarks in the Pacific. The summit is 760 feet high.

The Hawaiians called it *Leahi*. At its summit they built a *luakini heiau*, a temple used for human sacrifice. But since 1825, when British sailors found calcite crystals sparkling in the sun and mistakenly thought they'd struck it rich, it's been called Diamond Head.

In 1909 the US Army began building Fort Ruger at the edge of the crater. They constructed a network of tunnels and topped the rim with cannon emplacements, bunkers and observation posts. Reinforced during WWII, the fort has been a silent sentinel whose guns have never been fired. Today, there's a Hawaii National Guard base inside the crater as well as Federal Aviation Administration and civil defense facilities.

Diamond Head is a state monument, with picnic tables, rest rooms, a pay phone and drinking water. The best reason to visit is to hike up to the crater rim for the panoramic view. The gates are open 6 am to 6 pm daily.

Diamond Head Trail

The trail to Diamond Head summit was built in 1910 to service the military observation stations along the crater rim.

Don't expect a walk in the park, because it's a fairly steep hike with a gain in elevation of 560 feet. It is, however, only three-quarters of a mile to the top, and plenty of people of all ages hike to the summit. It takes about 30 minutes to reach the top. The trail is open and hot, so you might want to take along something to drink.

As you start up the trail, the summit is a bit to the left, at roughly eleven o'clock. The crater is dry and scrubby with *kiawe, koa haole*, grasses and wildflowers. The small, yellow-orange flowers along the trail are native *ilima*, Oahu's official flower.

About 20 minutes up the trail, you enter a long, dark tunnel. Because the tunnel curves, you don't see light until you get close to the end. It's a little spooky, but there is a handrail, and your eyes will adjust to make out shadows in the dark. Nevertheless, to prevent accidents, the park advises hikers to bring a flashlight.

SOUTHEAST OAHU

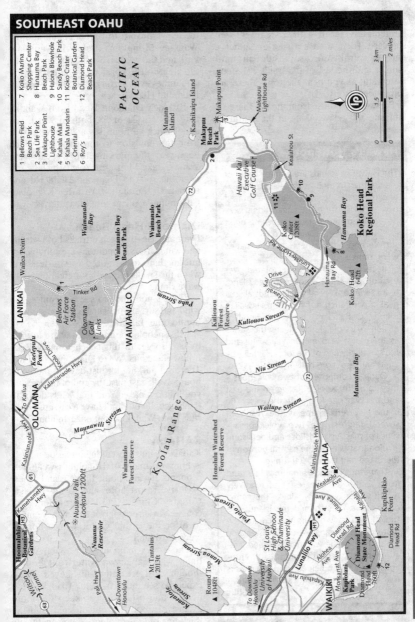

1 Bellows Field
   Beach Park
2 Sea Life Park
3 Makapuu Point
   Lighthouse
4 Kahala Mall
5 Kahala Mandarin
   Oriental
6 Roy's
7 Koko Marina
   Shopping Center
8 Hanauma Bay
   Beach Park
9 Halona Blowhole
10 Sandy Beach Park
11 Koko Crater
   Botanical Garden
12 Diamond Head
   Beach Park

PACIFIC OCEAN

Kaohikaipu Island

Manana Island

Makapuu Point

Makapuu Beach Park

Makapuu Lighthouse Rd

Kealahou St

Hawaii Kai Executive Golf Course

Koko Crater 1208ft

Koko Head 642ft

Hanauma Bay

Koko Head Regional Park

Lunalilo Home Rd

Hanauma Bay Rd

Kai Drive

Hawaii Kai

Wailea Point

Tinker Rd

Bellows Air Force Station

Olomana Golf Links

Waimanalo Bay

Waimanalo Bay Beach Park

Waimanalo Beach Park

LANIKAI

WAIMANALO

Kaelepulu Pond

Kailua Drive

To Kailua

Kalanianaole Hwy

OLOMANA

Kalanianaole Hwy

Maunawili Stream

Puha Stream

Kuliouou Forest Reserve

Kuliouou Stream

Niu Stream

Maunalua Bay

Koolau Range

Wailupe Stream

Waimanalo Forest Reserve

Honolulu Watershed Forest Reserve

Palolo Stream

Kalanianaole Hwy

KAHALA

Kealaolu Ave

Kilauea Ave

Nuuanu Pali Lookout 1200ft

Hoomaluhia Botanical Gardens

Nuuanu Reservoir

Pali Hwy

Kamehameha Hwy

Wilson Tunnel

To Downtown Honolulu

Mt Tantalus 2013ft

Round Top 1048ft

Manoa Stream

Kanewai Stream

University of Hawaii

To Downtown Honolulu

St Louis High School & Chaminade University

Lunalilo Fwy

Kapahulu Ave

Alohea Ave

Monsarrat Ave

Diamond Head Rd

Diamond Head State Monument

Diamond Head Rd

Diamond Head 760ft

Kapiolani Park

WAIKIKI

Kupikipikio Point

SOUTHEAST OAHU

PACIFIC OCEAN

0   1.5   3 km
0   1   2 miles

When you step out into the light, you're immediately faced with a steep, 99-step staircase. Then, there's a shorter tunnel, a narrow spiral staircase inside an unlit bunker and the last of the trail's 271 steps. Be careful as you near the top – there are some steep drops.

Persevere, because from the top there's a fantastic 360° view taking in the southeast

Hawaii's Hot Spot

The Hawaiian Islands are a linear chain of islands that formed as the Pacific Plate – one of Earth's tectonic plates – rotated over a hot spot on the ocean floor. Lava oozed out of this hot spot, building upon itself until it eventually reached the ocean's surface and, voilà, the Hawaiian Islands were formed.

Because the Pacific Plate rotated over the hot spot, there is not one huge island, but a series of several small islands all in a neat curving arch. Of the main Hawaiian Islands, Oahu clocks in at only about 2 million years old; Kauai claims the status as the oldest at 5 million years old; and the spring chicken of the lot is Hawaii (the Big Island) – a mere half-million years old.

Oahu is composed of two volcanoes – they form the Koolau Range on the east and the Waianae Range on the west. The island's current shape is the result of several factors: the two volcanoes, a series of massive landslides and persistent erosion that filled in the central portion of the island and the coastal fringe.

Diamond Head, Hanauma Bay and Koko Crater are the result of relatively recent volcanic activity. Unlike the gently oozing lava that formed the island, this trio of natural wonders was created by more violent means. As the lava reached the surface of the water, it exploded, creating small, steep tuff cones. Later eruptions and erosion helped form the craters that characterize all of these sites today.

Chris Gillis

coast to Koko Head and Koko Crater and the leeward coast to Barbers Point and the Waianae Mountains. Below is Kapiolani Park and the Waikiki Shell. You can also see the lighthouse, coral reefs, sailboats and sometimes even surfers waiting for waves at Diamond Head Beach.

To reach Diamond Head from Waikiki, take bus No 22 or 58, both of which run about twice an hour. It's a 20-minute walk from the bus stop to the trailhead, which begins at the parking lot. By car from Waikiki, take Monsarrat Ave (which begins near the zoo) to Diamond Head Rd and then take the right turn after Kapiolani Community College into the crater.

Diamond Head Beach

Diamond Head Beach attracts both surfers and windsurfers. Conditions are suitable for intermediate to advanced windsurfers, and when the swells are up, it's a great place for wave riding.

There's not much to see here unless the wind and surf are up. The beach has showers but no other facilities.

Most people coming this way are touring by car. To get to this beach from Waikiki, follow Kalakaua Ave to Diamond Head Rd. There's a parking lot just beyond the lighthouse. Walk past the end of the lot, and you'll find a paved trail that leads down to the beach. If you don't have a car, bus No 14 runs from Waikiki about once an hour.

KAHALA

Kahala, Oahu's most affluent seaside suburb, is home to many of Honolulu's wealthiest residents. It's also home to the island's most exclusive resort hotel and to the Waialae Country Club, a PGA tournament golf course. Not surprisingly, it doesn't have much to offer the casual visitor with a normal credit card limit.

The area's main drive, Kahala Ave, is lined with expensive waterfront homes, though most are rather low-keyed. Don't expect to see much from the road, because hedges and estate fences keep the more exclusive properties out of sight, and the thick line of houses blocks out virtually any view of the sea. Between the homes, there are a half-dozen shoreline access points that provide a right-of-way to the beach, but the swimming conditions aren't notable – it's mostly shallow, with sparse pockets of sand.

Places to Stay

Kahala Mandarin Oriental (☎ 739-8888, 800-367-2525, fax 739-8800, sales@mohg.com, 5000 Kahala Ave, Honolulu, HI 96816) is on its own quiet stretch of beach in swank Kahala. Formerly the Kahala Hilton, the 370-room hotel underwent a $75 million face-lift.

This is where the rich and famous go when they want to avoid the Waikiki scene, a 10-minute drive away. The guest list is Hawaii's most regal: Britain's Prince Charles, Spain's King Juan Carlos and Queen Sofia and the last six US presidents.

Rates start at $295 for garden-view rooms and $420 for rooms on the hotel's enclosed lagoon, where dolphins swim just beyond the lanais. The presidential suite tops off at $3530. The hotel can be booked through Mandarin Oriental Hotels worldwide. Visit the website for a preview (www.mandarin-oriental.com/kahala).

Places to Eat

You'll find a large selection of places to eat at the Kahala Mall, 4211 Waialae Ave, just off the highway. In addition to the usual fast-food chains, there are a number of local favorites: *Kozo Sushi* for good, inexpensive, fast-food sushi; *Patti's Chinese Kitchen*, with decent Chinese fare at cheap prices; and *Ba-Le*, with crispy French bread sandwiches and Vietnamese items for just a few dollars. The mall also has a couple of decent, moderately priced restaurants: *California Pizza Kitchen*, with good thin-crust gourmet pizzas, and *Yen King Restaurant*, popular for its northern Chinese dishes.

Kahala's top-end restaurant is *Hoku's* (☎ 739-8780, 5000 Kahala Ave, Honolulu, HI 96816) in the Kahala Mandarin Oriental hotel at the east end of Kahala Ave. This beachfront restaurant specializes in Pacific Rim cuisine with an emphasis on seafood, but also has traditional fine-dining fare such as rack of lamb. Dinner for two can easily top $100.

KOKO HEAD REGIONAL PARK

The entire Koko Head area is a county regional park. It includes Hanauma Bay, Koko Head, Halona Blowhole, Sandy Beach and Koko Crater.

Koko Crater and Koko Head are both tuff cones created about 10,000 years ago during Oahu's last gasp of volcanic activity. The area is backed by Hawaii Kai, an expansive development of condos, houses, shopping centers, a marina and a golf course – all meticulously planned and rather sterile in appearance.

Hanauma Bay Beach Park

Hanauma is a wide, sheltered bay of sapphire and turquoise waters set in a rugged volcanic ring. Hanauma, which means 'Curved Bay,' was once a popular fishing spot, and the fish population was nearly depleted by the time the bay was designated a marine life conservation district in 1967. Now that the fish are fed instead of eaten, they swarm in by the thousands.

Hanauma is both a county beach park and a state underwater park. It has a grassy picnic area, lifeguards, showers, rest rooms, changing rooms and access for the disabled. The bay is closed on Tuesday, but it is otherwise open 7 am until 6 pm daily in winter, until 7 pm in summer. Information about the park, including emergency closure, is available by calling ☎ 396-4229. There's a $3 admission fee for non-Hawaii residents.

The snack bar sells hot dogs, ice cream and soda. The beach concession stand, open 8 am to 4:30 pm, rents snorkel sets for $6 (you'll need to either hand over $30, a credit card or your car rental keys as a deposit).

Hanauma's biggest draw is the sheer number and variety of fish. From the overlook you can peer into crystal waters and view the entire coral reef that stretches across the width of the bay. You can see schools of glittering silver fish, the bright blue flash of parrot fish and perhaps a lone sea turtle. To see an even more colorful scene, put on a mask, jump in and view the bay from beneath the surface.

The park seems to get as many people as fish. With over a million visitors a year, it's often busy and crowded. The heavy use of the bay has taken its toll. The coral on the shallow reef has been damaged by all the action, and the food that snorkelers feed to the fish has increased fish populations in Hanauma well beyond what it can naturally support. In fact, many of the fish in the bay are not common to Hanauma but are more aggressive types that have been drawn in by the feeding.

A master plan that aims to normalize the fish distribution and reduce the number of beachgoers from 10,000 a day to just 2000 is under way. Fish feeding will soon be phased out – in the meantime, snorkelers shouldn't feed the fish anything but the fish food that can be purchased at the beach concession stand.

Paths lead along low ledges on both sides of the bay. The eastern path goes to the Toilet Bowl, and the western path goes to Witches Brew. When the surf is up, which is most high-wind days, the paths are gated shut and entry to the ledges is prohibited. At other times you can walk out along the ledges, but you should still be cautious; whenever the tide is high, waves can wash over the ledges – and of course a rogue wave can occur at any time.

A 15-minute walk out to the point on the left side of the bay brings you to the **Toilet Bowl**, a small natural pool in the lava rock. The Toilet Bowl is connected to the sea by an underwater channel that enables water to surge into the bowl and then flush out from beneath. People going into the pool for the thrill of it can get quite a ride as it flushes down 4 to 5 feet almost instantly. However the rock around the bowl is slippery and difficult to grip, and getting in is far easier than getting out. It definitely should not be tried alone.

A 10-minute walk along the right side of the bay will take you to a rocky point. The cove at the southern side of the point is the treacherous **Witches Brew**, so named for its swirling, turbulent waters. From here, there is

a nice view of Koko Crater, and green sand made of olivine can be found along the way.

More people drown at Hanauma than at any other beach on Oahu. Although the figure is high largely because there are so many visitors at this beach, people drowning in the Toilet Bowl or being swept off the ledges have accounted for a fair number of deaths over the years.

Snorkeling and diving are good all year at Hanauma Bay. Mornings are better than afternoons, because swimmers haven't yet stirred up the sand. The large, sandy opening in the middle of the coral, known as the Keyhole, is an excellent place for novice snorkelers. The deepest water is 10 feet, though it's very shallow over the coral, so if you have diving gloves, bring them. It's well protected and usually swimming-pool calm.

For confident snorkelers, it's better on the outside of the reef, where there are larger coral heads, bigger fish and fewer people; to get there, follow the directions on the sign near the snack bar, or ask the lifeguard at the southwest end of the beach. Keep in mind that because of the channel current, it's generally easier getting out than it is getting back in. Don't attempt to swim outside the reef when the water is rough or choppy. Not only will the channel current be strong, but there will be poor visibility due to the stirred-up sand.

Divers have the whole bay to play in, with clear water, coral gardens, sea turtles and lots of fish. When the surf is up, beware of dangerous currents, especially the Molokai Express, a treacherous current that runs just outside the mouth of the bay; the current is also dangerous near Witches Brew.

Getting There & Away Hanauma Bay is about 10 miles from Waikiki via Hwy 72. There's a large parking lot, although it sometimes has filled up by midday and on the weekend. It costs $1 to enter the parking area, but if you're unable to find a space, the fee will be refunded. Parking outside a marked space will result in a parking ticket.

Bus No 22, called the Beach Bus, goes to Hanauma Bay (and on to Sea Life Park). On weekdays the first buses leave Waikiki from

andy Beach is one of Oahu's hottest bodysurfing spots.

rothy breakers at Hanauma Bay

Ehukai Beach Park, on the North Shore, on a rare calm day

Swaying palms on the windward coast

Moku Lua, off the windward coast

The perfect beach: sun, sand and sea, Kailua Bay

KIM GRANT

Koko Head, a volcanic tuff cone on Southeast Oahu

LEE FOSTER

One of the island's lush tropical forests

LEE FOSTER

Waimea Valley Adventure Park, North Shore

the corner of Kuhio Ave and Namahana St at 8:15 and 9:15 am, with subsequent buses leaving at 55 minutes past the hour until 3:55 pm, and then a final bus at 4:25 pm. The Beach Bus also stops near the zoo at Monsarrat and Kalakaua Aves, but because of high demand, it often fills to capacity before it reaches that stop. It's best to catch the bus at Kuhio and Namahana.

Buses leave Hanauma Bay to return to Waikiki at least once every hour from 11:10 am to 5:40 pm. On weekends the buses are more frequent (roughly twice an hour), though the schedule is more sporadic.

Koko Head

Koko Head (not to be confused with Koko Crater) overlooks and forms the southwest side of Hanauma Bay. There are two craters atop Koko Head, as well as radar facilities on its 642-foot summit. The mile-long summit road is closed to casual visitors.

The Nature Conservancy maintains a preserve in the shallow Ihiihilauakea Crater, the larger of the two craters. The crater has a unique vernal pool and a rare fern, the *Marsilea villosa*. For information on work parties or weekend excursions to the preserve, call the Nature Conservancy (☎ 537-4508).

Halona Blowhole Area

About three-quarters of a mile past Hanauma is a **lookout** with a view of striking coastal rock formations and crashing surf.

A little less than a mile farther is the parking lot for the **Halona Blowhole**, where water surges through a submerged tunnel in the rock and spouts up through a hole in the ledge. It's preceded by a gushing sound, created by air as it's forced out of the tunnel by rushing water. The level of action depends on water conditions – sometimes it's barely discernible, while at other times it's a real showstopper.

Down to the right of the parking lot is **Halona Cove**, the little beach where the famous love scene with Burt Lancaster and Deborah Kerr in *From Here to Eternity* was filmed in the 1950s.

Immediately before the blowhole, a small stone monument sits atop Halona Point. It

NED FRIARY

Sandy Beach has a punishing shorebreak.

was erected by Japanese fishermen to honor those lost at sea.

Note: the public bus doesn't stop between Hanauma and Sandy Beach, so visiting the Halona Blowhole area is only practical if you have your own transportation.

Sandy Beach

Sandy Beach is wide, very long and, yes, sandy. It's frequented by sunbathers, young surfers and admirers of both. When the swells are big, board surfers hit the left side of the beach.

Sandy Beach is also the most dangerous beach on the island in terms of lifeguard rescues and broken necks. It has a punishing shorebreak, a powerful backwash and strong rip currents. Red flags flown on the beach indicate hazardous water conditions. Even if you don't notice the flags, always check with the lifeguards before entering the water.

Nevertheless, the shorebreak is extremely popular with bodysurfers who know their stuff, and it's equally popular with spectators who gather to watch the excitement as transparent waves toss the bodysurfers about.

SOUTHEAST OAHU

Not all the action is in the water, however. The grassy strip on the inland side of the parking lot is used by people looking skyward for their thrills – it's both a hang glider landing site and a popular locale for kite flying. If you want to try your hand at the latter, High Performance Kites sets up a van here on the weekend (10 am to 4 pm) and sells kites and offers free instruction.

The park has rest rooms, showers and a pay phone. Bus No 22 stops in front of the beach. *Local Chef*, a food wagon, sets up in the parking lot from around 11:30 am to 4 pm daily, selling cheap burgers, beef stew and $5 plate lunches.

Koko Crater

According to Hawaiian legend, Koko Crater is the imprint left by the magical flying vagina of Pele's sister Kapo. Kapo sent it flying from the Big Island to lure the pig-god Kamapuaa away from Pele.

Inside the crater there's a simple botanical garden of plumeria trees, oleander, cacti and other dryland plants. To get to the garden, take Kealahou St off Hwy 72 (it's opposite the northern end of Sandy Beach). Just over half a mile in, turn left onto the one-lane road to Koko Crater Stables and continue a third of a mile to the garden. (There's no public transportation to the crater.) It is open 9 am to 4 pm daily, and admission is free.

Places to Eat

The Koko Marina Shopping Center, on the corner of Lunalilo Home Rd and Hwy 72, is the main place to eat in this area, with more than a dozen restaurant choices ranging from fast food to waterfront dining.

Whole In One Bagels & Juice Rush opens at 7 am, has fresh juice and smoothies, makes a variety of decent bagels (75¢) and sells reasonably priced bagel sandwiches. The nearby *Kozo Sushi* has good, inexpensive takeaway sushi – you can get a small eight-piece set for $3 or a 15-piece lunch box for just $5; it opens at 9 am and is a popular stop for locals packing beach picnics.

Yummy Korean BBQ (☎ 395-4888) is also worth recommending for its local flavor. It offers barbecued meat dishes for $6 (the chicken is a good, lean choice), with 'two-scoop rice' and four tasty, marinated vegetable dishes or kimchis, including a terrific watercress and sesame variety. Though the food is prepared for takeout, there are waterfront tables adjacent to the marina where you can sit and eat.

For a sit-down restaurant, there's *Assaggio* (☎ 396-0756), which has good Italian food and a harbor view. The lunch menu (available 11 am to 2:30 pm) includes eggplant parmigiana or prosciutto sandwiches for $6 and house specialties such as calamari marinara or a tasty chicken with garlic and peppers for around $10. Dinner prices are a few dollars higher.

Koko Marina Shopping Center also has a *Foodland* grocery store, *McDonald's*, *Subway Sandwiches* and a *Taco Bell*. There's also a *Kokonuts Store* that specializes in shave ice. All the eateries in the center are open daily.

The best upmarket option in Southeast Oahu, and arguably the entire island, is *Roy's* (☎ 396-7697, Hawaii Kai Corporate Plaza, Hwy 72). Chef Roy Yamaguchi is one of the creative forces behind the popularity of Hawaii Regional cuisine, a style that emphasizes using fresh local ingredients and blending the lighter aspects of European cooking with Polynesian and Asian influences. An exhibition kitchen sits in the center of the dining room, where Roy orchestrates an impressive troupe of sous cooks and chefs.

Starters include salads, spring rolls and imu-oven pizzas for around $8. The crispy Thai stuffed chicken topped with a tasty chutney and macadamia curry sauce costs $16 and makes a delightful main dish. Most other meat dishes cost around $20, and fresh fish specials average $25. For dessert, the crème brûlée with fresh fruit is a decadent choice.

Roy's is a top choice for a special night out – the food is beautifully presented, the service attentive and the portions are a good size. The restaurant also has a superb reputation for matching moderately priced wines with its menu. It's open 5:30 (5 pm on

Saturday and Sunday) to 10 pm. Reservations are advised and can be made weeks in advance – request a table with a sunset view.

MAKAPUU HEAD AREA

Makapuu Head is the easternmost point of Oahu. The area, just east of Koko Head Regional Park, is reached via Hwy 72.

Makapuu Point

Just over a mile north of Sandy Beach is the 647-foot Makapuu Point and its coastal **lighthouse**. The mile-long service road to the lighthouse is locked to keep out private vehicles, but you can park off the highway, just beyond the gate, and walk in from there. Although not difficult, it's an uphill walk and conditions can be hot and windy. There are lovely coastal views along the way and from the lighthouse lookout. During the winter, you may spot whales offshore.

Back on the highway, about a third of a mile farther along, there's a scenic **roadside lookout** with a view down onto Makapuu Beach, with its aqua-blue waters outlined by white sand and black lava. It's an even more spectacular sight when hang gliders are taking off from the cliffs, which are Oahu's top hang-gliding spot.

From the lookout you can see two offshore islands, the larger of which is **Manana Island**, also known as Rabbit Island. This aging volcanic crater is populated by feral rabbits and burrowing wedge-tailed shearwaters. The birds and rabbits coexist so closely that they sometimes even share the same burrows. Amusingly, the island vaguely looks like the head of a rabbit, and if you try hard, you may see it, ears folded back. If that doesn't work, try imagining it as a whale.

In front of Manana Island is the smaller **Kaohikaipu Island**, which will not tax the imagination – all it looks is flat. Divers sometimes explore the coral reef between the two islands, but to do so requires a boat.

Makapuu Beach Park

Makapuu Beach is one of the island's top winter bodysurfing spots, with waves reach-

Sea Life Park is home to the red-footed boobie.

ing 12 feet and higher. It also has the island's best shore break. As with Sandy Beach, Makapuu is strictly the domain of experienced bodysurfers who can handle rough water conditions and dangerous currents. Surfboards are prohibited. In summer, when the wave action disappears, the waters can be calm and good for swimming.

The beach, opposite Sea Life Park, is in a pretty setting, with cliffs in the background and a glimpse of the lighthouse. Two native Hawaiian plants are plentiful – *naupaka* by the beach and yellow-orange *ilima* by the parking lot.

Sea Life Park

The Sea Life Park (☎ 259-7933) features an enormous 300,000-gallon aquarium filled with sea turtles, eels, eagle rays, hammerhead sharks and thousands of colorful reef fish. A spiral ramp circles the 18-foot-deep aquarium, allowing you to view the fish from different depths.

In one outdoor amphitheater, jumping dolphins and waddling penguins perform the standard park tricks. In another, the Whaler's Cove, a group of imported Atlantic bottlenose dolphins give a choreographed performance. The dolphins tail walk, do the hula and give rides to a 'beautiful island maiden' – all bordering on kitsch.

There's a large pool of California sea lions and a smaller pool with harbor seals. There's also a section with rare Hawaiian monk seals, comprised largely of abandoned or injured pups that have been rescued from the wild; once they reach maturity, they're released back into their natural habitat. The turtle lagoon holds green sea turtles, and another section of the park has red-footed boobies, albatrosses and great frigate birds, all seabirds indigenous to Hawaii.

Hanging from the ceiling of the park's little **Whaling Museum** is the skeleton of a 38-foot sperm whale that washed ashore off Barbers Point in 1980. The rest of the museum consists of a continuously playing video on whales and some posters on marine life and marine sanctuaries.

Sea Life Park is open 9:30 am to 5 pm daily. Admission to the park is a steep $25 for adults, $12.50 for children aged four to 12 (free for children under four). There's a $3 parking fee in the main lot; however, if you continue past the ticket booth to the area marked 'additional parking,' there's no fee.

You can visit the Whaling Museum and the park restaurant (sandwiches, salads and other cafeteria-style food) without paying admission. You can also get a free glimpse of the seal and sea lion pools from the walkway to the museum.

Public buses No 22, No 57 (Kailua/Sea Life Park) and No 58 (Hawaii Kai/Sea Life Park) stop at the park.

WAIMANALO BAY

Waimanalo Bay has the longest continuous stretch of beach on Oahu: 5½ miles of white sand that stretches from Makapuu Point to Wailea Point. A long coral reef about a mile offshore breaks up the biggest waves, thereby protecting much of the shore.

Waimanalo has three beach parks, all with camping facilities. The setting is scenic, although the area isn't highly regarded for safety.

Waimanalo Beach Park

Waimanalo Beach Park has an attractive beach of soft white sand, and the water is excellent for swimming. This is an in-town county park, with a caretaker, grassy picnic area, rest rooms, changing rooms, showers, ball fields, basketball and volleyball courts and a playground. Camping is allowed 8 am Friday to 8 am Wednesday. See Camping in the Facts for the Visitor chapter for details.

The park has ironwood trees, but overall it's more open than the other two Waimanalo parks to the north. The scalloped hills of the lower Koolau Range rise up *mauka* (toward the mountains) of the park, and Manana Island and Makapuu Point are visible to the south.

If you are driving, there's a parking lot. If you are relying on public transportation, bus No 57 stops here.

Waimanalo Bay Beach Park

This county park, about a mile north of Waimanalo Beach Park, has Waimanalo Bay's biggest waves, thus its popularity with board surfers and bodysurfers.

Locals call the park 'Sherwood Forest,' because hoods and car thieves used to hang out here in days past – it hasn't totally shaken its reputation, so keep an eye on your belongings.

The park itself is quite appealing, with beachside campsites shaded by ironwood trees. Camping is allowed from 8 am Friday to 8 am Wednesday. See Camping in the Facts for the Visitor chapter for details. There are barbecue grills, drinking water, showers, rest rooms and a lifeguard station.

Bus No 57 stops on the main road in front of the park, and from there it's a third of a mile walk to the beach and campground. The park gate is open 6 am to 7:45 pm.

Bellows Field Beach Park

The beach fronting Bellows Air Force Base is open to civilian beachgoers and campers on weekends only, from noon on Friday until 8 am on Monday. See Camping in the Facts for the Visitor chapter for details. This long beach has fine sand and is backed by ironwood trees. The small shore break waves are good for beginning bodysurfers and board surfers.

There are showers, rest rooms, drinking water, a lifeguard and a caretaker, and the 50 campsites are set among the trees. Although it's military property, camping permits are issued through the county Department of Parks & Recreation. See Camping in the Facts for the Visitor chapter for details.

The marked entrance to this beach park is a quarter of a mile north of Waimanalo Bay Beach Park. Bus No 57 stops in front of the entrance road and from there it's 1½ miles to the beach.

Places to Eat

Just north of Waimanalo Beach Park, near the post office, you'll find a *7-Eleven* convenience store; *Keneke's*, a local eatery serving plate lunches; and *Leoni's Ristorante*, a pizza and sub joint. A *food mart* and a *McDonald's* are just south of Waimanalo Bay Beach Park. About a mile north of Bellows Field is a shopping cluster with *Jack in the Box*, *Subway Sandwiches* and *Dave's Ice Cream*.

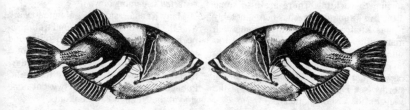

Windward Coast

- Enjoying a panoramic view of the windward coast from Nuuanu Pali Lookout
- Trying your hand at windsurfing or kayaking at lovely Kailua Beach Park
- Ringing the brass bell for luck at the picturesque Byodo-In temple in Kaneohe
- Stopping for a picnic and a swim at scenic Kualoa Regional Park

Windward Oahu, the island's eastern side, follows the Koolau Range along its entire length. The mountains looming inland are lovely, with scalloped folds and deep valleys. In places they come so near to the shore that they almost seem to push the highway into the ocean.

The main towns in this area are Kaneohe and Kailua, two nondescript bedroom communities for workers who commute to Honolulu, which is about 10 miles away. North of Kaneohe, the windward coast is rural Hawaii, where many Hawaiians toil close to the earth, making a living with small papaya, banana and vegetable farms. The windward side of the island is generally wetter than other parts of the island, and as a result, the vegetation here is lush and green.

Because the windward coast is exposed to the northeast trade winds, it's a popular area for anything that requires a sail – from windsurfing to yachting. There are also some attractive swimming beaches here – notably Kailua, Kualoa and Malaekahana – although many other sections of the coast are too silted for swimming. Swimmers should keep an eye out for the stinging Portuguese man-of-wars that sometimes wash ashore during storms (see Dangers & Annoyances in the Facts for the Visitor chapter).

Most of the offshore islets that you'll see along this coast are set aside as bird sanctuaries, providing vital habitat for ground-nesting seabirds.

Orientation

The windward coast runs from Makapuu Point in the south to Kahuku Point in the north. (For the Waimanalo to Makapuu area, see the Southeast Oahu chapter, earlier in this book.)

Two highways cut through the Koolau Range from central Honolulu to the windward coast. The Pali Hwy (Hwy 61) goes straight into Kailua, while the Likelike Hwy (Hwy 63) runs directly into Kaneohe. Although the Likelike (pronounced lee-kay-lee-kay) Hwy doesn't have the scenic stops the Pali Hwy has, in some ways it is more dramatic. Driving away from Kaneohe it feels as if you're heading straight into towering fairy-tale mountains – then you suddenly shoot through a tunnel and emerge on the Honolulu side, the drama gone.

If you're heading both to and from windward Oahu through the Koolau Range, take the Pali Hwy up from Honolulu and the Likelike Hwy back for the best views afforded by both.

VIA THE PALI HWY

The Pali Hwy (Hwy 61), which runs north from Honolulu toward Kailua, is a scenic little highway with a ridge lookout that offers a sweeping vista of the windward coast. If it's been raining heavily, every fold and crevice in the Koolau mountains will have a lacy waterfall streaming down it.

Many Kailua residents commute to work over the Pali, so Honolulu-bound traffic can be heavy in the morning and outbound traffic heavy in the evening. It's less of a problem for visitors, however, as most day-trippers will be traveling against the traffic. Public buses travel the Pali Hwy, but none stop at the Nuuanu Pali Lookout.

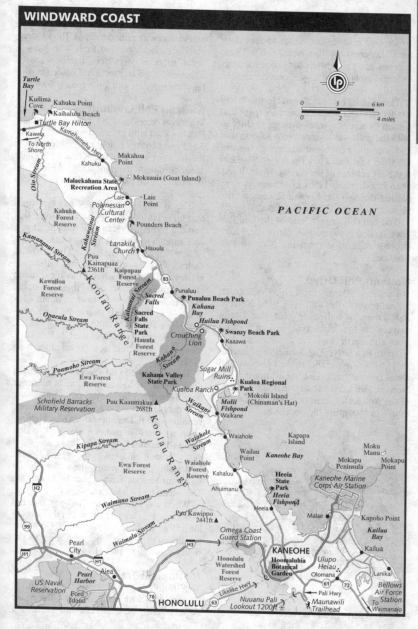

WINDWARD COAST

Turtle Bay
Kuilima Cove
Kaihalulu Beach
Turtle Bay Hilton
Kahuku Point
Kawela
To North Shore
Kamehameha Hwy
Makahoa Point
Kahuku
Oio Stream
Mokuauia (Goat Island)
Malaekahana State Recreation Area
Laie
Laie Point
Polynesian Cultural Center
Kahuku Forest Reserve
Pounders Beach
Kahawainui Stream
Lanakila Church
Hauula
Kamananui Stream
Puu Kainapuaa 2361ft
Kaipapau Forest Reserve
Punaluu
Sacred Falls
Punaluu Beach Park
Kahana Bay
Huilua Fishpond
Kawailoa Forest Reserve
Koolau Range
Kaluanui Stream
Sacred Falls State Park
Crouching Lion
Swanzy Beach Park
Kaaawa
Opaeula Stream
Hauula Forest Reserve
Kahana Stream
Sugar Mill Ruins
Poamoho Stream
Ewa Forest Reserve
Kahana Valley State Park
Kualoa Ranch
Kualoa Regional Park
Mokolii Island (Chinaman's Hat)
Molii Fishpond
Schofield Barracks Military Reservation
Puu Kaaumakua 2681ft
Waikane Stream
Waikane
Kipapa Stream
Waiahole Stream
Waiahole
Kapapa Island
Wailau Point
Kaneohe Bay
Moku Manu
Mokapu Peninsula
Mokapu Point
Ewa Forest Reserve
Waiahole Forest Reserve
Kahaluu
Heeia State Park
Heeia Fishpond
Kaneohe Marine Corps Air Station
Waimano Stream
Ahuimanu
Heeia
Malae
Kapoho Point
Puu Kawippo 2441ft
Omega Coast Guard Station
Kailua Bay
Pearl City
Aiea
Waimalu Stream
KANEOHE
Ulupo Heiau
Kailua
Lanikai
US Naval Reservation
Pearl Harbor
Ford Island
Honolulu Watershed Forest Reserve
Honolulu Botanical Garden
Hoomaluhia Botanical Garden
Olomana
Bellows Air Force Station
To Waimanalo
HONOLULU
Likelike Hwy
Nuuanu Pali Lookout 1200ft
Maunawili Trailhead
Pali Hwy

PACIFIC OCEAN

0   3   6 km
0   2   4 miles

Heading north up the Pali Hwy, just past the 4-mile marker look up and to the right to see two notches cut about 15 feet deep into the crest of the *pali* (cliff). These notches are thought to have been dug as cannon emplacements by Kamehameha the Great.

The original route between Honolulu and windward Oahu was an ancient footpath that wound its way perilously over these cliffs. In 1845 the path was widened into a horse trail and later into a cobblestone carriage road. In 1898 the Old Pali Hwy (as it's now called) was built in place of the carriage road. It was abandoned in the 1950s after tunnels were blasted through the Koolau Range and the present multilane Pali Hwy opened.

You can still drive a loop of the Old Pali Hwy (called Nuuanu Pali Drive) and hike another mile of it from the Nuuanu Pali Lookout.

Nuuanu Pali Drive

For a scenic side trip through a shady green forest, turn off the Pali Hwy onto Nuuanu Pali Drive, a half mile past the 2-mile marker on the highway. If you're coming from the north, look for the sign marked Nuuanu Pali Drive. The 2-mile-long Nuuanu Pali Drive runs parallel to the Pali Hwy and then comes back out to it before the Nuuanu Pali Lookout, so you don't miss any of the wonderful scenery by taking this side loop – in fact, quite the opposite.

This part of Oahu is lush and green.

The drive is through trees that form a canopy overhead, draped with hanging vines and wound with philodendrons. The lush vegetation includes banyan trees with hanging aerial roots, almond trees, bamboo groves, impatiens, angel trumpets and golden cup – a tall climbing vine with large golden flowers.

Nuuanu Pali Lookout

Whatever you do, don't miss the Nuuanu Pali Lookout with its broad view of the windward coast from a height of 1200 feet. From the lookout you can see Kaneohe straight ahead, Kailua to the right and Mokolii Island and the coastal fishpond at Kualoa Park to the far left.

This is *windward* Oahu – and the winds that funnel through the pali are so strong that you can sometimes lean against them. It gets cool enough to warrant having a jacket.

In 1795, Kamehameha the Great routed Oahu's warriors up the Nuuanu Trail during his invasion of the island. On these steep cliffs, Oahu's warriors made their last stand. Hundreds were thrown to their death over the pali as they were overcome by Kamehameha's troops. A hundred years later, during the construction of the Old Pali Hwy, more than 500 skulls were found at the base of the cliffs.

The abandoned Old Pali Hwy winds from the right of the lookout, ending at a barrier near the current highway about a mile away. Few people realize the road is here, let alone venture down it. Though you can hear highway noise, it otherwise makes a nice walk, taking about 20 minutes one way. There are good views looking back up at the jagged Koolau Mountains and out across the valley. Should you want to walk farther, see the Maunawili Trail section, which follows.

When you return to the highway, it's easy to miss the sign leading you out of the parking lot and go in the wrong direction. Go to the left if you're heading toward Kailua, to the right if heading toward Honolulu.

Maunawili Trail

The 10-mile-long Maunawili Trail connects Nuuanu Pali with Waimanalo on the coast. Popular with both hikers and mountain bikers, this scenic trail winds along the back side of Maunawili Valley, following the base of the lofty Koolau Range. Along the way, there are panoramic views of the valley, mountains and windward coast.

This trail consists of many climbs up and down gulches, across streams and along ridges. Going in an easterly direction is the less strenuous way, as you will be following the trail from the mountain crest down to the coast. Because Maunawili Trail is subject to erosion, mountain bikers are asked to stay off the trail when it's raining or if the trail is wet. If you come across muddy sections, always dismount and walk your bike.

For visitors on foot, it's generally most practical to take the trail for a couple of miles and then turn around and return the same way. Even hiking the trail for just an hour will reward you with some fine views of both the coast and Maunawili Valley's lush, forested interior.

Maunawili Trail can be accessed by continuing north on the Pali Hwy. Go about a mile past the Nuuanu Pali Lookout, and shortly after you go through the pali tunnel, pull off to the right into the scenic turnout, which is at the hairpin turn. There's parking here. Walk through the break in the guardrail; the trailhead is just beyond the small concrete drainage ditch.

The trail can also be picked up from the Nuuanu Pali Lookout by walking the mile-long stretch of the abandoned Old Pali Hwy that starts to the right of the lookout and ends near the Maunawili Trailhead.

KAILUA

In ancient times Kailua ('two seas') was a place of legends. It was home to a giant that turned into a mountain ridge, the island's first *menehunes* and numerous Oahuan chiefs. Rich in stream-fed agricultural land, fertile fishing grounds and protected canoe landings, Kailua once served as a political and economic center for the region. The area supported at least three *heiaus*, one of which, Ulupo Heiau, you can still visit today.

Kailua is the third largest city on Oahu, with a population of 38,000. Although the inland section may appear to be little more than an average suburban community, Kailua's shoreline is graced with miles of lovely beach – part set aside as public park, and the rest lined with oceanfront homes.

Kailua has long been known as a wind-surfing mecca and today it draws increasing numbers of kayakers too. The town has a generous variety of good restaurants relative to its size. It also has an agreeable mix of locals and visitors, making it a refreshing alternative to overtouristed Waikiki.

Information
The Bank of Hawaii, 636 Kailua Rd, is open 8:30 am to 4 pm Monday to Thursday, 8:30 am to 6 pm on Friday.

The Kailua post office, 335 Hahani St, is open 8 am to 4:30 pm on weekdays (to 6 pm on Wednesday) and 8 am to 2 pm on Saturday. For information on Internet access, see Stir Crazy.com in the Places to Eat section.

Bookends (☎ 261-1996), 590 Kailua Rd, next to the Times Supermarket, sells books, maps and newspapers. The Kailua Public Library, 239 Kuulei Rd, is open 10 am to 5 pm on Monday, Wednesday, Friday and Saturday and 10 am to 8 pm on Tuesday and Thursday.

The Kailua Laundromat, on the corner of Aulike and Uluniu Sts, is open 6 am to 10 pm daily.

Ulupo Heiau
Ulupo Heiau is a large, open-platform stone temple that is 30 feet high and 180 feet long. Its construction is attributed to the mene-hunes, the little people who, according to legend, created much of Hawaii's stone-work, magically building large projects overnight. Fittingly, Ulupo means 'night inspiration.'

In front of the heiau, which is thought to be a *luakini* type (a place of human sacrifice), is an artist's rendition of how the site probably looked in the 18th century, before westerners arrived.

If you walk the path across the top of the heiau, there is a view of **Kawainui Swamp**. Legend says the fishpond that stood here in earlier times had edible mud at the bottom and was home to a *moo*, or lizard spirit. In

WINDWARD COAST

KAILUA

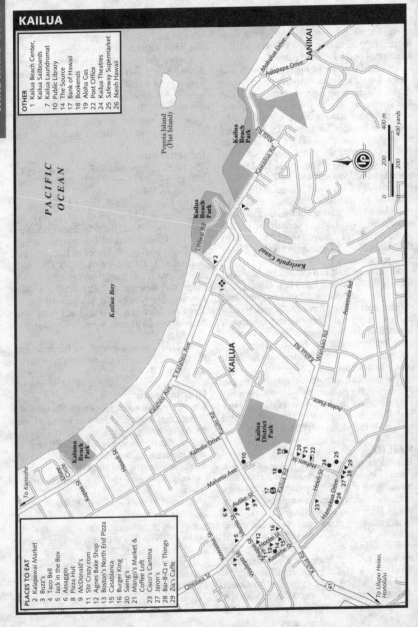

PACIFIC OCEAN

Kailua Bay

Popoia Island (Flat Island)

LANIKAI

Mokulua Drive

Aalapapa Drive

Kailua Beach Park

Kawailoa Rd

Aina Rd

Kaelepulu Canal

400 m

400 yards

200

200

0

Lihiwai Rd

Kailua Beach Park

KAILUA

Kalaheo Ave

S Kalaheo Ave

Kailua Rd

Wanaao Rd

Auwinala Rd

Kaelepulu Canal

Kuulei Rd

Kailua District Park

Aoloa Place

Kainalu Drive

Hahani St

Hekili St

Hamakua Drive

Kalama Beach Park

Kailua Rd

Kalapawai St

Hamakua St

Maluniu Ave

Oneawa St

To Kapeohe

Oneawa St

To Ulupo Heiau, Honolulu

61

Kailua Rd

Aulike St

Aulike St

Uluoa St

Uluniu St

Kihapai St

Hoolai St

Kailua Rd

Kainehe St

Makawao St

Wanaao St

the 1880s, the fishpond was converted into rice fields by Chinese farmers. However, in the early 20th century the fields were abandoned by the farmers, and they reverted to marshland. Today, Kawainui Swamp is one of Hawaii's largest habitats for endangered waterbirds.

Ulupo Heiau is 1 mile south of Kailua Center. To get there, go northwest off Hwy 61 onto Uluoa St (just northeast of the Hwy 72 junction); then turn right on Manu Aloha St and right again onto Manuoo St. The heiau is behind the YMCA.

Kailua Beach Park

Kailua Beach Park is a beautiful stretch of glistening white sand at the southeastern end of Kailua Bay. The beach is long and broad with lovely turquoise waters, and the park is popular for long walks, family outings and a full range of water activities. It draws a particularly large crowd on sunny weekends, when it can be a challenge to even find a parking space.

Kailua Bay is the top windsurfing spot on Oahu. Onshore trade winds are predominant and windsurfers can sail at Kailua year round. In different spots around the bay there are different water conditions, some good for jumps and wave surfing, others for flatwater sails. Two windsurfing companies, Naish Hawaii and Kailua Sailboards, give lessons and rent boards at the beach park on weekdays and Saturday mornings.

Kailua Beach has a gently sloping sandy bottom with waters that are generally calm. Swimming conditions are good all year, but sun bathers beware – the breezes favored by windsurfers also give rise to blowing sand. The park has rest rooms, showers, lifeguards, a snack shop, a volleyball court and large grassy expanses partly shaded by ironwood trees.

Kaelepulu Canal divides the park into two sections, although a sand bar usually prevents the canal waters from emptying into the bay. Because of pollution from runoff, the canal itself should be avoided. Windsurfing activities are centered to the west of the canal; there's a small boat ramp on the east side.

The island offshore, **Popoia Island** (Flat Island), a bird sanctuary where landings are allowed, is a popular destination for kayakers.

For more information on windsurfing and kayaking, see the Activities chapter, earlier in the book.

Kalama Beach Park

Kalama, a small beach park north of Kailua Beach Park, usually has one of the largest shorebreaks in the bay. When the waves are up, both board surfers and bodysurfers can find decent conditions here. Board surfers also sometimes head to the northern end of Kailua Bay to Kapoho Point (see the Kaneohe map), where they surf its break during swells.

Lanikai

If you follow the coastal road as it continues southeast from Kailua Beach Park, you will shortly come to Lanikai, which is a rather exclusive residential neighborhood. It is fronted by **Lanikai Beach**, which is an attractive stretch of powdery white sand. The sandy ocean bottom slopes gently, and the waters are calm, offering safe swimming conditions similar to those at Kailua Beach Park. Residential use has taken its toll, though, and much of the sand at Lanikai has washed away as a result

Kailua Bay is Oahu's top windsurfing spot.

of the retaining walls built to protect the beachfront homes.

Mokulua Drive, the coastal road that fronts Lanikai Beach, is a one-way road heading northwest. This means that if you want to go to Lanikai Beach and you are driving, you must take the one-way, inland Aalapapa Drive and loop around to Mokulua Drive. There are 11 narrow beach access walkways off Mokulua Drive. For the best stretches of beach, try the one opposite Kualima Drive, or try any of the next three walkways northwest of Kualima Drive.

The twin **Moku Lua islands**, Moku Nui and Moku Iki, sit directly offshore. Both islands are set aside as seabird sanctuaries. It's possible to kayak from Kailua Beach Park to Moku Nui, which has a lovely beach; for kayaking information, see the Activities chapter in the front of the book. Landings are prohibited on Moku Iki, the smaller of the two islands.

Places to Stay

Kailua has no hotels, but there are many furnished beachfront cottages, studios and Bed & Breakfast-style rooms in private homes. Although the majority are handled by the vacation rental services listed at the end of this section, the following places can be booked directly with the owners.

The **Sheffield House** (☎ 262-0721, sheffieldhouse@poi.net, 131 Kuulei Rd, Kailua, HI 96734), a short walk from Kailua Beach, has two cozy rental units in the home of Paul and Rachel Sheffield. There's a guest room with a wheelchair-accessible bathroom for $55 and a one-bedroom suite, which has a queen bed and a separate sitting area with a queen futon for $75. Each unit has a private entrance, bathroom, TV, microwave, toaster oven, coffeemaker, small refrigerator and ceiling fan. The Sheffields, who have three young children of their own, welcome kids. There's a three-day minimum stay; breakfast is not included in the rates, but coffee and tea are provided.

Paradise Palms Bed & Breakfast (☎ 254-4234, fax 254-4971, ppbb@pixi.com, 804 Mokapu Rd, Kailua, HI 96734) consists of two meticulously decorated studios at the side of Marilyn and Jim Warman's home, at the northwest end of Kailua. The Banyan Room has a queen bed and costs $65, and the Maile Room has a king bed and costs $70. Each has a private entrance, bathroom and a kitchenette with refrigerator, microwave, coffeemaker, toaster and electric skillet. The units also have cable TV, ceiling fan, air-con and phone.

Marilyn provides fresh-baked bread, fruit and coffee upon arrival. Smoking is not allowed. The minimum stay is three nights and the units often book up well in advance. There's a grocery store and fast-food restaurants just across the street. They maintain a website (www.pixi.com/ParadisePalms).

Manu Mele Bed & Breakfast (☎/fax 262-0016, manumele@pixi.com, 153 Kailuana Place, Kailua, HI 96734) consists of two attractive guest rooms in the contemporary home of English-born host Carol Isaacs. The largest, the Hibiscus Room, has a king bed and costs $80, and the smaller, but perfectly suitable, Pikake Room has a queen bed and costs $70. Each has a private entrance, bathroom, refrigerator, microwave, coffeemaker, air-con, ceiling fan and cable TV. There's a shared guest phone in the hall. A generous basket of fruit and baked goods is provided the first morning. The minimum stay is two nights. The house has a pool, and there's a short footpath to the beach nearby. Smoking is not allowed in the units. Carol maintains a website (www .pixi.com/~manumele).

Kailua Tradewinds (☎ 262-1008, fax 261-0316, 391 Auwinala Rd, Kailua, HI 96734) consists of two studio units at the home of Jona Williams. Breakfast is not provided, but each unit has a refrigerator, microwave, coffeemaker and toaster as well as a private entrance, bathroom, queen bed, TV and phone. One of the units also has a double futon. The rate is $70 for singles or doubles, plus $10 for each additional person. There's a swimming pool, and beach gear is available for guests to use. Visit their website to see photos (cyberrentals.com/hi/willaoahu .html) of the studios.

Papaya Paradise Bed & Breakfast (☎/fax 261-0316, 395 Auwinala Rd, Kailua, HI

96734), a vacation rental next door to Kailua Tradewinds, is a 15-minute walk from Kailua Beach. Bob and Jeanette Martz, the parents of Jona Williams, retired from the army and home most of the time, rent two rooms adjacent to their home. One room has a queen bed and a trundle bed, the other two twin beds; each has a private entrance, bathroom, phone, air-con, ceiling fan and TV. The rates are $75 for singles or doubles, including a continental breakfast. There is a $15 charge for a third person. Guests have access to a refrigerator and microwave. There's a pool and Jacuzzi. Boogie boards and snorkel gear can be borrowed for free. There's usually a three-day minimum stay. Visit their website for a preview (www.bnbweb.com/papaya .html) of the rooms.

Akamai Bed & Breakfast (☎/fax 261-2227, 800-642-5366, akamai@alohoa.net, 172 Kuumele Place, Kailua, HI 96734) has two pleasant studio units in a private home about 10 minutes' walk from Kailua Beach. Each is modern and comfortable and has a refrigerator, microwave, coffeemaker, small bathroom, cable TV and private entrance. Both units have a king bed as well as a sofa bed. The rate of $75 includes a fruit basket and breakfast items. There's a laundry room ($1 per load) and a quiet courtyard with a pool. The minimum stay is three days; smoking is limited to the outdoors. They have a website with photos (planet-hawaii.com/akamaibnb).

Vacation Rentals *Pat's Kailua Beach Properties* (☎ 261-1653, fax 261-0893, pats@aloha.net, 204 S Kalaheo Ave, Kailua, HI 96734) specializes in Kailua vacation rentals, handling a few dozen properties on or near the beach. These range from small studios that can sleep two people for $65/1600 a day/month to a beachfront home with four bedrooms and three baths that sleeps eight people for $425/8200 a day/month. They also maintain a website (www.10kvacationrentals.com/pats).

The two bed & breakfast services that follow each book more than 50 different Kailua-area accommodations.

Maria Wilson of *Affordable Paradise Bed & Breakfast* (☎ 261-1693, fax 261-7315, afford@aloha.net, 226 Pouli Rd, Kailua, HI 96734) books studios and B&Bs from $55 a double and cottages from $65. She can also arrange rooms in private homes starting at $45. This agency maintains a website (www .aicomm.com/hawaii).

All Islands Bed & Breakfast (☎ 263-2342, 800-542-0344, fax 263-0308, carlina001@ hawaii.rr.com, 823 Kainui Drive, Kailua, HI 96734) has B&B rooms from $55 to $70, studio apartments from $65 to $90 and a few cottages from $85. They have a website (www.hawaiialohaspirit.com/alisbnb).

In addition, *Naish Hawaii* (☎ 262-6068, 800-767-6068, fax 263-9723, 155A Hamakua Drive, Kailua, HI 96734) specializes in wind-surfing vacations with accommodations in Kailua, but they also book places for non-windsurfing travelers.

Places to Eat
Near the Beach *Kalapawai Market*, on the corner of Kailua Rd and Kalaheo Ave, is a popular place to stop for coffee on the way to the beach. You have a choice of fresh brews, with a 12oz cup costing just $1. They also have a few cheap eats, including bagels or chili and rice, and a good selection of wine and beer. It is open 6 am to 9 pm daily.

Kailua Beach Restaurant (☎ 263-2620, 130 Kailua Rd), in the Kailua Beach Center, has $3.75 pancake or omelette breakfasts, served with bacon and toast, until 10:30 am. At other times of the day, there are about 40 Chinese plate lunch options, such as chicken with broccoli, kung pao shrimp or stir-fry noodles, for $5 to $7. Open 7 am to 9 pm daily, it also sells Honolulu-made Dave's Ice Cream.

K & K Bar-B-Que Inn (☎ 262-2272, 130 Kailua Rd), also in the Kailua Beach Center, has plate lunches featuring barbecued ribs or chicken for around $5, as well as cheap sandwiches and burgers. It's open 9 am to 9 pm daily.

Also in the Kailua Beach Center is *Island Snow*, a popular shave ice shop with tropical flavors such as Maui mango and banzai banana. It's open 10 am to 6 pm weekdays, 10 am to 7 pm on weekends.

WINDWARD COAST

Buzz's (☎ *261-4661, 413 Kawailoa Rd*), opposite Kailua Beach Park, has lunches such as fresh fish burgers, sandwiches with fries and Caesar, spinach or Thai chicken salads – each for around $8. However, it's most popular as an evening steak house, with various cuts of beef from $14 to $25, including salad bar. It's open for lunch 11 am to 2:30 pm and for dinner 5 to 10 pm daily. Trivia buffs can find a plaque on one of the lanai tables marking the spot where Bill and Hillary Clinton ate dinner during one of their presidential trips to Hawaii. Credit cards are not accepted.

Town Center All of the following eateries are in the town center, within a mile of each other.

Boston's North End Pizza (☎ *263-7757, 29 Hoolai St*), just north of Kailua Rd, has excellent pizza. It sells huge slices, each equal to a quarter of a 19-inch pizza, for $2.50 to $4 depending on the toppings. Or for $10 to $16, you can buy a whole pie that easily feeds three or four people. Their spinach and fresh garlic version is awesome. It's open 11 am to 8 pm on weekdays and 11 am to 9 pm on weekends.

You can check your email down the street at *Stir Crazy.com* (☎ *261-8804, 45 Hoolai St*). This friendly little cafe prepares lattes and other coffee drinks, soups, salads and good tortilla-rolled sandwiches with lots of vegetarian options – everything costs $5 or less. Internet access costs $2.25 for 15 minutes, $7.50 for an hour. It's open 7 am to 9 pm weekdays, 8 am to 9 pm on Saturday and 8 am to 4 pm on Sunday.

Agnes Bake Shop, on Hoolai St opposite Stir Crazy.Com, is a good little bakery that makes whole-grain breads, inexpensive pastries and Portuguese *malasadas*. The malasadas take about 10 minutes to fry and cost 55¢ each. The shop also serves coffee, tea and Portuguese bean soup, and there are half a dozen cafe tables were you can sit and eat. It's open 6 am to 6 pm daily, except Monday.

A popular dining spot is *Jaron's* (☎ *261-4600, 201 Hamakua Drive*), which has a jazzy decor and a varied menu. Lunch prices range from $6 to $9, and the menu includes salads, such as blackened ahi Caesar or Thai chicken, and vegetarian, fish or meat sandwiches served with soup. The dinner menu has a large array of pasta, seafood and steak dishes priced from $12 to $20, a green salad included.

The sunset dinner ($9 to $11.50), available 4 to 7 pm, is an attractive deal that offers a choice of seven entrees, including chicken piccata and fresh salmon, served with salad and sourdough bread. It's open for lunch 11 am to 4 pm – except on Sunday when it offers brunch from 9 am to 2 pm – and for dinner 4 to 9 pm (to 10 pm on Friday and Saturday).

The bustling little *Zia's Caffe* (☎ *262-7168, 201 Hamakua Drive*), an open-air place next to Jaron's, has excellent Italian fare at honest prices. Various pastas, vegetable lasagna, shrimp scampi and a delicious eggplant parmesan are priced from $7 to $10. Appetizers include mussels marinara, a traditional antipasto plate and homemade minestrone. Zia's also has Caesar salads, meatball sandwiches, Philly cheese steak and Italian subs. It's open 11 am to 9 pm weekdays and 4:30 to 9 pm on weekends.

Bar-B-Q n' Things (☎ *261-7223, 201 Hamakua Drive*), next to Zia's, is a simple local eatery serving decent Japanese and Korean food. They dish up a plate of Korean barbecued meats or Japanese noodles for around $7. From 10:30 am to 2:30 pm weekdays, there are generous mixed plate lunch specials for $6. It's open 10:30 am to 9 pm Monday to Saturday and 4:30 to 9 pm on Sunday.

Cisco's Cantina (☎ *262-7337, 123 Hekili St*) is an unpretentious Mexican restaurant that serves generous portions at reasonable prices. You can get a taco for $6, a burrito for $8.50 or a two-item combination plate for $10, all served with rice and beans. It's open 11 am to 10 pm Sunday to Thursday and to 11 pm on weekends.

Mango's Market & Coffee Loft (☎ *263-6646, 319 Hahani St*), in the shopping center adjacent to the post office, is a small health food store that doubles as an informal cafe. There are Gardenburgers, burritos and spinach and feta sandwiches, each for $5, as well as fruit smoothies, bagels, coffee and a hearty soup of the day. It's open 7 am to 8 pm Monday to Saturday and 9 am to 7 pm on Sunday.

Saeng's (☎ 263-9727, 315 Hahani St), in the same little complex as Mango's, is a pleasant place with a full menu of Thai dishes, including curries, pad Thai, ginger chicken and crispy fish. Vegetarian entrees cost around $7, meat and seafood dishes $7.50 to $10. It's open 11 am to 2 pm on weekdays and 5 to 9:30 pm nightly.

Assaggio (☎ 261-2772, 354 Uluniu St) serves good, moderately priced Italian food in a somewhat upmarket setting. At lunch, sandwiches cost around $6 and hot dishes are just a few dollars more. The dinner menu is extensive, with numerous appetizers, including carpaccio, calamari or artichoke pepperonata for around $7, and more than 50 pasta, seafood, chicken and steak main dishes priced from $10 to $19. It's open 11:30 am to 2:30 pm weekdays and 5 to 10 pm nightly.

For an interesting night out, *Casablanca* (☎ 262-8196, 19 Hoolai St) has good, authentic Middle Eastern fare in an atmospheric dining room complete with Persian decor and seating on floor cushions. The fixed-price menu ($27.50) includes lentil-saffron soup, Moroccan salad, *b'stilla* (baked chicken in phyllo dough) and a choice of several main courses such as lamb brochettes, calamari or Cornish hen. Dessert is *chabbakia*, a honey-dipped cake, served with spearmint tea. No alcohol is served, but you can bring your own.

Out front, you can get reasonably priced falafels, kabobs and other simple food, but the real experience is the multicourse meal in the main dining room. It is open 6 to 9:30 pm Monday to Saturday.

The Source (32 Kainehe St) is a natural food store with bulk herbs and spices, vitamins, general food items and a small produce section. It's open 9 am to 9 pm on weekdays, 10 am to 5 pm on weekends. For a supermarket, there's a 24-hour *Safeway*

(200 Hamakua Drive), opposite Jaron's (see the Entertainment section that follows).

Kailua has numerous fast-food eateries centered in the downtown area, including *Burger King, Pizza Hut, McDonald's, Jack in the Box* and *Taco Bell*.

Entertainment

Jaron's (☎ 261-4600, 201 Hamakua Drive) has contemporary Hawaiian music, rock or reggae bands 10:30 pm to 2 am on Friday and Saturday; there's a dance floor and a small cover charge. *Cisco's Cantina* (☎ 262-7337, 123 Hekili St) sometimes has live music too.

The multiscreen *Kailua Theatres* (☎ 263-4171), Hahani St, opposite Jaron's, show first-run movies.

Getting There & Away

If traffic is light, by car it's a 20-minute drive along the Pali Hwy (Hwy 61) from Honolulu to Kailua. To get to Kailua Beach Park, simply stay on Kailua Rd, which begins at the end of the Pali Hwy and continues as the main road through town before reaching the coast.

Both bus Nos 56 and 57 run between the Ala Moana Center and downtown Kailua roughly once every 15 minutes from about 6 am to 10 pm; the trip takes about 40 minutes. To get to Kailua Beach Park or Lanikai, get off in downtown Kailua at the corner of Kailua Rd and Oneawa St and transfer to bus No 70 Lanikai-Maunawili. However, bus No 70 only operates about once every 90 minutes, so check the schedule in advance.

KANEOHE

Kaneohe, with a population of 36,000, is Oahu's fourth largest city.

Kaneohe Bay, which stretches from Mokapu Peninsula all the way to Kualoa Point, 7 miles north of Kaneohe, is the state's largest bay and reef-sheltered lagoon. Although inshore it's largely silted and not good for swimming, the near-constant trade winds that sweep across the bay are ideal for sailing.

WINDWARD COAST

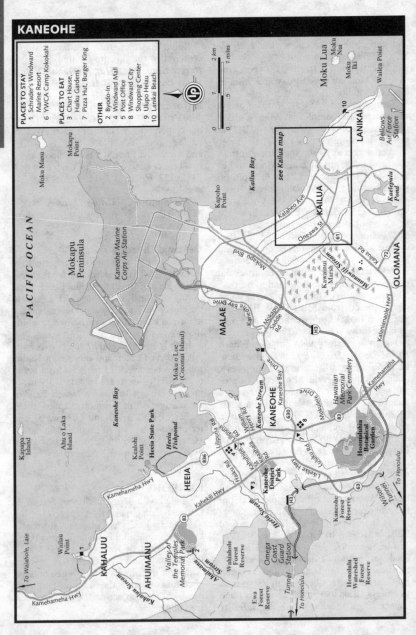

KANEOHE

PLACES TO STAY
1 Schrader's Windward
  Marine Resort
6 YWCA Camp Kokokahi

PLACES TO EAT
3 Chart House,
  Haiku Gardens
7 Pizza Hut, Burger King

OTHER
2 Byodo-In
4 Windward Mall
5 Post Office
8 Windward City
  Shopping Center
9 Ulupo Heiau
10 Lanikai Beach

Orientation

Two highways run north to south through Kaneohe. Kamehameha Hwy (Hwy 836) is closer to the coast and goes by Heeia State Park. The Kahekili Hwy (Hwy 83) is more inland and runs along the outskirts of Kaneohe, intersects the Likelike Hwy (Hwy 63) and continues on north past the Byodo-In temple. The Kahekili Hwy merges into the Kamehameha Hwy a few miles north of Kaneohe.

Kaneohe Marine Corps Air Station occupies the whole of Mokapu Peninsula. The H-3 Fwy terminates at its gate.

Information

There's a branch of First Hawaiian Bank at the Windward City Shopping Center on the Kamehameha Hwy. It's open 8:30 am to 4 pm Monday to Thursday and from 8:30 am to 6 pm on Friday.

The Kaneohe post office is at 46-036 Kamehameha Hwy, just east of the Windward Mall. It's open 8 am to 4:30 pm weekdays and 8 am to 2 pm on Saturday.

Valley of the Temples & Byodo-In

The Valley of the Temples is an interdenominational cemetery in a beautiful setting just off the Kahekili Hwy (the road in to the temple is about 1½ miles north of Haiku Rd). For visitors the main attraction is Byodo-In, the 'Temple of Equality.' It is a replica of the 900-year-old temple of the same name which is in Uji, Japan. This temple was dedicated in 1968 to commemorate the 100th anniversary of Japanese immigration to Hawaii.

Byodo-In sits against the Koolau Range. The rich red of the temple against the verdant fluted cliffs is strikingly picturesque, especially when mist settles in on the pali. The temple is meant to symbolize the mythical phoenix. Inside the main hall is a 9-foot-tall gold-lacquered Buddha sitting on a lotus.

Wild peacocks roam the grounds and hang their tail feathers over the upper railings of the temples. A carp pond with cruising bullfrogs and cooing doves fronts the temple. The 3-ton brass bell beside the pond

H-3

The recently opened H-3 Fwy, an idea that was born during the Reagan era, owes its existence in no small way to the heated Cold War mania of the day. Fought bitterly by environmentalists, the highway slices across formerly pristine valleys to connect the Kaneohe Marine Corps Air Station at one end and the Pearl Harbor Naval Base at the other. As the post-Cold War military presence in Hawaii decreases, the freeway's cost of $1.25 billion stands out as the biggest pork barrel project in Hawaii's history.

is said to bring tranquillity and good fortune to those who ring it.

It's all very Japanese, right down to the gift shop selling sake cups, daruma dolls and happy Buddhas. This scene is as close as you'll get to Japan without having to land at Narita.

Admission to the temple, which is collected 8 am to 4:30 pm daily, is $2 for adults, $1 for children younger than 12. There are no fees for visiting outside these hours and, as with most cemeteries, the grounds are accessible from sunrise to sunset.

On the way out, you might want to head up to the hilltop mausoleum with the cross on top and check out the view.

No buses go to Byodo-In, but bus No 55 can drop passengers off near the cemetery entrance on the Kahekili Hwy. From there, it's two-thirds of a mile to the temple.

Hoomaluhia Botanical Garden

Hoomaluhia, a 400-acre park in the uplands of Kaneohe, is the island's youngest and largest botanical garden. The garden is planted with groups of trees and shrubs from tropical regions around the world. It's a peaceful, lush green setting, with a stunning pali backdrop, and fittingly enough, the name Hoomaluhia means 'peace and tranquillity.' This is not a formal landscaped flower garden, but more of a natural preserve. A network of trails wind through the park and up to a 32-acre lake (no swimming allowed).

The visitor center (☎ 233-7323), although small, has displays on flora and fauna, Hawaiian ethnobotany and the history of the park, which was originally built by the US Army Corps of Engineers as flood protection for the valley below.

The park entrance is at the end of Luluku Rd, which is off the Kamehameha Hwy, about 2¼ miles north of its intersection with the Pali Hwy. Bus Nos 55 and 56 go to the Windward City Shopping Center, opposite the start of Luluku Rd, but there's no bus service to the park. It's 1½ miles up Luluku Rd from the highway to the visitor center and another 1½ miles from the visitor center to the far end of the park – so if you're getting around by bus, expect to do some walking.

The park is open 9 am to 4 pm daily and admission is free. Guided two-hour nature hikes are held at 10 am on Saturday and 1 pm on Sunday; call the visitor center for registration.

Weekend camping is allowed in Hoomaluhia garden; see the Places to Stay section that follows.

Heeia State Park

Heeia State Park is on Kealohi Point, just off Kamehameha Hwy. It has a good view of Heeia Fishpond on the right and Heeia-Kea Harbor on the left.

Before contact with the West, stone-walled fishponds used for raising fish for royalty were common along the coasts of Hawaii. The **Heeia Fishpond** is an impressive survivor that remains largely intact despite the invasive mangrove that grows along its walls and takes root between the rocks. You can walk around the grounds of Heeia State Park and take in the view, but otherwise there's not much to do here.

Coconut Island, just offshore and to the southeast of the fishpond, was a royal playground in times past. It was named for the coconut trees planted there by Princess Bernice Pauahi Bishop. In the 1930s it was the estate of Christian Holmes, heir to the Fleischmann Yeast fortune, who by dredging

doubled the island's size to 25 acres. During the war the estate served as an R&R facility for military personnel, and it briefly served as a hotel. Airbrushed shots of Coconut Island were used in opening scenes for the *Gilligan's Island* TV series. Today, the Hawaii Institute of Marine Biology of the University of Hawaii occupies a portion of the island, while the rest is privately owned.

Places to Stay

Hoomaluhia Botanical Garden (☎ 233-7323), at the base of the Koolau Range, has five grassy camping areas, each with rest rooms, cold showers and drinking water. The park can accommodate up to 650 people, but often only a couple of the areas need to be opened. If you don't mind being inland rather than on a beach, this botanical park makes an interesting camping option, and it's among the safest county parks on Oahu because it has a resident caretaker and gates that close to noncampers at 4 pm. On the minus side, it's out of the way for those who don't have their own transportation. There is no camping fee.

Camping is allowed on Friday, Saturday and Sunday nights only. You can get a permit in advance at any satellite city hall, or simply go to the park between 9 am and 4 pm Monday to Saturday; if you plan to get a permit the same day you intend to camp, call first to verify that space is available. If you prefer to apply for a permit in advance, send your request, along with a legal-sized, self-addressed and stamped envelope, to Hoomaluhia, 45-680 Luluku Rd, Kaneohe, HI 96744.

YWCA Camp Kokokahi (☎ 247-2124, kokokahi@gte.net, 45-035 Kaneohe Bay Drive, Kaneohe, HI 96744) is a budget option 1½ miles northeast of Kaneohe center. Although the camp gives priority to groups, it also accepts individual travelers. Accommodations are in simple cabins. You can opt for a tiny cabin all to yourself for $20, a double cabin with two single beds for $15 per person or a dorm bed in a five-person cabin for $15. Rates include a pillow, sheets and a blanket, as well as access to kitchen, lounge and laundry facilities.

You can also pitch a tent on the site for $8 per person. Though the camp overlooks Kaneohe Bay, the water is too silted for swimming, but there's a heated pool on the grounds. Two things to keep in mind: the place sometimes fills up completely, so call ahead to make reservations before heading all the way out; and check-in isn't allowed after 8 pm, so arrive early.

Bus No 56 (1¼ hours from Ala Moana Center) stops out front. The office is open 8 am to 5 pm on weekdays and 8:30 am to 5 pm on weekends. After 5 pm, the on-site caretaker is reached by dialing pager ☎ 549-4540 or 571-4407.

Alii Bluffs Windward Bed & Breakfast (☎ 235-1124, 800-235-1151, donm@lava.net, 46-251 Ikiiki St, Kaneohe, HI 96744) has two bedrooms in a cozy home filled with Old World furnishings, oil paintings, antique toys and collectibles. The Victorian Room has one double bed and costs $75, and the Circus Room has two twin beds and costs $60. Each room has a private bathroom. Originally from the Scottish Highlands, where his mother ran a B&B, host Don Munro and his partner De, a retired New York fashion designer, give guests the run of the house. Beach towels and coolers are provided; breakfast and afternoon tea are included in the rates. There's a small pool and a view of Kaneohe Bay. This B&B has a website (hawaiiscene.com/aliibluffs).

Offering you 57 units, *Schrader's Windward Marine Resort* (☎ 239-5711, 800-735-5711, fax 239-6658, 47-039 Lihikai Drive, Kaneohe, HI 96744) is a spread of simple low-rise wooden buildings in a residential neighborhood. Despite the name, the ambience is more like a motel than a resort. So many of the guests are military families that Schrader's provides free transport to the Kaneohe Marine Corps base. One-bedroom units range from $79 to $116, two-bedroom units from $110 to $200. All have refrigerators, microwaves, TVs, air-con and phones.

Places to Eat

The *Chart House* (☎ 247-6671), at Haiku Gardens, has a romantic, open-air setting with a picturesque view of a lily pond tucked beneath the Koolau Mountains. Open from 5:30 pm nightly, the restaurant features standard steak and seafood entrees ($17 to $30) accompanied by other dishes from a nice salad bar, though the real attraction is the setting. The gardens are flood-lit at night.

You can also drop by Haiku Gardens in the daytime and take a 10-minute stroll around the pond. From Kamehameha Hwy, head west on Haiku Rd (just past the Windward Mall); after crossing Kahekili Hwy, continue on Haiku Rd a quarter of a mile farther.

Chao Phya Thai Restaurant (☎ 235-3555), in the Windward City Shopping Center at the corner of Kamehameha Hwy and Kaneohe Bay Drive, is a family-run restaurant serving good Thai food. Most dishes – including green papaya salad, chili shrimp, pad Thai and vegetarian, fish or meat curries – are priced between $6 and $8. It's open 11 am to 2 pm Monday to Saturday and 5 to 9 pm daily. They don't serve liquor, but you can bring your own.

The Windward City Shopping Center also has *Kimo's Bagelman*, with 75¢ bagels and inexpensive salad and sandwiches; *Kozo Sushi*, an Oahu chain specializing in good takeaway sushi; a *Foodland* supermarket; *KFC* and *McDonald's*. *Burger King* and *Pizza Hut* are on the opposite side of the Kamehameha Hwy.

The Windward Mall, on Kamehameha Hwy at its intersection with Haiku Rd, is a large, two-level mall with chain department stores and shops. The *Windward Mall Food Court* is a sort of mini Ala Moana, with a row of food stalls selling hot cinnamon rolls, deli food, pizza by the slice and Japanese, Chinese, Mexican and Korean meals.

Getting There & Away

By car, the main route from Honolulu is the Likelike Hwy (Hwy 63), which leads into the Kamehameha Hwy (Hwy 836), Kaneohe's main commercial strip. By car from Kailua, it's only a 10-minute drive to Kaneohe if you take Hwy 61 south to the Kamehameha Hwy (Hwy 83).

Kaneohe is connected to Honolulu by bus No 55, with the first bus leaving the Ala

Moana Center at 6:15 am and then about every 30 minutes until 5:40 pm, with three more Kaneohe-bound runs (the last is at 10:15 pm). Bus No 65 covers the same route, but it departs only once an hour. Travel time between Honolulu and Kaneohe on either bus is about 35 minutes.

Bus No 56 connects Kailua with Kaneohe twice an hour between 5 am to 8 pm; the ride takes 20 minutes. You can also take this bus from the Ala Moana Center to Kaneohe, but it takes much longer, as it goes via Kailua.

WAIAHOLE & WAIKANE

The area north of Kaneohe has a sleepy, local feel to it, with some lovely beaches, interesting hiking opportunities and fine scenery. The Kamehameha Hwy, really just a modest two-lane road, runs the length of the entire coast, doubling as Main St for each of the small towns along the way. Waiahole and Waikane mark the beginning of rural Oahu. The area is home to family-run flower nurseries and small farms growing coconuts, bananas, papayas and taro.

If you want to pick up a little local flavor, stop at the Waiahole Poi Factory, on the inland side of the road in Waiahole, which processes island-grown taro and on weekends, it sells inexpensive pasteles – a snack of steamed bananas and pork.

Large tracts of Waikane Valley were taken over by the military during WWII for training and target practice, a use that continued until the 1960s. The government now

North of Kaneohe by Bus

Bus No 55 services the Kamehameha Hwy from Kaneohe to the Turtle Bay Hilton in Kahuku. From Kaneohe, the bus runs approximately every 30 minutes from dawn to 6 pm and then less frequently until 10:45 pm. By bus from Kaneohe, it takes about 30 minutes to reach Kualoa Regional Park, an hour to the Polynesian Cultural Center in Laie and 1⅓ hours to the Turtle Bay Hilton.

✿✿✿✿✿✿✿✿✿✿✿✿✿

claims the land has so much live ordnance it can't be returned to the families from whom it was leased, a source of ongoing contention with local residents who are angry that much of the inner valley remains off-limits.

KUALOA

Kualoa was once one of the most sacred places on Oahu. In fact, the name Kualoa means 'long ancestral background.' When a chief stood on the point, passing canoes lowered their sails in respect. The children of chiefs were brought here to be raised, and it may also have been a place of refuge where kapu breakers and fallen warriors could seek reprieve from the law. Reflecting its historic importance, the double-hulled canoe *Hokulea* landed at Kualoa in 1987, following a two-year voyage through Polynesia tracing the ancient migration routes.

Kualoa Regional Park

Kualoa Regional Park, a 153-acre county beach park on Kualoa Point, is bounded on the southwest by **Molii Fishpond**. From the road southwest of the park, the fishpond is visible through the trees as a distinct green line in the bay. Because of its rich significance to Hawaiians, Kualoa Regional Park is listed in the National Register of Historic Places.

Kualoa is a nice beach park in a scenic setting. The mountains looming precipitously across the road are called, appropriately enough, Pali-ku, meaning 'vertical cliff.' When the mist settles, it looks like a scene from a Chinese watercolor.

The main offshore island is **Mokolii**. In Hawaiian legend, Mokolii is said to be the tail of a nasty lizard or a dog – depending on who's telling the story – that was slain by a god and thrown into the ocean. Following the immigration of Chinese laborers to Hawaii, this cone-shaped island also came to be called Papale Pake, Hawaiian for 'Chinese hat.'

Apua Pond, a 3-acre brackish salt marsh on Kualoa Point, is a nesting area for the endangered *aeo* (Hawaiian stilt). If you walk down the beach beyond the park, you'll see a bit of Molii Fishpond, but it's hard to get a good perspective on it from there because its rock walls are covered with mangrove, milo and pickleweed.

The park is largely open lawn with a few palm trees. It has a long, thin strip of beach with shallow waters and safe swimming. There are picnic tables, rest rooms, showers, a pay phone and a lifeguard. Camping is allowed from Friday to Tuesday night. Camping here is free, and it requires a permit from the county. Kualoa, in one of Oahu's nicest beach settings, has an on-site caretaker and gates that are locked at night. See the Camping section in the Facts for the Visitor chapter for details on obtaining a permit.

Kualoa Ranch

The horses grazing on the green slopes across the road from Kualoa Regional Park belong to the Kualoa Ranch. The scenic ranch was used as a setting for the movies *Jurassic Park* and *Godzilla*. The ranch offers all sorts of activities, including horseback riding, kayaking and target shooting, with many of them packaged for Japanese tourists who are shuttled in from Waikiki. For more information on activities, call Kualoa Ranch (☎ 237-8515).

Back in 1850, Kamehameha III leased 625 acres of this land to Dr Judd, a missionary doctor who became one of the king's advisers, for $1300. Judd planted the land with sugarcane, built flumes to transport it and imported Chinese laborers to work the fields. His sugar mill trudged along for a few decades but went under just before a reciprocity agreement with the USA opened up mainland sugar markets.

Half a mile north of the beach park, right alongside the road, the remains of the sugar mill's stone stack and a bit of its crumbling walls are still visible.

KAAAWA

In the Kaaawa area, the road hugs the coast and the pali moves right on in, with barely enough space to squeeze a few houses between the base of the cliffs and the road.

Swanzy Beach Park, the neighborhood beach used mainly by fishers, is fronted by a shore wall. Camping is allowed on weekends (see the Camping section in the Facts for the Visitor chapter for more details). Across the road is a 7-Eleven store, a gas station and a postage-stamp-sized post office – pretty much the commercial center of town, such as it is.

Just north of Swanzy is a rock formation known as the **crouching lion**. In Hawaiian legend, the rock is said to be a demigod from Tahiti who was cemented to the mountain during a jealous struggle between Pele, the volcano goddess, and her sister Hiiaka. When he tried to free himself by pulling into a crouching position, the demigod was turned to stone.

The crouching lion is behind a restaurant by the same name (if you're driving north, it's just past the 27-mile marker). To find him, stand at the Crouching Lion Inn sign with your back to the ocean and look straight up to the left of the coconut tree. The figure, which to some people resembles a lion, is on a cliff in the background.

Places to Eat

The *Crouching Lion Inn* (☎ 237-8511, 51-666 Kamehameha Hwy) is the area's main sit-down restaurant, and it attracts a fair number of day-trippers. At lunch, 11 am to 3 pm, it serves sandwiches, salads and a few hot plates for $7 to $12. Most dinners are about double that, although from 5 to 7 pm there's an $11 early-bird special, usually a choice of kalua pig, mahimahi or chicken macadamia. Torches are lit at dinnertime, and there's a sea view that makes the restaurant's veranda a pleasant place to dine at sunset. It's open to 9 pm daily.

KAHANA VALLEY

In old Hawaii the islands were divided into *ahupuaa* – pie-shaped land divisions reaching from the mountains to the sea. They provided everything the Hawaiians needed for subsistence. Kahana Valley, 4 miles long and 2 miles wide, is the only publicly owned ahupuaa in Hawaii.

Kahana is a wet valley. Annual rainfall ranges from about 75 inches along the coast to 300 inches in the mountains. Before settlers arrived from the West, Kahana Valley was planted with wetland taro. Archeologists have identified the overgrown remnants of more than 130 agricultural terraces and irrigation canals, as well as the remains of a heiau, fishing shrines and numerous house sites.

In the early 20th century, the area was planted with sugarcane, which was hauled north to the Kahuku Mill via a small railroad. During WWII, the upper part of Kahana Valley was taken over by the military and used for training soldiers in jungle warfare. In 1965 the state bought Kahana Valley from the Robinson family of Kauai (owners of the island of Niihau) in order to preserve it from development.

About 30 Hawaiian families live in the lower valley. The upper valley remains undeveloped and is mostly used by local hunters who come here on weekends to hunt feral pigs.

While many of Kahana's archeological sites are deep in the valley and inaccessible, the park's most impressive site, the **Huilua Fishpond** on Kahana Bay, is visible from the main road and can be visited simply by going down to the beach.

Kahana Valley State Park

The entrance to Kahana Valley State Park is 1 mile north of the Crouching Lion Inn. If you are traveling south on the Kamehameha Hwy, there is a sign for the park entrance.

When the state purchased Kahana, it also acquired tenants, many of whom had lived in the valley for a long time. Rather than evict a struggling rural population, the state created a plan allowing the 140 residents to stay on the land. The concept is to eventually incorporate the families into a 'living park,' with the residents acting as interpretive guides. The development of the park is a slow process, but after two decades of planning and negotiating, the 'living park' concept is inching forward. A simple orientation center inside the park entrance is open and tours are being provided to school children and local organizations.

Although there are no tours for individual travelers, you can walk through the valley on your own. The orientation center, open 7:30 am to 4 pm weekdays, has the latest information on trail conditions and provides a map. Keep in mind that the trails can be slippery when wet, and this is the wettest side of Oahu.

The most accessible of the park trails is the 1¼-mile **Kapaeleele Koa and Keaniani Lookout Trail**, which begins at the orientation center. It goes along the old railroad route, passes a fishing shrine called Kapaeleele Koa and leads to Keaniani Kilo, a lookout that was used in ancient times for spotting schools of fish in the bay. The trail then goes down to the bay and follows the highway back to the park entrance.

If you want to visit the rain forest, there's the **Nakoa Trail**, which makes a 2½-mile loop through tropical vegetation. This trail makes a couple of stream crossings and passes a swimming hole en route. However, the start of the Nakoa Trail is 1¼ miles inland from the orientation center on a rough dirt road, so the total walking distance equals 5 miles.

The park also encompasses **Kahana Bay** with its tree-lined beach and fishpond. The bay is set deep and narrow, and the protected beach provides safe swimming, with a gently sloping sandy bottom. There are 10 beachside campsites that are used primarily by island families, so there may be some turf issues for tourists.

Camping here is free, limited to five nights per month, and a permit is required. For information on obtaining a permit, see Camping in the Accommodations section of the Facts for the Visitor chapter.

PUNALUU

Punaluu is a scattered little seaside community that doesn't draw much attention from tourists. At **Punaluu Beach Park**, a long, narrow beach offers fairly good swimming, because the offshore reef protects the shallow inshore waters in all but stormy weather. Be cautious near the mouth of the Waiono Stream and in the channel leading out from it, because currents are strong when the stream is flowing quickly or when the surf is high. If you are traveling to Punaluu by bus, take the No 55.

Places to Stay & Eat

Pat's at Punaluu (☎ 293-2624, 53-567 Kamehameha Hwy) is a 136-room condominium complex midway between the 23- and 24-mile markers. The place is largely residential, older and a bit neglected, but on the plus side, it's on the water, the units face the ocean and there's a swimming pool. There's no front desk. The units are handled by individuals and realtors, some of whom post their listings on the bulletin board in the lobby.

Bob and Jeanette Martz (☎/fax 261-0316, 395 Auwinala Rd, Kailua, HI 96734) rent a unit with a double bed, queen futon, full kitchen, TV, phone and washer/dryer for $490 a week. (The unit is in Pat's at Punaluu.) Most other rentals are by the month. However, *Paul Comeau Condo Rentals* (☎ 467-6215, fax 293-0618, PO Box 589, Kaaawa, HI 96730) handles studio units that cost $80 a day, one-bedroom units for $100 and three-bedroom units for $170, with a three-day minimum.

Punaluu House is a home in the center of Punaluu belonging to the owners of Hostelling International Honolulu (☎ 946-0591, fax 946-5904, 2323A Seaview Ave, Honolulu, HI 96822). Because there are only a couple of rooms and it's a cozy situation, the hostel prescreens potential guests – so if you want to stay at Punaluu House, you need to go to the Honolulu hostel first to meet with the staff there and get a referral. Punaluu House has a couple of guest rooms, one with twin beds, another with a double bed; there's a shared bath and a shared kitchen. House parents live on site. The cost is $20 per person.

Ahi's (☎ 293-5650, 53-146 Kamehameha Hwy), a third of a mile north of the 25-mile marker, is Punaluu's only restaurant. It specializes in fresh shrimp, and the menu includes shrimp scampi, deep-fried shrimp and tempura shrimp. There are various specials, but expect a shrimp meal to cost around $10. It's open 11 am to 9 pm Monday to Saturday.

Ching's Punaluu Store, a small grocery store just north of the 24-mile marker, is open 8 am to 6:30 pm daily.

SACRED FALLS STATE PARK

Sacred Falls is a 1374-acre state park that folds deeply into the Koolau Mountains. The central feature of the park is a **2-mile trail** leading up the narrow Kaliuwaa Valley. The moderately difficult hike, following Kaluanui Stream through a narrow canyon, takes about 1½ hours, involves a couple of stream crossings and ends at a dramatic 80-foot waterfall beneath high, rocky cliffs.

The falls may be sacred, but the hike isn't blessed. Because the canyon is narrow, it's subject to flash floods. Over the years, a number of hikers have been swept to their deaths when unexpected rainstorms unleashed sudden swells of water without warning.

Falling rocks pose another hazard and account for the park's single worst disaster. In May 1999, on a sunny Sunday afternoon, more than 50 people who were swimming and sunbathing at the base of the falls were injured when a landslide let loose directly above them. Eight people were killed by falling boulders and debris and a dozen others had to be hospitalized.

Although the trail to the falls has weathered other disasters, the instability that caused the landslide has cast doubts upon the park's future. Until geologists can make a positive determination on the soundness of the cliff face, it's unlikely that the park will reopen.

If Sacred Falls State Park does reopen, the trail will, as in the past, be closed any day when the weather is sufficiently bad or the water level is high. Entering when the gate is locked not only subjects hikers to potential natural hazards, but also to hefty fines. At the trailhead, the parks department (☎ 587-0300) posts a sign as to whether the trail is open or closed; you can also call to check on the park's status.

The park is on the inland side of Kamehameha Hwy, about a third of a mile north of the 23-mile marker.

HAUULA

Hauula is a rather tired-looking coastal town set against a scenic backdrop of hills and majestic Norfolk pines. There are some lovely hiking trails in the forest reserve behind the town.

The in-town beach is none too appealing for swimming, but it occasionally gets waves big enough for local kids to ride. The beach is actually a county park that allows camping, although it's mostly local families that camp there. Camping is allowed from 8 am Friday to 8 am Wednesday. For more details, see the Camping section in the Facts for the Visitor chapter.

The main landmark in town is the stone ruins of **Lanakila Church** (circa 1853). It's perched on a hill opposite Hauula Beach, next to the newer Hauula Congregational Church.

If you're in need of a quick bite to eat, Hauula has a 7-Eleven store and a couple of small eateries.

If you are traveling by bus, take the No 55.

Trails

The Division of Forestry & Wildlife maintains three trails in the forest reserve behind Hauula. All three share the same access point and head into some beautiful hills beneath the Koolau Range.

The most popular, best maintained and easiest of the three trails is the **Hauula Loop Trail**. It forks off to the right shortly after you enter the forest reserve and is a scenic 2½-mile trail that crosses gulches and climbs up to a ridge that provides expansive views of the lush forest interior, the ocean and the town of Hauula. The trail passes both native plants, such as ohia trees, and thickly planted groves of shaggy ironwood trees and towering Norfolk pines. The hike takes about two hours.

The **Maakua Ridge Trail**, which begins on the left about half a mile after entering the forest reserve, makes a 2½-mile loop that climbs in and out of gullies and follows the narrow Maakua Ridge. Much of the trail is open and dry, but there are sections that are closed in by thickets of acacia trees, creating a tunnel effect. There are ridge views of the coast and Hauula along the way. The hike takes about 2½ hours in all.

The **Maakua Gulch Trail** follows the narrow Maakua Gulch and leads 3 miles into the forest reserve. The farther inland you go, the narrower the gulch becomes. There are several stream crossings, and eventually the trail is squeezed into the streambed itself. The streambed rocks that hikers have to scramble over are very slippery and fallen trees provide further obstacles. There's a small waterfall and pool near the end, but because the trail gets rougher as it goes along, they can be a challenge to reach.

There are two hazards to be aware of: the potential for rock falling from the unstable cliff-face on the upper canyon and flash floods that occur suddenly and with little warning. The trail should not be hiked when rain is predicted or when the stream is high. Depending on how far in you hike, this difficult trail can take anywhere from a few hours to a good half day.

The signpost for the trailhead to all three routes is at a bend in Hauula Homestead Rd (in town, at the north end of Hauula Beach Park), about a quarter of a mile in from Kamehameha Hwy.

Backcountry camping is permitted near the mouth of Maakua Gulch, along the Maakua Gulch Trail, but a permit from the Division of Forestry is required. For details on obtaining a permit, see Backcountry Camping in the Accommodations section of the Facts for the Visitor chapter.

LAIE

Laie is thought to have been the site of an ancient *puuhonua* – a place where kapu breakers and fallen warriors could seek refuge. Today, Laie is the center of the Mormon community in Hawaii.

The first Mormon missionaries to Hawaii arrived in 1850. After an attempt to establish a Hawaiian 'City of Joseph' on the island of Lanai failed amidst a land scandal, the Mormons moved to Laie. In 1865 they purchased 6000 acres of land in the area and slowly expanded their influence.

In 1919 the Mormons constructed a **temple**, a smaller version of the one in Salt Lake City, at the foot of the Koolau Range. This stately temple, at the end of a wide promenade, is like nothing else on the windward coast. Although there's a visitor center

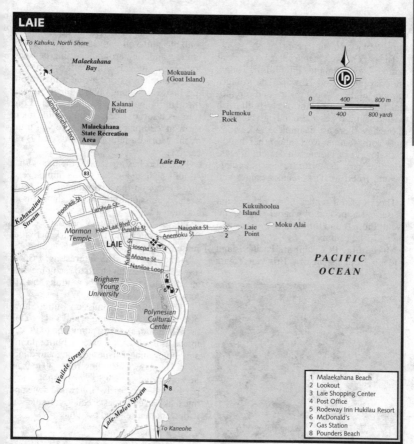

LAIE

To Kahuku, North Shore

Malaekahana
Bay

Mokuauia
(Goat Island)

Kalanai
Point

Pulemoku
Rock

Malaekahana
State Recreation
Area

Laie Bay

Kukuihoolua
Island

Naupaka St
Anemoku St

Laie
Point

Moku Alai

Mormon
Temple

Hale Laa Blvd
Puyahi St

Poohaili St
Lanihuli St

LAIE

Iosepa St

Moana St

Naniloa Loop

Brigham
Young
University

Polynesian
Cultural
Center

PACIFIC
OCEAN

Kahawainui
Stream

Kamehameha Hwy

83

Wailele Stream

Laie-Maloo Stream

To Kaneohe

1 Malaekahana Beach
2 Lookout
3 Laie Shopping Center
4 Post Office
5 Rodeway Inn Hukilau Resort
6 McDonald's
7 Gas Station
8 Pounders Beach

0   400   800 m
0   400   800 yards

where eager guides will tell you all about Mormonism, tourists are not allowed to enter the temple itself.

Nearby is the Hawaii branch of **Brigham Young University**, with scholarship programs that recruit students from islands throughout the Pacific.

Information

The Laie Shopping Center on Kamehameha Hwy, about half a mile north of the Polynesian Cultural Center, has a Bank of Hawaii open 8:30 am to 4 pm Monday to Thursday and 8:30 am to 6 pm on Friday.

The Laie post office, 55-510 Kamehameha Hwy, at the east side of the Laie Shopping Center, is open 9 am to 3:30 pm on weekdays and 9:30 to 11:30 am on Saturday.

There's a coin laundry, open 6 am to 9:30 pm Monday to Saturday, at the Laie Shopping Center.

Polynesian Cultural Center

The Polynesian Cultural Center (☎ 293-3333, 800-367-7060), called PCC by locals, is a 'nonprofit' organization belonging to the Mormon Church. The center covers 42 acres and draws more tourists than any other attraction on Oahu, with the exception of the USS *Arizona* Memorial. They have a website (www.polynesia.com).

The park's seven theme villages represent Samoa, New Zealand, Fiji, Tahiti, Tonga, the Marquesas and Hawaii. The villages contain authentic-looking huts and ceremonial houses, many elaborately built with twisted sennit ropes and hand-carved posts. In the huts there are examples of weavings, tapa cloth, feather work and other handicrafts. People of Polynesian descent dressed in native garb demonstrate poi pounding, coconut frond weaving, dances, games and the like.

There's also a replica of an old mission house and a missionary chapel representative of those found throughout Polynesia in the mid-19th century.

Much of the PCC staff are Pacific Island students from the nearby Brigham Young University, who pay their college expenses by working at PCC. The interpreters are amiable and you can easily spend a few hours wandering around chatting or trying to become familiar with a craft or two.

The admission price includes the following: boat rides along the winding waterway through the park; the Pageant of the Long Canoes, a sort of trumped-up floating talent show at 2:30 pm; and 35-minute van tours of the Mormon temple grounds and BYU campus.

PCC also has an IMAX theater with a 40-foot-high screen that shows films several times a day on the environment and Polynesia. Admission to the IMAX theater is an additional $5.

PCC is open 12:30 to 9 pm daily, except Sunday, though the theme park activities cease by 6 pm.

Although it can be interesting, PCC is also very touristy and hard to recommend at an admission price of $27 for adults and $16 for children ages five to 11.

There's also an 'Admission-Buffet-Show' ticket costing $47 for adults and $30 for children. It includes general admission to PCC, a movie at the IMAX theater, a buffet dinner and the evening Polynesian song and dance show. The show, which runs from 7:30 to 9 pm in winter and 8 to 9:30 pm in summer, is partly authentic, partly Hollywood-style and much like an enthusiastic college production, with elaborate sets and costumes.

Beaches

The 1½ miles of beach between Malaekahana State Recreation Area and Laie Point front the town of Laie and are used by surfers, bodysurfers and windsurfers.

Pounders Beach, a half mile south of the main entrance to PCC, is an excellent bodysurfing beach, but the shorebreak, as the name of the beach implies, can be brutal. There's a strong winter current. The area around the old landing is usually the calmest. Summer swimming is generally good, and the beach is sandy.

From the lookout at **Laie Point**, there's a good view of the mountains to the south and

Depiction of native Hawaiian, by John Webber

of tiny islands offshore. The island to the left, with the hole in it, is Kukuihoolua, otherwise known as Puka Rock. To get to Laie Point, head toward the ocean via Anemoku St, opposite the Laie Shopping Center, then turn right on Naupaka St and go straight to the end.

Places to Stay & Eat

Rodeway Inn Hukilau Resort (☎ 293-9282, 800-526-4562, fax 293-8115, 55-109 Laniloa St, Laie, HI 96762), right outside the Polynesian Cultural Center, is a two-story motel with 49 rooms surrounding a courtyard pool. Although not special, it's comfortable enough, and each room has a lanai, cable TV, air-con and mini-refrigerator. Rates start at $84, including a continental breakfast.

Laie Chop Suey (☎ 293-8022), in the Laie Shopping Center, is a local-style eatery with standard Chinese fare. Most main dishes cost $5 to $6, as do set lunch and dinner plates. It's open 10 am to 9 pm Monday to Saturday.

The shopping center also has a *Foodland* grocery store, *Subway Sandwiches* and *Domino's Pizza*. The *McDonald's*, on the highway at the north end of PCC, has a little more character than the usual McDonald's. Originally built as a restaurant for the hotel next door, the building resembles a Polynesian longhouse with a peaked roof, and there's even a small waterfall inside. The only Laie eatery open on Sunday, its hours are 6:30 am to at least 10 pm daily.

MALAEKAHANA STATE RECREATION AREA

This beautiful park is on the Kamehameha Hwy, north of Laie. **Malaekahana Beach** stretches between Makahoa Point to the north and Kalanai Point to the south. The long, narrow, sandy beach is backed by ironwood trees. Swimming is generally good year round, although there are occasionally strong currents in winter. This popular family beach is also good for many other water activities, including bodysurfing, board surfing and windsurfing. **Kalanai Point**, the main section of the state park, is less than a mile north of Laie and has picnic

tables, barbecue grills, camping, rest rooms and showers.

Mokuauia (Goat Island), a state bird sanctuary just offshore, has a nice, sandy cove with good swimming and snorkeling. It's possible to wade over to the island – best when the tide is low and the water's calm – but be sure to ask the lifeguard first about water conditions and the advisability of crossing. Be careful of the shallow coral and sea urchins.

You can also snorkel across to Goat Island and off its beaches. Beware of a rip current that's sometimes present off the windward end of the island where the water is deeper.

Malaekahana State Recreation Area has the best **campgrounds** at this end of the windward coast. You can pitch a tent in the park's main Kalanai Point section for free if you have a state park permit; camping is limited to five nights per month. For details on applying for a permit, see Camping under Accommodations in the Facts for the Visitor chapter.

You can also rent a cabin or camp for a fee in the Makahoa Point section of the park, which has a separate entrance off the highway, three-quarters of a mile north of the main park entrance. Friends of Malaekahana (☎ 293-1736 after 10 am), a local nonprofit group dedicated to cultural preservation, maintains this end of the park. The gates here are locked to vehicles between 7 pm and 7 am. Rustic cabins that can accommodate a maximum of eight people cost $66 on weekdays and $80 on weekends, tax included. Tent camping in this section costs $5 per person.

KAHUKU

Kahuku is a former sugar town with little wooden cane houses lining the road. The mill in the center of town belonged to the Kahuku Plantation, which produced sugar from 1890 until it closed in 1971. The operation was a relatively small concern, unable to keep up with the increasingly mechanized competition of Hawaii's bigger mills. When the mill shut down, Kahuku's economy skidded into a slump that still lingers today.

Kahuku Sugar Mill

A fledgling shopping center now occupies Kahuku's old sugar mill, with small shops set amongst the old machinery. The mill's enormous gears, flywheels and pipes are painted in bright colors to help visitors visualize how a sugar mill works. The steam systems are painted red, the cane-juice systems are light green, hydraulic systems are painted dark blue and so forth. It looks like something out of *Modern Times* – you can almost imagine Charlie Chaplin caught up in the giant gears.

The center has not been wildly successful, but there's a local plate-lunch eatery, food mart, gas station, post office, bank and a few other shops struggling along in the complex.

Kuilima Cove

The shallow Kuilima Cove, also known as Bay View Beach, is fronted by the Turtle Bay Hilton, the only hotel in Kahuku. This pleasant white sand beach, protected by a reef, is one of the area's best swimming spots. It also has a few coral patches that are good for snorkeling. While it's mostly used by Hilton guests, it's open to all.

The beach concession stand rents snorkel sets and boogie boards for $12 a day, floats and tubes for $10, lounge chairs for $4.

You can park at one of the free spaces for beachgoers, on the right just before the guard booth, and walk 10 minutes to the beach. Alternatively, there's parking inside the hotel lot for $1 for the first half-hour and 50¢ for each additional half-hour.

Kaihalulu Beach

Kaihalulu is a beautiful, curved, white-sand beach backed by ironwoods. Although a shoreline lava shelf and rocky bottom make the beach poor for swimming, it's good for beachcombing – you can walk east about a mile to Kahuku Point. Local fishers cast nets from the shore and pole fish from the point. The dirt road just inland of the beach is also used as a horse trail.

To get there, turn into the Turtle Bay Hilton and just before the guard booth turn right into an unmarked parking lot, where there are free spaces for beachgoers. It's a five-minute walk out to the beach; just walk east on the footpath that begins at the field adjacent to the parking lot. There are no facilities.

Places to Stay

Turtle Bay Condos (☎ 293-2800, fax 293-2169, Box 248, Kahuku, HI 96731) handles units at Kuilima Estates, a modern condominium complex on the grounds fronting the Hilton. Rates are $90 for a regular studio, $100 for a studio with a loft and from $110/150 for a unit with one/two bedrooms. Weekly rates are six times the daily rate; monthly rates are 2½ times the weekly rate.

Green Sea Turtles

Turtle Bay, the wide bay on the west side of the Turtle Bay Hilton, takes its name from the green sea turtles that swim into the bay to feed on algae.

Green sea turtles, which can weigh upwards of 200 pounds, are the most abundant of the three native species of sea turtles (*honu*) found in Hawaiian waters. The turtles are not permanent residents of the main Hawaiian islands. About once every four years they return to their ancestral nesting grounds in the remote French Frigate Shoals, 500 miles east of Oahu, where they mate and nest.

Hawaii's other two native turtles are the hawksbill, which is about the same size as the green sea turtle but far rarer, and the leatherback, a huge turtle that weighs up to a ton and is found in deep offshore waters.

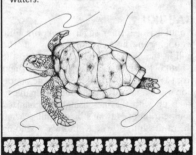

In addition, there's a $50 cleaning fee for all rentals, no matter how long you stay. Each unit has a complete kitchen, washer/dryer, TV, phone and lanai. The complex has two tennis courts and five pools.

Turtle Bay Hilton (☎ 293-8811, 800-445-8667, fax 293-9147, Kahuku, HI 96731) is a self-contained resort and the only major hotel on the windward and north shores. The Hilton is perched on Kuilima Point, between Turtle Bay and Kuilima Cove. All 485 rooms have ocean views. Room rates range from $165 to $265, and suite rates range from $400 to $1500. There are two golf courses, two swimming pools, horse stables and 10 tennis courts.

Places to Eat

If you like shrimp, look for *Giovanni's Aloha Shrimp*, a truck that parks along the highway just south of the Kahuku Sugar Mill, which is in the center of town. Popular with both locals and weekend sightseers from Honolulu, Giovanni's offers a choice of tasty shrimp scampi, conventional grilled shrimp or an ultra-fiery spicy shrimp. A plate with half a pound of jumbo shrimp and two scoops of rice costs $11. There's a covered picnic area where you can sit and eat. It's open 10:30 am to 6:30 pm daily.

There are also a few restaurants at the Turtle Bay Hilton, though the food's not particularly notable. The *Palm Terrace* has buffets for around $14 at lunch and $20 at dinner. The *Sea Tide Room* has a Sunday brunch 10 am to 2 pm for $27, and *The Cove* is the hotel's fancy dinner restaurant. In addition, the lobby-side *Bayview Lounge* serves a simple evening buffet, some nights a pizza and pasta spread and other nights a taco bar; the buffet is offered 5:30 to 8:30 pm and costs $10 for adults, $6 for children.

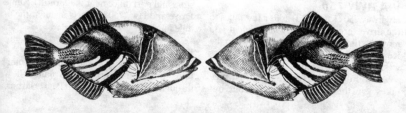

Central Oahu

Highlights

- Strolling among the grand old trees of the Wahiawa Botanical Garden

- Driving through the island's picturesque pineapple country

- Visiting the royal birthstones where Hawaiian queens went to give birth

Central Oahu forms a saddle between the Waianae Mountains on the west and the Koolau Mountains on the east. Wahiawa is the region's commercial center and is smack in the middle of Oahu. Three routes lead north from Honolulu to Wahiawa: H-2, the freeway, which is the fastest route; Hwy 750, the farthest west but the most scenic; and Hwy 99, the least interesting option, which hits the local traffic as it runs through Mililani, a nondescript residential community.

Most people just zoom up through central Oahu on their way to the North Shore. If your time is limited, this isn't a bad idea. There are a few sights along the way, but Wahiawa doesn't really warrant much more than a quick visit anyway.

From Wahiawa two routes, Hwy 803 (Kaukonahua Rd) and Hwy 99 (Kamehameha Hwy), lead through pineapple country to the North Shore. Hwy 803 is a slightly shorter route to Mokuleia, and both routes are about the same distance to Haleiwa. The two roads are equally picturesque, and if you're not circling the island, you might as well go up one and down the other.

VIA HWY 750

Highway 750 (Kunia Rd) adds a few miles to the drive through central Oahu, but if you have the time it's worth it. Follow H-1 to the Kunia Rd-Hwy 750 exit. The exit is 3 miles west of where H-1 and H-2 divide.

As you drive up Hwy 750, the first mile takes you through creeping suburbia, but then you enter plantation lands. The road runs along the foothills of the Waianae Mountains and the countryside is solidly agricultural all the way to Schofield Barracks.

Two miles into the drive, you'll come to a strip of cornfields planted by the Garst Seed Company. Three generations of corn are grown here each year, making it possible to develop hybrids of corn seed at triple the rate on the mainland. Incidentally, the little bags covering each ear of corn are there to prevent cross-pollination.

One of the prettiest pineapple fields in Hawaii is a bit farther north, a landscape without buildings or development – just red earth carpeted with long, green strips of pineapples stretching to the edge of the mountains.

From the Hawaii Country Club, just up the road on the right, there's a distant view of Honolulu all the way to Diamond Head.

Kunia

Kunia, a little town in the midst of the pineapple fields, is home to the field-workers employed by Del Monte. Rows of gray-green wooden houses with corrugated tin roofs stand on low stilts. Residents take pride in their little yards, with bougainvillea and other colorful flowers adding a splash of brightness despite the wash of red dust that blows in from the surrounding pineapple fields.

If you want a look at a current-day plantation village, turn west off Hwy 750 onto Kunia Drive, which makes a 1¼-mile loop through town. The Kunia Drive-Hwy 750 intersection is about 5½ miles north of the intersection of Hwy 750 and H-1 (there's a store and post office near the turnoff). Kunia Drive and Hwy 750 intersect again at the 6-mile marker.

Kolekole Pass

Kolekole is the gap in the Waianae Mountains that Japanese fighter planes flew through on their way to bomb Pearl Harbor.

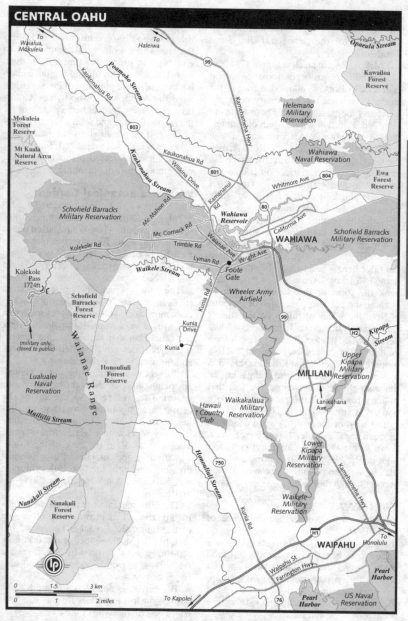

CENTRAL OAHU

Film buffs may recognize the landscape, as the historic flight was re-created here 30 years later for the classic war film *Tora! Tora! Tora!*

Kolekole Pass, at an elevation of 1724 feet, sits on military property above Schofield Barracks. Visitors are allowed as long as the base isn't on some sort of military alert.

Access the pass through Foote Gate, on Hwy 750, a third of a mile south of its intersection with Hwy 99. After passing through the gate, take the first left onto Road A, then the first right onto Lyman Rd. The pass is 5¼ miles up past the barracks, golf course and bayonet assault course. The parking lot is opposite the hilltop that has a big white cross that's visible from miles away.

From the parking lot it's a five-minute walk to the top of the pass, from which there is a view straight down to the Waianae Coast. The large, ribbed stone sitting atop the ridge here is said to have been a woman named Kolekole. According to legend, she took the form of this stone in order to become the perpetual guardian of the pass.

Note the series of ridges on the stone's side. One drains down from the bowl-like depression on the top. Shaped perfectly for a guillotine, the depression has given rise to a more recent 'legend' that Kolekole served as a sacrificial stone for the beheading of defeated chiefs and warriors. The fact that military bases flank the pass has no doubt had a little influence on this belief.

Just west of the pass the road continues through the Lualualei Naval Reservation down to the Waianae Coast, but you can't take it. The Navy base is a storage site for nuclear weapons, and there's no public access through that side.

WAHIAWA

Wahiawa, whose name means 'place of noise' in Hawaiian, is a GI town, sitting on the edge of Schofield Barracks, Hawaii's largest army base. Just about every fast-food chain you can think of is found in Wahiawa's center. Tattoo parlors and pawnshops are the town's main attractions, and if you're looking for a little excitement, there are some rough-and-tumble bars.

Despite its current drab commercial center, Wahiawa once played a significant role in Oahu's history. Just north of town is the site where women of royalty went to give birth in precontact times. Back then, vast stretches of this upland region, including the site of the present botanical garden, were thick with sandalwood trees. Unfortunately, foreign traders had a penchant for the fragrant wood, and soon after the arrival of the first merchant ships, the native sandalwood forests were depleted. Today, most of the former forested plains are planted with endless rows of pineapple.

Wahiawa Botanical Garden

The Wahiawa Botanical Garden (☎ 621-7321), 1396 California Ave, is a mile east of the Kamehameha Hwy. What started out in the 1920s as a site for forestry experiments by the Hawaii Sugar Planters' Association is now a 27-acre city park with grand old trees and a wooded ravine.

The park is a nice shady place to take a stroll. Interesting 70-year-old exotics such as cinnamon, chicle and allspice are grouped in one area. *Loulu* palms (fan palms), ginger and other Hawaiian natives are in other sections. The trees are identified by markers, and the air is thick with birdsong.

Two common, but unique, native Hawaiian plants are planted right by the visitor center. The tree ferns to the left of the center are *hapuu*, a fern that reaches heights of 20 feet and forms the understory in many of Hawaii's wetter forest areas. The silky 'wool' at the base of the fronds was used in ancient Hawaii as a surgical dressing, and until the late 19th century it was harvested commercially as filling for mattresses.

The other common native found here is the koa tree, which grows on the other side of the center. Koa reaches heights of 100 feet, has flat sickle-shaped leafstalks and a red-tinged wood favored by Hawaiians for crafts ranging from wooden bowls to outrigger canoes.

The garden is open 9 am to 4 pm daily. Admission to the park is free, as is a brochure describing some of the trees.

Healing Stones

Among the odder sights to be labeled with a visitors bureau marker are the 'Healing Stones' that are caged inside a small stone 'temple' next to the Methodist church on California Ave, half a mile west of its intersection with Kamehameha Hwy.

The main stone is thought to be the gravestone of a powerful Hawaiian chief. Although the chief's original burial place is in a field a mile away, the stone was moved long ago to a graveyard at this site. In the 1920s people thought the stone had healing powers, and thousands made pilgrimages to it before interest waned. The housing development and church came later, taking over the graveyard and leaving the stones sitting on the sidewalk.

A local group with roots in India perceive a spiritual connection between Hawaiian and Indian beliefs, so they visit the temple, leaving flowers and little elephant statues placed around the stones. The story of the healing stones is actually more interesting than the sight, however.

Royal Birthstones

Kukaniloko, just north of Wahiawa, is a site with royal birthstones and the place where Hawaii's queens gave birth. The stones are thought to date back to the 12th century. Legend held that if a woman lay properly against the stones while giving birth, her child would be blessed by the gods, and indeed, many of Oahu's great chiefs were born at this site.

These stones are at one of only two documented birthstone sites in Hawaii (the other is in Kauai). Many of the petroglyphs on the stones are of recent origin, but the eroded circular patterns are original.

To get to the site from town, go three-quarters of a mile north on Kamehameha Hwy from its intersection with California Ave. Turn left onto the red dirt road directly opposite Whitmore Ave. The stones, marked with a state monument sign, are a quarter of a mile down the road, through a pineapple field, among a stand of eucalyptus and coconut trees. If it's been raining, be aware that the red clay can cake onto your car tires,

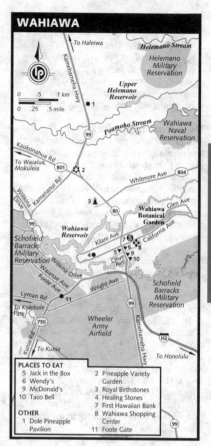

WAHIAWA

PLACES TO EAT
5 Jack in the Box
6 Wendy's
9 McDonald's
10 Taco Bell

OTHER
1 Dole Pineapple
   Pavilion

2 Pineapple Variety
   Garden
3 Royal Birthstones
4 Healing Stones
7 First Hawaiian Bank
8 Wahiawa Shopping
   Center
11 Foote Gate

and once back on the paved road, the car may slide as if you're driving on ice.

Pineapple Variety Garden

Del Monte maintains a little pineapple demonstration garden, which is at the intersection of Hwys 99 and 80.

Smooth cayenne, the commercial variety of pineapple grown in Hawaii, is shown in various growth stages. Each plant produces just two pineapples. The first takes nearly two years to reach maturity, the second about one year more. Other commercial varieties of pineapple grown in Australia, the Philippines and Brazil are on display, as are some varieties of purely decorative bromeliads (pineapples are in the Bromeliaceae family).

You can pull off to the side of the road and walk through the garden on your own at any time of the day or week.

Dole Pineapple Pavilion

The Dole Pineapple Pavilion is on Hwy 99, less than a mile north of its intersection with Hwy 80. This touristy complex in the heart of Oahu's pineapple country consists of a bustling gift shop, some simple bromeliad gardens and an expansive hibiscus hedge maze. Dole's processing plant sits across the street, and miles of pineapple fields surround the area.

The gift shop sells pineapple in many forms – juice, freezes, pastries and pineapples boxed to take home. Expect things to be a bit pricey, but the bromeliad gardens are free and make a nice opportunity to get out of the car and stretch.

If you feel like getting lost, you can wander through the 'world's largest maze,' a claim confirmed by the Guinness record book (and sorry, there's no helpful Lonely Planet map for this one, so you're on your own). The maze covers nearly 2 acres and contains 1.7 miles of pathways, and truth be told, there's a certain monotony to it. Most people take 15 to 30 minutes to get through. Admission costs $4.50 for adults and $2.50 for children. The maze is open 9 am to 5:30 pm daily, the gift shop until 6 pm.

Places to Eat

If you have a hankering for some fast food, then Kamehameha Hwy, the main drag through downtown Wahiawa, has in rapid succession a *Taco Bell*, a *McDonald's*, a *Wendy's* and a *Jack in the Box*.

Not far from the Kamehameha Hwy, at 823 California Ave, the Wahiawa Shopping Center has a couple of interesting places to eat. For example, *Wok & Grill Express* serves inexpensive Chinese fare. It is open 10 am to 9 pm daily (to 8 pm on Sunday). *Surf Taco* offers fish burritos and tacos at reasonable prices, and it's open 10:30 am to 10 pm daily. For a bargain breakfast, try the bakery in the *Foodland* supermarket. It makes a tasty, filling bread pudding ($1) and cheap doughnuts. Its hours are 6 am to 11 pm daily.

Getting There & Away

To go through town and visit the botanical garden, healing stones and royal birthstones, take Kamehameha Hwy (which is Hwy 80 as it goes through town, although it's Hwy 99 before and after Wahiawa). To make the bypass around Wahiawa, stick with Hwy 99.

Although exploring many of Central Oahu's sights is only practical for those with their own transportation, you can get from Honolulu to Wahiawa and onward to Haleiwa via bus No 52 (see the North Shore chapter for details). Wahiawa is also reached via bus No 62, which leaves the Ala Moana Center about once every 30 minutes, takes approximately 1½ hours and stops by the botanical garden.

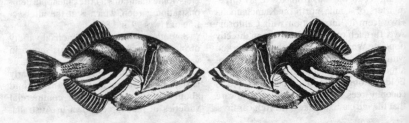

North Shore

Oahu's North Shore is synonymous with surfing and wicked winter waves, but long before it was a surfing hot spot, Polynesian settlers were drawn to the North Shore by the region's rich fishing grounds, cooling trade winds and moderate rainfall. The areas around Mokuleia, Haleiwa and Waimea all once had sizable Hawaiian settlements, and abandoned taro patches still remain in the upland valleys.

By the early 20th century, the Oahu Railway & Land Company had extended the railroad from Honolulu to the North Shore, and the first beachgoers began to arrive. Hotels and private beach houses sprang up to accommodate the tourists, but when the railroad stopped running in the 1940s, the hotels shut down for good (sections of abandoned railroad track are still found along many of the beaches).

Waikiki surfers started taking on the enormous North Shore waves in the late 1950s. Sunset Beach, the Banzai Pipeline and Waimea Bay are among the world's hottest and most famous surf spots, and they attract top surfers from around the globe. Other North Shore surf breaks may be less well known, but with names such as Himalayas and Avalanche, it is obvious that they are for experts, rather than surfing neophytes.

Big-time surf competitions are a North Shore tradition. The Triple Crown, comprised of three major surf contests, is the most prestigious event of all. The events take place in early winter, with prize purses in the six figures.

Surf mania prevails – even in the restaurants, which serve up omelettes with names such as 'Pumping Surf' and 'Wipe Out.' When the surf's up, half the North Shore population can be found on the beach. On winter weekends, convoys of cars make the trip from Honolulu to watch the surfers ride the waves. If you want to avoid the traffic, simply head up to the North Shore on a weekday.

Getting There & Away

By car, the quickest route from Honolulu is to take the H-1 Fwy west and then exit north onto the H-2 Fwy to Wahiawa, where you can continue north via the Kamehameha Hwy. The Kamehameha Hwy (Hwy 83), which is a two-lane coastal road once it reaches the North Shore, connects Haleiwa

Water Conditions

With the exception of Haleiwa Beach Park, the North Shore's beaches are notorious for treacherous winter swimming conditions. There are powerful and dangerous currents along the entire shore. If the water does not look as calm as a lake, it is probably not safe for swimming or snorkeling.

During the summer, surf conditions along the whole North Shore mellow out. Shark's Cove in Waimea becomes a prime snorkeling and diving site, and Waimea Bay, internationally famous for its winter surf, turns into a popular spot for swimming and snorkeling.

NORTH SHORE

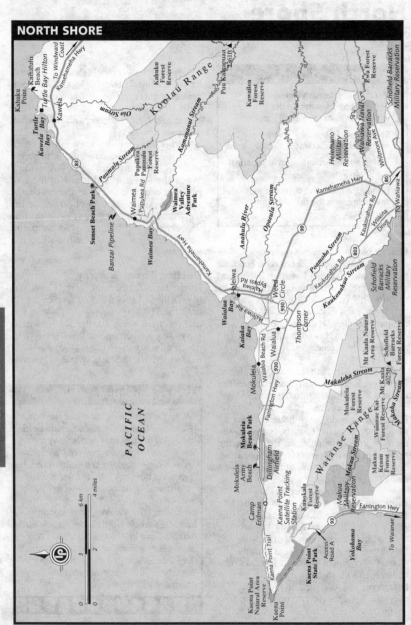

with the North Shore's main sight-seeing locales and beaches.

Bus No 52 is the main line serving the North Shore. It runs from the Ala Moana Center in Honolulu all the way to the Turtle Bay Hilton in Kahuku. En route, the bus stops in Wahiawa (1¼ hours), Haleiwa (1½ hours), Waimea Bay (1¾ hours) and Sunset Beach (two hours) before terminating at the Turtle Bay Hilton (2¼ hours). The bus leaves the Ala Moana Center twice an hour from 6:10 am to 5:20 pm and then again at 6:20 pm and 8 pm.

Bus No 52 bypasses Waialua, but local bus No 76 connects Haleiwa and Waialua once every 40 minutes from 6 am to 6:40 pm; travel time between the two towns is 15 minutes.

WAIALUA

Waialua, a small former plantation town a mile west of Haleiwa, is centered around the dusty Waialua Sugar Mill. The mill shut down in 1996, bringing an end to the last commercial sugar operation on Oahu.

Although the Waialua area remains economically depressed, with many of the surrounding fields overgrown with uncultivated sugarcane, other sections are newly planted with coffee trees – a labor-intensive crop that holds out promise for new jobs. In fact, Waialua coffee is now available on the market.

The old Waialua Sugar Mill now serves as the coffee operation's headquarters. There is a small visitors center (☎ 637-2411), but at this point there's not much to see. You can try Waialua coffee here – a small sample is free, and a full cup is $1. The visitors center is free and open 9 am to 4 pm daily.

As for other sights, this sleepy town has a handful of period buildings, the most interesting being the local watering hole, the *Sugar Bar* – it occupies the old Bank of Hawaii building down by the mill.

The most scenic route between Haleiwa and Waialua is via Haleiwa Rd.

MOKULEIA

The Farrington Hwy (Hwy 930) runs west from Thompson Corner to Dillingham Airfield and Mokuleia Beach. (Both this road and the road along the Waianae Coast are

Coffee Buzz

Hawaii is the only state in the USA where coffee is commercially grown. Christian missionaries introduced the first coffee trees to Hawaii in the 1820s, and by the end of the 19th century it was an important cash crop throughout the islands. However, the erratic rise and fall of international coffee prices eventually drove coffee farmers out of business on all the Hawaiian Islands except the Big Island, where highly regarded Kona coffee kept a small, but loyal, market.

In the early 1980s, a rising interest in gourmet coffee led to an increased demand for Kona coffee, and its price skyrocketed. Hoping to get in on the lucrative market, the other main Hawaiian Islands started planting coffee on a commercial scale. Oahu is the most recent to get on board, with the establishment of the Waialua coffee plantation.

Coffee, a relative of the gardenia, produces fragrant white blossoms in February. By early summer the trees have green berries that turn red as they ripen. The fruit is harvested in the fall, and the trees must be hand-picked several times a season, because not all the berries ripen at the same time.

called Farrington Hwy, but they do not connect, and each side reaches a dead end about 2½ miles short of Kaena Point.)

Mokuleia Beach is a 6-mile stretch of white sand running from Kaiaka Bay toward Kaena Point. Although some GIs and locals come this way, the beaches don't draw much of a crowd, and the area feels a bit like the boondocks. This is certainly not a popular tourist area – there's little traffic and no bus service. The only beach facilities are at Mokuleia Beach Park, and the nearest store is back in Waialua.

Dillingham Airfield is a takeoff site for glider rides and skydiving. For details, see the Activities chapter in the front of the book.

Mokuleia Beach Park

Mokuleia Beach Park, opposite Dillingham Airfield, has a large, open grassy area with picnic tables, rest rooms, showers and a pay phone. Camping is allowed with a county camping permit. For details, see Camping in the Facts for the Visitor chapter.

Mokuleia is sandy, but it has a lava shelf along much of its shoreline. It has fairly consistent winds, making it a popular spot with windsurfers, particularly in spring and fall. In the winter there are dangerous currents.

Mokuleia Army Beach

Mokuleia Army Beach, opposite the western end of Dillingham Airfield, is the widest stretch of sand on the Mokuleia shore. Once reserved exclusively for military personnel, the beach is now open to the public, but the army no longer maintains it, and there are no beach facilities.

The beach is unprotected, and there are very strong rip currents, especially during winter high surf. Locals sometimes surf here in the winter, but water conditions can be dangerous, and this beach has had a number of fatalities over the years.

Army Beach to Kaena Point

From Army Beach, you can drive another 1½ miles south, passing still more white-sand beaches and aquamarine water. You'll usually find someone fishing, and occasionally you'll see a few local people camping.

The paved road goes past Camp Erdman, a facility run by the YMCA, and then ends at a locked gate. The terrain is scrubland,

reaching up to the base of the Waianae Range, and the shoreline is wild and windswept. The area is not only desolate, but can also be a bit littered, and this is certainly not a must-do drive.

From the road's end, it's possible to walk 2½ miles to Kaena Point, but it's a more attractive walk from the other side of the point (for details, see Kaena Point State Park in the Waianae Coast chapter).

HALEIWA

Haleiwa is the gateway to the North Shore, and the town caters to the multitude of day-trippers who make the circle-island ride (see the boxed text 'Circle-Island Route' in the Getting Around chapter).

The 2500 townspeople are a mix of multi-ethnic families who have lived in Haleiwa for generations and more recently arrived surfers, artists and New Age folks.

Most of Haleiwa's shops are on Kamehameha Ave, the main drag through town, and the town has a picturesque boat harbor that is bordered on both sides by beach parks. The south side is known for its winter surfing, and the north side is known for the North Shore's safest year-round swimming conditions.

The Anahulu River flows into the boat harbor and is spanned by the Rainbow Bridge, so nicknamed because of its distinctively curved arches. From the bridge, take a glimpse up the river. It's still a lush green scene, and it's easy to imagine how this area must have looked in ancient Hawaii, when the riverbanks were lined with taro patches.

Information

There's a Bank of Hawaii in the Haleiwa Shopping Plaza and a First Hawaiian Bank farther north on Kamehameha Ave. Both are open 8:30 am to 4 pm Monday to Thursday and 8:30 am to 6 pm on Friday.

The Haleiwa post office, on Kamehameha Ave, at the south side of town, is open 8 am to 4 pm on weekdays and 9 am to noon on Saturday.

Surf-N-Sea (☎ 637-9887), 62-595 Kamehameha Ave, north of the Rainbow Bridge, rents surfboards, boogie boards, windsurfing

House of the Frigate Bird

In the summer of 1832, John and Ursula Emerson, the first missionaries to the North Shore, built a grass house and a missionary school beside the Anahulu River. They called the school Haleiwa, meaning house (hale) of the great frigate bird (iwa). Over time, the name came to refer to the entire village.

❀❀❀❀❀❀❀❀❀❀❀❀❀

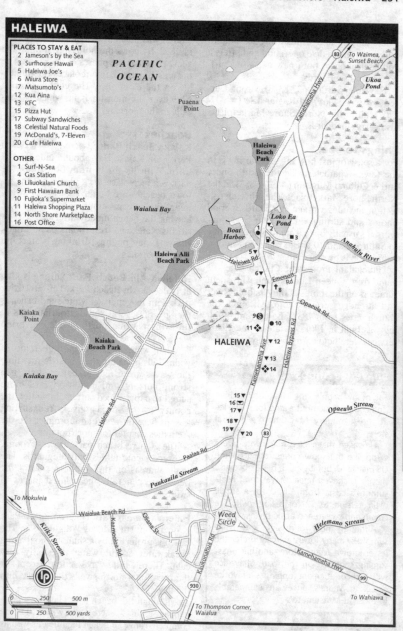

HALEIWA

PLACES TO STAY & EAT
2   Jameson's by the Sea
3   Surfhouse Hawaii
5   Haleiwa Joe's
6   Miura Store
7   Matsumoto's
12 Kua Aina
13 KFC
15 Pizza Hut
17 Subway Sandwiches
18 Celestial Natural Foods
19 McDonald's, 7-Eleven
20 Cafe Haleiwa

OTHER
1   Surf-N-Sea
4   Gas Station
8   Liliuokalani Church
9   First Hawaiian Bank
10 Fujioka's Supermarket
11 Haleiwa Shopping Plaza
14 North Shore Marketplace
16 Post Office

PACIFIC OCEAN

To Waimea, Sunset Beach

Ukoa Pond

Kamehameha Hwy

Puaena Point

Haleiwa Beach Park

Loko Ea Pond

Anahulu River

Waialua Bay

Boat Harbor

Haleiwa Rd

Emerson Rd

Opaeula Rd

Haleiwa Alii Beach Park

Kaiaka Point

HALEIWA

Haleiwa Bypass Rd

Kamehameha Ave

Kaiaka Beach Park

Kaiaka Bay

Opaeula Stream

Haleiwa Rd

Paalaa Rd

Paukauila Stream

To Mokuleia

Kiikii Stream

Waialua Beach Rd

Ohana St

Kaukonahua Rd

Weed Circle

Helemano Stream

Kamehameha Hwy

To Wahiawa

930

To Thompson Corner, Waialua

99

0   250   500 m
0   250   500 yards

NORTH SHORE

equipment, diving gear and snorkel sets and offers surfing and windsurfing lessons. In addition, it has a dive operation and offers a good selection of both new and used surfboards and sailboards.

Hawaiian Surf (☎ 637-8316), Strong Current (☎ 637-3406) and Raging Isle (☎ 637-7707), all in the North Shore Marketplace, also carry surfboards.

Things to See

For a sense of just how integral surfing is to the town's character, visit the **North Shore Surf & Cultural Museum** (☎ 637-8888), in the North Shore Marketplace. The museum collection includes vintage surfboards, period photos and surfing videos. Run by volunteers, it's usually open 9 am to 6 pm Monday to Saturday and 10 am to 6 pm on Sunday. Admission is by donation.

Liliuokalani Protestant Church takes its name from Queen Liliuokalani, who spent summers on the shores of the Anahulu River and attended services here. Although the church dates from 1832, the current building was built in 1961. As late as the 1940s, services were held entirely in Hawaiian.

The unusual seven-dial clock inside the church was donated by Queen Liliuokalani in 1892. It shows the hour, day, month and year, as well as the phases of the moon. The queen's 12-letter name replaces the numerals on the clock face. The church is open whenever the minister is in, which is typically in the morning.

Beaches

Kaiaka Beach Park 53-acre Kaiaka Beach Park is on Kaiaka Bay, about a mile west of town. With its shady ironwood trees, the park is a nice place for a picnic, but the in-town beaches are better choices for swimming. Two streams empty into Kaiaka Bay, leaving the beach muddy after heavy rainstorms. Kaiaka has rest rooms, picnic tables, showers, pay phones, drinking water and seven campsites.

Haleiwa Alii Beach Park Surfing is king at Haleiwa Alii Beach Park. This attractive park with its generous white-sand beach is the site of several surfing tournaments in the winter, when north swells can bring waves as high as 20 feet.

When waves are less than 5 feet, lots of young kids bring out their boards. Any time the waves are 6 feet or better, there is a strong current and conditions are more suited to experienced surfers. In winter, the county (☎ 637-5051) gives free surfing lessons here on weekend mornings; see the Activities chapter for more details.

The 20-acre beach park has rest rooms, showers, picnic tables and lifeguards. The shallow areas on the southern side of the beach are generally the calmest places to swim.

Haleiwa Beach Park Haleiwa Beach Park is on the north side of Waialua Bay. The beach is protected by a shallow shoal and a breakwater, so the water is usually very calm. There's little wave action, except for the occasional north swells that ripple into the bay.

Although the beach isn't Haleiwa's most appealing, this 13-acre county park has the complete range of beach facilities, as well as

Shave Ice Shops

For many people, the circle-island drive isn't complete without a stop for shave ice at the legendary **Matsumoto's** general store.

Hawaiian shave ice is made with sweet syrup like the snow cones found on the US mainland, but it's much better, because the ice is shaved finer. Shave ice at Matsumoto's costs from $1.20 for a small, plain version to $2 for a large with ice cream and sweetened azuki beans.

Although most tourists flock to Matsumoto's, many locals actually prefer the lesser-known **Miura Store**, another unassuming spot just up the road. Shave ice with a coconut cream topping is a favorite choice at Miura's; prices are comparable to those at Matsumoto's.

basketball and volleyball courts, an exercise area and a softball field. It also offers a good view of Kaena Point.

Places to Stay

Surfhouse Hawaii (☎ 637-7146, surfhouse@ aol.com, 62-203 Lokoea Place, Haleiwa, HI 96712) is a budget place on the north side of Haleiwa. Situated on 2 acres behind Lokoea Pond, Surfhouse Hawaii offers three accommodation options. There are a half dozen campsites, some with platforms, at a cost of $9 for one camper or $15 for two. The second option is a dormitory-style cabin with a lanai, kitchen and six beds for $15 per person. The third option, for $45, is a private room with a double bed and shared bath in the home of Lee and Sofie, the couple who run the place.

All guests have access to kitchen facilities. Bicycles and water-sports equipment are available for rent; if you don't have a tent, that can be arranged for a small fee as well. Sofie speaks French. The location, on a quiet side road immediately north of Rainbow Bridge, is within walking distance of both the beach and town center. Surfhouse Hawaii maintains a website at www.surfhouse.com.

The other option is camping at *Kaiaka Beach Park*, where the county allows camping (permit required) from Friday to Tuesday night. It is free. For details on obtaining a permit, see Camping in the Facts for the Visitor chapter.

In addition, rooms are occasionally for rent in private homes. Look for notices on the bulletin boards at the Coffee Gallery, Celestial Natural Foods and Haleiwa Super Market.

Places to Eat

Cafe Haleiwa (☎ 637-5516, 66-460 Kamehameha Ave), on the south side of town, is an unpretentious eatery that serves good, reasonably priced food. An institution of sorts on the North Shore, it has long been a haunt for local surfers and day-trippers. A large burrito with terrific home fries costs $6, and two large pancakes loaded with blueberries cost $3.50. Lunch is predominantly sandwiches and Mexican fare, aver-

aging $7 to $8. It's open 7 am to 2 pm daily, with breakfast available until 12:30 pm (2 pm on Sunday).

Celestial Natural Foods (☎ 637-6729, 66-443 Kamehameha Ave), opposite Cafe Haleiwa, sells bulk foods, granolas, fresh produce, yogurts and just about everything else you'd expect to find in a good health-food store. The store has a tiny cafe, open 10 am to 5 pm, that sells vegetable chili over brown rice for $3, sandwiches and salads for around $5 and a few Middle Eastern dishes for a tad more. The store is open 9 am to 6:30 pm Monday to Saturday and 10 am to 6 pm on Sunday.

The popular *Kua Aina* (☎ 637-6067, 66-214 Kamehameha Ave), in the center of town, prepares the North Shore's best burgers and fish sandwiches. Each costs about $5. It's open 11 am to 8 pm daily.

The *Coffee Gallery* (☎ 637-5571, 66-250 Kamehameha Ave), in the North Shore Marketplace, is a good alternative to the burger and plate-lunch scene. It has coffees, scones and bagels at reasonable prices. Breakfast fare, such as granola with yogurt and fruit, costs around $5, as do soups, sandwiches, quiche and salads. There's open-air seating at the side of the cafe; food can also be ordered for takeout. It's open 8 am to 8:30 pm daily.

Cholo's (☎ 637-3059, 66-250 Kamehameha Ave), in the North Shore Marketplace, has good Mexican fare, though finding a free table on a busy day can be a challenge. You can choose from a variety of combination plates for $7 to $10. A good choice, when it's available, is the fresh ahi taco for $3.50. Cholo's is open 8 am to 9 pm daily.

There's a more expensive Mexican restaurant, *Rosie's Cantina* (☎ 637-3538), as well as a pizza place, *Pizza Bob's* (☎ 637-5093), and a bakery, *Haleiwa Bake Shop*, in the Haleiwa Shopping Plaza.

For fast-food fare there are *McDonald's*, *Subway Sandwiches*, *Pizza Hut*, *KFC* and *7-Eleven*, all on the south side of town, on Kamehameha Ave.

The local favorite for a more upmarket meal is *Haleiwa Joe's* (☎ 637-8005, 66-001 Kamehameha Ave), which has a pleasant harbor-view setting at the north side of town. Dinners, priced $13 to $20, include tasty options such as herb-roasted chicken with garlic potatoes, blackened ahi with spicy soba noodles, or tempura coconut shrimp with rice. You can add a green salad for $1.50. Appetizers include tempting ahi spring rolls, sushi or sashimi for $5 to $10. Dinner is served from 5:30 pm nightly. Lunch, available 11:30 am to 4:30 pm daily, includes burgers, fish sandwiches and salads in the $6 to $10 range.

Jameson's by the Sea (☎ 637-4336, 62-540 *Kamehameha Ave*), north of the Rainbow Bridge, is a long-standing North Shore institution. It serves dinner 5 to 9 pm Wednesday to Sunday in its 2nd-floor dining room, which has views of the boat harbor. Seafood is the specialty, with entrees from around $20. You can also eat in a more casual pub setting downstairs from 11 am to about 5 pm daily, with sandwiches and salads in the $8 to $10 range.

Haleiwa has two main grocery stores: *Haleiwa Super Market*, in the Haleiwa Shopping Plaza, is open 8 am to 8 pm Monday to Saturday and 8:30 am to 5:30 pm on Sunday; across the street is *Fujioka's Supermarket*, which is open 8 am to 8 pm Monday to Saturday and to 5 pm on Sunday.

WAIMEA

Waimea Valley was once heavily settled. The lowlands were terraced for growing taro, the valley walls were dotted with houses, and the ridges were topped with *heiaus* (stone temples). Just about every crop grown in Hawaii thrived in this valley, including a rare pink taro that was favored by the *alii* (royalty).

Waimea River, now blocked at the beach by a sandbar, originally emptied into the bay. The river served as a passage for canoes traveling to villages upstream. Surfing was immensely popular here centuries ago, and the early Hawaiians rode Waimea's huge waves on their long boards.

In 1779, when Captain Cook's ships sailed into Waimea to collect water (shortly after Cook's death), an entry in the ship's log noted that the valley was uncommonly beau-

tiful and picturesque. However, contact with the West did nothing to preserve that beauty. Logging and the clearing of land to build plantations caused deforestation above the valley.

One of the consequences of the massive deforestation was a devastating flood in Waimea in 1894. In addition to water damage, an enormous volume of mud washed through the valley, so much so that it permanently altered the shape of Waimea's shore. After the flood, most of the area's residents abandoned the formerly beautiful valley and resettled elsewhere.

The church of **St Peter & Paul** stands beneath the tall, unassuming tower on the northern side of Waimea Bay. The structure was originally a rock-crushing plant that was built to supply gravel for the construction of the highway in the 1930s. After it was abandoned, the Catholic church converted it into Oahu's most unlikely chapel.

Puu O Mahuka Heiau State Monument

Puu O Mahuka is a long, low-walled platform temple perched on a bluff above Waimea, at an elevation of 300 feet. The largest heiau on Oahu, its stacked-stone construction is attributed to the legendary *mene-hunes* (magical 'little people'). Its name means 'hill of escape,' a bit ironic given that it was a luakini heiau where human sacrifices took place.

The terraced stone walls are a couple of feet high, although most of the heiau is now overgrown with plants. Collectively, the three adjoining enclosures that form the main body of the heiau are more than 550 feet in length. This was a dramatic site for a temple, and it's well worth the drive for the view, especially at sunset. The site, which is under the jurisdiction of the state park system, is a national historic landmark.

For a view of Waimea Valley and Waimea Bay, walk from the parking lot, along the left side of the heiau. To the west, you can see the coast all the way to Kaena Point.

To get to the heiau, turn up Pupukea Rd (at the Foodland supermarket). The marked turnoff to the heiau is about a half mile up

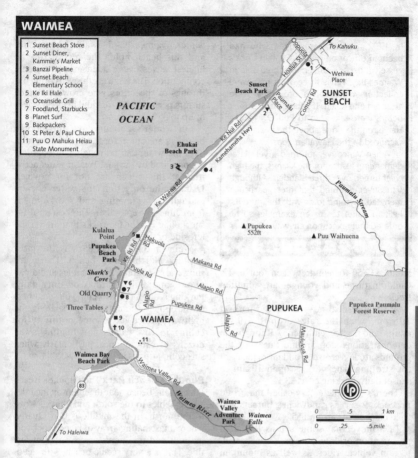

WAIMEA

1 Sunset Beach Store
2 Sunset Diner,
  Kammie's Market
3 Banzai Pipeline
4 Sunset Beach
  Elementary School
5 Ke Iki Hale
6 Oceanside Grill
7 Foodland, Starbucks
8 Planet Surf
9 Backpackers
10 St Peter & Paul Church
11 Puu O Mahuka Heiau
  State Monument

NORTH SHORE

the road, and from there it's three-quarters of a mile in to the site. On the drive up, there's a good view of Pupukea Beach Park.

Waimea Valley Adventure Park

Waimea Valley Adventure Park (☎ 638-8511), across from Waimea Bay Beach Park on Hwy 83, is a combination botanical garden and cultural theme park.

The main park road, which leads up the Waimea Valley to a waterfall, is flanked by extensive naturalized gardens that include sections of ginger, hibiscus, heliconia and medicinal plants (many of the plants have

identification labels, and there are several rare species under propagation).

The park has ancient stone platforms and terraces and some replicas of thatched buildings similar to those used by early Hawaiians. Traditional hula dances, Hawaiian games and other demonstrations are held during the day. In addition, several times a day, a cliff diver plunges 60 feet into the waterfall pool, thrilling spectators.

Although much of the valley's natural beauty is nicely preserved, and the park is pleasant to wander through, the cost of admission has climbed to a steep $25 for

Human Sacrifices

In 1792, Captain Vancouver, who had been an officer on one of Captain Cook's vessels a decade earlier, anchored ship in Waimea Bay. While three of his men were collecting water on shore, they were attacked and killed. It's thought that their bodies were taken up to Puu O Mahuka Heiau, on the ridge above the beach, and sacrificed to the Hawaiian gods.

When Vancouver returned a year later demanding justice for the killings, the high chief turned over three islanders. Although Vancouver doubted that these particular men had anything to do with the murders, he had come to set an example, so he ordered their execution anyway.

❀❀❀❀❀❀❀❀❀❀❀❀❀

adults, $12.50 for children aged four to 12. Children three and younger are admitted free.

A cheaper deal is to go to the park at 4:15 pm, when the rates drop to $10 for adults and $5 for children. Although the demonstrations stop around this time, the grounds are less crowded and more pleasant for strolling. The park is open 10 am to sunset daily. Parking costs $3.

There's a simple eatery called the Proud Peacock. It serves sandwiches, burgers and fried chicken for around $5.

In a move that some see as less than preservation-oriented, the park now has all-terrain vehicle rides, as well as mountain biking and horseback riding. Each activity costs $35.

Bus No 52 stops on the highway in front of the park, from where it's a half-mile walk to the entrance of the park.

Beaches

Waimea Bay Beach Park Waimea Bay is a beautiful, inset bay with turquoise waters and a wide white-sand beach that is almost 1500 feet long. Ancient Hawaiians believed its waters were sacred.

Waimea Bay's mood changes with the seasons: It can be tranquil and as flat as a lake in summer, then savage with incredible surf and the island's meanest rip currents in winter. Waimea has Hawaii's biggest surf, and this beach holds the record for the highest waves ever ridden in international competition. The huge north swells bring out throngs of spectators who crowd to watch surfers perform near-suicidal feats on waves of up to 35 feet.

On winter's calmer days, the boogie boarders are out in force, but even on calm days the water can be rough, and boarders get pounded by the surf. Winter water activities at this beach are not for novices. Usually, the only time the water is calm enough for swimming and snorkeling is from June to September. The best spot for snorkeling is near the rocks that are on the left side of the bay.

Waimea Bay Beach Park is the most popular North Shore beach. There are showers, rest rooms, picnic tables and a pay phone, and a lifeguard is on duty daily. Parking is often tight. Even if you see others do it, don't be tempted to park along the highway; police have some notoriety for calling in tow trucks and hauling away dozens of cars at once, particularly when surf competitions are taking place.

Pupukea Beach Park The Pupukea Beach Park, a long beach near the highway, includes Three Tables to the south and Shark's Cove to the north. In the middle is **Old Quarry**, where a fascinating array of jagged rock formations and tide pools are exposed at low tide. This is a very scenic beach, with deep-blue waters, a varied coastline and a mix of lava and white sand. The waters off Pupukea Beach are protected as a marine-life conservation district. The rocks and tide pools are tempting to explore, but be careful – they're razor sharp, and if you slip, it's easy to get a deep cut. Pupukea, incidentally, means 'white shell.'

There are showers and rest rooms in front of Old Quarry. The entrance to the beach is opposite an old gas station; bus No 52 stops out front. Snorkel sets and other water-sports equipment can be rented from Planet Surf, at the side of the Foodland supermarket.

Three Tables, at the southern end of the beach, gets its name from the ledges rising above the water. In summer when the waters are calm, Three Tables is a good place for snorkeling and diving. It's possible to see some action by snorkeling around the tables, but the best coral and fish, as well as some small caves, lava tubes and arches, are in deeper water farther out. It's a summer-only spot. In the winter dangerous rip currents flow between the beach and the tables. Beware of sharp rocks and coral in the water.

Shark's Cove is beautiful, both above and below the water's surface. The naming of the cove was done in jest – sharks aren't a particular problem. In the summer, when the seas are calm, Shark's Cove has good snorkeling and swimming conditions, as well as Oahu's most popular cavern dive. A fair number of beginning divers take lessons here, and the underwater caves will thrill advanced divers.

To get to the caves, swim out of the cove and around to the right. Some of the caves are very deep and labyrinthine, so exercise caution when exploring them. There have been a number of drownings in these caves.

The large boulders out on the end of the Kulalua Point, at the far right of the cove, are said to be followers of Pele, the Hawaiian volcano goddess. To acknowledge their loyalty, Pele gave her followers immortality by turning them to stone.

Ehukai Beach Park Even in old Hawaii, Ehukai was known for its powerful breaking surf – the name means 'sea spray.' The main reason people come to Ehukai Beach Park is to watch the pros surf the world-famous **Banzai Pipeline**. The Pipeline is a few hundred feet south of the park. It breaks over a shallow coral reef and can be a death-defying wave to ride. The Pipeline takes its name from the near-perfect tubes that are formed when huge westerly swells hit the shallow reef, exploding into a forward curl as they break.

At Ehukai Beach itself, many board riders and bodysurfers brave a hazardous current to ride the waves. Water conditions

Surf mania prevails on the North Shore.

mellow out in summer, when it's good for swimming, but even then there are occasionally strong currents. Some of the Triple Crown surfing events that take place in late November and early December are held at Ehukai Beach (others are held at nearby Sunset Beach).

The entrance to Ehukai Beach Park is opposite the Sunset Beach Elementary School. The beach has a lifeguard, rest rooms, showers and a pay phone. Because the beach is small, parking is limited; if you park on the highway, you risk getting towed.

Sunset Beach Park Sunset Beach Park, north of Ehukai Beach Park, is a pretty, white-sand beach that invites sunbathing, but the main action is in the water. This beach is Oahu's classic winter surf spot, with incredible waves and challenging breaks.

Because of the tremendous surf activity in winter, the slope of the beach becomes increasingly steeper as the season goes on. In the summer, as the sand washes back in, the shoreline begins to smooth out. Winter swells create powerful rips. Even when the waves have mellowed in the summer, there's still a current along the shore that swimmers have to deal with.

Despite Sunset Beach's legendary reputation, unless there's a surf meet going on, the site is surprisingly low-key. Toilets and a lifeguard tower are the only beach facilities.

NORTH SHORE

Backyards, the surf break off Sunset Point, at the northern end of the beach, draws many top windsurfers. There's a shallow reef and strong currents to contend with, but Backyards has the island's biggest waves for sailing.

Places to Stay

In addition to the places listed here, the bulletin board at Pupukea Foodland has roommates-wanted notices and the occasional vacation rental listing.

Backpackers (☎ 638-7838, fax 638-7515, backpackers@aloha.net, 59-788 Kamehameha Hwy, Haleiwa, HI 96712), opposite Three Tables, is pretty much a surfers' hangout. A durable place that's been in business for 20 years, it has a few different setups, most of them beach-house casual. The main house has four bunks to a room for $15 a bed; a three-story house behind it has simple double rooms for $50. Both houses have shared bathrooms and kitchens. Expect spartan decor and aging furniture, but if you just want a place to crash between waves, then it's an option that won't take a deep bite out of your wallet.

A small beachfront motel across the road has eight studios with TVs, kitchens and great views. Units on the bottom floor have dorm beds for $17, and private rooms on the top floor are $80 to $95.

The third property, a few hundred yards away on the inland side of the road, consists of nine cottages with either two or three bedrooms. Dorm beds are $15; an entire cottage, which sleeps six to eight people, costs $110 to $150. Around noon each day, Backpackers makes a run to the airport in Honolulu. The ride is free, and you can get dropped off in Waikiki as well. There is a website (backpackers-hawaii.com).

Debbie Rezents (☎/fax 638-9402, 58-335 Mamao Place, Haleiwa, HI 96712) rents a pleasant studio above her garage in a residential area near Sunset Beach. It has a deck with a peek of the ocean, two twin beds, TV, bathroom with tub and limited kitchen facilities that include a refrigerator, microwave and hot plate. The cost of the studio is a reasonable $50.

Thomsen's Bed & Breakfast (☎ 638-7947, fax 638-7694, 59-420 Kamehameha Hwy, Haleiwa, HI 96712), near Ehukai Beach Park, is one large studio unit above the garage of a private home. It has a king-size bed, queen-size sofa bed, bathroom, kitchen, private entrance, phone, TV and a lanai facing the mountains. It's a good value at $65, but despite the name, breakfast is not included in the rate. Smoking is not allowed on the premises. The house is up for sale, so things may change, but it's worth calling to inquire.

Ironwoods (☎ 293-2554, fax 293-2603, 57-531 Kamehameha Hwy, Kahuku, HI 96731), 2 miles north of Sunset Beach, is a studio in the beachside home of Ann and Richard McMann. The studio has a private entrance; a loft bedroom with one king-size bed (or two twin beds) – it's reached via a steep ladder staircase; and a downstairs sitting area with cable TV, a bathroom, a couch that can be converted into a single bed and a kitchenette equipped with a refrigerator, microwave, toaster, coffeemaker and hot plate. The cost is $65 a night with a simple breakfast, or $400 a week with no breakfast; there's a three-night minimum stay.

The unit is recommended for two people, but three can be squeezed in if it's a family situation. The road is nearby, so expect to hear the traffic noise, though it's usually drowned out by the sound of the waves lapping the shore. The beach is literally in the backyard, just footsteps from the house. Ann speaks a little German.

Ulu Wehi B&B (☎/fax 638-8161, 59-416 Alapio Rd, Haleiwa, HI 96712) is 1½ miles up the hill from Pupukea Beach Park. Tina Jensen and her French husband, Bernie Moriaz, an artist, operate a small nursery at their home and rent out a simple studio unit. The unit has both a double bed and a single bed, a TV (no cable, but there's a VCR and movie collection), a microwave, a refrigerator, a toaster and a coffeepot. The toilet and shower are in a rustic bathhouse in the rear garden. The cost is $85 for singles/doubles, plus $15 for a third person; there's a $10 nightly discount on weekly stays.

A breakfast of Kona coffee, tropical fruit and baked goods is included. The house has a lovely 75-foot lap pool in the backyard and a poolside barbecue that guests are free to use. Smoking is not allowed.

Another option is *Ke Iki Hale* (☎ 638-8229, 59-579 Ke Iki Rd, Haleiwa, HI 96712), where a dozen simple apartments front a beautiful white-sand beach just north of Pupukea Beach Park. Although the furnishings are worn and the amenities are basic (the units have kitchens, but no TV or phone), the location is a gem. The management is scheduled to change, so conditions may change as well. Rates are $132 for a one-bedroom unit and $174 for a small two-bedroom unit. There are also a couple of separate streetside units for $85.

North Shore Vacation Homes (☎ 638-7289, 800-678-5263, fax 638-8736, luckyc@ibm.net, c/o Marilyn Cole, 59-229C Ke Nui Rd, Haleiwa, HI 96712) consists of four pleasant beachside houses sharing a 1-acre lot that is between Sunset Beach and Turtle Bay. The cheapest unit, which has two bedrooms, one bath and a living room with a sofa bed, costs $130/150 in the low/high season (these rates cover four people).

The other three units have three bedrooms and two baths and cost $175 to $190 in the low season, $195 to $220 in the high season (these rates cover six people). Each house has a full kitchen, a ceiling fan, washer and dryer, cable TV, a phone and a spacious deck looking out over the ocean. There's typically a seven-night minimum stay, but shorter stays can sometimes be arranged. There is a website (www.teamrealestate.com).

Places to Eat

You can get burgers, sandwiches and $6 plate lunches at *Sunset Diner*, opposite Sunset Beach Park. It's open 9:30 am to 8 pm daily. Food supplies are available at *Kammie's Market*, next to Sunset Diner, or at *Sunset Beach Store*, just north of Sunset Beach.

However, the best grocery prices and selection on the North Shore are at the *Foodland* supermarket that is opposite Pupukea Beach Park. It also has a deli with good, inexpensive fried chicken. *Starbucks* coffee shop, inside Foodland, sells regular coffee for $1.25 and specialty coffees such as lattes for double that. Starbucks also has bagels, scones and brownies for under $2, but if you don't want to eat on the premises, you can find cheaper bakery items at Foodland itself. Both places open at 6 am daily. Starbucks closes at 8 pm and Foodland closes at 10:30 pm, except on weekends when both close an hour later.

The popular *Oceanside Grill*, a little white trailer that parks along the highway 100 yards north of Foodland, sells hamburgers, cheeseburgers or vegetarian Gardenburgers for around $4. There are a few tables where you can sit and eat, with a view of the beach across the road. It's open 11 am to about 5:30 pm daily.

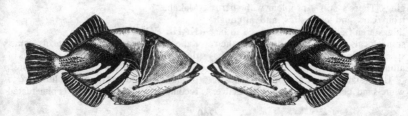

Waianae Coast

The Waianae Coast is the arid, leeward side of Oahu. In 1793, English captain George Vancouver was the first westerner to drop anchor here. He found a barren wasteland with only a few scattered fishing huts. Just two years later, Kamehameha the Great invaded the island, and the population density along the remote Waianae Coast swelled with Oahuans who were forced to flee from their homes elsewhere on the island. This isolated area of Oahu became their permanent refuge.

Today, leeward Oahu still stands separate from the rest of the island. There are no gift shops or sightseeing buses on the Waianae Coast. When you get right down to it, other than watching surfers at Makaha, there aren't a whole lot of sights to see. Although developers are beginning to grab Waianae farmland for golf courses, leeward Oahu remains the island's least-touristy side.

The area has a history of resisting development and a reputation for not being receptive to outsiders. In the past, visitors have been the targets of assaults and muggings. There's still a problem with thefts from cars and campsites, and although things aren't as hostile as they used to be, some locals aren't keen on sharing their space with tourists. Overall, you need to be attuned to the mood of the people.

The Waianae Coast has long stretches of white-sand beaches, some quite attractive, others a bit trashed. In winter, swimming conditions are treacherous at most beaches, but at the same time, these conditions offer some of the island's more challenging surfing opportunities. Although the towns themselves are ordinary, the cliffs and valleys cutting into the Waianae Range form a lovely backdrop.

Getting There & Away

This is basically a one-road region. All through traffic, both by car and bus, is along the Farrington Hwy (Hwy 93), the coastal road connecting Waianae's towns and beaches.

Bus Nos 51 and 51A connect Honolulu with the Waianae Coast, stopping in every town as far north as Makaha. If you're going to Makaha Beach Park, bus No 51 is the more direct option, because it stays along the coast. Bus No 51A goes up Makaha Valley Rd to the golf course and the Makaha Valley Towers condominiums and then comes down Kili Drive to the beach.

The two buses, which alternate throughout the day, run the same route before reaching the Makaha area. From the Ala Moana Center in Honolulu, buses run an average of every 30 minutes from 5:30 am (slightly later on weekends) to 7:30 pm, and then less frequently until 11:15 pm, except on Sunday, when they run until 9:15 pm. Travel time from Honolulu is about 1½ hours to Nanakuli and 1¾ hours to Maili. Bus travel to Makaha Beach from Honolulu takes about two hours on bus No 51 and 2¼ hours on bus 51A.

There is no public bus service beyond Makaha.

KAHE POINT

Kahe Point Beach Park, despite its name, does not have a beach, just the rocky cliffs of Kahe Point. The park has running water, picnic tables and rest rooms, but little else to recommend it. The backdrop is punctuated

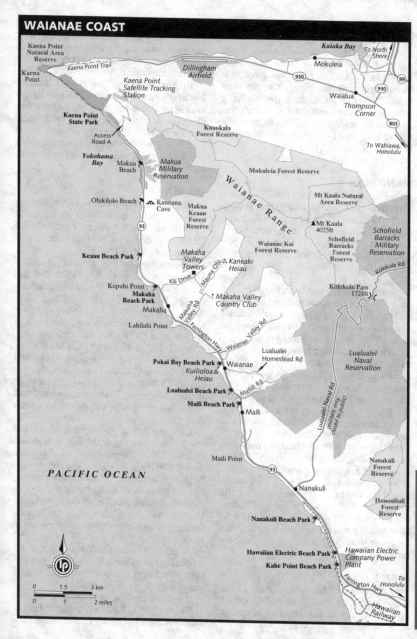

by the smokestacks of the electric power plant across the way.

Hawaiian Electric Beach, a sandy beach north of Kahe Point, is more commonly known as Tracks. The name was given to it by beachgoers who used to go there by train before WWII. In the summer this is a fairly calm place to swim, and in the winter it's frequented by surfers. To get there, take the first turnoff after the power plant and drive over the abandoned railroad tracks. There are rest rooms and a lifeguard station.

NANAKULI

Nanakuli, with a population of 9500, is the biggest town on the Waianae Coast. The site of a Hawaiian Homesteads settlement, Nanakuli has one of the largest native Hawaiian populations on Oahu. The town doesn't have much – just supermarkets, a courthouse, a bank and a few fast-food places.

Nanakuli is lined by a broad, sandy beach park. This area has swimming, snorkeling and diving during the calmer summer season. In winter, high surf can create rip currents and dangerous shore breaks.

To get to the beach park, turn left at the traffic lights on Nanakuli Ave. This is a community park, with a playground, sports fields, beach facilities and campsites. Camping is allowed 8 am Friday to 8 am Wednesday. See the Camping section in the Facts for the Visitor chapter for details. Note: Because of turf issues and an undercurrent of resentment that some residents have for outsiders, camping along the Waianae Coast is not recommended for nonresidents.

Nanakuli's eateries are along the Farrington Hwy. In the shopping center at the south side of town you will find *McDonald's*, *Nanakuli Chop Suey* and a *Sack 'n' Save* grocery store; there are a *KFC* and a *7-Eleven* store a bit north of the shopping center.

MAILI

Maili is fronted by **Maili Beach Park**, a long, grassy roadside park with an endless stretch of white-sand beach. Like other places on the Waianae Coast, the water conditions are

often treacherous in winter but usually calm enough for swimming in summer. The park has a lifeguard station, a playground, beach facilities and a few castrated coconut palms that provide limited, but safe, shade.

To the north of Maili Beach Park is **Lualualei Beach Park**. Its shoreline is less desirable than Maili Beach and not suitable for swimming; this park is mainly used by local fishers and campers. Camping is allowed 8 am Friday to 8 am Wednesday (summer only). See the Camping section in the Facts for the Visitor chapter for details.

WAIANAE

Waianae, with a population of 8800, is the second largest town on the leeward coast. It has a beach park, a protected boat harbor, a satellite city hall, a police station, supermarkets and lots of fast-food places.

Protected by both Kaneilio Point and a long breakwater, **Pokai Bay Beach Park** has the calmest year-round swimming conditions on the Waianae Coast. Waves seldom break inside the bay, and the sandy beach slopes gently into the water, making it a popular spot for families with children.

Snorkeling conditions by the breakwater are fair – fish gather around the rocks. The bay is also used by local canoe clubs, and you can watch them rowing if you happen by in the late afternoon. There are showers, rest rooms and picnic tables, and a lifeguard is on duty daily.

Kaneilio Point, which runs along the south side of the bay, is the site of **Kuilioloa Heiau**. Partially demolished by the army during WWII, the heiau (a stone temple) has been reconstructed by local conservationists. Because part of Kaneilio Point was destroyed, some sections of the reconstruction had to be modified from the heiau's original design in order to fit the smaller space.

To get to the beach park and heiau, at the traffic light immediately after the Waianae post office, turn makai (toward the ocean) onto Lualualei Homestead Rd.

If you are looking for something quick to eat, there are a *7-Eleven*, a *Pizza Hut*, a *Burger King*, a *McDonald's*, a *KFC* and a *Taco*

Bell along the Farrington Hwy. If you prefer cheap – but not chain – there are also a couple of inexpensive local *Chinese restaurants* in the Waianae Mall Shopping Center (it's behind the Burger King).

MAKAHA

Makaha means 'ferocious,' and in days past the valley was notorious for the bandits who waited along the cliffs to ambush passing travelers. Today, Makaha is best known for its world-class surfing. It also has a fine beach, a golf course, a few condominiums and Oahu's best-restored heiau.

Makaha Valley

For a little loop drive, from Farrington Hwy take Kili Drive, opposite Makaha Beach Park, toward the mountains. The road skirts up along scalloped green cliffs into Makaha Valley. If you're in the area around midday, stop to visit Kaneaki Heiau – one of Hawaii's most authentically restored heiaus.

To get to the heiau, take Kili Drive to the Makaha Valley Towers condominium complex and turn right onto Huipu Drive. A half mile down, make a left onto Mauna Olu St, which leads a mile into Mauna Olu Estates and Kaneaki Heiau.

To complete the loop, head back on Mauna Olu St. Go left at its intersection with Huipu Drive. When you reach Makaha Valley Rd, head to the right. This will take you back to Farrington Hwy and complete the loop.

Kaneaki Heiau The Kaneaki Heiau sits in the geographic center of Makaha Valley, midway between the valley's wet, forested uplands and its dry, coastal lowlands. Its construction dates to around 1545, and the heiau was originally a temple dedicated to Lono, the god of agriculture. As with many Hawaiian temples, over time it went through transformations in both its physical structure and its use. In its final phase it was rededicated as a *luakini* (war) temple, and it's thought that Kamehameha the Great used Kaneaki Heiau as a place of worship after he conquered Oahu. The heiau remained in use until his death in 1819.

Kamehameha worshiped at Kaneaki Heiau.

The social and religious upheaval introduced by Kamehameha's successors resulted in the abandonment of Kaneaki Heiau – and all the other Hawaiian temples as well. Although many of Hawaii's more accessible coastal heiaus were dismantled and their stones used to build cattle fences and other structures, Kaneaki Heiau, protected by its remoteness, survived largely intact.

Constructed of stacked basalt rocks, Kaneaki Heiau has two terraced platforms and six enclosed courtyards. Its restoration, undertaken by the Bishop Museum, was completed in 1970. The heiau was authentically reconstructed using ohia logs handhewn with adzes and thatch made from native pili grass gathered on the Big Island. The project added two prayer towers, a taboo house, a drum house, an altar and god images – items representative of those that would have been at the heiau.

For those interested in precontact Hawaiian culture, it's a special place; the immediate setting surrounding the heiau remains undisturbed, even though the site is in the midst of a residential estate.

An estimated 3000 wild peacocks live in the Makaha Valley, including about two dozen white ones. They can be spotted, or at least heard, throughout the upper valley, and if you visit the heiau, it's not unusual to see

HAWAII STATE ARCHIVES

WAIANAE COAST

them performing their courting rituals in the field adjacent to the parking lot.

The guard at the Mauna Olu Estates gatehouse usually lets visitors enter to see the heiau between the hours of 10 am and 2 pm Tuesday to Sunday. However, you might want to call the gatehouse (☎ 695-8174) in advance to inquire, as they can be a bit inconsistent in providing access. Also, you'll need to show your rental vehicle contract and driver's license, and there's typically no access if it's raining. There's no admission charge.

Makaha Beach Park

Makaha Beach is broad, sandy and crescent-shaped, with some of the most daunting winter surf in the islands. Experienced surfers and bodysurfers both hit the waves here.

Over the years Makaha Beach has hosted a number of major surf events. In the early 1950s it was the site of the Makaha International Surfing Championships – Hawaii's first international surfing competition. Although the biggest surfing events have since shifted to Oahu's North Shore, Makaha is still a site that is favored by longboarders, and in 1997 it hosted the World Longboard Championship.

When the surf's not up, Makaha is a popular beach for swimming (when the surf is up, rip currents and a strong shorebreak make swimming hazardous). In the summer the slope of the beach is relatively flat, but in winter it has a steeper drop due to the turbulent wave action. The beach sand is slightly coarse and of calcareous origin, with lots of mollusk shell fragments. As much as half of the sand temporarily washes away during winter erosion, but even then Makaha is still an impressive beach. The beach has showers and rest rooms, and lifeguards are on duty daily.

Snorkeling conditions here are good during the calmer summer months. Makaha Caves, out where the waves break offshore, feature underwater caverns, arches and tunnels that reach depths of 30 to 50 feet. It's a popular spot for diving on the leeward coast.

Places to Stay & Eat

Makaha doesn't have many accommodations for short-term visitors. There are a handful of condos geared primarily to permanent residents, but none are terribly appealing and they generally require you to stay for at least a week.

Makaha Surfside (☎ 695-9574 or 524-3455, riess@aloha-cafe.com, 85-175 Farrington Hwy, Makaha, HI 96792) is a four-story cinder-block apartment complex a mile south of Makaha Beach. Although it's predominantly residential, some of the 450 units are rented out on a weekly basis. The cost is around $300 for a studio and $400 for a one-bedroom unit, both with a full kitchen. There's nothing special about this place, although it does have pools and barbecue grills.

Makaha Shores (☎ 696-8415, fax 696-1805, Hawaii Hatfield Realty, 85-833 Farrington Hwy, suite 201, Waianae, HI 96792) is a condo right on the northern end of Makaha Beach, with lanais overlooking the water. Studios cost $450 for one week, $650 for two weeks and $900 for a month, plus a $50 cleaning fee. There are also one-bedroom units for around 20% more. It can be tough to book accommodations in the high season, because many retired people winter here.

Hawaii Hatfield Realty also handles similarly priced units in *Makaha Valley Towers*, the high-rise complex that's tucked into the valley.

There aren't many places to eat in this area. *Makaha Valley Country Club*, overlooking the golf course at the east end of Makaha Valley Rd, is a popular lunch spot with a varied menu that includes items such as fried chicken and teriyaki beef for around $7 and sandwiches for about half that price. Lunch is served 10:30 am to 2 pm on weekdays and until 3 pm on weekends. From 7 am (6 am on weekends) until 10:30 am there are pancakes, omelettes and similar breakfast fare at reasonable prices.

For something on the run, the *7-Eleven* store on the corner of Farrington Hwy and Makaha Valley Rd sells inexpensive doughnuts, turnovers and simple fast-food items.

The *Makaha Drive-In*, opposite the beach and about 150 yards north of the 7-Eleven, serves $5 plate lunches and burgers, chili and sandwiches for around $2. There are no places to eat north of Makaha.

NORTH OF MAKAHA

Keaau Beach Park is a long, open, grassy strip that borders a rocky shore. It has campsites, showers, drinking water, picnic tables and rest rooms. A sandy beach begins at the very northern end of the park, although a rough reef, sharp drop and high seasonal surf make swimming uninviting.

Camping is allowed from 8 am Friday to 8 am Wednesday. See the Camping section in the Facts for the Visitor chapter for details.

Driving north along the coast you'll see lava cliffs, white-sand beaches and patches of kiawe (a relative of the mesquite tree). On the inland side you'll get a glimpse into a run of little valleys.

Kaneana Cave, a massive cave on the right-hand side of the road, about 2 miles north of Keaau Beach Park, was once underwater. Its impressive size is the result of wave action that wore away loose rock around an earthquake crack. Over the millennia, the cavern expanded as the ocean slowly receded. It's a somewhat uncanny place – often strong gusts of wind blow near the cave, while just down the road it's windless.

Hawaiian kahunas (priests or sorcerers) once performed rituals inside the cave's inner chamber. Older Hawaiians consider it a sacred place and won't enter the cave for fear that it's haunted by the spirits of deceased chiefs. From the collection of broken beer bottles and graffiti inside, it's obvious not everyone shares their sentiments.

From **Ohikilolo Beach,** which is below the cave, you can see Kaena Point to the north. Ohikilolo Beach is sometimes called Barking Sands, because the sand is said to make a woofing sound when it's very dry and someone walks on it.

Scenic **Makua Valley** is open, wide and grassy, backed by a fan of sharply fluted mountains. It serves as the ammunition field of the Makua Military Reservation. The makai road, opposite the south end of the

Nanaue the Shark Man

Hawaiian legend tells of a child named Nanaue who was born with an open space between his shoulders. Unbeknownst to Nanaue's mother, the father of the child was the king of sharks, and he had taken on the guise of a man to woo her. Nanaue was born half human, half shark. He was human on land, but when he entered the ocean, the open space on his back became a shark's mouth. After a nasty spell in which many villagers were ripped to shreds by a mysterious shark, Nanaue's secret was discovered, and he was forced to swim from island to island as he was hunted down. For a while he lived near Makua and took his victims into Kaneana Cave via an underwater tunnel.

✿✿✿✿✿✿✿✿✿✿✿✿

reservation, leads to a little graveyard that is shaded by yellow-flowered be-still trees. This solitary site is all that remains of the Makua Valley community that was forced to evacuate during WWII when the US military took over the entire valley to use for bombing practice. War games still take place in the valley, which is fenced off with barbed wire and signs that warn of stray explosives.

Over the years, numerous protests have been held at Makua, demanding the return of the valley to native Hawaiians. The Earthjustice Legal Defense Fund has taken up the cause and filed a lawsuit requesting that an environmental impact statement be undertaken to examine the consequences of military activities in the valley.

Makua Beach, the white-sand beach opposite the military reservation, was a canoe landing in days past. A movie set was built on the beach for the 1966 movie *Hawaii,* based on James Michener's classic novel, but no trace of the set remains.

Immediately before the gate to Kaena Point State Park, a road leads up to **Kaena Point Satellite Tracking Station,** which is operated by the US Air Force. The tracking station's antennae and domes sit atop the mountains above the point, where they resemble giant white golf balls.

There are hiking trails above the tracking station, including a 2½-mile ridge trail that leads to Mokuleia Forest Reserve. To get past the air force's guard station, you will need to obtain a hiking permit in advance from the Division of Forestry & Wildlife (call ☎ 587-0166).

Kaena Point State Park

Kaena Point State Park is an undeveloped 853-acre coastal strip that runs along both sides of Kaena Point – the westernmost point of Oahu. Until the mid-1940s, the Oahu Railway had a route that brought passengers up the Waianae Coast. The attractive, mile-long sandy beach on the south side of the point is Yokohama Bay, named for the large numbers of Japanese fishers who came here by train during that time.

Winter commonly brings huge, pounding waves, making Yokohama a popular spot for surfing and bodysurfing. It is, however, best left to the experts, because of the submerged rocks, strong rip currents and dangerous shorebreak. Swimming is pretty much limited to the summer, and then only during calm conditions. When the water's flat, it's possible to snorkel; the best spot with the easiest access is at the south side of the park. Rest rooms, showers and a lifeguard station are also at the south end of the park.

In addition to being a state park, Kaena Point is designated as a natural area reserve because of its unique ecosystem. The extensive dry, windswept coastal dunes that rise above the point are the habitat of many rare native plants. The endangered Kaena akoko growing on the talus slopes is found nowhere else. In the winter you can identify it by its pale green leaves, but it drops all of its leaves in the summer.

Some common plants also grow here, including the beach naupaka, a native shrub with white flowers that look like they've been torn in half; pau-o-hiiaka, a vine with blue flowers; and beach morning glory, sometimes found entwined with the ka-unaoa, a parasitic vine that looks like orange fishing line.

Seabirds that are common to Kaena Point include shearwaters, boobies and the common noddy – a dark-brown bird with a grayish crown. In addition to birds, there are often schools of spinner dolphins off the beach, and in winter humpback whale sightings are not unusual.

Dirt bikes and 4WD vehicles once created a great deal of disturbance in the dunes, but since Kaena Point became a natural area reserve in 1983, vehicles are restricted and the situation has improved. The reserve is once again a nesting site for the Laysan albatross, and Hawaiian monk seals occasionally bask in the sun here.

Kaena Point Trail A 2½-mile (one way) coastal trail that utilizes an old railroad bed runs from the end of the paved road at Yokohama Bay to Kaena Point. This easy-to-follow hike offers fine views the entire way, with the ocean on one side and the lofty cliffs of the Waianae Range on the other. Along the trail there are tide pools, sea

---

Kaena Point Legends

Early Hawaiians believed that when people went into a deep sleep or lost consciousness, their souls would wander. Souls that wandered too far were drawn west to Kaena Point. If they were lucky, they were met there by their *aumakua* (ancestral spirit helper), who led their soul back to their body. If unattended, their soul would be forced to leap from Kaena Point into the endless night, never to return.

On clear days, the island of Kauai is visible from Kaena Point. According to legend, it was from this point that the demigod Maui attempted to cast a huge hook into Kauai. He wanted to pull it next to Oahu and join the two islands. But the line broke and Kauai slipped away, with just a small piece of it remaining near Oahu. Today, this splintered rock, off the end of Kaena Point, is known as Pohaku O Kauai.

❀❀❀❀❀❀❀❀❀❀❀❀❀

arches and a couple of lazy blowholes that occasionally come to life on high-surf days.

The hike typically takes three to four hours roundtrip. The trail is exposed and lacks shade (Kaena means 'the heat'), so take plenty of water. Be cautious near the shoreline, because there are strong currents, and the waves sometimes reach extreme heights. In fact, winter waves at Kaena Point are the highest in all of Hawaii, sometimes towering in excess of 50 feet.

Don't leave anything valuable in your car. Telltale mounds of shattered windshield glass litter the road's-end parking area used by most hikers. Parking closer to the beach rest rooms or leaving your doors unlocked can decrease the odds of having your car windows smashed.

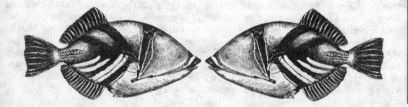

Ewa Area

Highlights

- Learning about Oahu's multiethnic society at Hawaii's Plantation Village
- Enjoying a day of sun, sea and sand at the lagoons of Ko Olina Resort
- Taking a journey back in time on the Hawaiian Railway Society's OR&L line

The southwestern side of Oahu is an area in transition. It encompasses some curious extremes – Waipahu, a former plantation town with a foot in the past, and Kapolei, a new boomtown that's the state's fastest growing community. It is also home to the former Barbers Point Naval Air Station, a 3700-acre military base that was demilitarized in 1999. The base is in the early stages of being converted to civilian use.

In Waipahu, the Hawaii's Plantation Village complex preserves important remnants of the sugar plantation era. Ewa, the village southwest of Waipahu, also has its roots in sugar, and its main attraction – the restored OR&L rail line – takes visitors back in time with antique trains.

The area's other attractions are designed around water – the splashy thrills of the new Hawaiian Waters Adventure Park and the manufactured lagoons at Ko Olina Resort.

The public beaches in this area are mostly used by local residents and military personnel. The best of the lot is Ewa Beach, a decent span of white sand, of which 5 acres is a county beach park, with much of the rest set aside for the military. Oneula Beach and Nimitz Beach are predominantly rocky, with marginal swimming conditions, and Barbers Point Beach, just south of the industrial park, is outright unappealing.

HAWAII'S PLANTATION VILLAGE

Making a visit to Hawaii's Plantation Village (☎ 677-0110), in Waipahu, will reward you with a glimpse of plantation life and a deeper understanding of the Hawaiian Islands' multiethnic heritage.

The 50-acre site is composed of 30 homes and buildings set up to re-create a typical plantation village of the early 20th century. The houses are furnished with period pieces illustrating the lifestyles of the eight different ethnic groups (Hawaiian, Japanese, Okinawan, Chinese, Korean, Portuguese, Puerto Rican and Filipino) that worked Hawaii's sugar plantations. The Chinese cookhouse (circa 1909) was originally on this site, and the Japanese shrine (1914) was moved here; the other structures were built to authentically replicate the architecture of the time and place.

The setting is particularly evocative, because Waipahu was one of Oahu's last plantation towns, and its sugar mill, which operated until 1995, still looms on a knoll directly above the village. There's also a small museum detailing the lives and cultural backgrounds of plantation workers. Artifacts on display include a Japanese *ofuro* bath, a Korean flute, straw slippers and various tools for working on a sugar plantation. All in all, it's a nice, community-based production.

Guided tours of the village begin on the hour between 9 am and 3 pm. It's open 9 am to 4 pm Monday to Saturday. Admission costs $5 for adults, $4 for seniors and children aged five to 17.

To get to Hawaii's Plantation Village by car, head west on the H-1 Fwy, take exit 7, turn left at the end of the off-ramp onto Paiwa St, then turn right onto Waipahu St, drive past the sugar mill and turn left into the complex. The distance from H-1 is about 1⅓ miles. If you are taking public transportation, bus No 47 runs between Waikiki and Waipahu every 30 minutes from 6 am until 6:30 pm, and then once an hour until 11:30 pm. The bus takes about 1¾ hours. Ask the driver to let you off at Waipahu Cultural Garden Park.

EWA AREA

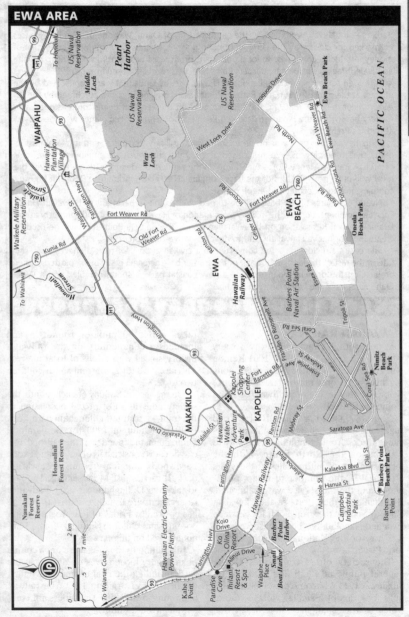

Life after the Navy

Barbers Point Naval Air Station, at the southwest tip of Oahu, was one of 97 military bases earmarked for closure by the US government in 1993. Military bases pump a good deal of money into local economies, so local politicians often resist base closings. However, despite ambivalent feelings in Hawaii, Barbers Point NAS was formally closed in July 1999.

Although some military installations in Hawaii occupy lands that were confiscated by the military at the start of WWII, the Barbers Point base is on land that was purchased by the US government in 1940. In 1941, the property was on the verge of being commissioned as a military base when the Japanese attacked Pearl Harbor. Three dozen planes were destroyed at Barbers Point that day.

In its heyday the base was home to some 5000 military personnel, and it had almost as many civilian employees. When it closed in 1999, its personnel and employees were relocated to Kaneohe Marine Corps Air Station on the windward side of the island. However, the navy will retain nearly a third of the base's original 3700 acres, including a 950-unit housing complex, a medical center and a golf course.

Nearly 600 acres of the base will be turned over to the Department of Hawaiian Home Lands as compensation for the military's occupation of Hawaiian Home Lands property at the Lualualei Naval Reservation on the Waianae Coast. The Barbers Point tract will be used to create jobs for native Hawaiians and to develop native-run businesses.

The base's airfields are being converted to a civilian airport for recreational planes. The fate of the rest of the land, about half of the former base acreage, is still being plotted. Other projects on the drawing board include a new coastal park, a sports complex and a West Oahu campus of the University of Hawaii.

HAWAIIAN RAILWAY

The nonprofit Hawaiian Railway Society (☎ 681-5461, fax 681-4860), 91-1001 Renton Rd, Ewa, offers narrated train rides along 6½ miles of restored railroad track that once belonged to the Oahu Railway & Land Company (OR&L).

From 1890 until 1947, the OR&L carried sugarcane and passengers along its narrow-gauge tracks, from Honolulu all the way to Kahuku on the North Shore. With the increasing use of automobiles in the years after WWII, the number of riders plummeted and the rail service was abandoned. But thanks to the efforts of the Hawaiian Railway Society, the stretch of track between Ewa and Nanakuli has been preserved, and it is now on the National Register of Historic Places.

The society offers train rides to the general public at 12:30 and 2:30 pm on Sunday. A 1944 Whitcomb diesel locomotive pulls four cars of a similar vintage, one of which is wheelchair accessible. Each ride takes about 90 minutes roundtrip and includes a commentary on the railway's history, spiced with tidbits of local interest. The fare is $8 for adults and $5 for children two to 12.

On the second Sunday of each month, the society adds its most prized possession to the train – a restored Dillingham parlor car. Built on Oahu in 1900 for Benjamin F Dillingham, the founder of the railroad, this classic car is constructed of native and exotic hardwoods and features an observation deck. It carries just 14 passengers. The fare to take the Dillingham car is $15; advance reservations are usually essential (if no one has booked by Friday of that week, it won't go out); and children younger than 13 are not allowed on this car.

In addition to the ride, there are a couple of stationary locomotives on display in the yard, including the coal engine that pulled the first OR&L train in 1889. The railway maintains a website (members.aol.com/hawaiianrr/index.html).

To get to the Hawaiian Railway, take exit 5A off the H-1 Fwy, drive south 2½ miles on Fort Weaver Rd and then turn right at the 7-Eleven store onto Renton Rd. The railway is 1½ miles down, on the south side of the road.

You can get there on bus No 48. It departs from Alapai and Hotel Sts in downtown Honolulu every hour from 7:35 am to 5:25 pm. The bus takes about 1¼ hours.

KAPOLEI

Kapolei is a new planned community that has been created to shift Oahu's future growth to the less-developed southwestern side of the island. Since first 'opening' in 1992, nearly $500 million has been invested in construction projects, ranging from state government offices to Hawaii's first water amusement park. It is envisioned that Kapolei will eventually grow into an urban center that will be second only to Honolulu, and indeed, it's already been dubbed 'the second city' by developers.

So far, 20,000 new homes have been built, ranging from million-dollar properties overlooking golf course greens to smaller houses geared to first-time home buyers. If all goes according to plan, Kapolei will triple in size over the next decade. A recent slowdown in sales, however, is beginning to put a damper on new building projects and the dizzying pace of the boom appears to be slowing down.

For visitors, Kapolei's main attractions are the waterpark and Ko Olina Resort, an upscale development at the western outskirts of the city.

Hawaiian Waters Adventure Park

Hawaiian Waters Adventure Park (☎ 945-3928), off the Farrington Hwy in Kapolei, is a $14 million waterpark that claims to be one of the largest parks of its type in the world. Covering 29 acres, the park features water slides and a variety of other water activities, such as Hurricane Bay, a wave pool the size of a football field. It generates 3-foot waves geared for bodysurfing. There's also Kapolei Kooler, a relaxing inner-tube cruise down a 800-foot continuous river.

Other attractions include Cliffhanger, a seven-story speed slide; Waterworld, the 20,000-sq-foot multilevel, multiactivity pool; Keiki Kove, with water slides designed especially for young children; a teen activity pool with rope ladders; and an adults-only swimming pool that features a swim-up bar.

The park is open 10:30 am to 6 pm daily. Admission, which includes unlimited access to all attractions, costs $30 for adults and $20 for children aged 3 to 11. Visit the website for a preview (www.hawaiianwaters.com).

Ko Olina Resort

In the late 1980s, a coastal tract at the southwestern end of the island was earmarked to become Hawaii's newest resort development. Named Ko Olina, it was to be Oahu's rival to the Kaanapali and Wailea resorts on Maui. The area lacked good beaches, but the state allowed the resort to carve out little protected swimming coves and haul in tons of white sand.

The grand design for Ko Olina Resort envisioned eight resort hotels and thousands of condominium units fronting four artificial lagoons. Now, more than a decade later, only one hotel (Ihilani Resort & Spa), a golf course and a small condominium project are completed. The original financing for the project dried up in the wake of Japan's banking crisis, but the undeveloped acreage has passed to new owners. The development plan is now focused on building upmarket housing and a 350-slip marina for yachts.

The four artificial lagoons at Ko Olina Resort have attractive, white-sand beaches that are open to the public. The largest lagoon, more than 200m across, borders the Ihilani Resort & Spa; the other three are about half that size. The lagoons are constructed with small islets at their mouths, a design that creates channels for water circulation; sometimes there is a strong seaward current going out through the middle channels. Signs posted at each lagoon detail water safety issues.

If you're up for a walk, a shoreline path connects the four lagoons. Each lagoon has rest rooms and parking spaces for about 20 cars.

Places to Stay & Eat

Ihilani Resort & Spa (☎ 679-0079, 800-626-4446, fax 679-0080, 92-1001 Olani St, Kapolei, HI 96707) is a modern luxury resort hotel with extensive spa facilities. The 387 rooms are equipped with private lanais, deep soaking tubs, thermostatic air-con, large-screen TVs, minibars, room safes and extra touches such as Japanese-style *yukata* robes and slippers. The grounds include six Kramer-surfaced tennis courts and a championship golf course that has hosted PGA tournaments. The resort's spa specializes in Thalasso therapy, which utilizes warmed seawater, and it offers other hydrotherapy such as Vichy showers and Roman pools.

Rates are $295 for garden-view rooms and $440 for oceanfront rooms; packages that include spa treatments and golf are available. Visit the resort's website for a preview (www.ihilani.com).

The Ihilani Resort & Spa has five eateries. At the low end, there's *Naupaka (☎ 679-0079)*, a poolside grill that is open 6 am to 10 pm daily. It serves lunchtime burgers and sandwiches for $10 and salads and hot dishes for around $15. There's also *Niblick (☎ 676-6703)*, which overlooks the golf course and serves similar fare at similar prices. It's open 8:30 am to 7 pm daily. At the top end is *Azul (☎ 679-0079)*, an expensive, fine-dining dinner restaurant specializing in Mediterranean cuisine. It is open 6 to 9 pm Monday, Wednesday and Friday.

Outside the resort, the Kapolei Shopping Center, on the Farrington Hwy, has a bevy of fast-food establishments as well as a *Safeway* supermarket.

Getting There & Away

Kapolei is near the western terminus of the H-1 Fwy. To get to the Kapolei Shopping Center by car, take exit 2 off H-1; to get to Hawaiian Waters Adventure Park, take exit 1, which circles around to the park entrance. The road to Ko Olina Resort is off the south side of the Farrington Hwy.

Bus Nos 51 and 51A connect Honolulu with the Waianae Coast, and they make stops in Kapolei at both Hawaiian Waters Adventure Park and the shopping center. The bus ride to Kapolei takes about an hour from the Ala Moana Center in Honolulu. Buses run an average of every 30 minutes from 5:30 am (slightly later on weekends) to 7:30 pm, and then less frequently until at least 9:15 pm.

There's no bus to the Ko Olina Resort – the bus stops along the Farrington Hwy, and from there it's a mile walk to the nearest beach. It's a destination best suited for people with their own transportation.

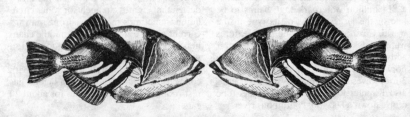

Glossary

ahi – yellowfin tuna

ahu – stone cairns used to mark a trail; or an altar or shrine

ahupuaa – traditional land division, usually in a wedge shape that extends from the mountains to the sea

aikane – friend

aina – land

akamai – clever

aku – skipjack tuna

akua – god, spirit, idol

akule – bigeye mackerel

alii – chief, royalty

aloha – the traditional greeting meaning love, welcome, good-bye

aloha aina – love of the land

amaama – mullet

amakihi – small, yellow-green bird; one of the more common native birds

ao – Newell's shearwater (a seabird)

apapane – red native Hawaiian honeycreeper

au – marlin

aumakua – ancestral spirit helper

auwe – Oh my! Alas!

awa – kava, made into an intoxicating brew; milkfish

awapuhi – wild ginger

bento – the Japanese word for a box lunch

cilantro – coriander leaves (also known as Chinese parsley)

crack seed – snack food, usually dried fruits or seeds; can be sour, salty or sweet

elepaio – a brownish native bird with a white rump, common to Oahu forests

gyoza – a grilled dumpling made of minced pork and garlic

hala – pandanus plant; the leaves are used in weaving mats and baskets

hale – house

hana – work; a bay, when used as a compound in place names

haole – Caucasian; literally 'without breath'

hapa – half; person of mixed blood

hau – indigenous lowland hibiscus tree whose wood is often used for outrigger canoes

haupia – coconut pudding

Hawaii nei – all the Hawaiian Islands taken as a group

heiau – ancient stone temple, a place of worship in Hawaii before contact with the West

Hina – Polynesian goddess (wife of Ku, one of the four main gods)

holoholo – to walk, drive or ramble around for pleasure

holoku – a long dress similar to the *muu-muu*, but more fitted

holua – sled, or sled course

honu – turtle

hoolaulea – celebration, party

huhu – angry

hui – group, organization

hukilau – fishing with a seine (a large net), involving a group of people; the word can also refer to the feast that follows

hula – traditional Hawaiian dance

hula halau – *hula* school or troupe

humuhumunukunukuapuaa – rectangular triggerfish

iiwi – a bright-red forest bird with a curved, salmon-colored beak

iliahi – Hawaiian sandalwood

iliili – stones

ilima – native plant, a ground cover with delicate yellow-orange flowers

imu – underground earthen oven used in traditional *luau* cooking

kahili – a feathered standard, used as a symbol of royalty

kahuna – wise person in any field, commonly a priest, healer or sorcerer

kahuna nui – high priest

kaiseki ryori – a formal Japanese meal consisting of a series of small dishes

kalua – traditional method of baking in an underground oven *(imu)*

kamaaina – native-born Hawaiian or a longtime resident; the literal meaning is 'child of the land'

Kanaloa – god of the underworld

kane – man; also the name of one of four main Hawaiian gods

kapu – taboo, part of strict ancient Hawaiian social system

kaunaoa – a thin, parasitic vine

kava – a mildly narcotic drink made from the *Piper methysticum*, a pepper shrub

keiki – child, children

kiawe – a relative of the mesquite tree introduced to Hawaii in the 1820s, now very common; its branches are covered with sharp thorns

kii – image, statue

ko – sugarcane

koa – native hardwood tree often used in woodworking of native crafts

kohola – whale

kokua – help, cooperation

kona – leeward, or a leeward wind

koolau – windward side

Ku – Polynesian god of many manifestations, including god of war, farming and fishing (husband of Hina)

kukui – candlenut tree; the official state tree, its oily nuts were once burned in lamps

kuleana – an individually held plot of land

kupuna – grandparent

kuula – fishing shrine

Laka – goddess of the hula

lanai – veranda

lauhala – leaves of the *hala* plant used in weaving

laulau – bundles of pork or beef with salted fish that are wrapped in leaves and steam cooked

lei – garland, usually of flowers, but also of leaves or shells

lilikoi – passion fruit

limu – seaweed

lio – horse

lolo – stupid, crazy

lomi – raw, diced salmon marinated with tomatoes and onions

lomilomi – massage

Lono – Polynesian god of harvest, agriculture, fertility and peace

loulu – native fan palms

luakini – a type of *heiau* (temple) dedicated to the war god Ku and used for human sacrifices

luau – traditional Hawaiian feast

mahalo – thank you

mahimahi – also called 'dolphin,' but actually a type of fish unrelated to the marine mammal

maile – native plant with twining habit and fragrant leaves; often used for *leis*

makaainana – commoners; literally 'people who tend the land'

makaha – a sluice gate, used to regulate the level of water in a fishpond

makahiki – ancient four-month-long winter-harvest festival dedicated to Lono, during which sports and celebrations replaced all warfare

makai – toward the sea

makaku – creative, artistic *mana*

malasada – a fried dough served warm, similar to a doughnut

malihini – newcomer, visitor

malo – loincloth

mana – spiritual power

manini – convict tang (a reef fish); also used to refer to something small or insignificant

mano – shark

mauka – toward the mountains; inland

mele – song, chant

menehune – 'little people' who, according to legend, built many of Hawaii's fishponds, *heiaus* and other stonework

milo – a native shade tree with beautiful hardwood

moo – water spirit, water lizard or dragon

mu – a 'body catcher' who secured sacrificial victims for the *heiau* altar

muumuu – a long, loose-fitting dress introduced by the missionaries

naupaka – a native shrub with delicate white flowers

Neighbor Islands – the term used to refer to the main Hawaiian Islands outside of Oahu

nene – a native goose; Hawaii's state bird

nisei – people of Japanese descent

noni – Indian mulberry; a small tree with yellow, warty, smelly fruit, used medicinally
nuku puu – a native honeycreeper with a bright-yellow underside

ohana – family, extended family
ohia lehua – native Hawaiian tree with tufted, feathery, pom-pom-like flowers
olo – surfboards used by Hawaiian royalty
onaga – red snapper
ono – delicious; also the name of the wahoo fish
opae – shrimp
opakapaka – pink snapper
opihi – edible limpet

pakalolo – marijuana; literally means 'crazy smoke'
pali – cliff
palila – native honeycreeper
pau – finished, no more
Pele – goddess of fire and volcanoes
pho – a Vietnamese soup of beef broth, noodles and fresh herbs
piko – navel, umbilical cord
pili – a bunchgrass, commonly used for thatching houses
pilikia – trouble
pipikaula – salted, dried beef that is broiled
poha – gooseberry
poi – a gooey paste made from taro roots; a staple of the Hawaiian diet
poke – chopped raw fish marinated in soy sauce, oil and chili pepper
Poliahu – goddess of snow
pua aloalo – a hibiscus flower
puka – any kind of hole or opening

pupu – snack food, hors d'oeuvres; shells
puu – hill, cinder cone
puuhonua – place of refuge

saimin – a Japanese noodle soup

tabi – Japanese reef-walking shoes
talk story – to strike up a conversation, make small talk
tapa – cloth made by pounding the bark of the paper mulberry tree, used for early Hawaiian clothing (*kapa* in Hawaiian)
taro – a plant with green heart-shaped leaves; cultivated in Hawaii for its edible rootstock, which is mashed to make *poi* (*kalo* in Hawaiian)
teishoku – Japanese word for fixed-plate meal
teppanyaki – Japanese style of cooking using an iron grill
ti – common native plant; its long shiny leaves are used for a variety of things, including wrapping food and making *hula* skirts (*ki* in Hawaiian)
tout – an irritating and persistent person who solicits customers
tutu – aunt, older woman

ukulele – a stringed musical instrument derived from the 'braginha,' which was introduced to Hawaii in the 1800s by Portuguese immigrants
ulu – breadfruit

wahine – woman
wana – sea urchin
wikiwiki – hurry, quick

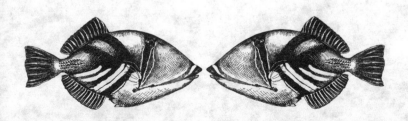

Toll-Free Numbers

Accommodations

Best Western	☎ 800-528-1234
Doubletree	☎ 800-367-6070
Hilton	☎ 800-445-8667
Holiday Inn	☎ 888-992-4545
Hyatt Regency	☎ 800-233-1234
Outrigger Hotels	
from the USA and Canada	☎ 800-688-7444
from Australia, Japan, Hong Kong, New Zealand and the UK	☎ 800-688-74443
from Germany	☎ 0800-181-8598
Sheraton	
from the USA and Canada	☎ 800-325-3535
from Australia	☎ 008-07-3535
from Japan	☎ 1-120-003535

Airlines

Air Canada	☎ 800-776-3000
Air New Zealand	☎ 800-262-1234
All Nippon Airlines	☎ 800-235-9262
Aloha Airlines	☎ 800-367-5250
America West Airlines	☎ 800-235-9292
American Airlines	☎ 800-433-7300
Canadian Airlines	☎ 800-426-7000
China Airlines	☎ 800-227-5118
Continental Airlines	☎ 800-525-0280
Delta Air Lines	☎ 800-221-1212
Garuda Indonesia	☎ 800-342-7832
Hawaiian Airlines	☎ 800-367-5320
Island Air	☎ 800-323-3345
Japan Airlines	☎ 800-525-3663
Korean Air	☎ 800-438-5000
Northwest Airlines	☎ 800-225-2525
Philippine Airlines	☎ 800-435-9725
Qantas Airways	☎ 800-227-4500
Singapore Airlines	☎ 800-742-3333
TWA	☎ 800-221-2000
United Airlines	☎ 800-241-6522

Car-Rental Agencies

Alamo	☎ 800-327-9633
Avis	☎ 800-831-8000
Budget	☎ 800-527-7000
Dollar	☎ 800-367-7006
Hertz	☎ 800-654-3131
National	☎ 800-227-7368

Cruise Lines

Holland America Cruise Line	☎ 800-426-0327
Norwegian Cruise Line	☎ 800-327-7030
Princess Cruises	☎ 800-568-3262
Royal Caribbean Cruise Line	☎ 800-327-6700

Money

American Express	☎ 800-528-4800
for lost traveler's checks	☎ 800-221-7282
Diners Club	☎ 800-234-6377
Discover	☎ 800-347-2683
MasterCard	☎ 800-826-2181
for lost traveler's checks	☎ 800-223-9920
Visa	☎ 800-336-8472
Western Union	☎ 800-325-6000

Acknowledgments

THANKS
Many thanks to the travelers who used previous editions of Lonely Planet's *Hawaii* and *Honolulu*, the titles on which this book is based, and wrote to us with helpful hints, useful advice and interesting anecdotes:

Robin Adlerblum, Nate Anderson, Connie Baker & John Sabo, Magdalena Balcerek, Rolf Ballmoos, Anna Banerji, Jane Battersby & Neil Griggs, Nano Beivi & Iris Dietisheim, Vincent Boisvert, Walter Bono, Monique Bonoo, Helan Bottrill, Dave Brown, Alexander Brucker, Mike Buckley, Anne Burgess, Andrea Caloini, Tess Camfield & Graham Rivers, Gayle M Campbell, Andrea & Edward Canapary, Katherine Carroll, Alessandra Cassar, Deivy Centeio, Sumeet Chhibber, Danielle Clode, Matt Collier, Marisa & Andrea Daniele, James Davis, Mark Davis, Juli Dent, Andre Desjardins, Sam & Osa Detrick, Ava Dolan, Mark Domroese, Kylie Duthie, John Dyer & Gavin Lock, Greg & Juli Edward, Andrew & Louise Edwards, Jesse Elliott, Padraig Eochaidh & Dawn Sentance, Justin Farley, Marietta Fedder, Pam Feinstein, Craig Foss & Matthew Staley, Dan Fowler, Sheila Freita, Phyllis Frey, Chirag Gandhi, Will Gardner, Annemone Goldschmied, Lori Gonder, Gerd Gopel, James Gordon, John Gropp, Nadine Guitton, Anja Hansen, W John Harker, TS Heaton, Jack & Linda Hibbard, Lori Higa, Chuck & Nancy Hooper, Lee Howard, Beverley Jennings, Stig Jepsen, Brian L Jester, Liz Jones, Lloyd Jones, Sarah Kettley, Min Kim, Olliemarie Kingston, Marge & Tom Kinney, John Kosowski & Kristen Rogers, Thomas Krahenmann, Ann Krumboltz, Dr Angela Kung, Larry Kwiatkowski, Frances Kwok, Hau Boon Lai, Kay Lamier & Charlie Stokes, Karen Latter, Rosemary & Randy Leach, Barbara Lohoff, Francine Marshall, Heather Martin & Forrest Roberts, Simon McHugh, E McRae, Anne Marie McTrowe, Joan & Bill Meikle, Russ Michaels, Ann Miya, Roz Morris, Frank Murillo, Trish & Bruce Murray, Chris Murray, Anna Mya, Anja Niewolik, Ken & Joyce Norris, Kevin P O'Connell, David & Sharyn Olive, Nort Petrovich, Karen White Pettigrew, Bill Pollington, Joel & Maria Teresa Prades, Tom Regan, K Rogers, Herwig Rombauts, Dan Sabath, Michael Schuette, Janna Scopel, Darren Scott, Terri Scott, Jacob Siboni, Andrew Sinclair, Christos Siopis, Teresa Sivilli, Catherine Smith, Dawn Smith, Michelle Smith, Sue Smith, Sandra Starke, Alexandra Stern, Kevan & Cindy Strube, Tim Sturge, Tammy Svoboda, Eleanor Swain, Giselle Sweet-Escott, Mike Tailor, Kathleen Thomas, Mike Tuggle, Judy Uhart, Anne Vaile, Erwin & Diana van Engelen, Maggie & Martin Varco, Amanda & Ian Vernalls, Jim R Walker, S Bruce Warthman, Catherine Watkins, Mary Wells, Dörte Wendlandt, Jodie Wesley, Arvis & Ken Willetts, Ann Wilson-Wilde, Milse Wolbe, Simon Wood, Hannah & Bart Wright, Erin Zoski.

LONELY PLANET

Phrasebooks

Lonely Planet phrasebooks are packed with essential words and phrases to help travellers communicate with the locals. With color tabs for quick reference, an extensive vocabulary and use of script, these handy pocket-sized language guides cover day-to-day travel situations.

- handy pocket-sized books
- easy to understand Pronunciation chapter
- clear & comprehensive Grammar chapter
- romanization alongside script to allow ease of pronunciation
- script throughout so users can point to phrases for every situation
- full of cultural information and tips for the traveller

'...vital for a real DIY spirit and attitude in language learning'
— *Backpacker*

'the phrasebooks have good cultural backgrounders and offer solid advice for challenging situations in remote locations'
— *San Francisco Examiner*

Arabic (Egyptian) • Arabic (Moroccan) • Australian *(Australian English, Aboriginal and Torres Strait languages)* • Baltic States *(Estonian, Latvian, Lithuanian)* • Bengali • Brazilian • Burmese • Cantonese • Central Asia • Central Europe *(Czech, French, German, Hungarian, Italian, Slovak)* • Eastern Europe *(Bulgarian, Czech, Hungarian, Polish, Romanian, Slovak)* • Ethiopian (Amharic) • Fijian • French • German • Greek • Hebrew • Hill Tribes • Hindi/Urdu • Indonesian • Italian • Japanese • Korean • Lao • Latin American Spanish • Malay • Mandarin • Mediterranean Europe *(Albanian, Croatian, Greek, Italian, Macedonian, Maltese, Serbian, Slovene)* • Mongolian • Nepali • Papua New Guinea • Pilipino (Tagalog) • Quechua • Russian • Scandinavian Europe *(Danish, Finnish, Icelandic, Norwegian, Swedish)* • South Pacific Languages • South-East Asia *(Burmese, Indonesian, Khmer, Lao, Malay, Tagalog Pilipino, Thai, Vietnamese)* • Spanish (Castilian) *(also includes Catalan, Galician and Basque)* • Sri Lanka • Swahili • Thai • Tibetan • Turkish • Ukrainian • USA *(US English, Vernacular, Native American languages, Hawaiian)* • Vietnamese • Western Europe *(Basque, Catalan, Dutch, French, German, Greek, Irish)*

LONELY PLANET

Lonely Planet Journeys

JOURNEYS is a unique collection of travel writing – published by the company that understands travel better than anyone else. It is a series for anyone who has ever experienced – or dreamed of – the magical moment when they encountered a strange culture or saw a place for the first time. They are tales to read while you're planning a trip, while you're on the road or while you're in an armchair in front of a fire.

These outstanding titles explore our planet through the eyes of a diverse group of international writers. JOURNEYS books catch the spirit of a place, illuminate a culture, recount a crazy adventure or introduce a fascinating way of life. They always entertain, and always enrich the experience of travel.

FULL CIRCLE
A South American Journey
Luis Sepúlveda (translated by Chris Andrews)

'A journey without a fixed itinerary' with Chilean writer Luis Sepúlveda. Extravagant characters and extraordinary situations are memorably evoked: gauchos organising a tournament of lies, a scheming heiress on the lookout for a husband, a pilot with a corpse on board his plane … *Full Circle* brings us the distinctive voice of one of South America's most compelling writers.

WINNER 1996 Astrolabe – Etonnants Voyageurs award for the best work of travel literature published in France.

GREEN DREAMS
Travels in Central America
Stephen Benz

On the Amazon, in Costa Rica, Honduras and on the Mayan trail from Guatemala to Mexico, Stephen Benz describes his encounters with water, mud, insects and other wildlife – and not least with the ecotourists themselves. With witty insights into modern travel, *Green Dreams* discusses the paradox of cultural and 'green' tourism.

DRIVE THRU AMERICA
Sean Condon

If you've ever wanted to drive across the USA but couldn't find the time (or afford the gas), *Drive Thru America* is perfect for you. In his search for American myths and realities – along with comfort, cable TV and good, reasonably priced coffee – Sean Condon paints a hilarious road-portrait of the USA.

'entertaining and laugh-out-loud funny'– *Alex Wilber, Travel editor, Amazon.com*

SEAN & DAVID'S LONG DRIVE
Sean Condon

Sean and David are young townies who have rarely strayed beyond city limits. One day, for no good reason, they set out to discover their homeland, and what follows is a wildly entertaining adventure that covers half of Australia.

'a hilariously detailed log of two burned out friends' – *Rolling Stone*

Lonely Planet Travel Atlases

Lonely Planet has long been famous for the number and quality of its guidebook maps. Now we've gone one step further and produced a handy companion series: Lonely Planet travel atlases – maps of a country produced in book form.

Unlike other maps, which look good but lead travellers astray, our travel atlases have been researched on the road by Lonely Planet's experienced team of writers. All details are carefully checked to ensure the atlas corresponds with the equivalent Lonely Planet guidebook.

- full-colour throughout
- maps researched and checked by Lonely Planet authors
- place names correspond with Lonely Planet guidebooks
- no confusing spelling differences
- legend and travelling information in English, French, German, Japanese and Spanish
- size: 230 x 160 mm

Available now: Chile & Easter Island • Egypt • India & Bangladesh • Israel & the Palestinian Territories • Jordan, Syria & Lebanon • Kenya • Laos • Portugal • South Africa, Lesotho & Swaziland • Thailand • Turkey • Vietnam • Zimbabwe, Botswana & Namibia

Lonely Planet TV Series & Videos

Lonely Planet travel guides have been brought to life on television screens around the world. Like our guides, the programs are based on the joy of independent travel, and look honestly at some of the most exciting, picturesque and frustrating places in the world. Each show is presented by one of three travellers from Australia, England or the USA and combines an innovative mixture of video, Super-8 film, atmospheric soundscapes and original music.

Videos of each episode – containing additional footage not shown on television – are available from good book and video shops, but the availability of individual videos varies with regional screening schedules.

Video destinations include: Alaska • American Rockies • Argentina • Australia – The South-East • Baja California & the Copper Canyon • Brazil • Central Asia • Chile & Easter Island • Corsica, Sicily & Sardinia – The Mediterranean Islands • Cuba • East Africa (Tanzania & Zanzibar) • Ecuador & the Galapagos Islands • Ethiopia • Greenland & Iceland • Hungary & Romania • Indonesia • Israel & the Sinai Desert • Jamaica • Japan • La Ruta Maya • The Middle East (Syria, Jordan & Lebanon) • Morocco • New York • North India • Northern Spain • Outback Australia • Pacific Islands (Fiji, Solomon Islands & Vanuatu) • Pakistan • Peru • The Philippines • South Africa & Lesotho • South India • South West China • South West USA • Trekking in Uganda • Turkey • Vietnam • West Africa • Zimbabwe, Botswana • Namibia

The Lonely Planet TV series is produced by: Pilot Productions
The Old Studio
18 Middle Row
London W10 5AT, UK

Lonely Planet On-line
www.lonelyplanet.com *or* AOL keyword: lp

Whether you've just begun planning your next trip, or you're chasing down specific info on currency regulations or visa requirements, check out Lonely Planet On-line for up-to-the minute travel information.

As well as mini guides to more than 250 destinations, you'll find maps, photos, travel news, health and visa updates, travel advisories, and discussion of the ecological and political issues you need to be aware of as you travel. You'll also find timely upgrades to popular guidebooks which you can print out and stick in the back of your book.

There's also an on-line travellers' forum where you can share your experience of life on the road, meet travel companions and ask other travellers for their recommendations and advice.

And of course we have a complete and up-to-date list of all Lonely Planet travel products including travel guides, diving and snorkeling guides, phrasebooks, city maps, travel atlases, travel literature and videos, and a simple on-line ordering facility if you can't find the book you want elsewhere.

Lonely Planet Diving & Snorkeling Guides

Beautifully illustrated with full-color photos throughout, Lonely Planet's **Pisces Books** explore the world's best diving and snorkeling areas and prepare divers for what to expect when they get there, both topside and underwater.

Dive sites are described in detail with specifics on depths, visibility, level of difficulty, special conditions, underwater photography tips, and common and unusual marine life present. You'll also find practical logistical information and coverage on topside activities and attractions, sections on diving health and safety, plus listings for diving services, live-aboards, dive resorts and tourist offices.

LONELY PLANET

Guides by Region

L onely Planet is known worldwide for publishing practical, reliable and no-nonsense travel information in our guides and on our Web site. The Lonely Planet list covers just about every accessible part of the world. Currently there are thirteen series: travel guides, shoestring guides, walking guides, city guides, phrasebooks, audio packs, city maps, travel atlases, diving and snorkeling guides, restaurant guides, first-time travel guides, healthy travel and travel literature.

AFRICA Africa – the South • Africa on a shoestring • Arabic (Egyptian) phrasebook • Arabic (Moroccan) phrasebook • Cairo • Cape Town • Cape Town city map • Central Africa • East Africa • Egypt • Egypt travel atlas • Ethiopian (Amharic) phrasebook • The Gambia & Senegal • Healthy Travel Africa • Kenya • Kenya travel atlas • Malawi, Mozambique & Zambia • Morocco • North Africa • South Africa, Lesotho & Swaziland • South Africa, Lesotho & Swaziland travel atlas • Swahili phrasebook • Tanzania, Zanzibar & Pemba • Trekking in East Africa • Tunisia • West Africa • Zimbabwe, Botswana & Namibia • Zimbabwe, Botswana & Namibia travel atlas
Travel Literature: The Rainbird: A Central African Journey • Songs to an African Sunset: A Zimbabwean Story • Mali Blues: Traveling to an African Beat

AUSTRALIA & THE PACIFIC Auckland • Australia • Australian phrasebook • Bushwalking in Australia • Bushwalking in Papua New Guinea • Fiji • Fijian phrasebook • Islands of Australia's Great Barrier Reef • Melbourne • Melbourne city map • Micronesia • New Caledonia • New South Wales & the ACT • New Zealand • Northern Territory • Outback Australia • Out To Eat – Melbourne • Papua New Guinea • Papua New Guinea (Pidgin) phrasebook • Queensland • Rarotonga & the Cook Islands • Samoa • Solomon Islands • South Australia • South Pacific Languages phrasebook • Sydney • Sydney city map • Tahiti & French Polynesia • Tasmania • Tonga • Tramping in New Zealand • Vanuatu • Victoria • Western Australia
Travel Literature: Islands in the Clouds • Kiwi Tracks • Sean & David's Long Drive

CENTRAL AMERICA & THE CARIBBEAN Bahamas and Turks & Caicos • Bermuda • Central America on a shoestring • Costa Rica • Cuba • Dominican Republic & Haiti • Eastern Caribbean • Guatemala, Belize & Yucatán: La Ruta Maya • Jamaica • Mexico • Mexico City • Panama • Puerto Rico
Travel Literature: Green Dreams: Travels in Central America

EUROPE Amsterdam • Amsterdam city map • Andalucía • Austria • Baltic States phrasebook • Barcelona • Berlin • Berlin city map • Britain • British phrasebook • Brussels, Bruges & Antwerp • Budapest city map • Canary Islands • Central Europe • Central Europe phrasebook • Corsica • Czech & Slovak Republics • Denmark • Dublin • Eastern Europe • Eastern Europe phrasebook • Edinburgh • Estonia, Latvia & Lithuania • Europe • Finland • France • French phrasebook • Germany • German phrasebook • Greece • Greek phrasebook • Hungary • Iceland, Greenland & the Faroe Islands • Ireland • Italian phrasebook • Italy • Lisbon • London • London city map • Mediterranean Europe • Mediterranean Europe phrasebook • Norway • Paris • Paris city map • Poland • Portugal • Portugal travel atlas • Prague • Prague city map • Provence & the Côte d'Azur • Romania & Moldova • Rome • Russia, Ukraine & Belarus • Russian phrasebook • Scandinavian & Baltic Europe • Scandinavian Europe phrasebook • Scotland • Slovenia • Spain • Spanish phrasebook • St Petersburg • Switzerland • Trekking in Spain • Ukrainian phrasebook • Vienna • Walking in Britain • Walking in Ireland • Walking in Italy • Walking in Switzerland • Western Europe • Western Europe phrasebook
Travel Literature: The Olive Grove: Travels in Greece

INDIAN SUBCONTINENT Bangladesh • Bengali phrasebook • Bhutan • Delhi • Goa • Hindi/Urdu phrasebook • India • India & Bangladesh travel atlas • Indian Himalaya • Karakoram Highway • Kerala • Mumbai • Nepal • Nepali phrasebook • Pakistan • Rajasthan • Read This First: Asia & India • South India • Sri Lanka • Sri Lanka phrasebook • Trekking in the Indian Himalaya • Trekking in the Karakoram & Hindukush • Trekking in the Nepal Himalaya
Travel Literature: In Rajasthan • Shopping for Buddhas

Mail Order

Lonely Planet products are distributed worldwide. They are also available by mail order from Lonely Planet, so if you have difficulty finding a title please write to us. North and South American residents should write to 150 Linden St, Oakland, CA 94607, USA; European and African residents should write to 10a Spring Place, London NW5 3BH, UK; and residents of other countries to PO Box 617, Hawthorn, Victoria 3122, Australia.

ISLANDS OF THE INDIAN OCEAN Madagascar & Comoros • Maldives • Mauritius, Réunion & Seychelles

MIDDLE EAST & CENTRAL ASIA Arab Gulf States • Central Asia • Central Asia phrasebook • Hebrew phrasebook • Iran • Israel & the Palestinian Territories • Israel & the Palestinian Territories travel atlas • Istanbul • Istanbul city map • Istanbul to Cairo • Jerusalem • Jerusalem city map • Jordan & Syria • Jordan, Syria & Lebanon travel atlas • Lebanon • Middle East on a shoestring • Syria • Turkey • Turkish phrasebook • Turkey travel atlas • Yemen
Travel Literature: The Gates of Damascus • Kingdom of the Film Stars: Journey into Jordan

NORTH AMERICA Alaska • Backpacking in Alaska • Baja California • California & Nevada • Canada • Chicago • Chicago city map • Deep South • Florida • Hawaii • Honolulu • Las Vegas • Los Angeles • Miami • New England • New Orleans • New York City • New York city map • New York, New Jersey & Pennsylvania • Pacific Northwest USA • Puerto Rico • Rocky Mountain States • San Francisco • San Francisco city map • Seattle • Southwest USA • Texas • USA • USA phrasebook • Vancouver • Washington, DC & the Capital Region • Washington, DC city map
Travel Literature: Drive Thru America

NORTH-EAST ASIA Beijing • Cantonese phrasebook • China • Hong Kong • Hong Kong city map • Hong Kong, Macau & Guangzhou • Japan • Japanese phrasebook • Japanese audio pack • Korea • Korean phrasebook • Kyoto • Mandarin phrasebook • Mongolia • Mongolian phrasebook • North-East Asia on a shoestring • Seoul • South-West China • Taiwan • Tibet • Tibetan phrasebook • Tokyo
Travel Literature: Lost Japan

SOUTH AMERICA Argentina, Uruguay & Paraguay • Bolivia • Brazil • Brazilian phrasebook • Buenos Aires • Chile & Easter Island • Chile & Easter Island travel atlas • Colombia • Ecuador & the Galapagos Islands • Latin American Spanish phrasebook • Peru • Quechua phrasebook • Rio de Janeiro • Rio de Janeiro city map • South America on a shoestring • Trekking in the Patagonian Andes • Venezuela
Travel Literature: Full Circle: A South American Journey

SOUTH-EAST ASIA Bali & Lombok • Bangkok • Bangkok city map • Burmese phrasebook • Cambodia • Hanoi • Healthy Travel Asia & India • Hill Tribes phrasebook • Ho Chi Minh City • Indonesia • Indonesia's Eastern Islands • Indonesian phrasebook • Indonesian audio pack • Jakarta • Java • Laos • Lao phrasebook • Laos travel atlas • Malay phrasebook • Malaysia, Singapore & Brunei • Myanmar (Burma) • Philippines • Pilipino (Tagalog) phrasebook • Singapore • South-East Asia on a shoestring • South-East Asia phrasebook • Thailand • Thailand's Islands & Beaches • Thailand travel atlas • Thai phrasebook • Thai audio pack • Vietnam • Vietnamese phrasebook • Vietnam travel atlas

ALSO AVAILABLE: Antarctica • The Arctic • Brief Encounters: Stories of Love, Sex & Travel • Chasing Rickshaws • Lonely Planet Unpacked • Not the Only Planet: Travel Stories from Science Fiction • Sacred India • Travel with Children • Traveller's Tales

FREE Lonely Planet Newsletters

We love hearing from you and think you'd like to hear from us.

Planet Talk

Our FREE quarterly printed newsletter is full of tips from travellers and anecdotes from Lonely Planet guidebook authors. Every issue is packed with up-to-date travel news and advice, and includes:

- a postcard from Lonely Planet co-founder Tony Wheeler
- a swag of mail from travellers
- a look at life on the road through the eyes of a Lonely Planet author
- topical health advice
- prizes for the best travel yarn
- news about forthcoming Lonely Planet events
- a complete list of Lonely Planet books and other titles

To join our mailing list, residents of the UK, Europe and Africa can email us at go@lonelyplanet.co.uk; residents of North and South America can email us at info@lonelyplanet.com; the rest of the world can email us at talk2us@lonelyplanet.com.au, or contact any Lonely Planet office.

Comet

Our FREE monthly email newsletter brings you all the latest travel news, features, interviews, competitions, destination ideas, travellers' tips & tales, Q&As, raging debates and related links. Find out what's new on the Lonely Planet Web site and which books are about to hit the shelves.

Subscribe from your desktop: www.lonelyplanet.com/comet

Index

Bold indicates maps.

Boxed Text

Bold indicates maps.

MAP LEGEND

BOUNDARIES

- International
- State
- County

HYDROGRAPHY

- Water
- Reef
- Coastline
- Beach
- River, Waterfall
- Swamp, Spring

ROUTES & TRANSPORT

- Freeway
- Toll Freeway
- Primary Road
- Secondary Road
- Tertiary Road
- Unpaved Road
- Pedestrian Mall
- Trail
- Walking Tour
- Ferry Route
- Railway, Train Station
- Mass Transit Line & Station

ROUTE SHIELDS

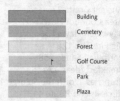

- (H1) Interstate Freeway
- (11) State Highway

AREA FEATURES

- Building
- Cemetery
- Forest
- Golf Course
- Park
- Plaza

- ✪ NATIONAL CAPITAL
- ◉ State, Provincial Capital
- ● LARGE CITY
- ● Medium City
- ● Small City
- ● Town, Village
- ○ Point of Interest

- ■ Place to Stay
- ▲ Campground
- RV Park
- Shelter

- ▼ Place to Eat
- Bar (Place to Drink)
- Café

MAP SYMBOLS

- ✈ Airfield
- ✈ Airport
- Archaeological Site, Ruins
- ⑤ Bank
- Baseball Diamond
- Beach
- Buddhist Temple
- Bus Depot
- Castle
- Cathedral
- Cave
- † Church
- Dive Site
- Embassy
- Footbridge
- Garden
- Gas Station
- Hospital, Clinic
- ⓘ Information
- Lighthouse
- Lookout

- Monument
- ▲ Mountain
- Museum
- ← One-Way Street
- Park
- P Parking
-)(Pass
- Picnic Area
- ★ Police Station
- Pool
- Post Office
- ⓞ Public Toilet
- Shinto Shrine
- Shopping Mall
- Stately Home
- Surfing
- Taoist Temple
- ☎ Telephone
- Trailhead
- Winery
- Zoo

Note: Not all symbols displayed above appear in this book.

LONELY PLANET OFFICES

Australia
PO Box 617, Hawthorn 3122, Victoria
☎ 03 9819 1877 fax 03 9819 6459
email talk2us@lonelyplanet.com.au

USA
150 Linden Street, Oakland, California 94607
☎ 510 893 8555, TOLL FREE 800 275 8555
fax 510 893 8572
email info@lonelyplanet.com

UK
10A Spring Place, London NW5 3BH
☎ 020 7428 4800 fax 020 7428 4828
email go@lonelyplanet.co.uk

France
1 rue du Dahomey, 75011 Paris
☎ 01 55 25 33 00 fax 01 55 25 33 01
www.lonelyplanet.fr

World Wide Web: www.lonelyplanet.com *or* AOL keyword: lp
Lonely Planet Images: lpi@lonelyplanet.com.au